Zelie Girl

Zelie Girl
A Memoir

by Amy McKay Core

edited by Sarah Core

Core Press
2021

First Printing: April 2021

ISBN: 978-1-7367871-9-9 (paperback)
ISBN: 978-1-7367871-8-2 (e-book)

Cover design by Sarah Core

Printed in the United States of America

Core Press
Washington, Pennsylvania

Life is busy. Time with family and friends is brief. Our conversations are about the present and perhaps future plans. Only fleeting bits of the past are mentioned. This is an attempt to share my memories and get them out of the computer and into print for anyone who might be interested.

My college roommate and lifelong friend, Jean Archer Rothermel, set an example for me when she wrote her own autobiography. She consulted with me by phone on details of our college years. This was a wonderful legacy to leave for her family. Often when speaking to my family, I'm told that I'm either repeating myself or neglecting to tell everyone the story. So, this is for my children Gordon, Philip, and Amy Jane. This is what they may not know about me.

I have been part of a monthly writing class at my retirement community for the past twenty years. Suggestions or prompts are given out as assignments and the members of the class learn about each other when we meet and read our papers. My contributions are episodes from the past, though eventually some present creeps in. Over the years, I have forwarded these stories on to friends and family through print and email, and sometimes have published them in local newsletters. Our teacher, retired English professor Nancy E. James, who has written a number of books and leads writing seminars, encouraged me to write a book. That's when I realized I had already written a book through all of the essays and stories I'd submitted over the years. My neighbor Mary Koepke, a published poet, gave me sage advice: "You have to get an editor!"

What better editor could I find than my granddaughter Sarah Core, with a master's degree in journalism. Happily, she has the editing and computer skills, combined with an interest in family history, to help flesh out my stories. This could not have happened without her. Thank you, Sarah.

I have been accused of "artistic license" when someone remembers things differently than I do. I am calling it "creative writing" when it improves upon a story.

Enjoy!

Amy M. Core

Contents

One
Childhood

A Beginning

The most important day of my life was the beginning, of course, on April 22, 1921. Naturally I have no memory of that day, but it is recorded in Harrisburg, Pennsylvania on a birth certificate as "baby girl" McKay, duly signed by the attending physician. This event took place the day before my mother's thirty-fifth birthday and two days before my parent's first wedding anniversary (the date is inscribed on the back of their silverware). That meant that when I had a birthday cake, we had leftover cake for Mother and Father the next day.

My parents were Marie Christine Gelbach, of Zelienople, Pa., named for her aunt Maria "Marie" Christina Buhl Boggs, and Hugh McKay, born in Ozark, Alabama. My mother came from a long line of German-Americans who had immigrated to Pennsylvania in the early 1800s, while my father's family were Scottish settlers who had arrived around the same time in the South.

My father was a telegrapher for the Baltimore and Ohio Railroad at the time when there were few long-distance phone lines. The railroad maintained lines along its right of way and when the public needed fast communication, they relied on the telegrams carried along those lines. This job took him all over the country. He had worked in Connellsville, Pa. before being transferred to Zelienople. He roomed in Widow Frederick's large boarding house on High Street. She liked the shy young man and played matchmaker for Marie, the daughter of her long-time friend Frederica Buhl Gelbach. She not only arranged their introduction, but went with them as chaperone on their first date to the theatre in Pittsburgh. This was 1918 and there were few entertainments in a small town. Mother's diary from 1919 tells of long walks and going to the movies with Hugh and seeing each other at church events.

In her thirties, Mother was considered an old maid. She lived at home with her parents on Clay Street in the large house they had built. Her hopes of becoming

9

a kindergarten teacher were quashed by her father's Victorian attitudes and beliefs. He was a prosperous man and could well have afforded her a college education. However, he believed in staking his two sons, Floyd and Harry, to land, which was in Missouri, and supporting his daughters at home until they married. Mother was his dependent for many years, but more than paid her way by the help she gave her mother and the business letters she wrote for her father in her large, bold hand.

By 1919, Hugh was overseas in France in the abyss of the cold, muddy trench warfare of World War I. He and Mother corresponded as best they could. Upon Hugh's safe return, their courtship blossomed into an engagement. They had a small home wedding on April 24, 1920 officiated by her minister, Rev. Leidy. Marie wore a white, sheer cotton dress with lots of tucks and lace insets. I have a picture of them in their honeymoon attire on a small bridge near her parents' home.

My mother and I with my perfectly round head

The newly married couple moved to a small house on a hill overlooking the Connoquenessing Creek, on a street called Madison just across from Allen's Bridge in Zelienople. Their landlady, Mrs. Sisson, lived in the larger adjacent house. Mother called it their honeymoon cottage. It was close to the railroad station and also to the trolley stop. At some point my father left the railroad job because he didn't want to be subject to a further transfer. He then had an office job at the National Tube Company's steel plant in Ellwood City. This was a short streetcar commute.

The attending physician at my birth, Dr. Ralston, had a tiny office beside his Main Street home. That was all that was needed, for he was out day and night on house calls covering every kind of case, including delivering babies. Only privileged city dwellers went to a hospital for childbirth. Mother's labor was long and difficult and may have entailed much time and several visits. It was finally decided to use forceps to bring the baby's head out of the birth canal. There is a scar on my left forehead under the hairline as a reminder of this.

The trauma of my birth must have shocked them to the extent that they were unprepared with any name. It was three weeks later before my name was decided on. My first name, Amy, was short and one that they liked. My second name,

Eleanor, was in tribute to a close friend, Eleanor "Nora" Wild, who had moved West. I only knew about her through Mother's correspondence.

My parents were thrilled with my final safe arrival, and even though my head was misshapen and scarred, Mother saw me through eyes of love. My grandmother, who had borne eight children, later told me that she had looked at me and said to herself, "this child will never be right."

Fortunately, Mother had an experienced, practical nurse named Mrs. Hildebrand, who came to help every day and spent much time gently molding my soft baby skull to a normal shape. For that I can be very thankful.

It was for perhaps a year or more that the honeymoon cottage was my home. Then, due to my grandfather's failing health, we moved to the large house on Clay Street to help Grandmother with his care in his final days. Finally, my parents bought the new house at 310 East Spring Street that was home from then on. It was a modest red brick with a peaked Tudor-style roof, different from most of the square wooden frame houses in town. I was an only child for six years before the birth of my sister, Lucille Buhl McKay. There were no babysitters then. I went everywhere with my parents or stayed with my grandmother. The vague memories of those days now have meaning.

Such was my beginning.

The Rescue

There were all the classic elements of a medieval romance. The story had an innocent young maiden, very young, and a wild, wide plain ending at a precipice above a dangerous chasm. Then there was the handsome passing knight on a bicycle and even a touch of humor at the end of the rescue.

My maternal grandparents' spacious brick home on Clay Street was built on land that had been owned by Grandmother's paternal grandfather, Christian Buhl, who had helped pioneer the town of Zelienople just over a century before. Constructed in an L shape, there was a covered back porch along the rear wing and a side porch at the front. By the entrance from the street to that porch was a wide sewer tile that held flowering plants and which served as my sandbox. Every child needs a place to dig.

The few things that I remember of that house when I lived there as a toddler were the deep windows and the large shady bathroom. A chain was attached to a tank high on the wall and the handles on the chain had to be pulled to flush the toilet. Mother toured me around town in a big wicker buggy.

There were also short walks for my short legs. Not far away from Clay Street was a wonderful attraction, Stokey's Pond, where there were large goldfish. The pond was encircled by a wooden railing, but since it was above my head, I was always held firmly by the hand and kept well back from the edge. Mr. Stokey had a log house by the pond and an old stone spring house at the other side of his house where people often stopped for a taste of the special water that started on East Spring Street.

Beside my grandparents' house was an empty lot and a small stream along the side street. The stream was usually only a trickle except during spring rains. At the age of three, the small sandbox became boring, and one day I set off to see the world across the field. It must have been a fall day as I was wearing a jacket and little round cap and the leaves had fallen, leaving just weeds and brambles along my path. When I came to the bank along the small, dry stream, I didn't stop but tumbled down the stony slope into a tangle of thorns and small bushes. Panic set in. I was lost and began to cry loudly.

The small maiden in distress was heard by the newspaper boy doing his deliveries. The brave youth got off his bicycle to pull me back up the bank and to take me back to the house. But, in addition, he had to also rescue my "beanie" hat, which was caught on a tree branch. After I had been comforted and scolded in equal measure, I told Mother proudly that my hat on the tree looked just like Christmas.

From an early age, I was interested in exploring my world and found my own backyard too confining. Since there were no fences, it was easy for me to wander off and visit around the neighborhood. On one embarrassing day, as a punishment for this wanderlust, my mother tied a long clothesline to my ankle and fastened it to the support of the grape arbor. There I was commanded to stay and play.

When I was a teenager, the sound of the train whistle echoing around our small-town valley would fill me with longing. Trains took people places in those days. Eventually, I married and ended up living all over the country with my husband, and when he retired, traveling the world with him.

There have been no broken bones or worse injuries in my travels than in that first great adventure and thrilling rescue. Still the wanderlust lingers on. My lifelong hero took me to see the world and when the train's horn sounds throughout the day and night, it is no longer sad, but nostalgic.

Childhood Pleasures

As a little girl born to somewhat older and doting parents, and the youngest grandchild for some time, I could have been spoiled and showered with gifts. That was not the case in this practical family.

 All of my toys were kept in a large fancy fruit basket under the kitchen table. There were blocks, a top, metal cars and small dolls or bits of dolls all in a jumble. I was fiercely possessive of my collection, even the broken things, and when my mother suggested that the basket should be sorted out and some things thrown away, I stubbornly refused. It is still hard to throw anything away!

My father made me a rope swing with a wooden seat that was hung from the grape arbor near the kitchen door. When winter came, the swing was unhooked and hung in the cellar from rings in the stout rafters. The best swinging, however, was on visits to see my country cousins, where a swing was suspended from a tall old tree. That really felt like flying into space, better than a backyard swing set or playground equipment.

My best friend and neighbor, Jeanie Beighley, had a wooden dollhouse with a hinged back that opened to reveal two floors and lighted with a pointed Christmas tree bulb. I envied that dollhouse because my dollhouses were made from shoe boxes. I used spools for table and chairs and bits of fabric for curtains and the rug. Little celluloid dolls dressed in bits of cloth from Mother's scrap basket lived in these rooms.

I had requested a baby sister repeatedly, but Lucille, whom we called Ceil, was a great disappointment to me, since I couldn't play with her like a living doll as I, at five-and-a-half years old, had expected. Then when she could walk and talk, she became a great nuisance because she was always following me around. Due to the difference in our ages, it was many years before we became best friends, but then it was a lifelong friendship that even included being neighbors.

On rainy days, the dining room table made a playhouse with the chairs around it turned down and covered with old sheets or blankets. In the summer on the front porch were two large wicker chairs that could be turned over and covered for a small hideaway.

Ceil and I on the front porch at 310 East Spring Street

One summer I cleaned the lattice space under the back porch of spiders and bugs and put down an old grass porch rug. The space was uncomfortably low and was soon abandoned. In the back yard a six-foot lilac bush grew near the garage and next to it was a snowball bush of equal size. The space between the two bushes made a small retreat.

My father bought an Army pup tent that he put up in the side yard with ropes and tent pegs stretching from the front and rear poles that held it up. It was fine for the first half hour and sometimes on a rainy day. But with no air except the front flap, it was soon suffocating on a summer day. It never saw a second summer. He also built a sandbox, but with no shade in that side yard, it also was too hot. The sand dried out so quickly that it would not stay shaped into roads or even mud pies. The boy next door, Owen Rape, had a sandbox that enjoyed some shade and was filled with finer sand, so that was where we played.

My grandmother, who by now lived by herself in a house five doors up the street from us, provided an unusual playhouse or me. She bought the body of an old automobile from a relative and arranged to have it put on the back corner of our lot. The wheels and hood had been removed. The sedan's back seat made a built-in couch. The flat dashboard in front became a table and a folding stool completed the furnishing. For a luxury touch, there was a built-in glass holder for flowers. The windows could roll down so the playhouse was comfortable and weatherproof.

We played hopscotch on the front walk so a chalk supply was prized. We used a length of clothes line as a jump rope. Roller skates that clamped on over shoes and could be adjusted for size were fun. The skates had to be tightened often so everyone had a skate key on a string hung from the neck. I had a three-wheel tricycle and a scooter which were passed on to my little sister.

Grandmother gave all of her grandchildren a gold coin for Christmas until the country went off the gold standard. After that it was a five-dollar bill. I learned that I could count on this annual bonanza and that the money went much further in the after-Christmas sales.

The year I was ten I was able to buy a large Flexible Flyer sled from the local hardware store. Another year I bought a secondhand girl's bicycle with warped wooden wheels from a girl I knew. I spent many evenings that winter in the basement sanding and repainting this ancient wooden bike. My mother had deemed a bicycle too dangerous and had refused all pleas for one, but when I had survived two or three years on that old bike, even with bad brakes, she finally weakened. On my fourteenth birthday, I was given a beautiful new metal bicycle with shiny chrome fenders. We sometimes played bicycle hockey in the evening on Clay Street where there was a smooth level surface at the foot of East Spring Street.

As teenagers, a group of girlfriends had bike hikes to Pine Run in Fombell, Pa. We would build a fire on the flat rocks by the stream and cook pancakes with bacon added in, wade in the water, and try to catch crayfish. The bicycle was used even after college as transportation to my wartime job at Johns-Manville. In good weather, it was an easy downhill in the morning, but a long upgrade at the end of the day returning home. It was only after I was married that the bicycle was sold to a young neighbor girl. Since no bicycles were being made during wartime, it probably fetched as much as its original cost.

Childhood pleasures were simple and innovative and nothing was plastic!

Out to Lunch

It was a momentous occasion in childhood, so much so that it has stayed with me all of my life. I was six years old when I was entertained at my first "ladies" lunch by Mother's cousin Lillian Gelbach Whittaker. She was not only a cousin but also a good friend of my mother's and we often visited her at her house. But this day, I had been sent on some small errand all by myself. Cousin Lillian invited me into the kitchen where we chatted for a bit. Then she asked if I'd like to have lunch with her and she would phone my mother for permission.

Cousin Lillian lived with her husband Doc Whittaker in a spacious brick house at 108 Grandview Avenue that also served as his physician's office. He was our family physician. It was three blocks away from my house, with only two streets to cross. In our small town, the streets were narrow and the cars went slowly. A side door under the porte-cochère opened to his waiting room, office and dispensary. A door from the waiting room led into their house and we never had to sit with other patients when Cousin Lillian was at home. She always welcomed us into the living room to visit until it was our turn to be seen.

There were no secretaries and assistants in those days, it was just Doc. The second room on his side was the office and at the rear was the examining room with built-in cupboards and glass enclosed shelves where the medicines were stored. He gave out his own pills and potions and only rarely was there a prescription that had to be filled at the drugstore. Most interesting to me as a child – and somewhat gruesome – were some body parts preserved in formaldehyde in his office.

She served a luncheon menu of chou-chou sandwiches, milk and cookies. Cousin Lillian didn't aspire to French cuisine, but the peanut butter sandwich went by the name chou-chou because it included crisp iceberg lettuce. That keeps the peanut butter from sticking to the roof of your mouth. Ever since then I have considered it much superior to plain peanut butter and jelly, and have served it at many a children's luncheon. The most elegant part of all was that the crusts of bread were trimmed off and the sandwich was cut in dainty triangles. At home I had to eat those crusts and was never allowed to leave them on the plate. Mother said it was wasteful. My mother was ordinarily a most truthful

Dressed up and ready to go out with my doll

person. However, in the case of my hair, she lied. She told me that if I ate all of my bread crusts, my hair would become curly. Well, it never did. It stayed fine, thin and straight.

I have attended some lovely ladies' luncheon parties since that day, but I couldn't tell you what the menu was in any of those elegant places. My fondest memory is of my first luncheon invitation when I was treated like a grown-up. Peanut butter has never been quite as special as it was that day.

Rural Zelienople

Although Zelienople was founded in 1802, it was not incorporated as an official borough until 1840. Part of the reason for the town's formal organization was to solve some local problems. Most residents had horses, cattle, and pigs, along with the barns to house them. Beside the Passavant House on Main Street, where the Zelienople Historical Society is now located, there was a large barn, which became the site of a filling station.

Main Street was an unpaved road and had several small streams running across it. Over the years, the runs which drain the hillsides have been piped under the streets and parking lots. One of the early problems of the local borough was the condition of Main Street, where small streams had to be forded by townspeople and where the mud was an attraction for wandering pigs that loved to wallow. The shops in town had hitching posts in front for their customers' horses. There was a stable on Main Street that remained in existence as late as the 1930s, before becoming an A&P grocery store.

An early regulation of the town fathers was a cow curfew. Apparently, many cows were free to wander in town during the day. They were required to be under control of their owners by eight o'clock in the evening. A two-dollar fine was imposed (which was significant back then) on any owner who did not comply. One dollar went to the person who reported the offence and the other dollar went into the borough treasury.

The livestock is long gone, and even chickens are no longer allowed in town, so the early morning crow of roosters is never heard. But if you know where to look, you will still find traces of the many small streams flowing toward the Connoquenessing Creek.

School Days

In 1927, there were no organized play groups, nor preschool or kindergarten, so it was thrilling to be old enough to go to school at last. Before that the play time was with other children of a similar age in the neighborhood. There was Owen, the boy next door (and owner of the best sand pile), and my best friend, Jeanie Beighley, who lived three doors away. School days began when you were six years of age. Years later, I can close my eyes and see clearly the large, sunlit room that was our first-grade classroom.

Before one could start school, there was a mandatory smallpox vaccination. It often left a large white scar on the upper arm. Dr. Ralston was thoughtful in choosing a less conspicuous place on my upper thigh.

Zelienople Grade School, with classes one through six, was in an impressive brick building on the southeast corner of Main Street and Grandview Avenue. Built in an L shape, it was topped with a bell tower. It was entered directly from the street but there were trees at the side and back of the land that made up the playground at recess. The building had been the high school where my mother had attended the first classes, then a borough building, and when I was there it was the grade school (the building is long since gone and today it is a park).

The first three grades were on the first floor and a broad staircase, which divided, led to the upper three classrooms. The teachers then, in grade order, were Miss Edith Sitler, Miss Sara Wise, Miss Evelyn Scott, Miss Lois Blayney, Miss James and Miss Leone Hart.

The bell tower had a rope hanging down in the front hall. The janitor, Mr. Bicker, rang the bell for morning and afternoon school opening. Everyone went home for the lunch hour. He was a stout, kindly man and would go to the door and look up the street and motion any laggards to hurry before ringing the bell.

Our first-grade teacher was slim, dark-haired Miss Edith Sitler who we all adored. The classrooms each had a cloakroom for coats and school supplies. It was also the place where private punishment was sometimes administered. Spanking was quite acceptable then. I don't recall that she needed to do that. The other punishment was staying after school. We felt honored when we were asked to clean the blackboard, take the thick felt erasers outside the door for cleaning, or do anything to assist her.

The room had wooden floors, a high ceiling supported by poles in the middle of the room, tall windows and a door with a glass transom window above. Between the two poles was a low table with upright sides that made a tray. It was filled with sand. Small

My first-grade school portrait

villages could be created or maps drawn across the sand. The holidays and seasons could be marked with a sand table scene. Houses and figures were constructed of oak tag paper, a lightweight tan-colored cardstock, or colored construction paper. In the spring, we learned about Japan by making a Japanese village that had fans, kites, dolls and blossoming peach trees. The trees were made of short branches with twists of pink crepe paper blossoms. Later in life, when I visited Japan, I was surprised to find the customs that I had learned about in first grade were still practiced.

At the start of the day, we all sang:

"Good morning, good morning, good morning to you,
Good morning, dear teacher, and how do you do?"

This was followed by the Pledge of Allegiance. The alphabet was printed above the blackboard. There was also a cardboard coffee pot and a cardboard milk bottle. The teacher would ask if anyone had drunk coffee for breakfast, which was a bad thing. Then the coffee pot would chase the milk bottle. If no one had coffee, the milk bottle would chase the coffee pot. Long sheets on each side of the door had the "it" family and the "at" family and we learned to add letters of the alphabet for word building.

A side door opened to the playground. Recess was an important part of the morning when we went outside to play, and we had small glass bottles of white or chocolate milk. We brought milk money, and even then, were aware of a few pupils who brought no money because their families were on relief during the Depression.

Once I was kept after school for sitting on my desk with my feet on the seat. I had persuaded my friend Helen to do this, too. She never forgot her punishment, both at school and then at home afterward when her parents found out why she was late coming home.

In fourth grade, I got braces to have my teeth straightened. The local dentist, Dr. Dunkin, wasn't really an orthodontist, but there wasn't one in town so he was doing his best. Braces then weren't like they are today. They were made of metal that went all the way around your teeth and rubber bands were used to force your teeth into proper alignment.

One afternoon I was sitting in class and I grew bored. So, I worked the rubber bands loose in my mouth and told Miss Blayney I needed to see the dentist. And she let me leave school! I walked two blocks up Grandview Avenue to the dentist's office, got my rubber bands tightened, and then walked home. I never returned to school that day. It's hard to imagine getting away with playing hooky like that today. My teeth never did get straightened and, when it was time for my sister, Ceil, to have braces, Mother took her to a real orthodontist in Pittsburgh.

Married women were not hired as teachers back then. Husbands were expected to support their families. Miss Sitler lived with her widowed father in a spacious house on East New Castle Street. Some years later, she married "Curly" Stover, a popular widower with a little girl. As a skilled teacher, an exception was made for her and she continued to teach for many years as Mrs. Stover. Times were changing.

Miss Sara Wise

Miss Sara Wise, a tall, blonde young woman, was my second-grade teacher. I can still see her stooping over to help her young pupils with their schoolwork.

Miss Wise lived on the same street as I did, East Spring Street, and my grandmother lived even closer to her. My great-uncle and aunt Edward Winter and Matilda Buhl Winter lived next door to the Wise family. All of this gave me a feeling of closeness to her, almost like she was an extended part of my family.

The Bobbsey Twin books, with Betty and Bob as the main characters, were popular reading at the time. I was sorry not to be named Betty, which was a much more fashionable name than Amy. The consolation was that Amy was a short name. I felt sorrier for my first cousin Geraldine Humphrey, who had such a long name to write on the top of her school papers.

Second grade was exciting because we were writing a book about Betty and Bob. Each day we came to school with ideas for a page. Miss Wise would write out the story for the day on the blackboard, enlisting our help in the spelling of new words. Then we would copy the story for our growing book. We were unaware that she was incorporating a spelling lesson, a reading class and a writing exercise in a project that engaged our full attention. By the end of the year, we made cardboard covers, punched holes in the lined pages, and tied it together with bright yarn. Everyone had their own copy.

The fact that I had to wear long underwear with dark stockings and high-top shoes was the bad part of that year. Supporters held up the stockings, which were always lumpy over the long underwear. Time was required to dress and the result was still embarrassing.

Sara Wise was such a fine teacher that she soon went off to work in the Pittsburgh school system, where the salary was greater. Prestige was involved in being a teacher in the city. I only saw her fleetingly after that.

Somewhere over the years, my second-grade book was lost, but not the memory of the wonderful teacher who made our class so interesting.

First Fish, First Shorts

Blanche Beringer was a maiden lady who was Grandmother Gelbach's live-in housekeeper for many years until Grandmother passed away. When Blanche had time off, she went to stay with her aunt on New Castle Street or her married sister who lived along the streetcar route at May Stop beyond Evans City. Blanche and Grandmother got along well. Grandmother did not need waiting on and she was never idle. She gardened and made homemade noodles. She wore glasses to hand-sew quilt pieces. Her goal was to make a quilt for each of her five adult children. Her mind was keen and she was not seriously ill until the last three weeks of her life before she died at age eighty-seven.

When Grandfather died after several years of illness, Grandmother sold the big Clay Street house and bought a smaller, newly built house just five doors away from our home. The family was concerned about Grandmother living alone and persuaded her to have a dog at the new house. Her grown children considered her delicate. The gift of the dog proved to be more trouble than company. It is doubtful that it was any help or protection.

Before long Grandmother had a live-in housekeeper named Mrs. Graham, a tall thin widow lady. Grandmother shared in the cooking. She enjoyed making pies and doing a bit of canning and jelly making. When Mrs. Graham departed this world, her place was taken by a Mrs. McKinney, who was the widowed aunt of her neighbor Florence French. When she died, the next housekeeper was Blanche, who was younger and survived Grandmother. While my grandmother appeared to be frail, she was sturdy enough to outlast two housekeepers and lived well into her eighties.

My first fish caught in my first pair of shorts

Blanche was very much part of the family and enjoyed cooking for Grandmother's guests. She made lamb-shaped cakes with white coconut icing for my sister's birthdays. My sister, Ceil, was near in age to Blanche's nephews and often she took her along to play with them when she made visits there.

Blanche and her sister had inherited their family farm. The house had burned down. There was only a barn and a small shed where the caretaker lived. Blanche said he was a hermit, which made me curious. I once sneaked a peek in the open door of the shack and saw only a cot, a table and a wooden chair.

That was on the summer day she had invited us to picnic there and to fish in the farm pond. Mother drove us. I wore my one-piece shorts outfit of which I was very proud. This was my first pair of shorts. Mother said that it would have to be my last pair of shorts as I would soon be too old to wear shorts. If she only knew!

Rugs had been delivered to the house wrapped around bamboo poles that we had never thrown away. That became my fishing pole. I don't remember if I had a proper hook or just used a safety pin. Either way, a cork was tied on the line as a bobber. That was how I caught my first fish. It was a small catfish and I insisted that Mother cook it for us, though it made only a few bites.

Although it was my first fish, it was not my first pair of shorts. Times have changed and shorts are acceptable at any age now.

Oakwood

Henry and Christina Speyerer Buhl were the parents of eight children: four daughters named Maria "Marie" Christina, Frederica, Emma, and Matilda; and four sons named Frederick, Henry, Jr., Christian (who died in infancy), and Benjamin. They were both first generation German-American immigrants from Bavaria.

Henry's father, Christian, a hatter and furrier, was an early pioneer of Zelienople. He arrived in America in 1802, walking over the mountains from the eastern part of Pennsylvania. He was one of only two households recorded living there in 1804, building a log cabin near the creek. Later he would erect a substantial brick house for his family, which still stands today as a museum in downtown Zelienople. The Speyerers hailed from Frankethal where Christina's father, Frederick, was a successful merchant. The family fled to Heidelberg when Napoleon's army invaded during the French Revolution before immigrating to America.

The white brick home outside of town where Henry and Christina raised their family was an early split-level style house built into the hillside, not far above the Connoquenessing Creek where Henry had a mill. Oakwood still stands on Buhl Hill in Forward Township, Butler County. Originally, it had a circular carriage drive to the front entrance on the upper level. A wide hall led through to a rear veranda. There was a double parlor on the right and bedrooms to the left with more bedrooms upstairs. The covered veranda provided a shelter for the lower floor and gave a view of the valley. The kitchen and dining room were on the ground floor with the laundry and fruit cellar built into the hillside. The house is well-maintained and can be seen from old Route 68 between Evans City and Butler. A closer view of the house is available by taking old Route 68 and winding past what was once the mill on the river.

Their eldest daughter, Marie, married Russell Hurd Boggs, the business partner of her brother Henry Buhl, Jr. They founded Boggs & Buhl, a successful department store in Allegheny City, now the North Side of Pittsburgh. The younger daughters, Emma and Matilda, married two Winter brothers, sons of a Zelienople minister. Frederick was a well-known local farmer, while the youngest brother, Benjamin, went out West to farm near Hurdland, Mo. where his descendants live today. Their middle child, Frederica, was my grandmother.

Frederica Justina Buhl Gelbach
1852 – 1941

Grandmother was a small, slim lady just under five feet tall. She was modest in manner and dress, though she did take pride in her slender wrists and ankles that she could circle with her thumb and forefinger. Her hair was gray, parted in the middle and braided down her back, and the braid was coiled into a bun in the daytime. She wore nearly ankle-length dresses that she had made for her. In the winter, she wore black with small white prints and a high-necked white collar. In the summer, it was the reverse. The background was white with small black designs and, occasionally, it was a white-lavender figured print. That was as daring as she allowed herself.

These dresses were handmade for her and there were always extra scraps of material to put into the quilt tops that she kept busy in piecing. Her goal was to finish a quilt for each of her children. These were utilitarian quilts to be used for warmth as well as not to waste any material. As her brother-in-law W. Henry would say, he didn't understand these women who would buy good cloth, cut it up and then sew it back together again. She usually paid to have the tops quilted by a group of church women, though there were a few winters when there was a quilting frame set up by the dining room double windows where the light was best and where neighbors would often spend some sewing and visiting time.

The only clothing that came from the store were her coats and hats. She expected to get her wear from these garments and, as her eightieth birthday approached, she was reluctant to invest in a good coat that she felt she might not live to wear out.

My grandmother, Frederica Buhl Gelbach

Grandmother's only jewelry was a plain gold wedding band. She also used some small decorative pins under two inches long that were referred to as "beauty pins" and were used to fasten the black velvet band she wore around her throat when dressing for church or visiting. I felt that she needed more rings and, for several years at Christmas, I presented her with a carefully chosen ring from the local five and dime store. I was thanked, but the ring was never worn. It probably would have turned her finger green. When I learned to knit, she was pleased with gifts of knee warmers and wristlets, which she did wear. My small allowance was never increased before Christmas, so my funds were extremely limited and gifts were homemade. Once I made a footstool from a wooden box to which I attached four legs and covered it with green Indian head cotton. It was not a thing of great beauty, but apparently, it was useful because Grandmother kept it beside her rocking chair in the living room.

Grandmother was nineteen years old when she and Grandfather were married on April 6, 1871. Grandfather was a twenty-five-year-old farmer who lived nearby. My cousin Julia said that they had a difficult time when they were first married. They had a house fire, their only horse died and their first child, a daughter named Emma, born in 1872, lived only for a month. In 1879 their fifth child, a son Charles, died at the age of one. Grandmother tended the graves of those little ones in an abandoned cemetery for many years, and her grandson Warren Eakin helped her and carried on for many years later. Those graves are lost and forgotten today, but the names and dates are inscribed on the Gelbach marker in the family plot in Zelienople.

They had six other children who lived to adulthood, four daughters and two sons. Laura, born in 1873, was the eldest, followed by Henry (Harry), Eva, Floyd, Lillian and my mother Marie, the youngest, born in 1886. One way that grandmother managed this large family was by having the oldest girl, Laura, take care of her younger sister, and the second oldest girl take care of the next-youngest girl, and so on. Laura never married and died before my birth in 1916 at the age of thirty-seven. She was remembered as a wonderful needlewoman. My first cousin Laura Eakin was named in her honor.

Grandfather Jacob was the eldest son of a German-American family of seven, born to Philip and Sophia Dambach Gelbach in 1848. They had two daughters and five sons: Jacob, Philip, Louisa, William Henry, Julia, Christian and John. Heinrich "Henry" Gelbach, his grandfather, came from Bavaria in 1832, settling with his large family in Harmony, Pa. Jacob was the oldest of

The mustachioed Gelbach brothers

Philip's children. A large picture of the five sons adorned the living room wall growing up. I always thought that the Gelbach men, all mustached, looked like the illustration on the Smith Brothers cough drops wrapper.

My grandfather died when I was just three years old, so I have only vague memories of a bearded old man seated in a wooden, round-backed chair. There are not too many affectionately remembered family stories, either. The only tribute paid to his memory was that he was a "good business man." He was a hard-headed German with Victorian-era ideals. Music was considered frivolous to Grandfather. There were music lessons for his oldest daughter, but when she didn't practice, he declared that no more money would be wasted on any of the rest of the family. It was not a question of money with Grandfather. He invested his funds in the form of personal notes and mortgages to others, rather than investing in his family. A civic investment to his credit was the financing of the municipal water system for the borough.

In the year before he died, my parents moved into their home on Clay Street to help Grandmother. I was two years old. Grandfather had a male nurse and companion, an old friend who came in daily. My older cousin Laura said that she had heard that Grandfather once drank. This was never breathed in our family, but it could have been the reason that his family were such teetotalers. Grandmother did keep on hand a jug of blackberry wine for "medicinal purposes" and, later in life, to her embarrassment, had to resort to the state liquor store when she no longer made her own wine.

Grandmother was a modest person who lived simply and did not have expensive tastes. However, she had a weakness for fine linens. Her husband deemed these extravagant and she rarely bought new linen sets. After he died, she gave, as Christmas gift sets to each member of the family, a brand new fine linen tablecloth with a dozen napkins. The napkins came in a long strip that was cut apart and hemmed by hand with a narrow-rolled hem.

She also owned an elegant sterling silver fruit basket that had been bequeathed to her by her sister-in-law Louise Miller Buhl in 1922. In Louise's will, she had detailed not only specific items for certain people, but explained in which room of her two mansions the items could be found. This lovely Art Nouveau silver piece was kept in the dining room china closet and was the centerpiece for all of the family holiday dinners. After Grandmother's death, it was inherited by her youngest daughter, my mother, Marie, who kept it brightly polished and used it for special occasions. On the day of Mother's funeral, it sat in a place of honor on the dining room table, filled with golden mums. I inherited the Buhl basket and recently gifted it to my own daughter-in-law, who in turn will pass it on to my granddaughter one day. Thus, it has been passed down through five generations of women in our family.

The Clay Street house where Grandfather and Grandmother Gelbach lived was erected on family land, as it backed onto the property of her grandfather Christian Buhl, whose home, the oldest one in Zelienople, still stands at 221 South Main Street. The property was purchased from Grandmother's cousin Jane Buhl Randolph, who inherited it in appreciation for the years of care that she gave her grandfather and grandmother, Christian and Frederica Dorothea Goehring Buhl, in their twilight years. There was a small barn in back in which the horse and buggy were kept. The house was built in an L shape and had a side porch on the back-frame wing and a side porch at the front.

After Grandfather died at age seventy-eight, the spacious brick house was too big and so it was sold to the funeral director, Oliver W. Zeigler. I have a faint memory of being with Mother and Grandmother in an upstairs office of the funeral director. There was a gas stove heating the small room filled with a rolltop desk, at which papers were being signed. Before the move, an auction of the furnishings was held, with the exception of what was to be moved to the new three-bedroom house we were to live in. The funeral director used the barn out in back for casket storage and for his hearse. It is still standing today.

After she finished selling the Gelbach family home, Grandmother purchased a house at 338 East Spring Street, which was being built up. A new yellow-brick house was going up across the street that was soon occupied by Mrs. Schiever, a widow near Grandmother's age. Her name was Sarah and they became good friends, but were never on a first-name basis. To childhood friends, Grandmother was Freddy, or Aunt Freddy to her relatives.

She wouldn't quite be described as a "merry widow," but in her widowhood, she enjoyed life, particularly because she could afford to treat others. She invited all the family to be her guests for a weekend at a hotel on Lake Conneaut. Another summer, she realized a lifelong dream to travel on an Ohio riverboat. Her father, Henry, had been a riverboat pilot early in his life and she had watched the boats when visiting her maternal grandparents, Frederick Charles and Maria Christina Justine Stoessel Speyerer, in Rochester. Grandmother took as many of the family as were free to join her on a weeklong round trip from Pittsburgh to Cincinnati. It was the start of the Great Depression and the last summer that there was recreational passenger traffic on the Ohio River for many years. One winter she hired two horses and a bobsled filled with hay to give the children of the neighborhood a sleighing experience. Several years later, she wondered aloud at her audacity, saying, "It could have been dangerous – what if there had been an accident and I was responsible."

Grandmother faithfully attended Grace Reformed Church in Harmony, Pa. and since her hearing was poor, she occupied a pew in the front. A new church had just been built in front of the original building. She gave money to furnish the Ladies Sunday School room, a lounge that the committee filled with so many overstuffed couches and chairs that it looked like a furniture store display. The church expansion took place just before the Great Depression and brought the congregation a huge debt that the members had to work years to repay. There were many church suppers. We were taken to all of these affairs as her guests, together with many others. The chicken and dumplings, apple pies and angel food cakes were delicious. The church women worked hard in a windowless basement kitchen equipped only with laundry tubs for dishwashing. Grandmother was a generous supporter of all the church fundraising activities.

Grandmother had a grape arbor off a semi-enclosed back porch in the East Spring Street house. There was a small back lawn and every year she grew a decorative border of salvia, cannas and castor beans that screened the vegetable garden. On the porch, which went across the front of her house, there was a swing, porch furniture and bountiful hanging baskets. The local florist filled them each spring with an assortment of flowering plants.

The living room was a long room and opposite the front door was a doorway leading to an inner hall and stairway. This was on one side of the fireplace and double glass doors to the dining room were on the other side. A library table sat in the middle of the room with a dictionary and condensed encyclopedia showing pictures of unbelievable underwater life. They were things that I couldn't imagine until years later when we lived in the Bahamas and I finally saw them for myself. The kitchen was in the back corner of the house with a door to the porch and a stairway to the basement. On the stair landing, just inside the side door, was the icebox where the iceman made his regular ice deliveries.

Grandmother's large attic was always dark and dim. In the daytime, the only light came from a small window at either end and after dark there was one lone lightbulb hanging in the center. No one spent much time there since, depending on the season, it was too hot or too cold. Three large trunks held pillows, blankets and quilts. There were two tall antique chests of drawers and a few other bits of furniture left from her former large home on Clay Street.

Grandmother had two favorite chairs. One was the rocking chair in the living room by the double window where she could see people going by on the sidewalk. The other was an East Lake chair by the double window in the dining room. That was the sewing chair. From this position, she could see the rear of our lot and the garage and knew when the garage doors were open and the car was missing that Mother was out.

Thanksgiving and Christmas dinners were at Grandmother's with my Aunt Eva Eakin and Pittsburgh cousins in attendance. Then, in the summer, there were visits from Gelbach relatives from out West, primarily Missouri and Illinois, for longer stays. Occasionally, Grandmother hosted afternoon card parties for her friends. I can remember sitting under the table, quietly playing and listening to the women talking about local news and gossip as they played popular card games of the era.

I usually made an afternoon stop at Grandmother's house after school, since she got the Pittsburgh Press, the afternoon paper. At home, we had the Pittsburgh Post-Gazette, which was the morning paper. I was addicted to the funnies and so my visit wasn't purely social. My favorite way of reading the comics was on the floor and the housekeeper complained that I spread the paper out in the doorway. Often, I had tea with Grandmother. She called this cambric tea and it was warm milk with sugar and a small amount of her tea added. There were homemade cookies, too.

I was forbidden coffee as a child, which naturally made it seem very attractive. One day, when helping to clear the table, I decided to taste the coffee left in the bottom of a cup. What a terrible disappointment that was…cold and bitter. That made me a confirmed tea drinker for the rest of my life and I could never bring myself to learn to like coffee or even coffee-flavored candy.

There were no babysitters in my youth but my sister, Ceil, and I spent time at Grandmother's house on many occasions. Grandmother was a wonderful confidant and I felt free to tell her many things that I wouldn't have told my mother. She listened and never lectured.

Aunt Tillie and Uncle Ed Winter

Matilda "Tillie" Buhl and Edward Winter were married in Zelienople, Pa. on September 29, 1898. She was the daughter of Henry Buhl, Sr. and Christina Wilhelmina Carolina Speyerer. Tillie was thirty-seven years old and Ed was a forty-six-year-old widower with two young children, Albert and Jean. It was a case of sisters marrying brothers, for her older sister Emma had married his brother Ferdinand A. Winter of Altoona in May 1875. So, they had been well-acquainted in-laws for many years.

The Winters were sons of a local United Evangelical minister, Rev. Ernest Ferdinand Winter. The couple lived in a spacious red brick house on the corner of Beaver Street facing High Street. Henry Buhl, Sr. had died in their home in Zelienople in 1898, just a month before Tillie and Ed were married.

It was not until I was over fifty years old that I learned from a cousin that Great-Aunt Tillie, my grandmother's sister, had been divorced before she married Ed. It was something that my mother never told me and was never spoken of, to my knowledge. Apparently, she had made an unfortunate marriage at a young age, had one child that died in infancy and then started divorce proceedings against him in 1885. She lived with her parents before marrying Ed in 1898. Great-Uncle Ed worked at Boggs and Buhl's department store for his brothers-in-law at some time after their marriage. He was a charmer and a favorite relative of mine.

Tillie and Ed moved to Zelienople in 1927 and built a lovely house on East Spring Street just two doors away from my grandmother, Freddy, who was her older sister. I remember Great-Aunt Tillie as being always beautifully dressed, wearing her hair on top of her head and usually with a black velvet ribbon around her throat. People seldom saw her in simpler attire, but though she had no need to do any housework, she did wear more modest house dresses and had a back path that she walked to visit her sister's house when she was not dressed up.

Edward's son, Albert, was one of the two casualties of my hometown from World War I. His sister, Jean, married a local boy, Frank French, and at that time they were living in New York City. Frank was an employee of American Express, then still an express transportation company.

Great-Uncle Ed was a fitness buff and ahead of his time. He was devoted to exercise and planned to live to be ninety. He was often seen by the neighbors doing exercises outside, to their amazement. To entertain us as children, he would bring the mat into the elegant living room and do forward and backward somersaults, stand on his head and help us to do the same. We loved that attention. Great-Aunt Tillie was not amused by this activity in her elegant living room. When it was summertime and the gymnastics were outside on the grass, she was more tolerant.

Tillie and Ed's beautifully landscaped home at 352 East Spring Street was on a double lot. It was a

A snapshot of Uncle Ed and Aunt Tillie on their East Spring Street front porch

mansion with three bedrooms and two baths on the second floor. The large master bedroom had an adjoining study. There were additional bedrooms and a bath for servants on the third floor. On the first floor, there was a long living room to the left of the wide hallway with a fireplace opposite the doorway and French doors

27

leading to a tiled-covered porch on both sides of the fireplace. The rear wall of the room had high windows with glass-fronted bookcases completely across the wall and, in front of the bookcases, was a grand piano.

A dining room to the right also had a fireplace opposite the door and a large convex gold-framed bulls-eye mirror, above which reflected the display of silver on the mahogany buffet. A swinging door led to a butler's pantry and the kitchen and then to a breakfast room. Tucked under the main staircase was a powder room. The steps led up to a wide landing with a window seat before turning to the upstairs. A two-car detached garage was at the end of the side driveway. A pergola shaded one side of the garage and led to the professionally landscaped garden, rare at that time in our small community.

They had German staff – Antonia, their maid, known as Annie, and Karl Minzel, their chauffeur and gardener – to care for the property. It was all very elegant and completely out of place in comparison with the other houses on the street. Aunt Tillie must have really loved her sister to build in that location.

Uncle Ed loved cars and had a big black Lincoln sedan that he drove sedately down East Spring Street. It was said that he speeded up his pace outside of town. The limousine had glass vases for flowers fixed beside the rear doors and, most fascinating to me, was the compact built into the armrest on one side of the rear seat and the cigarette case on the other side.

Ladders led to a large storage area above the garage and that became a clubhouse when his granddaughter, Mary French, came to live in Zelienople while her parents were posted overseas. Her aunt Florence French and cousins Bill and Ruth lived just a few doors away on the opposite side of the street. She was actually named Ellen Mary French but didn't use Ellen at that time. We were pen pals when she lived in Buenos Aires with her parents and always thought of ourselves as cousins. Our mothers had been close friends growing up together.

I remember one exciting evening in the master bedroom after Aunt Tillie and Uncle Ed had been to Europe and they were unpacking their souvenirs and had gifts for everyone. My gift was a soft decorated Florentine leather coin purse that I used for years.

When Aunt Tillie passed away in 1931, Uncle Ed kicked his heels up in a modest way. Uncle Ed was left the house and her estate went to their adopted daughter, Edna Hotham Putts of Erie, who was, in reality, a distant Buhl cousin. He continued to be active in the Rotary and even became an honorary member of a Native American tribe when a visiting group put on a program at the high school. Uncle Ed went to Florida for the winter for several years.

Annie and Karl, their former servants, had married each other. Later the Minzels were employed by the Passavant family and lived on their farm beyond town where they raised two daughters.

One winter, my grandmother had a letter from Florida from her brother-in-law, telling her that he had just remarried a widow, Mary Martin Warren, and they would be returning in a month. There was much speculation as to the age, appearance and personality of this new neighbor and family member. The day after they arrived, we were invited to come in the evening to meet the new bride.

It was a feminine delegation headed by my grandmother, my mother, my little sister and I, and also mother's sister, Eva, and her daughter, Julia Eakin, from Pittsburgh. There was tension in the air. That was soon dispersed when we met Mary. She was from Prospect, Pa. and had been a childhood sweetheart of Uncle Ed. She and Grandmother found they had many friends in common. She was a warm, unassuming person that we fell in love with immediately. We called her Aunt Mary and, in fact, I felt closer to her than some of my real aunts. She was not a social person but they did give a large party to meet his friends. One of the kind things that she did was to feature Uncle Ed's blind sister, Nettie Winter, who played the piano during the evening celebration.

Great-Uncle Ed didn't get to celebrate his ninetieth birthday as he had wished. He died in 1935 at the age of eighty-three from pneumonia caught after walking on the beach in Florida. Aunt Mary returned to Zelienople and we continued to be close. She had a home in Prospect where she spent the summers and rented modest rooms in town during the winter. Mother usually drove her to church with us until her death in 1944.

Digging for Black Gold

There is a modest sign outside the small town of Evans City in Butler County, Pa. that states it is the "City of Black Gold." Few people remember that time or even know what "black gold" refers to. Today the gasoline from this product at the gas pump is carrying out that name.

With the worldwide interest in oil and the exploration for oil in so many places, it is hard to realize that this all started in Pennsylvania with the drilling of the earliest wells by Colonel Edwin Drake, the first American to successfully drill for oil. This was rapidly followed by discovery of oil in Butler County.

Small amounts of oil had been known about for years, mostly for medicinal purposes. The Native Americans had a hidden spring in the hills where the water was covered by a film of oil. They went there for sacred ceremonies, during which they would light the oil on the water on fire.

The history of Butler County is filled with companies formed for drilling. They tell the names and locations of the wells that were drilled and what the output in barrels was daily. So many companies were formed and disappeared, according to the dry wells. Of the names that appeared, only one local company, T.W. Philips, still remains active, since it has long since expanded to other areas. There are many names of present-day county families, like mine, who moved on from oil and gas to careers in merchandising, banking, law and other businesses, which may have been financed initially by this natural resource.

I do not know how successful of a farmer my grandfather Jacob Gelbach was before his land in Butler County produced "black gold." This crop of oil enabled him to leave farming and become a banker. The family moved to town where a private bank was opened on Main Street. They lived in part of what was known as the Bank House in Zelienople until they built the brick home at what is now 208 South Clay Street.

My grandfather Jacob Gelbach

My grandfather was apparently still a farmer at heart, for he seems to have been a silent partner with most of the banking business being carried on by two of his brothers. With the money from the oil, he was able to become a gentleman farmer. He built a barn at the rear of the house where he kept a horse and buggy, which he drove to a small farm that he had purchased just north of town on a hill on Fanker Road. There he could supervise a tenant man who did the farming for him. In town, he watched over his investments until his health failed.

At some point, the bank was sold and his brothers went on to found other banks. Christian founded the Mars Bank, which is still in existence today. William Henry married the daughter of the head of the Evans City Citizens Bank and their brother John headed a bank in Ellwood City. So, oil played a large part in the family moving into finance.

Brother Philip was the great tragedy in the family. He stayed on his successful farm with a large house on Brownsdale Road. He was happily married and had three sons and five daughters. The train into Pittsburgh ran near the farm and would pick up passengers on request. He boarded the train one summer day in 1908 for what was presumed to be a business trip. He carried little of value but his gold watch and chain and a few coins for travel. He was never seen again.

Pittsburgh police were not very interested in the case, and so his four brothers and older sons united in going into the city, checking hospitals and the morgue and searching as best as they could. No one could understand what could have happened, as he wasn't carrying a large sum of money or many valuables. Nor were any funds withdrawn from his bank account before or after his disappearance.

The newspapers speculated that he had committed suicide. He'd given his son authority over his bank accounts by letter, postmarked from Pittsburgh after leaving town, and had recently drawn up a will. But no evidence ever appeared suggesting what had happened to him. The family feared the worst.

His wife hired the Perkin's Detective agency and sought information on his whereabouts, spending upwards of $1,000 to try and trace her husband, but none of their efforts were successful. Without results or clues, he was finally declared dead by the courts seven years later. Today, it remains a Gelbach family mystery.

"Aunt Kate" stayed on the farm until after the marriage of her youngest daughters and sons. She then moved to Grove City where her daughter Clara was a successful business woman. Son Dan lived with her, as well. He had lost part of an arm in a farming accident. He was a genial fellow and liked to demonstrate to me and my young cousins what he could do with the stub of his arm below the elbow. Her son Henry lived in Evans City and had a feed mill store across Main Street from his spacious home. It was a convenient location with the railroad tracks and station there. Some distance in back of his house was a large horse barn and hay storage. It was the site of a large fire, said to have been ignited by sparks from a passing locomotive. Some horses were rescued, others died and the building was a complete loss.

In today's times, we talk about the Recession, but then there was the Depression. There was a housing boom in the 1920s. No mortgages were amortized and only interest payments were required. It was believed that amortization would mean that people would be able to finance homes over a period of years by paying toward the principal and the interest. Somehow, with the bundling of mortgages and the unreal appraisals and removal of local lenders, a great many things went wrong.

Henry and his wife, Carrie, had one son, Philip, and two daughters, Katherine and Ruth. They lived well and belonged to the Ellwood City Country Club. But the feed mill business was suffering. With the fire loss and mounting debts, Henry went to his garage one night and ended his life by running his car and breathing the exhaust fumes. It was 1934, the height of the Depression. He is buried in Evans City Cemetery. Only many years later did any of the family admit it was a suicide.

The mortgaged house became part of the estate of his late Uncle Jacob, my grandfather. His widow, Carrie, stayed on paying a small rent to the family until the children finished high school. Then she became a house mother at Allegheny College where all her children graduated, perhaps with the financial help of her brother, who was a prosperous doctor. Her son, Philip, became a doctor in Detroit. Katherine married an Episcopalian minister, Robert Appleyard, who became the bishop of Western Pennsylvania. Ruth married a lawyer, Douglas Cochran, who joined the foreign service. They lived alternately in Washington, D.C. and many places around the world.

Grandfather felt that the men of the family should handle business affairs. When he died, he had appointed his brother John, the Ellwood City banker, as his executor. He was a shareholder in his brother's bank, had trusted his brother with an unsecured $25,000 personal loan and was heavily invested in a mortgage pool managed by his brother John's two sons, Myron and Loring.

With the bank closings mandated under President Franklin D. Roosevelt, much of his estate went up in smoke. As a shareholder in the Ellwood City Bank, my grandmother Frederica lost heavily at that time and a family schism ensued with the Ellwood City relatives that was never bridged. Grandmother and her children discovered they had become landlords for a great many properties, as inflated mortgages had been foreclosed on. As a youngster, I can recall the heated political discussions, during which Roosevelt was branded a demon.

Unlike today's market, the people living there were allowed to stay on in their homes, paying rent in lieu of interest. Mother, who had no previous business experience, but was the only family member near at hand, bought a car, learned to drive and found herself coping with foreclosed mortgages, collecting rents and trying to do what she could with the remains of Grandfather's estate.

I remember driving around to see the various houses in Ellwood City that our family now owned and relied on for income. They looked very different from the descriptions on paper. One brick house of four bedrooms sounded more promising than some others until it was viewed in person. The location was on the edge of the National Tube Company dumping grounds.

Henry Buhl, Jr.
1848 – 1927

As the last living Buhl descendent who knew Henry Buhl, Jr., it is time to record my faint childhood memories of him and his estates. My great-uncle Henry loomed large in my mind as a small child because of the special gifts that were sent to us from his business, the Boggs and Buhl department store. There was a patent leather hatbox, which I packed when going up the street to spend the night at my grandmother's house. Another gift he gave me was a little pink monkey that opened into a tiny mirrored compact. The presents I usually received from my parents and maternal grandparents were much more practical things. The sterling silver flower basket that his wife willed my grandmother still sits in a place of honor among my silver collection.

My grandmother was Henry's younger sister. When my parents, Marie and Hugh McKay, bought their first automobile, a Star, they were able to take my grandmother to visit him in Pittsburgh on the North Side. There at the Buhl mansion at 1241 Western Avenue, we were shown upstairs, where Great-Uncle Henry was sitting in a chair with a robe over his knees. While they conversed, I was turned over to the care of the two German maids, who played hide-and-seek with me in the large house while the adults enjoyed each other's company. Mindful of his German heritage, Henry Buhl usually hired young immigrant German girls to give them a good start in this country. The maids seemed to have had an ongoing battle with the Japanese butler-chauffeur, named George Inou. They taught me "du bist ein esel" and told me to go and say that to the butler. It is still the only German that I know and it can rarely be used in polite conversation, as I later learned it translates to "you are a jackass."

We all had dinner together in a large, dark formal dining room. I must have been seated across from the doorway, since I remember there being a wide stairway situated opposite. It was my first experience having a butler serve us dinner, which he did from silver dishes. The meal felt very grand and imposing.

I also recall a visit to Great-Uncle Henry's summer estate in Sewickley Heights. Prior to building his own summer residence, he and his wife, Louise, would summer at Twin Hollows in Edgeworth. It was a large home that still stands at 404 Beaver Road, northwest of the city. In 1901 Henry purchased 41 acres of land in Leet Township along Camp Meeting Road for $17,000. There he built a mansion named Cloverton Hills and from then on, that was where the family would spend their summers. Just down the road was his brother-in-law and business partner Russell Hurd

My great-uncle Henry Buhl, Jr.

Boggs' summer home, Hohenberg. I remember with great fun rolling down a steep grassy hillside at Cloverton Hills one summer day. Inside the house, the doorway to the dining room was decorated with hanging silver, large spoons, ladles and serving pieces. This fascinated me as a child. I have a mirror collection hanging in my own home that somewhat mimics the silver collection at Cloverton Hills. Neither the mansion on the North Side nor the summer home survives today. The street sign "Buhlmont Drive" in Sewickley Heights is all that remains of Uncle Henry's grand estate.

After Henry's wife, Louise, died in 1922, he asked his sister and brother-in-law, Matilda and Ed Winter, to come live with him. Aunt Tillie managed his homes on North Avenue and his summer estate in Sewickley Heights while Uncle Ed worked in the offices of Boggs and Buhl. When we went shopping at the store, we would visit Uncle Ed and several more of Mother's handsome Winter cousins who also worked there.

Uncle Henry never had any children, but he was a family-oriented man who took care of his relatives. Not only did he hire many of his nieces, nephews and cousins to work in the store, when Aunt Tillie needed to divorce her first husband, William C. Bradford, her brother stepped up. Newspaper records show that he publicly supported her court proceedings, otherwise, she may not have been able to get the divorce. Divorce in the Victorian era was rare and, in Pittsburgh, it was decided by a jury. Without his wealth and social power, the all-male jury may not have sided with her. Her case took two years to wend its way through the court before they granted her a divorce on grounds of cruelty in 1887.

When Henry's first cousin Emma Simpson Hotham died of cholera at the age of just twenty-nine, she left behind three young daughters. Their grandmother had been a Buhl and, with their father unable to care for them, Uncle Henry took charge. He petitioned the Orphan's Court to appoint him as the guardian for Blanche, Emma, and Edna. Then they were split among Buhl relatives who had the means to care for them. His sister, Marie, adopted and raised the middle daughter, Emma, with her husband, Russell Boggs. His parents and Aunt Tillie, who was living with them, took in Edna. The eldest, Blanche, was sent to live with Rev. Josiah Titzel and his wife, Elizabeth, a Buhl cousin from another branch of the family who lived in Mercer County. The Hotham girls became well-educated misses and Blanche graduated from Thiel College where Rev. Titzel taught.

When Henry Buhl died in 1927, he left his sister, Matilda, a legacy of $150,000 plus the personal property in the summer home. To Edward there was a bequest of $25,000. Aunt Tillie also inherited her choice of Henry's personal effects from both estates. That was when she and Uncle Ed returned to Zelienople and built their large house on East Spring Street.

Boggs and Buhl was an elegant shopping venue for many years until the decline of the North Side. At its height, it boasted sixty-nine retail departments, featured a fine lunch counter, a post, freight and express office, telegraph and telephone operations, had a personal tailoring department and a carpentry shop, a private men's club for their clerks, a stable full of 110 of the finest horseflesh for their delivery wagons and employed roughly 1,750 staff on the average workday. The store and fireproof warehouses covered nine acres of land. Boggs and Buhl was the heart of the North Side.

My great-aunt Louise Miller Buhl
as a young married woman

They were also known for their efficient delivery service, which meant that you could order a fur coat there in the morning and have it delivered the same afternoon. When I had my first job, I bought a fur scarf there from an older clerk who told me, "Mr. Buhl really knew furs." My last major purchase there was my wedding gown in 1944. By 1958 the department store had shuttered as suburbia boomed and the first indoor shopping malls were built. After eighty-nine years in business, Boggs and Buhl was no more.

Looking back at the past, one can wonder what would happen if something had been done differently or what the outcome would have been.

Henry Buhl, Jr. was a multi-millionaire. He had set up an early Pittsburgh charitable trust, The Buhl Foundation, dedicated to the memory of his beloved late wife. She was the love of his life and had always encouraged his philanthropy. His will was skillfully crafted and was so well-written that it was a case study for the law school at the University of Pittsburgh for many years. My husband's class studied the will when he attended there. Uncle Henry had provided for his surviving siblings, nieces, nephews, cousins, in-laws and employees after his death. His sisters received $150,000 each; his brother received $75,000 and the farm in Hurdland, Mo.; and his nieces and nephews received bequests anywhere from $10,000 to $35,000 each. Even his butler, George, received $5,000. But the bulk of his estate was for the Foundation.

Two of his nieces, Cousin Nettie Glenn and her sister, Tiny Wahl, considered contesting the will and came to my grandmother with the idea. They would have needed the cooperation of a majority of the heirs to do this and thought they might be able to persuade Benjamin Buhl, his younger brother, to join their suit.

Grandmother was a person of great integrity. She was indignant at the idea of contesting the will and refused to go against the wishes of her brother. She firmly opposed any such move and told them that her brother had been generous in remembering all of them and that it would be a sacrilege to be greedy and go against his good intentions. Without her support, the well-constructed will could not be opposed and the plan fell apart.

My wonderful husband once pointed out to me that, if my mother had been the beneficiary of a large sum of money, I probably would have attended a prestigious college in the East and we would never have met. I am eternally grateful for my grandmother's wise and thoughtful decision.

Great-Aunt Marie and Great-Uncle Russell Boggs

By contrast, my great-uncle Russell Boggs, who married Henry's sister, Marie, had a fortune equal in size to his brother-in-law. The bulk of Uncle Boggs' investments went into projects like an interurban streetcar railway called the Harmony Line and various North Side real estate. His fortune was lost when the neighborhood declined and cars became the primary mode of transportation into the city. The rest was dispersed among his family, including his adopted daughter,

Emma, upon his death. All that is left of the Boggs legacy is his mansion on North Avenue, which is now a bed and breakfast.

The Buhl family name would surely have died out if the fortune had been dispersed among our family after his death. Instead, The Foundation preserved his name and legacy in the city of Pittsburgh. In 1939 when I was a college freshman, we were invited to attend a private preview of the Buhl Planetarium and the unveiling of Henry Buhl Jr.'s portrait. When the Buhl Planetarium and Observatory was rebuilt at the Carnegie Science Center in 1991, my family, including my grown children and grandchildren, were invited back to the grand re-opening.

Today his Foundation is stronger than ever and continues its good works for the people of Pittsburgh.

The Coulter E. Glenn House

There were many family stories about Coulter E. Glenn, Sr. who built his mansion in Evans City during the days of the oil boom there and in Forward Township. Evans City was known as the town of black gold. He made a fortune, lived lavishly, lost money in dry wells and made another fortune.

When I visited the Glenn mansion at 233 North Washington Street with my mother, we were calling on his widow, Nettie, a Buhl cousin. Although the house was not in its glory days, it was still most impressive. The wide hallway beyond the front entrance porch held not a living room on the left, but what was called the library. The feature that Cousin Nettie showed us with pride was the tiled section in front of the log-burning fireplace that concealed a dumbwaiter box. It brought logs up from the basement and took away the ashes.

The room to the right of the front hall was called the music room. It had several floor-to-ceiling gold-framed mirrors, a grand piano, and a harp. Christine, a daughter who died in her thirties of pneumonia, played the grand piano. Her daughter, Lucille, who taught school in Evans City for a time, played the harp. After having a mental breakdown (which was the talk of the town, for she had run down the street naked) she found a teaching job in Connellsville, Pa. Nettie's son, Coulter, Jr. played the trumpet and had his own jazz group at one time. There was a ballroom with a mirrored ceiling, which may have been on the second floor, and the kitchen was quite modern for its time with many white cabinets and a collection of blue and white dishes on the walls.

By the time we got a chance to visit, the merry-go-round at the Glenn house was long gone. The turn-table in the garage was later sold to H. B. Beighley in Zelienople, who installed it in the garage beside his East Spring Street home. It is there to this day, but no longer operates since the motor has burned out. His grandchildren from New Jersey loved to visit there in the summer. He would take the car out of the garage and put chairs on the turn-table so they could have their own merry-go-round.

We would also visit Nettie's sister, Mary Christina "Tiny" Wahl, who lived much more modestly just a block away. Tina, or Tiny as she was called by the family, had once lived outside Evans City with her husband on her father Fred Buhl's farm, which became known as the Buhl-Wahl farm. Now she and her husband, daughter and son-in-law lived together in town. They had a large garden and did a great deal of canning. Part of the visit there was a trip to their spic-and-span basement to admire the rows of jars of everything that Tiny and her daughter had put up for the winter.

She was close to her sister and they visited by phone every day until Nettie's phone service was cut off for non-payment. Tiny missed their visits and so she gave Nettie money to pay the telephone company each month, but to her dismay, Nettie sometimes used the money for other needs.

Cousin Nettie was having problems with arthritis as well as finances and, while she mentioned these, she managed to laugh and say that things were going to get better. The Glenn mansion was heavily mortgaged to a Butler attorney, who was patient for many years. Neither Nettie's health or finances improved, and, finally, she was forced to move to a small house on the side street across from the mansion. She owned three houses there. One was lived in by Coulter, Jr. and his family. She moved into the middle house, where her hospital bed was in the front room along with the harp, which now was missing many of its strings. There were sagging front steps up to the porch. It was sad to see the tiny house jammed with some of the fine china and lovely things that Nettie refused to part with but would never use again. Lucille was teaching out of town and came home on weekends. Eventually, Nettie died in the home of her daughter in Connellsville.

Snooping

In the summer, we kept our windows open, for there was no air-conditioning in those days. Living in a small town, our houses were close together and backyards often faced either other. As a youngster, I was amazed at what I could overhear on any given summer night from my bedroom window. It could not really be described as snooping, for the quarreling of a neighboring couple was too loud to be ignored at any open window.

The husband, Carl, liked his beer and his wife did not. She complained loudly and that was the start of a battle that went on for hours with screaming and shouting and crying. On some nights, the wife, Clara, would threaten and sometimes call her father, who lived a short block away to come and defend her. He usually responded and then more shouting and carrying-on happened.

In my youthful innocence, I kept expecting that, after each knock-down, drag-out fight, there would be news of a divorce pending. Somehow, to my surprise, that never happened. All the neighbors knew, of course, but pretended that they never heard what went on during those summer nights.

The Girl Scout

In early spring, the hillside to the north of Zelienople is gray with the trunks of trees and their interlacing branches. Before the trees come into leaf, it is possible to see the bare ground and the places where the Girl Scout hikes of my youth took place.

Those were the years when the Girl Scout Handbook was my bible. It was, and still is, a wealth of information on a world of practical things: how to build a fire, Morse code, compass reading, care of the flag, signaling with semaphore flags, first aid, poisons and many other things. The daunting requirements for the various Scout badges were outlined. Most of them seemed too difficult to attempt. Therefore, I selected the Canning Badge, knowing that my mother would be available to help me.

The Pittsburgh department stores all had a small Girl Scout section in the girls' department. These special items and the uniforms were expensive in Depression years. For my birthday, Mother bought the official gray-green yardage and made me a uniform. It was not as crisply tailored as those in the store, but it served me well. Not many of the troop had uniforms. My grandmother bought me an official dark green canvas backpack embellished with the Scout insignia. It was my pride and joy.

The Girl Scout meetings were held weekly after school in the American Legion rooms. This was an apartment above Metz's men's store on Main Street. There were as many as three leaders during my time, volunteers being soon exhausted with our youthful hijinks. Tony was one of them. She was Antoinette Frauenheim, whose parents had a summer home in Zelienople. It was on the outskirts of town with considerable land and a long driveway off Route 68. The family may have had financial reverses during the Depression for they lived there full-time for a number of years. For three years during college, I led a Girl Scout troop at a Pittsburgh church and was much more of a disciplinarian. My only regret was that, with a group of twenty-five to thirty girls, I could not encourage any badge work, as I had no extra time for individual help.

Scouting was full of challenges and opportunities. An employee of the local power company taught us first aid in a class that met at the Community Room of the Municipal Building. We were prepared to rescue others as we learned about tourniquets, made arm slings, bandages and splints for broken limbs. Perhaps there was a badge for this course. Fortunately, none of those emergencies has ever occurred in my life (so far). Our hikes and a weekend at a cabin in Ellwood City were without incident. Like the Boy Scouts, we shared the motto: "Be Prepared."

Backpacks were originally designed for hiking. When our group went on one of the first hikes, it was to the hill above the town. I was well-prepared. My new scout pack held a skillet, matches and paper to start the fire, food, small books for wildflower and tree identification and even a first aid kit, to the amusement of the leader. She looked on in awe as I pulled out the contents of my pack.

The Girl Scout Handbook is faded and worn but has never been discarded because it is so packed with things I should know and can't always remember.

Musical Memories

My mother made piano lessons a high priority for her daughters. Perhaps it was because this was something that had been denied her. Her oldest sister, Laura, was given a few piano lessons, didn't practice and soon gave up. That was enough to convince their stern father that piano lessons were a waste of time and his money. Therefore, the following three daughters never had a chance for any musical education. Mother was disappointed that she didn't get the chance to learn to play and vowed that no child of hers would miss out on piano lessons, whether they wanted them or not.

In 1929, when I was eight years old, the major family purchase was a piano. My mother was frustrated by the fact that she had wanted and never had piano lessons, so this was very important to her. So when I was deemed to be of the age for piano lessons, my mother and father enlisted the help of a German music teacher living in our small town in choosing a piano.

A special trip was made to a large Pittsburgh music store with the "Professor." He selected a Kurtzman upright. It was a big and shining black piano with a clear tone and a stiff action that never relaxed over the years. The Professor was my first music teacher. He was stout and balding with a fringe of white hair. As a very fine musician himself, he was not patient with stupid little children. I went to his house for my lessons. I found him quite frightening, as he would get red in the face and mutter in German as he sat beside the keyboard watching me poorly plunk out my notes.

The only attraction at his house was a parrot in a big cage that I liked to try to talk to when I went there for lessons. It sat in the dining room of their house and was the first parrot that I had ever seen. I was warned away from the cage and told that the parrot's sharp beak could bite off a finger if given the chance. I was secretly pleased when I was told that I would not be going to his house for lessons anymore, as the Professor had died. As a child, I wondered if I had caused his apoplexy during my lessons and felt a bit guilty.

The Professor was followed by several piano teachers that came to my house weekly. They were unmemorable with a lot of boring scales, Czerny exercises and insipid pieces. I spent a lot of time staring at the picture that hung above our piano, a view of the Grand Canal of Venice. I marveled at this strange city where the streets were made of water, and boats were used to get around instead of automobiles or streetcars. It was a great achievement when I finally learned two hymns that I could play for Sunday school.

Finally, a local organist at the English Evangelical Lutheran Church, Mrs. Ruth Covalt Burrell, was hired to teach me. She was an encouraging piano teacher who lived nearby on North Clay Street. A new bride with a young daughter, she became an older friend to me. She promoted classic piano pieces for her annual recitals. Most importantly, she taught me to sight read notes, and music became an important part of my high school social life.

In junior high school there were clarinet lessons in preparation for entering the high school band. In the fall, this was a marching band for football season and

Armistice Day parades. In the winter and spring, this was a concert band for school programs and area and state-wide forensic competitions. The travel for the forensic contests was exciting.

In high school, we formed small musical groups based on combinations of instruments, for which there was available music, and also based on friendships. Playing for school events and sometimes local lodge meetings helped us get over stage fright. We sometimes played for Sunday school at the Reformed Church. I went with Reverend Brown, a neighbor and popular minister at the United Presbyterian Church, when he held a monthly Sunday afternoon service at the Knights of Pythias Home to play the piano.

On rare occasions, we went to concerts in Pittsburgh's impressive Syria Mosque concert hall, built in 1911 in Oakland. The concert that stands out most was a piano recital by famed pianist, composer and conductor Sergei Rachmaninoff. Accompanied by the Pittsburgh Symphony Orchestra, this was during the large-scale tour across the country he undertook in the 1930s. Even in his sixties, he was impressively tall and gaunt, with long arms, huge hands and an exuberant style. The audience gave him a rousing and well-deserved standing ovation. He returned to Pittsburgh often to perform before his death in 1943. How lucky I was to see him in person as a high schooler, and hear his music performed by his own hands.

A new arrival in town was Jane Davis, the only person we knew who played an accordion. She was a petite, quiet girl. Her family lived outside town and was anxious for her to make friends. We often went to her house on a Sunday afternoon. There was a baby grand piano in the living room stacked with sheet music. We could rummage through the old songs. People chose favorite tunes and several of us took turns playing them at the piano while others sang along. Mr. and Mrs. Davis always had hot chocolate and cookies for us in the dining room afterward.

Not all musical memories are positive. My most embarrassing time was when my memory failed at a piano recital. When I reached the mid-point of the piece, which I knew so well from memory, my mind went blank. So I went back to the beginning and started over again. The same thing happened at the mid-point. I was so embarrassed I had to get up and leave. I walked home, crying all the way.

I wanted to take organ lessons, but my request to take lessons and practice at the Presbyterian church where we belonged was refused. Thanks to the influence of my grandmother, who was a pillar of the Grace Reformed Church in Harmony, one town over, I was given permission to use that organ. My teacher was Miss Alice Strohecker, a humorless but demanding instructor. These were summer lessons and she walked to Harmony to meet me at the church. I usually rode my bicycle. Thanks to this beginning I was able to get an organ scholarship for lessons in college. Much of my social life in college revolved around music, too.

Looking back, I am grateful that my mother gave me so many musical opportunities that have enriched my life.

Shopping Days

Some of my memories are connected with major family purchases. Our first car was a Star automobile, which was made by the Durant Motors Company in the 1920s. That was a big event since it first involved building a garage in the backyard. My parents had the cement foundation poured and then built the garage themselves. It is still standing! During the winter, cars couldn't be driven because the roads were too bad. My father took the streetcar into work at the National Tube Company in Ellwood City. Meanwhile, the car was put up on cement blocks and the air was let out of the balloon tires to preserve them, as they were made of real rubber. The second car was a Hupmobile, another early car company no longer in business.

As a telegraph operator, Daddy took a great interest in the beginnings of the radio. His first one was a table model, about 36-inches long and 12-inches high. This radio required tuning with many dials and it was listened to with ear phones, one person at a time. As radios improved, we had a tall cabinet model on legs that stood in the dining room. This too required some adjusting of the dials.

Another big investment was a General Electric refrigerator, a square white box on legs with the big coils on the top. This was our family's first refrigerator. We bought it when I was six years old, as it was deemed a necessity with the birth of my sister, Ceil. Prior to that, food preservation in winter was by a window box that was fastened outside the kitchen

My sister Ceil and I in our new winter coats

window. There was a fruit room with a dirt floor in the cellar where potatoes, onions, apples, preserved eggs, butter, milk and canned fruits were kept. One of my childhood chores was to take things up and downstairs for my mother.

Heberling's Variety Store was on Main Street. A Mr. Heberling was never seen, but Mrs. Heberling was always present and usually the only person tending store. At holiday times, there might be one of her children helping her. The small shop was just a half-block away from my grade school on the opposite side of the street and this is where I did my important shopping for penny candy. It was dark and incredibly cluttered inside. Walls were covered with packed shelves and merchandise was hanging from the ceiling. A little bell tinkled as the door opened.

Down the left-hand aisle was the candy counter, the case covered with curved glass. Mrs. Heberling stood behind the case, endlessly patient as I debated my choice of coconut bacon strips, chewing gum, jaw breakers, chewy green mint leaves, licorice strips, sugar cigarettes, lollipops or wax bottles filled with sweet-colored liquid. She would put the purchase in a small white paper bag as I counted out my pennies.

On the right side of the store were sewing notions, handkerchiefs, games, jacks, balls, paper doll books, celluloid baby dolls (which were very fragile, as they were an early form of plastic and could easily melt) and more permanent items. Rolls of four-inch-wide taffeta ribbon was sold by the yard for my Sunday dress-up hair bows, as well as the holders to gather the bow and fasten it to the hair on top of my head. That was what every well-dressed little girl wore. It took even longer to make decisions in this part of the store and no salesperson interrupted my dreaming. This was also where my savings were used for Christmas presents, such as handkerchiefs for five or ten cents, which made good gifts. From a tray of ten-cent rings I chose one for my grandmother, since she only wore a gold wedding band and I felt she needed more rings. An expensive purchase for my father was a pack of cigarettes. No one questioned my buying them back then!

Another store on Main Street was Graff's 5&10 Store a block away. It was much larger and carefully arranged and presided over by the stately, gray-haired Mr. Graff. Sometimes he was assisted by his wife, as they lived right above the store. Mr. Graff followed me around the store and, if I touched anything, he would adjust its place by a quarter of an inch in a disapproving manner. He never smiled. Mrs. Graff was much less threatening.

Shopping at Mrs. Heberling's was a much more pleasant and a form of treasure hunting among the jumble, which I enjoy doing to this day. Most of all it was an early exercise in independence.

Feeling the Fabric

My feeling for fabric began as a youngster when my mother made most of my clothes. I was allowed to go with her to Lizzie Ketterer's dry goods store and help chose the patterns and the materials. The big pattern books of McCalls, Betterick, Simplicity and Vogue were on a low wooden counter with several stools in front. The selections for children's fashions were unfairly small. Even so, it took a long time to make a choice. Once a pattern was selected, it took even more time to find just the right fabric, and feeling was an important part of the process.

Two small dressing rooms were in the back of the store where a few racks of ready-made dresses were available. A dress or two might be displayed in the front windows along with hats, gloves, purses and umbrellas. Ladies in town always were interested in their attractive window displays.

Lizzie Ketterer was tall and dark-haired and noted for wearing large, colorful earrings. Her sister, Sophie, managed the store with her and was endlessly patient with customers young and old. Both spinsters, they built an attractive house on East New Castle Street where their mother lived with them.

From time to time, Mother enlisted the help of a dressmaker who came to the house for the cutting and fitting of dresses. A second fitting at the dressmaker's home in Harmony usually followed several weeks later. No material was wasted, for Grandmother used leftovers for her quilts, which became a history of past dresses. Mother never attempted making coats. Mrs. Myers was the dressmaker who worked on coats and furs. She seemed able to speak with a mouthful of pins and that is the way that I remember her.

As a teenager, I did a lot of sewing beyond the required apron that was the first project in home economics class. I had some ready-made clothes from the Boggs and Buhl department store in Pittsburgh, Offuts and Troutmans in Butler, and Ketterer's store only when there was a seasonal sale.

My sewing skills came in handy years later when living in Nassau, Bahamas. I was able to make my daughter's school uniforms, unlike many other mothers, who had to rely on a dressmaker. St. Andrew's School had numerous entertainments which required costumes and my husband was a member of the Nassau Players and occasionally needed a costume. For one Shakespearean play I had to create a codpiece!

The British Red Cross held an annual fundraising fair in Government House Gardens in Nassau. The Bay Street merchants, who handled yard goods, never sold remnants. These were donated to a committee for a sewing booth at the Fair. Several months earlier, the committee would host a morning coffee where all the remnants were displayed and given out. Volunteers could feel the fabrics and decide what they might be able to create. These pieces were signed out to each person. It was amazing to see the end results at the fair.

With the increased cost of patterns and fabric these days, home sewing has been relegated to the past. But I am still fascinated by ideas for remnants and love to feel the fabric in the few remaining yard goods store sections. And fabric is one of the best travel souvenirs. It packs easily and can have a of myriad uses. There is still a drawer of bits and pieces in my cottage, just in case!

Hair Days

No one ever said my hair was my crowning glory. I was born with a bit of fuzz which became fine blonde hair. The best solution for that was a Dutch boy haircut with square bangs and straight sides done by the local barber, Mr. Klinefelter. Mr. Klinefelter was a fat, jovial man who was our next-door neighbor. He made me feel very important when he put a board across the arms of the barber chair for my seat and then a too-short ride up. A big striped apron was tied around my neck. I gazed at myself in the mirror and admired the shaving mugs on the shelves beside the mirror. Some of the mugs had floral decorations and a few had the names of the mugs' owners.

I had to shut my eyes when my bangs were cut. The shaver tickled the back of my neck. The final flourish was the long soft brush, then a dab of bay rum and a sprinkle of talcum powder. I never minded going to the barber and this was my hairstyle throughout my elementary school years. From being blonde in my childhood, my hair darkened to "dishwater blonde" as I grew older.

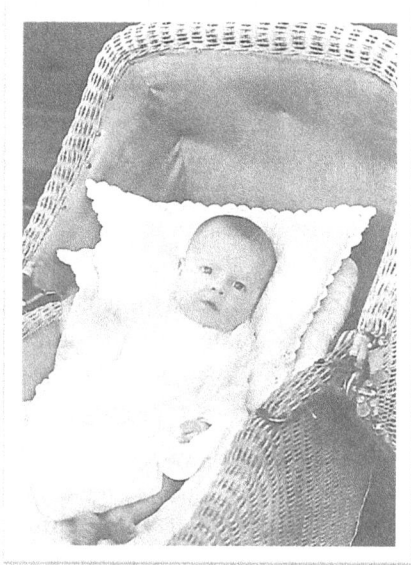

My earliest "bit of fuzz" days

My playmate, Jeanie, had long hair that her mother put up with strips of rags. This made long sausage-like curls. For Sundays and dress-up occasions, we wore big four-inch taffeta ribbon hair bows gathered in a specially designed hair clasp.

Beauty shops were far in the future. My friend Hope Mitchell's mother had a gas-heated curling iron that we experimented with in junior high school. Her mother sometimes did "Marcels" for neighbors that produced bumpy waves rather than end curls. Soon after this came ocean-like waves. These were achieved with a liberal dousing of a gummy setting mix applied to the hair, which was then pushed into place with a series of long combs. Those waves never lasted long in my fine hair. In college, most of the girls had long hair that was put up every night in pin curls. Few had permanents. When you had a date on a rainy or even just a damp night, the result was that the end curls straightened out, leaving one looking droopy.

Mary Haverstraw opened the first beauty shop in her Grandview Avenue home in the 1930s. My mother went there to have her hair set in the current style, even though she had naturally curly hair. The first permanents were about to arrive. To demonstrate the safety of the process, Miss Haverstraw rented the high school auditorium and invited the public to a demonstration of a permanent wave.

There on center stage was a large stand topped with a metal hood, from which many wires hung down with clasps on each end. Miss Haverstraw's white-haired aunt, Mrs. Kloffenstein, was the model. The process took a long time but the audience sat entranced. I thought it was like watching grass grow. The final result was a mass of curls. Everyone surreptitiously watched Mrs. Kloffenstein for weeks afterward to see if her hair would fall out or turn yellow.

Permanents provided the cycle of a haircut – a too curly head of hair, some weeks of reasonably natural curl, and the inevitable growing out. The hair still needed to be set. Then, for some time, home permanents could be purchased at the drugstore. Young housewives embraced this cost savings and usually enlisted the help of a friend to help with the process. The results were often unpredictable, which is why they disappeared years ago.

My first experience with the bouffant hair style was during a holiday in Mandeville, Jamaica. My hair was teased to a size that amazed my family. It was not easy to maintain. This style marked the demise of the millinery industry, since hats would crush the hairdo. It was terrible to see women in the grocery with their big rollers not even covered by a scarf. It was difficult not to comment on their appearance.

For many years I styled my hair with permanents that gave it that curl I so desperately wanted when I was younger. But perms were no longer taking well as I became older. The first puff of wind or drop of rain would destroy the beauty shop's setting. I finally accepted my fate, that my hair would always be straight. The wheel has turned full circle and now straight hair is acceptable, the longer, the better.

For a time, my bangs remained and the sides were pulled back into a bun as I aged. My hair was dyed a very light ash blonde to hide the mix of gray. Then at ninety-two, I threw out the bun and the dye and my all-white hair got a fashionable, no-fuss pixie cut. Straight hair has finally come back in style!

Haystacks

Haystacks aren't what they used to be. Once they would have been small golden stacks dotting the newly mown field or towering mounds waiting to be stored inside barns. In Europe, the small mushroom-shaped stones that anchored haystacks to the ground are now turned into garden ornaments. Today the hay may be rolled into bundles that resemble a loaf of bread and they are often wrapped in plastic and stored in the corner of a field near a barn.

I remember two wonderful haystack experiences.

After oil was discovered on his Forward Township farm outside Evans City, Pa., my grandfather moved to Zelienople to join the world of banking. Leaving most of the banking business to his brothers, he bought a small farm on a hillside out of town and became a gentleman farmer. There was a small house on the property and a bank barn. He hired a man to do the farming and kept a horse and buggy in town, by which he went to the farm almost daily.

The farm house was usually uninhabited, and as a girl, my mother and her friends often camped there in the summers. They had a sign made christening it "Camp Overlook" for its view over the valley below. Pictures show them as teenagers lined up on a fence behind the sign in their long full skirts, leg-of-mutton-sleeved blouses and Gibson girl hairdos. This was adventure camping in 1905.

Years later my mother took me to the farm for a picnic with friends of hers and their children. It was fun to explore the small, empty farmhouse and the nearby barn built into the hillside. Wide doors opened into the shadowy floor and the cool darkness inside. Opposite these doors was a somewhat smaller door that stood open to the top of a story-high haystack.

My playmate, Jeanie, and I discovered that we could run through the barn and leap out the rear door to the top of the haystack. It was like being a bird for a second and the closest I would ever come to flying. We made a soft landing in the hay and slid down the slippery stack to run around the side of the barn and leap again and again. It was a sensation never to be forgotten.

Years later, I had another lovely haystack experience during the summer of my sophomore year of college when I was a counselor at Camp Redwing of the Pittsburgh Girl Scout Council. We were on duty with the girls all day, every day. Some of each unit's counselors were allowed free time after nine o'clock to leave the camp. One moonlight night, three of us left camp for a hike. We crossed a number of fields, and a small wood, sometimes climbing over or under fences and finding a stile at one fence line. The summer evening was getting cool and we sat on a log for a smoke. I didn't smoke, but tried a cigarette and found the taste bitter. But the warmth of the lit cigarette was pleasant to hold.

We found an isolated haystack away from any barn or buildings and climbed to the top. We had a snack and made our beds in the hay, covering ourselves against the dew of the night with the ground cloth we had brought from camp. It was a magical night but rather short, for the sun awakened us early in the morning. We slid down the hay and found a blackberry patch where we had some quick refreshment before returning to camp in time for breakfast.

Now the times are different and so are haystacks! Rolled and wrapped in plastic, there isn't much of an opportunity for haystack flying.

Amelia Earhart and Me

I saw Amelia Earhart, I heard her speak, and I fell in love with her when I was eight years old. That was the experience of many people after she spoke in the amphitheater of the Chautauqua Institution on July 20, 1929 to an audience of about five thousand.

My family often vacationed in Chautauqua, N.Y. Chautauqua was a favorite place of Mother's. Our holiday was always just an easy one-day drive from home. We also would visit her cousin Ida Gelbach Shank and her husband in nearby Jamestown.

During the two-month season at Chautauqua there was a little theater, some music classes, a resident symphony orchestra, workshops, lectures and a bevy of activities. There was a Boys Club and a Girls Club and all ages were provided for. I was enrolled in the Girls Club for our brief stay, but the lessons on canoeing are still remembered. We learned how easy it was to tip over a canoe; that it was important not to try to swim away from the canoe; how to right the canoe and get into it again. Even when the canoe was filled with water, it would float and keep you safe and could be hand-paddled.

The central amphitheater was the site of morning, afternoon and evening programs. The audiences were white, church-going and very conventional. Amelia Earhart was the featured nationally-known speaker one afternoon. The older audience viewed her appearance with a great deal of skepticism. This was the 1920s, after all; what was this young woman doing in the developing world of the airplane?

That sunny day, the thirty-two-year-old landed her airplane dramatically on the 14th fairway of the Chautauqua Golf Course. After a private luncheon, she was to speak about the 20-hour and 40-minute flight she'd taken across the Atlantic the year before in the tri-motored Fokker plane, "Friendship."

Amelia Earhart came on stage wearing an ankle-length dress of brown cotton eyelet, looking very feminine. She had been presented with an orange corsage and her light brown hair was short and curling. She spoke with enthusiasm and the conviction of her dreams. She described the joy and freedom of flying. She pointed out the value of her travel to advance the knowledge of flight. She was utterly convincing. The mood of the audience warmed and changed completely as her appearance and her words won them over. Many, like me, must have fallen in love with her.

In 1996, author Jane Mendelsohn wrote her first novel, *I Was Amelia Earhart*, that combined fact and imagination about that charismatic woman. As I read it, the book brought back the memory of seeing Amelia Earhart in the flesh – and how to handle a tipped canoe.

The Monster

The monster that lived in the cellar was big and black and round. Its multiple fat arms extended in many directions. A fire glowed in its belly all winter. The beast had to be fed frequently with coal shoveled into an opened door. Much regular attention was required by way of a lever to shake out dead ashes and then a lower door opened to remove the dusty ash.

In the fall, a coal truck would arrive to fill the basement coal cellar. A metal chute would be put from the truck through the high window to bring the black coal clattering down the chute. A cloud of black dust enveloped the process. The garden hose wetting down the coal helped a bit to keep down the dust.

In time, an innovation was installed that helped to feed the monster's appetite. A conveyor belt ran from the coal cellar to the fiery mouth. However, the conveyor had to have coal shoveled into it. The shaking and ash removal went on as usual.

The house was chilly every morning until the furnace came to life. A small gas heater in the bathroom was where we got dressed in the morning. Then the monster responded with welcome warmth for another day.

A wonderful change took place when the monster had its insides replaced by a gas burner and no longer had to be fed the dirty soft coal. Some years later the huge beast was replaced by a neat shiny clean gas furnace. The soft sooty days were over at last.

People who speak of the "good old days" have forgotten their past struggles with Monsters.

Losing My Father

In the fall of 1929, my father, Hugh, became ill and could no longer work at his office job at the National Tube Company in Ellwood City, but there seemed to be no definite diagnosis. Uncle Ed and Aunt Tillie Winter were ardent followers of Dr. Hay's Diet and were convinced that would be a benefit to Daddy, and so he spent a month alone in January 1930 at the Hays Sanatorium in East Aurora, N.Y. Mother and Daddy had gone together to the sanatorium, but a week later she had to come home, after she received word that I was ill.

My father, Hugh McKay

That was a terrible winter. I had developed scarlet fever and was quarantined for a month. When my father returned from New York, he did the shopping for our house and left it outside the quarantine sign-posted door. My sister, Lucille, and Daddy stayed with Grandmother Gelbach up the street. After the month of isolation was over and everything was thoroughly fumigated, they returned home. A month later, Ceil came down with scarlet fever herself, so it was my turn to stay with Grandmother and my father for a month.

My father died May 22, 1930 at the age of forty, leaving a heartbroken widow with two small daughters to care for. I was nine years old and Ceil was only three. His death was registered officially as myocarditis, an inflammation of the heart, which is usually brought on by a viral infection. Mother felt that his wartime months in the muddy trenches during World War I had weakened his immune system.

Grandmother was a pillar of support at that time. Funeral services were held at our East Spring Street home and then a military graveside interment was held at the family plot across from the Zelienople Mausoleum. There was ample space beside the road near the mausoleum, and for many years the American Legion held their Memorial Day services there at the end of May. For me, it was like my father's funeral was being painfully repeated every year.

I never knew much about my father's service during World War I. But in 1962 at the age of forty-one, I had the chance to go to France on a vacation with my family. As we drove through the French countryside the poppies were blooming, and I thought of my father.

The Yankee

I was eleven years old when I found out that I was a Yankee. The Civil War was just a date in my history book with no connection to me. I was born and raised in Pennsylvania where my maternal family had lived for generations.

My father was from Alabama. He had grown up in Eufaula, which was a gracious small town on the banks of the Chattahoochee River. Eufaula is a Native American name and the town was spared the destruction of the Civil War, so it has many lovely old homes in a historic district. His father was a first-generation Scottish-American named Farquhar McKay and his mother was Lonnie Bert Greene. She could trace her ancestry back to Revolutionary War Colonel Christopher Greene and the English minister theologian Roger Williams, who founded the colony of Rhode Island.

Hugh had a brother Donald (named for his paternal grandfather) and two sisters, Louise and Winnie (named for his paternal grandmother). Travel was expensive, and so there was little opportunity for us to visit his brother Donald and his sister Winnie in the South. Men are seldom good at writing letters, so contact with our cousins was minimal. Daddy did teach Mother to cook grits. Two years after my father died, my mother wanted us to maintain closer connections with his family.

So we traveled by train, my mother, my five-year-old sister, Ceil, and me. I remember the majesty of the Cincinnati Railroad Station where we changed trains. I had never seen anything so grand. Then, when we got to Georgia, I was amazed, looking out the train windows, at the soil that was so red and the farm cabins that looked so very poor.

We were met in Atlanta by Uncle Don McKay and stayed with him and his wife, Aunt Ruth, and their three girls. Josephine was several years older than me; Mildred was my age; and Marjorie was a bit younger. They were very hospitable and took us sightseeing. One day we went to Stone Mountain, which was the nearby local wonder. Another day we saw the Cyclorama, an astounding diorama of the burning of Atlanta, keeping the memory of the Civil War vivid and alive.

From Atlanta we went to Rockwood, Ala. and visited Aunt Winnie and her husband, Grady Farley. They had an older daughter, Mary, a son, Grady, Jr., called Mac, who was fourteen, and Ann, the youngest, who was ten. Rockwood was a tiny place centered around the limestone quarry where Uncle Grady was superintendent, so we visited the quarry and I brought home a piece of polished limestone. It was our first experience with Southern cooking. Saturday was cooking day and a huge amount of food was prepared, which was served for Sunday dinner and repeated most of the week. It probably saved cooking in the heat of the summer. Aunt Winnie's cooking and her Southern fried chicken is one of the strong memories I have of the South. After we returned home, Aunt Winnie wrote friendly letters to us, as did Aunt Ruth, Uncle Don's wife, until she died.

When we returned to Pennsylvania, I asked Grandmother Gelbach, who was born in 1854, what she remembered about the Civil War. She was about my age at the time and she said she recalled troop trains coming through Rochester, Pa.

along the Ohio River when she was visiting her Speyerer grandparents there. She remembered Lincoln's funeral train and the national period of mourning. Everyone wore black for months. Store windows were draped in mourning cloth with black drapes around Lincoln's picture.

Years later I had the chance to read some of her paternal grandfather's letters, which were written during the Civil War. Although Christian Buhl had at least three grandsons fighting on the Union side, he was opposed to the war. He had come from a German province to ply his trade as a hatmaker at the age of twenty-five and to escape the European conflicts so the last thing he wanted was to be in the middle of a war again.

Mother did not drive so, following my father's death, she sold the Hupmobile. Several years later she realized that a car was a necessity not only for us but also for the business she was doing for Grandmother. She told a local car salesman "Red" Ziegler that she would buy a car from him if he would teach her to drive. He accepted the challenge and she bought a Plymouth sedan for $600.

One of the longer day trips that we made was to Akron, Ohio to meet Father's other sister, Aunt Louise, for the first time. Her husband was Hugh Little and they had three daughters and one son. We didn't meet her husband and the visit seemed short and awkward. A few annual Christmas cards were all that came of that meeting.

The McKay Cousins: Me, Josephine, Ceil and Mildred

A few years later two of our Atlanta cousins, Josephine and Mildred McKay, came North to visit us as teenagers. They were terrified on the train ride from the railway station in Cincinnati, Oh., where they changed trains to Pittsburgh and then on to Zelienople, because the train cars were not segregated and they had to share a car with black people. We found their behavior odd. We had an outdoor sleepover at Jane Davis' home in the country, went swimming and they were there for a special tea room dinner party for my grandmother's birthday. Train travel was a big adventure for them.

I made a return trip to Atlanta and was entertained royally by my cousins and their friends. There were home parties, a blind date with a short red-haired boy who wanted to hold hands and put his arm around me at the movies, dancing and a watermelon "cuttin'." In contrast to Pennsylvania, watermelons were cheap and so at these outside picnics only the sweet, ripe red heart of the melon was eaten.

Mildred and I were of an age and had the most in common, so we corresponded regularly after our return home.

The Atlanta McKay girls couldn't have friends over to their house. Their maternal grandmother had come to live with them following their mother's death, and she was ostensibly supposed to be running the household. However, the girls did all the housework and cooking. There was no diagnosis or word for their grandmother's condition then, but she certainly was in the depths of senility or dementia. She alternated between crying and screaming about everything that went on. Uncle Don and the girls were imprisoned in her fretful world and it made their home life very difficult.

Cousin Mildred died in 1947 at the age of twenty-six, ending my close contact with the Atlanta kin. Later in life, her sister, Josephine, provided me with copies of pages from the family Bible showing that my grandfather, Farquhar McKay, was born in Louisville, Barbour County, Ala. With this information, I wrote to the Barbour County courthouse asking for copies of records of my father's parents. In return, there was a letter from a genealogist to whom my inquiry was referred. She explained her fees for time, travel and copying and, upon receipt of a deposit, would send me what information she could find.

With the help of the genealogist, my sister and I learned that our great-grandfather Donald McKay, also called Daniel, was born in 1812 in Scotland and was a farmer near Louisville, Ala. We decided to make a trip to follow-up on the records that she had produced, which included cemeteries, churches, census reports from over twenty years and the estate which he left when he died in 1855 before the Civil War.

We enrolled in a five-day Elderhostel program at George T. Bagley State Park in Georgia, which was not far from Eufaula, Ala. We rented a car at Columbus, Ga. airport and spent the weekend in Eufaula before the start of the Elderhostel.

I had a letter of introduction to a local resident who took us to a Saturday morning meeting of the county historical society and also took us out to dinner that night at the country club. Sunday morning, we went to the First Presbyterian Church where the McKays had been members. We were greeted warmly, but given little specific information. We were early for the service and enjoyed strolling along the wide street lined with beautiful pre-Civil War homes. These houses were kept intact, we were told, due to a friendship the townspeople had with the Union general who had captured the land in Georgia across the Chattahoochee River. That afternoon we found the graves of our great-uncle Alexander McKay and his family.

Recently, the anniversary of the Civil War has called attention to a dark time in our country's history. Discussion in the media was whether the Civil War was about the abolition of slavery or the issue of states' rights. Rarely was anything mentioned about the economic impact of the end of slavery and the fact that the South was fighting for cold, hard cash. This was the money, often their entire wealth, that they had invested in buying slaves, and those enslaved people were what they depended on for cheap labor.

Great-grandfather Donald McKay's estate was very revealing. The assets were named down to the exact number of bushels of corn and wheat, as well as the worth of his 250-acre farm. He had five slaves of varying values and the most valuable slave was worth twice as much as the farm acreage. The total value of the slaves made up the bulk of his estate. The census revealed that his widow, Winney McKay, and her unmarried sister, Ann McRae, who lived with them, stayed on the farm for twenty years after his death, until her five children were grown and on their own.

The following weekend we returned to the same motel in Eufaula and drove to the county seat of Barbour County. We went to the courthouse to look at records and were shown into a room full of shelves filled with huge, dusty volumes. We were given free rein. It was overwhelming, an impossible task as we didn't know where to begin. We were grateful for the information gleaned by an experienced researcher.

Sunday morning, we drove to the Pea River Presbyterian church in the country beyond Louisville. A highway marker near the church identified the area as "Little Scotland" because of the number of Scots who settled there. We were early for the morning service and had ample time to explore the adjoining cemetery. There we found the grave of Farquhar McKay in one plot with the name of his lodge, and, in an earlier section of the graveyard, the tombstone of his first wife Rosa Faison. Beside it were the graves of their two young boys, who did not survive to adulthood.

Our grandmother, Lonnie Bert, his second wife, died many years after him, probably at the home of her daughter Winnie, and was buried in Russellville, Ala. There were no gravestones for Donald McKay and his wife in any of the cemeteries we visited, and presumably they were both buried on the farm property, which was common in earlier days.

Two strangers in the small Pea River congregation aroused some curiosity that morning. We told the friendly questioners of our family search and then attended the Sunday service. When the minister gave his announcements, he welcomed "our Yankee visitors." I whispered to my sister, "At least he didn't say damn Yankees!" Following the service, we met a woman who was the church historian. She took my address and kindly sent me church records showing the family participation.

The records of the Pea River Presbyterian Church, where my McKay and McRae ancestors attended, showed that the "negroes" were full members of the church. They sat in the balcony of the church and were given the polite euphemism of "servants" rather than slaves. The number of white members was listed and the number of black members in the records. Unsurprisingly, in 1876, the congregation suddenly became completely white when the blacks gained independence and formed their own church in that part of Alabama.

So many lives are lost in wars that are basically about greed and power. The tragedy lives on for centuries in whispered designations such as "Yankee."

Two

Coming of Age

Junior High School
1933 – 1934

It was exciting to be in Zelienople Junior High School at last. Our world seemed to expand even though we were the two lowliest classes in one wing of the buff brick high school on High Street.

Miss Lois Gallagher was the seventh-grade homeroom teacher. One of the older teachers in the school, she was capable, dignified and often dull. She warmed to the subject of geography, however. She had attended a summer school course on Central and South America and delighted in pronouncing and teaching us the multi-syllable names of faraway capitals, mountains and lakes.

Mrs. Bertha Meeder was a petite blonde widow who taught eighth grade and English classes. She was a favorite teacher of mine and I spent time with her after school seeking advice on what my future career should be.

For the first time in my educational career there were some male teachers. The high school athletic director was a tall, angular blond man named Mr. Mauno Siljander. He was often tongue-tied and awkward when away from the football field or basketball court. He taught an uninteresting health class. I can't recall the name of the little man who taught a history class, but I will call him Mr. Gray since that was his character. He was older than most of the faculty and said to be the only teacher with a prestigious master's degree. He was short with a balding hairline and wore a gray three-piece suit with a vest over a slightly protruding waist. His advanced degrees had not given him any teaching skills. He may have been the perpetual academic. His discipline was poor and his classes were dull and gray.

To the left of the big building were two small wooden buildings called "portables." They were originally meant as temporary housing, but had been permanent for years. The woodshop was in one and the music room in the other.

53

The boys had woodshop in one of the "portable buildings" where they made book holders as first projects. The girls had a cooking class in the school kitchens in the basement. There was no school cafeteria. We worked in teams and it was a complicated exercise in assembling all the utensils needed, the ingredients and the recipe to produce a simple but inedible bowl of cream of wheat.

Later, in home economics, we sewed half-aprons. There was the opportunity to take music lessons on band instruments which could lead to future participation in the high school band. I had a clarinet and some private lessons in the summer with music teacher Mr. Paul Inglefield who lived a block away. The clarinet was eventually passed down to my sister, Ceil. She was six years younger so there was never any passing down of clothing, but she did get the clarinet.

A visiting teacher came to oversee writing classes of the Peterson method, which emphasized arm movement. This was to be achieved by exercises making endless circles, waves, and points with the arms rather than fingers. I had top grades in all subjects but this writing class was my nemesis. In order to leave eighth grade, you had to pass writing and that was a tight squeeze for me.

Our house was within sight of the high school and within earshot as well. I never went to school until the first bell rang, knowing there would be ample time to get there before the second and last bell. If books or assignments were forgotten, it was easy to nip home between periods. Then there were times when a teacher might need something.

My childhood home was neither affluent nor deprived, but we had only one silver-plated grapefruit spoon. That was never a problem since my mother was the only one who liked grapefruit. She would cut it the night before and cover the cut half with sugar to soak in overnight and thus make the sour fruit edible. Much sweeter-tasting grapefruit has been developed since then. In home economics class, the teacher wanted to illustrate the difference between a soup and a bouillon spoon, a salad and a dinner fork, and so on, and so the grapefruit spoon went to school.

At an estate sale many years later, there was a set of eight silver-plated grape fruit spoons that somehow looked familiar. After buying the set and getting them home, I found that they were the identical pattern to Mother's lone spoon.

There was a great deal of freedom outside of school. Our town was small with narrow brick streets. We could walk everywhere or skate or ride bicycles. There was a small section of Clay Street at the foot of East Spring Street that was smooth and almost flat and we sometimes played bicycle polo using hockey sticks and a flattened tin can for a puck. In the back of Miss Emma Passavant's house, there was a tennis court on the Clay Street end of her property. This was a favorite summer hangout, watching others and waiting for a turn to play. She had a shed where the net was stored, along with a roller for the dirt court and a marker that was filled with lime to mark the lines. The older boys took care of that.

In winter, we went sled riding on Endress Hill and ice skating on the Connoquenessing Creek. The sturdiest wool snowsuits were worn. An ice-skating outfit could never have been worn for we sat on a log near a fire making a muddy puddle by the creekside while putting on our skates. We set off on the creek below the Main Street bridge on Lava Crucible property. The ice on the creek could be unpredictable. No one fell in, which was miraculous since we sometimes skated along the narrow ice bridge of the creek edge with water coming up onto the ice between the frozen sections. For a brief time, Mr. Archer, president of the borough council, persuaded the city fathers to open a shallow city reservoir for skating. Some wooden steps were built down the bank and also a warming shed. Volunteers cleared the snow from the ice.

Carl "Sparky" Glenn had parties at his house. He was the only child of the local funeral director and his parents were pleased to host parties in their spacious quarters for his friends. These were the first girl and boy parties with post office and spin the bottle games. The large living room was also the setting for funerals. Double doors at the end of the room led into the casket display area. Sparky delighted in showing off the latest stock there, which included innerspring mattresses and the satin linings that were embellished with hundreds of tucks. That was spooky! He was the first boy to give a favored girl candy or flowers and he set an example for others. He followed his father into the funeral business, as one might guess.

Transition to the high school was easy for us city kids who were in the same building, had taken part in school assemblies, and had attended all of the basketball and football games. This would not be the case for half of the incoming ninth graders, who came from all the country schools in the area, where their classes ended with eighth grade. The high school was then the center of almost all community activity.

Zelienople High School
1935 – 1939

Broad steps led up from the High Street sidewalk to a wide walk crossing an open lawn to the entrance of Zelienople High School. The buff brick two-story rectangular building with its flat roof had none of the grand features of the older grade school. Steps inside the double doors led to the first-floor hallways on either side and directly into the school auditorium was an all-purpose room that served as a gymnasium as well. It was the setting for plays, concerts, lectures, school assemblies and community events.

The small group of thirty to thirty-five pupils who started first grade together had few changes over the years. Now we were to begin four years of high school. Suddenly, the class size more than doubled from the influx of students who had been in the first eight grades in Harmony, the Orphans Home and Farm School, and other communities in the area. There were now two homerooms for each grade. Our close-knit group was somewhat uncomfortable with all of these newcomers. It was probably even more of a change for the new students. There was no school cafeteria so they had to bring lunches and manage transportation. A few boarded in town.

The Orphans Home students were not permitted to take part in extra-curricular activities because they had to return to the home promptly for work duties. The girls helped with cooking, cleaning and mending and the boys took care of the farm chores. We were social butterflies by comparison.

The auditorium had a stage in front with two doors on either side that led to the downstairs locker rooms. The open floor was a basketball court with hoops at each end. It took up so much of the space that spectators in the first row of the raised seats might have to duck a ball or else have a player land in their lap. During the school day, the gym classes and the volleyball games took place there. Fixed seats in the back half of the room ascended to the second floor and accommodated the whole school for assembly programs and school dances. For school plays, concerts and meetings the floor was filled with folding chairs that were kept in storerooms under the tiered seats. The band practiced before classes started in the morning. In football season the band marched on nearby East Spring Street or on the football field for their halftime performance practices.

Posing with bandmates and my clarinet before a parade in downtown Zelienople in 1937

Invitations to parades in the area meant fun trips for the band. Parades are not as glamorous for the band as for the spectators. There is a great deal of standing around for the parade to get underway. The parade route is usually longer than expected. Players have to keep in step, keep their eyes on their music and avoid stepping in any potholes. By the end of high school, it was evident to me that the band uniforms were either too hot or not warm enough for the prevailing weather.

The clarinet was my band instrument, and in time, I graduated to the second chair in that section. I sang in the girls' chorus as well. Spring was a busy time for the music department with extra rehearsals to prepare the designated numbers for the district forensic competitions. These were often two-day events in different parts of the state and involved travel and some overnight stays. My mother often chaperoned us and drove a carload of students.

In the summer of my junior year in high school, I worked in the town's community library assisting Mrs. Beighley, the librarian. I helped people find books and returned books to shelves, but I was never allowed to stamp books out or take them in. There were always interesting people coming into the library. One frequent patron came with a shopping bag and read the entire shelf of books written by Grace Livingston King. She was irate that there were no more by that author. A shy girl took out books on how to be popular. My reward at the end of the summer was the gift of a book.

The state requirements for graduation from high school at that time was sixteen credits. I also earned additional credits in typing, music, and home economics. I took everything but advanced algebra and calculus. Mr. Ronald "Pappy" Clouse, the science teacher and later principal, told the junior chemistry class that the next year's physics class was demanding. Any girls who needed science credits to go into nursing were the only girls who should take the class. I considered this a challenge and signed up with the only other girl who actually was planning to be a nurse. It was a small class and I enjoyed the freedom it involved. One fall afternoon, Mr. Clouse took us down the street to his house and demonstrated pulleys in a backyard tree.

George Gage was the high school principal and taught Civics classes as well. It was a thorough grounding in state and federal governments and how they work. He made it interesting with his warm personality. Two favorite teachers, who later became lifelong friends, were Ed Young in History and Eleanor Stout in English. Mr. Young could always amplify current events with an in-depth background. Later, I discovered that his source was none other than the New York Times. In her English classes, Miss Stout would ignore students who knew the answers in favor of bringing out the shy or needy pupils. She coached the school plays and persuaded me to take the role of the nasty mother-in-law in the junior class play. I discovered that it was fun to get audience reactions and laughs. Don Meiser was in charge of music. In addition to being young and talented, he seemed like one of us. Mr. Clarence Wardle taught business and typing. My graduation present was a big, black, heavy and extremely noisy standard Underwood typewriter purchased for $25 at the school's trade-in price. Using it in college, I was called "Rosie the Riveter" by my dormmates.

Such courses as Driver's Education were long in the future. Mother hired a neighbor with steel nerves to teach me to drive and I got my driver's license shortly after my eighteenth birthday. The test was given and I passed at the Pittsburgh site on Washington Boulevard. Getting there was hair-raising, as I had to negotiate from the north side of the city along the narrow cobblestoned East Street, which had street car tracks running down the middle, slick from recent rain.

I was editor of the yearbook and active in so many activities that I had the inflated impression that the school could not go on without me. In spite of looking forward to college, there was a reluctance to leave familiar surroundings.

With graduation approaching, Mr. Gage thought that the ceremonies could be made more pertinent if the speeches could be tied to a subject of local interest, namely the steel industry. To that end, he took the leading three students of the class to tour the Clairton Plant of United States Steel Company. He hoped that we could incorporate this experience into our talks. However, this proved to be beyond any of us.

The Strand Theatre

The Strand Theater was the only movie house in Zelienople and our main source of entertainment in junior high and high school. In Depression years, attendance was spurred by offering a free dish or piece of glassware on certain nights. We went to movies on our own, and the Saturday matinees were the high spot of the week. They began with a cartoon comedy, a preview, and in addition to the main feature, there was a serial that ended in a "cliffhanger," a situation so threatening that moviegoers had to return the next week to find out what happened next. I would float homeward bedazzled, regretting that small-town life was not like the movies.

A tiny ticket booth was under the front marquee that showed the current attraction above. Admission was ten cents for those under twelve. It was a source of pride to reach this age, but difficult to acknowledge this birthday when having to buy a more expensive ticket. It was a severe moral test when the twelfth birthday was achieved and you had to decide whether you should own up to this big day and now pay an adult admission. There was no popcorn or refreshment stand. A long center aisle had eight wooden seats on each side. Fortunately, the flip-up seats had curved bottoms for some comfort. On the left side, halfway down, a break in the seats provided an exit in case of fire and after the show was over. Some dim sidelights were on before the movie started.

At the beginning, there was a piano that provided the emotional setting for the silent movies in black and white. My best friend, Jeanie, and I went to see The Cradle Song. The plot has long since been forgotten. I just remember that it was extremely sad, a real tearjerker. There we were, sobbing our eyes out, with only one cloth handkerchief between the two of us (there was no Kleenex in those days). We each shared a corner. The situation became so ridiculous with our soggy handkerchief that we both began to giggle hysterically. The audience around us was distracted and disgusted by such silly kids. I think that we ended up leaving early!

The Strand Theatre was closed for many years, as most small-town movie houses have disappeared. But recently, an initiative was formed to save the theater from the "wrecking ball" and once again the theater's marquee lights up Main Street.

Christmas Eve

Teenagers love to stay up late and sleep in the next morning (or any morning). In a small town where the sidewalks roll up at seven o'clock and everyone is home by ten o'clock, it is difficult to find a good excuse for a late night out.

On Christmas Eve most of the local churches had their children's Christmas programs and family services early in the evening. The only exception was the Catholic Church on the other end of town where there was a midnight mass.

We were a small group of Protestant teens, fortified by hot cocoa and popcorn, as we set out well-bundled on a snowy night's walk to St. Gregory's. None of us had ever been to a Catholic service before, so there was some apprehension about entering this unknown world.

The small white church was already well-filled when our group arrived. We bypassed the holy water just inside the entrance and squeezed into a pew together. We later noticed that regular members each bowed to the altar before entering a pew. Looking around we saw statues on either side of the candlelit altar. There were also holy decorations spaced along the side walls. The organ and choir were not front and foremost, but on a balcony in the rear of the church.

The priest in his resplendent white robes did a lot of things at a shrine in front with his back turned to the congregation. Latin made the service even more mysterious, though there was a brief sermonette in English. We had to be alert for the standing up, sitting down and kneeling and took our cues from the actions of the people in the rows ahead.

There was a lot of movement from people leaving and others coming in later. The crowded church became very warm and there was the mingled scent of incense and whiskey in the air. Apparently, some of the parishioners had begun their holiday celebration early.

The service ended at midnight and my friends and I went out into the cold darkness feeling that we'd had a real adventure. We trudged homeward and agreed to do this each Christmas. We made the pilgrimage again for several years.

Dancing Days

In junior high we watched the high school dances with envy and I wanted to own a long skirt in the worst way. But before the dances could happen there were dancing classes. These were sponsored by the Woman's Community Club and were held on the second floor of the borough building on West New Castle Street, in a large room available for meetings and community activities.

Mrs. Anita Pawley, a slim, elegant woman with a delightful Southern accent, was the teacher. She had come to town with her two pretty daughters of junior high school age and they were living with her parents. These were Depression years, so no one knew or asked if it was financial problems that kept her husband in New York City. Aside from the modest class fees, much of her motivation for teaching probably was to provide social training for her daughters and their friends. My piano teacher, Mrs. Ruth Burrell, provided the piano music.

Girls and boys sat on opposite sides of the room. Pupils were paired by lining up against the walls. The proper etiquette of dance was taught and the boys were instructed to cross the room, make a slight bow and invite a girl to dance by offering a hand. You could never refuse. At the end of the dance, he was to escort her back to her seat and thank her with another bow and an awkwardly executed 'thank you.'

Lessons began with the box step and progressed through foxtrot, waltz, tango and samba. That was exotic for Zelienople! Each series of classes was capped by a final Cotillion to which everyone wore their Sunday best and the girls wore short white gloves. That helped with sweaty palms. Punch and cookies were served and sometimes parents came to watch. I didn't get a long dress but remember vividly my calf-length gold taffeta that had short puffed sleeves, a round collar edged with pleating and a full-length front panel edged with pleated taffeta. I could sketch that dress to this day.

At high school dances there were dance cards that looked like tiny programs. Many times these were quite elaborate and carried out the colors and the theme of the evening. They were bound by ribbon with a tiny pencil attached. The first and last dances were with your date, as well as the numbers before and after intermission. We dipped and twirled and the jitterbug era began. The last dance was always Hoagy Carmichael's classic song "Stardust." A multitude of memories must surround that number for thousands of people of that era. It was sad, dreamy, yearning and the prelude to goodnight kisses. The boy's responsibility was to fill up the card by exchanging dances with friends. Sometimes an infatuated couple ignored these rules to dance only with each other. This was frowned upon as being anti-social. Girls saved their cards in their scrapbooks along with lumpy pressed flowers and cards from their corsages.

The first formal gown that I was allowed to select for myself was a huge event my sophomore year. It was made of a plum interchangeable silk taffeta that alternated between wine and purple. Made on fairly straight lines, it had a jacket with large puffed sleeves. When the jacket was removed, there were modest wide straps. My mother approved of my choice, for the most part, but didn't think I should remove the jacket.

My first long dress was a thrill, but it did look awkward under an ordinary coat. By my junior year in high school, my fondest wish was for a black velvet evening coat. This was a glamorous Christmas gift that I was given early in time to wear for the holiday dances. Lined with white satin, there was no interlining so it gave no real warmth, but it looked smashing. I suffered in my glory and would never have admitted that I was freezing.

In addition, there was a Christmas dance held by the Junior Woman's Club. These affairs were held in the all-purpose high school auditorium, where one side was filled with elevated, fixed-seating bleachers up to the second floor. At each end of the room were basketball hoops, for this was also the basketball court. The stage facing the seats was for the orchestra. Crepe paper was used lavishly for decorating and a false ceiling could be created, often centered around a large revolving mirrored ball that cast sparkling lights onto the dancers. The final task of the decorating committee was to sprinkle powdered wax on the hardwood floor, which they did liberally, and slide around on it to spread the wax.

No one went to a dance without a date. You hoped that a favorite boy would be the first to invite you. You were doomed to accept the first invitation or miss attending the dance. In such a small school, no excuses could be made.

At one dance I had two escorts. One was my invited date and the other was a good friend who didn't have a date. He danced with me and with others and sat out with some of the chaperones. My best friend, Jeanie, was escorted by her older brother, Ozzie. After the dance, he left and Jeanie made up a foursome when we went out for breakfast at the Portersville twenty-four-hour truck stop.

Once, a private dance was held at a large country home owned by the Redmonds, friends whose father was a Pittsburgh eye doctor. The house had a wide central entrance where the stairway went up. This connected with a formal parlor and a large dining room. The rooms had been cleared of furniture and rugs. There was a three-piece orchestra from Pittsburgh. The rear library accommodated the adult guests. This was a special event in our small town.

At the woman's college that I attended, the girls issued the invitations for dances and were responsible for filling their own dance cards. The dance chairperson headed a receiving line usually accompanied by the dean of the college, the president of the college and his wife, thus adding dignity to the event. It was interesting to learn how to manage a receiving line. You should speak clearly in giving the guest's name to the next person in the line. This was no time for conversation. Using this technique, you grasp a guest's hand firmly and pull them along while introducing them. It speeds up loquacious friends. With intermission came tiny cookies and punch topped with floating sherbet. There was always live music.

College proms were held off-campus at Oakland's Schenley Hotel ballroom, the University Club with its dramatic curved staircase, or the patrician setting of the Twentieth Century Club. Full-skirted ball gowns were worn with long white kid gloves that extended above the elbows and fastened with tiny pearl buttons. These were expensive, a challenge to put on and to keep clean. Looking back at those Depression-era dances, it is amazing how graciously we managed to live.

Many years and many miles later I came to know Wayne Carmichael, a cousin of Hoagy Carmichael and also a fine musician. He played at fashionable hotels in Nassau, Bahamas on Friday and Saturday nights in the 1960s. On Sunday mornings he was the church organist at St. Andrew's Kirk where my family attended church. He had married the attractive young blonde widow of a wealthy doctor, so they were not dependent on his musical earnings. His talents enabled him to switch from jazz to hymns and he was known for his clever improvisations.

A friend of my generation died recently and there was a traditional Protestant funeral service. It was conventional and religious with the exception of the last musical number, which was Stardust. That seemed so appropriate.

First Boyfriends

The Accessioning Committee of the Zelienople Historical Society was meeting and we were recording recent donations of trivia and books for the Genealogical Library. One of the books was a publication of cemetery records for an adjacent township. I tried to find the proper Dewey Decimal number to mark and list it and remarked about the person who had compiled such a detailed and yet boring tome. Opening the book at random, my eyes landed upon the name of my earliest boyfriend. A flood of memories came to me when I saw his name – Ronnie Sitler. He was my first crush in eighth grade. He lived up East Spring Street with his brother and his grandparents. He was tall for his age with blond, curly hair and blue eyes and aimed to go out for football. Actually, he was awkward and I soon realized rather dumb, so the attraction was short-lived.

My high school sweetheart, Harlan Fiser, lived up the street and always had to walk past my house on the way to school. Harlan walked on the opposite side of the street until he came to the corner where he turned toward the school. I would watch from the dining room window and then stroll out the side door in time to be at the corner so he could scarcely avoid walking the short distance to school with me.

He was a French horn player and a star of the band. For three years he won the top place in the state-wide contests for the instrument. I could provide some piano accompaniments for his simpler solos but the required contest numbers even challenged the music teacher handling the difficult accompaniments. Harlan practiced diligently.

Harlan's senior portrait

Harlan was a big reason for my interest in band. I played the clarinet and eventually graduated to the second chair of that section. The band had early morning practices to prepare for concerts and marching practices to prepare for a half-time show at football games. Then there were parades when the march proved to be long and the band uniforms were too hot or not warm enough for the current weather.

We were in the same church youth group, which had roller skating parties, ice skating, sled riding and other group events. He was to be my date for the Junior Prom in his senior year. A week before the big night, I came down with mumps and looked like a squirrel with fat cheeks. This was a teenage tragedy. Harlan and his sister, Della, had both had the mumps before and they came to my house to keep me company. We spent the evening of prom playing Chinese checkers. He gave me his graduation picture. He had fine posture and dark wavy hair. The picture had a place of honor on my bedside table.

The summer after his graduation, his family moved about thirty miles away. He was looking for a job to earn money for college. His parents, with a family of five, could not help him. It was very hurtful when he told me that he wouldn't be dating me anymore. I was devastated and didn't realize at the time that it was because he would not have the time or money.

I was still thinking of Harlan and his picture went to college with me. I saw it daily on my dresser. But as a college freshman there were many young men to meet at fraternity parties and dances at Pitt and Carnegie Tech. There were blind dates and exchange events with Washington & Jefferson College, the nearest men's college. This was no time to sit and look back.

As World War II began, we on the home front found ourselves writing to all the men we knew and even some that we didn't know. I was hearing from Harlan, who was a bomber pilot stationed in China and flying over the Burma Road between China and India. As an officer, his mail was not censored and so he sent me pictures of Mt. Everest taken from his plane. It did not convey much to me, for, from the air, one mountain looks much like another to the unpracticed eye.

Then came the day when Harlan wrote asking me to "wait for him" when the war was over. It was a loving letter and I wanted to reply in kind. I thanked him for wonderful high school memories, his kindness that I would never forget and told him that he had been my first love. But by now I had a new love, Dan Core, who was writing me daily from a Texas Army post about our possible future.

Harlan's reply was that he understood and appreciated my loving letter. If it hadn't meant so much personally, he said he would have published it as a wonderful way to be let down gently. This was the era when a great many "Dear John" letters were written, and Harlan's was not the last I received.

Paul Baldwin

Paul Baldwin and I met on Grandmother Gelbach's front porch on a June afternoon. He had brought his mother from Rochester to call on Grandmother. Elizabeth Baldwin was the daughter of Grandmother's late cousin Herman J. Speyerer, from the Speyerer side of the family. Paul was the youngest of her three sons. The eldest son lived in Boston and taught at MIT. John was an attorney and Paul was a physicist working for Pittsburgh Plate Glass. They both lived at home. Their father was a judge and active in the community and on Lutheran church boards.

Paul was tall with thick, wavy light brown hair and was considered the handsome son. He had graduated from Carnegie Tech and done a further graduate year. I was about to enter my senior year in high school. He appeared at a time when I was coping with the loss of my high school sweetheart. Paul escorted me on interesting dates. Although he commuted to work in a noisy jalopy that he referred to as the Ford Symphony, he borrowed the family's elegant gray Packard to escort me. One evening that summer we had dinner and concert with his parents on the outdoor terrace of the Schenley Hotel. He took me to plays in Pittsburgh, such as Helen Hayes in *Victoria Regina* and *I Married an Angel*. He was very considerate and worried that the latter play might be too risqué.

At Thanksgiving, I was invited to the Baldwin extended family dinner. Mother insisted that I attend our own family gathering, which was fine with me. She liked Paul but felt that I shouldn't get too involved. He was a distant cousin, after all, perhaps three generations removed. The time when families tried to marry off cousins to each other was long past, I thought.

During high school, I took a full load of academic courses as well as home economics, music and typing and had more than enough credits for graduation. After the junior year of algebra, I did not sign up for calculus, but did take physics. Paul helped me with my project on Polaroid glass by providing samples. Paul liked to talk about math and physics to the point where the two melded into philosophy. Most of this was over my head, but I was a good listener.

The Junior Woman's Club sponsored an annual Christmas dance that was a community event. Before the dance, my friend Sunny White's parents had a supper party for house guests from Washington, Pa. I was invited to come with a date and invited Paul. He fit in well with our crowd and gave me my first orchid corsage. That Christmas he gave me a huge box of Yardley's English lavender that even included smelling salts and hair pomade.

When I graduated from high school, Paul presented me with an adorable black Scottie puppy. He had purchased it from a cousin of his who bred the pedigreed dogs. It came with the kennel association papers as well as a daunting list of instructions. There would be house breaking, special food, an egg yolk a day, vitamin drops, vet checks and many other requirements. My sister fell in love with the dog immediately. Mother pointed out that I would be going to college in three months and leaving all this to her. Therefore, the puppy was quickly returned. Ceil was the one who missed the puppy the most.

Paul and I had some dates that summer, but when college started, I found myself too busy most of the weekends. There were war clouds in the air and Paul joined the Army Air Corps. He was an officer because of his scientific background and was sent to England to fly with the RAF as a scientific observer, though America was not yet at war.

He wrote to me from England in April, saying that the poet's account of "Oh, to be in England, now that April's here" was sadly off the mark. His letters from there portrayed a cold, dreary country in the grip of war.

He brought me back a necklace which was an imitation of gold, made from a special formula that was lighter than gold and nontarnishable (I learned many years later that this was antique "pinchbeck"). I wore it rarely as it was rough against the neck. I answered his letters, as we were all writing letters to those in the service that we knew.

Paul was not especially romantic, but he must have decided early on that I would make a suitable bride and he seemed to cling to that notion for many years. I was attractive, intelligent and of a good family so he was prepared to wait. He proposed by mail. From his posting in Kissimmee, Fl., he sent a detailed marriage proposal, listing his savings, his monthly pay and the additional marital allowance he would receive once we were wedded. A lakeside cottage could be rented for $100 to $125 a month, he informed me. Needless to say, I was not swept away by this bevy of information and turned him down politely.

Paul turned up unexpectedly in April 1943 during my senior college year. I had become engaged over the phone on New Year's Eve to my beau, Dan Core.

This was Dan's first Army leave on his way to Officer Candidate School and we had been spending every possible minute together, to the disregard of my studies. Dan stopped by with a friend and we went downstairs to look at the bowling alley. We were not going out since I had to cram for an exam the next morning. The maid came in and said, with some reluctance, that a military officer was calling for me in the great hall. We went upstairs where introductions were made and Dan had to salute Paul, who was his superior in rank.

Dan was usually friendly, but on this occasion, he glared, and must have wondered what was going on. On this unannounced visit, Paul had brought his mother, his brother, and his brother's fiancée for a tour of Mellon Hall. What an awkward scene!

Paul wrote during his time in the service and continued to write after my marriage, even when I stopped replying. But our paths were destined to cross again. After the war, he married a girl named Helen Bentel from his hometown church, and they had a son, Paul, Jr., and a daughter, Christine. I learned that he was teaching at the University of Pittsburgh, Johnstown campus. Also on the faculty there was my former high school principal, George Gage.

Thirty-five years later, Dan and I were living in Minnesota when I had a letter from Paul. He had traced my address through my high school English teacher, Eleanor Stout, who was a friend of George Gage. Paul's wife had died within the past year and he was sad. The letter said that he realized that he had many lonely years ahead. I asked Dan how I should respond. We agreed on a sympathy note that should include the fact that Dan was in good health. After that there were occasional Christmas cards. When Paul retired, he returned to Rochester to a small apartment so that he could help his widowed brother, who was in poor health.

Dan and I decided, after many happy retirement years, that we wanted to be closer to my sister and our family, who were all in the Pittsburgh area. We put our names on a waiting list for a cottage for independent living. After waiting for two years, we were finally accepted, and made arrangements to move as soon as our house was sold. Shortly before moving, we learned that Paul Baldwin was living in the same retirement community. Dan was not pleased, but we were long-committed to this move. For some time after we arrived, Dan regarded Paul warily. Later, as he got to know Paul, he realized that he had never been any competition for him and he grew to be on good terms as we renewed our friendship.

We learned that Paul's son was married and his daughter Christine was a librarian in Washington, D.C. She decided to accept a position as a librarian in New Castle, Pa., and, with her father's help, she bought a house there. He moved to New Castle. Later Christmas cards showed addresses in Delaware, though Paul kept his membership in Grace Lutheran Church in Rochester. Thus, I learned of his death in 2008, when he would have been over ninety. I never had any romantic leanings toward Paul, but in retrospect I appreciate his gentlemanly escort and friendship at a time when I needed it.

A Pen Pal in India

Helen Supplee was my first-grade classmate. Her parents were Baptist teaching missionaries on furlough from their school in Kohima, Assam, India. Her mother's family lived in Zelienople, so they made their base there for their year of home leave, renting a house nearby. Her father had taught high school in Zelienople before becoming a missionary. We were playmates and good friends.

Helen and I had a connection even before we met. Her aunt and my mother were longtime friends and I was sometimes pressed into service to try on clothing that was being sent to India for Helen since we were the same age. After returning to India, Helen grew much taller than me, taking after her father who was a tall, well-built man. We became sporadic pen pals for many years.

Due to the Great Depression of the 1930s, the usual seven years of home leave for missionaries was extended to nine years. Helen again became a classmate of mine in our freshman year of high school. Returning to the United States after all this time must have been a cultural shock for her. In India, her mother taught school at the mission and Indian servants ran the household there. The family had grown to two girls and two boys. Now they were back and able to rent the same small house in Zelienople where they'd lived before.

The stateside time was not really a vacation for Mr. Supplee. He had to make the rounds at Baptist churches, showing movies of the mission school and raising funds to support it for their next trip. But Mrs. Supplee enjoyed being close to her family again.

Helen became a fun member of our crowd as well as getting excellent grades and we nicknamed her "Soup." The local church youth group sometimes had skating parties at the Evans City rink. She may have attended those with us. But Helen definitely did not attend the high school dances or go to movies at the Strand Theatre. According to her Baptist upbringing, these were sinful activities and she tried her best to "save" us. Luckily, card playing and drinking were not among our sins. Of course, the Supplees had home movies and shared them with us. Her dad took us to the Warrendale swimming pool and recorded movies there. We loved to see them run backwards as the person came up out of the water and landed on the diving board.

The neighborhood gang saying goodbye to the Supplees - I'm kneeling with Helen in the front

When the Supplees returned to India, Helen went to boarding school in Darjeeling. We wrote more often back and forth. She returned to attend Wheaton College near Chicago. There she met another "missionary kid" by the name of Robert Jongewaard. Their marriage ceremony was performed by a fellow classmate, the now-famous Rev. Billy Graham. Bob went to medical school with the goal of returning to India as a medical missionary. World War II brought many changes and independence to India, with the result that outsiders were banned for many years. At the outset of the war, Mr. Supplee had stayed behind his family and worked with native Indians on the Burma Trail. The Indian government banned him and all of his family from returning.

Helen and her husband, Bob, settled in a small town in Iowa where he became a country doctor. They were leaders in their evangelical church and the surrounding area. He was often paid in sausage, butter, apples and farm products as much as he was in cash. They had four children to educate, two of whom became doctors. My husband and I stopped to see them on a visit to Iowa. They lived in a small house with no garage for their three tired-looking cars, but they were happy.

We gave them a standing invitation to visit us in Minnesota. They called us one July with plans for a weekend visit since Duluth, Minn., on Lake Superior, is much cooler than Iowa is in the summer. Dan's best man and Army buddy, Frank Crnic, and his wife, Kate, from Pittsburgh also had a long-standing invitation to visit us. They phoned with plans to arrive the same weekend.

Although we had ample space for both couples, we were alarmed. They would have nothing in common and it would be like mixing oil and water. The Crnics were Catholics of Polish background that Helen might try to "save." It was a frightening prospect! We couldn't turn either one away though, so the double-booked weekend was on. Frank and Kate were driving from Pittsburgh and they got as far as Chicago when they had word that their daughter, Margaret, was ill. They phoned us with apologies and turned back home. What a relief. They finally made their visit several months later.

When "Doctor Bob" died, Helen moved to a retirement apartment near one of her sons. She had a granddaughter living in Pittsburgh. Helen came to see her and her granddaughter brought her to Zelienople for a drive around her childhood town and an afternoon visit to the retirement cottage where we were living.

A year later Helen was driving to play the piano for a friend's funeral and was killed in a traffic accident. I think of her fondly, and know she is surely in Baptist heaven.

Remembering Sunny

His name was Charles White and his parents called him Sonny. I always thought of him as Sunny as this was his disposition. He was my classmate in first, second and third grades in the brick elementary school at the corner of Grandview and Main Streets in Zelienople. Our classes were seated in alphabetical order, which meant that White was at the back of the room. There Sunny was inattentive.

He would make jokes which the class enjoyed. The teachers found him disruptive and graded him accordingly.

Sunny's father was Harold White, president of the Lava Crucible Company, which was one of the town's biggest industries. His mother was a social leader in the community. They were understandably concerned about his failing grades when he was so clever outside of the classroom. Arrangements were made for him to go to the Orphan's Home and Farm School in town where the classes were smaller. By coincidence, the head of the Orphan's Home was the Reverend Harold White with a son Charles, called Bud, a few years older. Although there was some improvement in his grades, it was not up to Sunny's potential, so he was sent to military school near Baltimore.

There it was finally discovered that Sunny was hard of hearing. He was taught lip reading and, with tutoring, he caught up and graduated from McDonough School. He was admitted to Kenyon College, then an Episcopal men's school in Ohio. The big lure at Kenyon was their polo team. He played polo on the local Old Furnace team with his father. During summer vacations, Sunny went to the YMCA Camp Kon-O-Kwee nearby and later was a counselor.

The Whites lived in a lovely big Victorian house a block away from my home. Our two younger sisters were playmates. During Sunny's years away at school, he had lost touch with most of his former classmates. He was ill at ease with girls as he was embarrassed by his hearing problem. He often missed questions and found himself tongue-tied. We had a comfortable friendship since, if I forgot to speak directly to him, he didn't mind asking me to repeat. We had a good time together and a true friendship. When he came home for Christmas and spring breaks, his mother wanted him to have a good time. She would arrange parties and also dates with me. His parents must have arranged the Pittsburgh evening when we double-dated with Mary from Kittanning and her date, Fred, who was from nearby Ford City where his father was a PPG executive. Her family chauffer took us to the Duquesne Club for dinner and to the Duquesne Gardens in Oakland for the Ice Capades.

During my college years, I entertained a small group at my home for dessert before we all went off to the Junior Women's Christmas dance at the nearby high school. I invited Sunny to bring a date. He did come, but did not have a date and so went on to the dance with the group. It was the only time that I had two escorts, who alternated, dancing with other girls and sitting with my mother on the side lines.

During the war, Sunny joined the Army. His military school background and his horsemanship meant that he was made an officer in the Army Cavalry. He breezed through testing with his lip-reading skill. The Army changes slowly and the cavalry division was a holdover from World War I. Sunny wanted to see more action and applied for transfer to the Army Air Corps. He was given the usual battery of tests. This time his hearing was tested in a soundproof booth where he had to understand words through a speaker system. For the first time, the Army learned of his hearing problem, so his transfer was denied. He stayed in his same rank and place throughout the war.

In the spring of my senior year in college, I was invited by Mrs. White to spend a weekend with the family, when Sunny would be home on leave. They were now living on a country estate outside Butler. It was great to see him again and get caught up on each other's lives. I shared the secret of my engagement, which would not be announced until after my graduation. We had a good time riding around on a tractor on a bright March afternoon. Dinner was at the nearby country club.

On Sunday morning, we went to the small Episcopal church with Mrs. White. His mother was eager to show him off there. Sunny was a handsome young man and looked dashing in his officer's uniform with his high-polished boots. We were well-aware that the church ladies saw us as a romantic young couple. After church there was an impromptu invitation to lunch at a country estate. They only had to alert their help to set three extra places.

That lovely spring weekend was the last time that Sunny and I were together. Several years later, his parents attended my wartime wedding. My husband had met Sunny at the Christmas dance and knew of our longtime friendship. He was surprised when Mrs. White clasped his hand at the receiving line and wished him the best, saying that she had hoped that it would be otherwise. I think she was being both flattering and exaggerating since Sunny and I never had even a mild flirtation.

Sunny and I kept in touch for many years with Christmas cards. He married a woman named Barbara. They had twins and lived near Chicago. Our rare friendship ended sadly when he died of a heart attack in his early forties.

The Cute Little Cape Cod Cottage

The cute little Cape Cod cottage was built by Burton and Leone Hall prior to WWII at the corner of Clay and Culvert Streets. Driving by it every time I enter my retirement community, I remember the family who first made it home.

Leone was a teacher when she married Burt and they first rented a small row house on Clay Street. Later they moved to 219 East Spring Street at the corner of Oliver Avenue. They had no children.

Leone was the oldest child of the Hart family from Ellwood City. Her mother was widowed, so she helped out her mother and two younger sisters often. When her brother, Leo, the baby in the family, was a teenager, he attended high school in Zelienople and lived with them on East Spring Street, just down the street from us. He became my sister Ceil's high school sweetheart.

Ceil went off to college and Leo went to work at the local news-stand. He later married the news-stand owner's daughter, Jane Greer, and eventually gained ownership of the shop. It was a happy arrangement, for he became the son the owner always wanted, someone who shared his interests in hunting, fishing and woodwork. Leo and his wife had two sons, one a doctor and the other a distinguished organist.

Burt and Leone had a wide circle of friends. Leone led in their social activities and Burt was quiet and affable as a host. Leone had been my sixth-grade teacher and she gave one of my bridal showers in their new Cape Cod, located at 204 Culvert Street. We kept in touch at Christmas and whenever my husband and I visited Zelienople.

Sports glamour came to town in the form of Cal Hubbard, an outstanding football star for the Green Bay Packers and later a baseball hero. He is the only person in both the Football and Baseball Hall of Fame. In retirement, he became a popular umpire. He was married to Ruth Frishkorn and they lived with her family in their home at 501 South Main Street. He led some of the local hunters in trips to Missouri and persuaded several of them to move there. That is when Burt and Leone sold their Cape Cod cottage. After a number of years, their adventure in Missouri ended and they returned to Zelienople where Burt ran a men's store. They bought and remodeled an old brick house at 100 High Street, which was at the corner of East New Castle Street and High Street. Eventually, they built their final one-story home in a more secluded area at 206 Northview Drive. It was a lovely setting for their antiques and country-style furnishings.

When Leone died, Burt's world collapsed. Soon it was apparent that he was not taking care of himself or their home. Leo and his wife, Jane, became reluctant caregivers, as they were the only family nearby. It became necessary to take over his affairs and get him into assisted living care at New Haven Court in the Passavant Retirement Community. Sometime after his moving there, he had a complete change of personality. From being simply quiet, later withdrawn, he suddenly became very talkative, flirtatious, giggly and exuberant. He romanced a widowed resident and it was a gala affair when they married at New Haven in the beautiful foyer.

It's possible this was when his senility started, for sadly more personality changes were in store for Burt. After a time, the staff became aware that he had become abusive toward his new wife and it was necessary to separate the couple. Soon after that, he was moved to nursing. His wife visited him faithfully to the end of his days in nursing.

Such is the saga of the family in the cute little Cape Cod cottage.

The Centennial

The town of Zelienople was laid out by Baron Detmar Basse shortly after he purchased 10,000 acres of Depreciation Land in the valley known as Creek Meadows. This was in 1802. He laid out the town and named it for his eldest daughter, Zelie, with the Greek suffix "-nople" added for the city. He was temporarily "land poor" until making a modest profit by selling 4,060 acres in 1804 to Father Rapp, the leader of a German separatist group who moved his followers over the next five years to a town they named Harmony.

It was not until the year 1840 that the town was officially incorporated as the Borough of Zelienople. A grand centennial celebration was planned for the summer of 1940. Local merchants, organizations and even churches combined to sponsor events. The whole community was involved. A theatrical producer from Philadelphia was hired to write and direct a historical pageant. The weeklong outdoor production was staged on the local football field using those bleachers and all the funeral home chairs. Nearby was a carnival with a Ferris wheel, merry-go-round and all the usual carnival attractions. The pageant was made up of historical episodes, each involving a different group. So many people of all ages were included that it was a mystery who could be left to form the audience.

My high school senior portrait

The merchants had special sales. The churches had suppers and special services. A book was printed that pictured and described the banks, industries, businesses and other organizations involved. No one was omitted.

There were many community groups such as the lodges, the Elks, the Odd Fellows, the Masons, a woman's sorority, the Woman's Community Club and the Junior Community Woman's Club, and they were all given a role to play. The Woman's Community Club was to select a court of four young women to reign over the festivities: namely, a Miss Centennial, a Miss Zelienople, a Miss America and a Miss Liberty.

The committee ladies of the Woman's Community Club were disturbed when they heard the rumor that the word around town was that there was to be a beauty contest and that girls were already considering what bathing suits and evening dresses they would wear. This was a shocking development. The committee was alarmed at the prospect of running a beauty pageant. This didn't fit with their ideas of decorum and they threatened to have nothing further to do with such an undertaking.

Finally, a compromise was reached. The committee would choose girls who were descendants of the earliest settlers. Thus, Virginia "Sis" Passavant, a distant cousin, was named Miss Centennial, I was named Miss Zelienople, Anna Jane Kelly was Miss America and Marjorie Zehner was Miss Liberty.

Sis and I were both away at school at the time, and we came home to find that we had won a beauty contest "in absentia" and our duties were already laid out for us. There may have been some nepotism involved, for Mother's cousin Lillian Whittaker was on the committee and was well-informed on the local history.

The court girls were supplied with long velvet capes to be worn over their own formal gowns. We each had a small speech in the program. There were many pictures taken and a full-page spread with our portraits was in the local newspaper. A dinner dance was held in our honor at Duffmont on Main Street, the local tearoom and bed and breakfast on the hill.

This proved to be an embarrassing problem for I needed an escort. My high school sweetheart, Harlan, had moved away and said 'goodbye.' My current college boyfriend had given me his fraternity pin upon leaving for his home in Chicago. My suitable, but too-eager escort, Paul, was already in England with the RAF. And my good friend, Sunny, was nearby but serving as a counselor at the YMCA Camp Kon-O-Kwee and couldn't get time off. Many boys seemed to be going steady. At this point, I can't recall who I finally dragooned for the affair.

Few people still recall the all-out celebration of 1940 besides the historical society. My children, who don't have my memories of Zelienople, find my short-lived fame as Miss Zelienople quite amusing.

Pomp and Circumstance

Jeanie Beighley was my closest childhood playmate. She was several years older than I, but it never seemed to make a difference. As we grew up, it seemed only natural to tag along with her school classmates and she didn't seem to mind. Her high school friend was Betty Passavant. She was a tall, attractive girl that I

Valedictorian for the class of 1939, leading my peers to our commencement ceremony

admired greatly. I watched what she wore, the nicest skirts and sweaters, and I copied the way that she walked. She was double-jointed and could move in amazing ways. She sometimes stood pigeon-toed, so I did too.

High school commencement ceremonies were impressive in our small town. When Jeanie and Betty graduated from high school, the commencement ceremonies were open to all, so, of course, I was there. Betty was the class valedictorian and led the procession into the school auditorium, walking alone. The black-robed classmates followed, two by two. It was at that moment that I decided that I wanted to copy Betty and be the valedictorian of my class. Since my class standing was fairly high, it wasn't too difficult to put in the extra effort needed to fulfill my dream.

My dream of leading the class into the auditorium as valedictorian was achieved by just working a little bit harder during my senior year. It was a brief moment of glory to lead the 75-member senior class into the auditorium as valedictorian. My robe was black and the mortarboard had the school colors, purple and gold in the tassel. The two other top honor students walked together wearing purple robes and mortar boards with gold tassels. This was impressive against the rest of the black robes. A local uniform salesman had provided the special gowns for the occasion in the hopes of selling them to the school.

The stage was decorated with peonies, iris and palms on that May night as we made an impressive exit from high school. The high school band, in which I had played clarinet for four years, was seated below the stage. They played Elgar's traditional Pomp and Circumstance march and I winked at my bandmates as I passed by. I have no memory of who the main speaker was at graduation. Though one member of the class cried during my valedictory speech, it was certainly not memorable to me since I can't remember a word of it. We left high school that night with the perfume of the flowers that edged the stage and went in many different directions.

That was my "swan song." In the fall, it was on to college where once again I found myself at the bottom of the academic ladder, among a freshman class filled with many other valedictorians. So much for passing glory!

Somehow, I survived another four years to march to the sound of the organ at the Third Presbyterian Church playing Pomp and Circumstance once again. I wasn't at the top of this class this time, but in addition to my bachelor of arts degree in English, I had an engagement ring hidden on a chain around my neck.

Three
College Girl

Dormitory Life
1939 – 1941

Woodland Hall was the only dormitory on the campus of the Pennsylvania College for Women in 1939, now known as Chatham University. The long, undistinguished brick building sat on the side of the hill overlooking Woodland Road with its quaint gaslights glowing at night. A few gables topped the three-story building and a partial basement held the kitchens.

The dormitory entrance was at one end, just a few yards away from the tall old Victorian Berry Hall with its later additions, which was the first building at the college. If you overslept, it was a simple matter to roll up your pajamas, throw on a raincoat and make it to class just in time. The college enrolled 600 women, but more than half were day students commuting to class by streetcar. Many of them who might otherwise have gone away to Eastern schools were now living at home during the Depression and going to a local college.

Just to the right of the front door was the housemother's suite for Miss Ethel Bair. She reigned over the sign-out sheets and the check-ins with an eagle eye. She was not very motherly. Down the front hall was a large, gloomy living room dominated by a grand piano and a non-working fireplace. The only daylight came from the adjacent sunroom. A staircase to the second-floor dorm rooms went up from there. Upstairs there were several extra-large rooms at the corner of the building, which were snared by seniors. The smaller doubles fell to the freshmen. The majority of the rooms had a doorway into a tiny hall with closets on both sides and doors into two separate rooms. The communal bathroom down the hall had a wall of sinks, a row of brown varnished toilet stalls and two bathtub sections.

My first roommate, Mary Louise Henry, and I corresponded before meeting in order to coordinate bedspreads and curtains. Our one window looked into a steep bank below the playing field above. We each had a single bed, dresser and a single drawer desk with a bookshelf top and chair. We shared the only closet in the room. Somehow, we managed to exist peacefully, though we had little in common. Her mind was in her hometown of Greensburg with her boyfriend, George. An identical room one floor above held Jean Archer and her roommate

Jean Archer and I on her wedding day

Priscilla Jean Sweet (who also went by Jean). She scarcely fit the rest of her name, as she was neither Prissy or Sweet. She was an orphan, raised by two maiden aunts. College was a time to "feel her oats." This was another unfortunate freshman roommate mismatch. Luckily, Jean Archer and I hit it off. We were roommates for the next three years of college together and became lifelong friends.

Fellow students were warm and welcoming. Upper class big sisters were assigned to each freshman and made the transition easier. Instant friendships developed, in a way that was different from high school years. We lived each other's lives, sharing small triumphs and disappointments (if Nancy didn't get a letter from her boyfriend, Dave, we all sympathized). Clothes were exchanged, particularly evening gowns. It was considered good luck to contribute something to the wardrobe of someone who was going away for a college weekend.

This happy beginning to college almost came to a halt when, prior to heading off to school, the school doctor conducted a more thorough examination of me than the family doctor had. She found that I was anemic and had lung scars that could indicate tuberculosis. In those days, many people in Western Pennsylvania burned soft coal in their homes and died of its effects. Would I end up in a sanatorium in Arizona instead of college?

After some frightening consultations, it was determined that I could stay in Pittsburgh with an anemia treatment of pills and twice weekly iron shots. The shots and blood checks took place at Dr. Irene Ferguson's residence, which was within walking distance of campus. I was excused from exercise other than ping pong and walking. That continued all freshman year. Peg Miller was the other student I knew on the restricted regime.

We soon got into trouble with Miss Bair, when following a freshman mixer dance, some boys returned with milkshakes and snacks that we were to get by lowering a basket from our room. The boys were routed and we were lectured and put on probation.

Breakfast, lunch and dinner were served in the large first-floor dining room at assigned tables that were changed weekly. Service was family-style with a hostess at each table and dishes brought in by uniformed maids and scholarship students. It had been just a few years earlier that Thursday night formal dress was required on campus. The hostess at each dining table was skilled in judging the correct portions to be served. In the case of broccoli, many declined that serving. That turned out to be a mistake, for if any broccoli remained in the serving dish and was returned to the kitchen, it was often creamed and repeated at another meal. We learned to take a portion so that this did not happen. Friday night was fish night, which was also unpopular, so groups of girls often went to Sodini's, a small Italian restaurant on Wilkins Avenue, for a cheap spaghetti dinner. The drugstore beside Sodini's was the closest source of Coca-Cola, which was carried back to school in six-packs.

Uniformed maids cleaned the rooms once a week and supplied fresh towels and linens. They were also on duty on Friday and Saturday nights to open the door for dates and come up to the rooms to announce the visitors who waited in the living room.

Skirts and sweaters, dirty saddle shoes and handknit ankle socks were the uniform of the time. I learned to knit socks, turn a heel and make a double heel. Day students who travelled to classes via streetcar had to wear skirts. But jeans could be worn on campus. No women's jeans were made then, so, ill-fitting boy's jeans topped with a boy's white dress shirt with the tails out were worn. Dressing up was reserved for Friday and Saturday date nights. Then we could go all out! Day students had a lounge in Berry Hall, but often came over to spend time with dorm friends. There were many unorthodox continuing bridge games that went on between classes where a bridge hand was passed on to someone else when it was time to leave.

The dormitory dining room was cleared for informal mixers, when men from the University of Pittsburgh and Carnegie Tech were invited for dancing. The chapel floor in Berry Hall was used for regular college dances and the prom was held off-campus at locations like the Schenley Hotel, the University Club or the Twentieth Century Club.

The infirmary was located first on a third floor and later in the first-floor wing off the dining room. Once my roommate, Jean Archer, was in the infirmary there with a severe case of athlete's foot, which definitely kept her from an informal dance that was being held just outside. Several of us girls took fellows in to commiserate with her. The school nurse, a proper English spinster, was shocked at what she considered the invasion of her infirmary and the indecency of visiting someone of the opposite sex in bed. All kinds of dire threats were made (in vain, fortunately). Jean and I enjoyed our time together in Woodland Hall.

Biology 101

Biology was a required freshman course at Pennsylvania College for Women. It carried three credits with one hour of lecture and two lab hours three times weekly. The professor was Dr. Laura Hunter, a tall, nervous woman. She had light brown hair that was cut short and she was usually wearing a white lab coat. Her manner was vague and her lectures were also, particularly when it came to the mating patterns of animals. After discussing other details of animal behavior at length, when it came to their sex life she would blush and say, "you will find the rest on page seventy."

Lab work was no problem even though it came immediately after lunch with the strong smell of formaldehyde. The broader concepts of ecology were what gave me problems. My answers and papers revealed that I wasn't getting it.

By the second semester, we were dissecting embryo pigs and using a ruler to measure the length of the intestines after they were uncurled and stretched out. Each student had her own pig. The great mystery to be solved was the sex of each pig since the tiny organs were hidden inside with no outward signs. When solved, it sometimes meant changing the name of your pig.

I was really concerned about my biology grades. One afternoon in late March, Dr. Hunter approached my bench in the lab. I was alarmed and then surprised when she asked me if I would like to go on an Audubon Society trip to Pymatuning Dam the first Sunday in April. Hoping to get in her good graces, there was no way that I could refuse this invitation.

Special permission had to be secured from Miss Bair, the housemother, for we would be leaving Pittsburgh at two o'clock in the morning. This was in order to reach Pymatuning Lake and be in the marsh before sunrise to see the geese take off. I had a date that Saturday night and signed into the dorm at midnight. It wasn't worthwhile going to bed, so I amazed my dormmates by changing from dress clothes into layered outdoor attire, including sturdy boots. Two middle-aged school teachers picked me up, together with a senior student and Dr. Hunter. We drove through the deserted city and then a long way on Route 19 North in the darkness.

At the tiny town, we met the other group of about twenty-five birders at a rustic hotel and boarding house. They were dressed in an amazing variety of attires and were draped with binoculars, cameras and canteens. There were bulging pockets with notebooks and bird books. We had coffee and doughnuts and a brief lecture before we set out. There were strict instructions against any conversation since we were supposed to creep silently in the darkness among the tall grasses of the swamp. We did indeed see the geese fly up and then the welcome sunrise. For those who recognized them, there were different species. It was all just cold and damp to me.

After the morning drama, the group returned to the hotel for a full hunters' breakfast. The time was about half past eight in the morning but it seemed like the middle of the day. There was another lecture, after which we set out again with a park ranger through barren land among leafless trees. This time we were to search the ground for owl fewmets. These were little gray bundles which when opened would reveal what small animals the owl had been feasting on. What excitement!

Whether or not this great effort improved my biology grades is uncertain. Among the society members that day was the Girl Scout executive of Allegheny County and we were together on part of the hike. This slight acquaintance helped me to get a job the following summer as a counselor at Camp Redwing.

It was about noon when tired and muddy, we left for the three-hour trip back to the city. I did pass Biology 101, but not quite with flying colors.

In later life, I had a friend who was a loyal member of the Audubon Society. Jean Clark prevailed on me to help fill the bus for field trips in Wisconsin and Minnesota. Even with my own binoculars borrowed for the occasion, it was difficult to get focused on birds that were pointed out with excitement and identified for me. By the time the glasses were adjusted, the birds were long gone. These people recognized bird songs and knew them by their flight patterns. When I realized that not only was it necessary to identify the bird by its coloring of each sex, but also the plumage could change according to the season that made it hopeless for me.

My preference is plants. They remain in one place to be identified by the leisurely perusal of the illustrated wildflower book. They have interesting names and histories and a wide variety of uses. I am for the plant kingdom!

Holding for Miss Held

The small women's college Music Department had a staff of three spinsters. The senior heading the department taught theory and instruments, primarily piano lessons. A younger colleague gave voice lessons and was the capable director of the college choir. Miss Lillie B. Held, the assistant professor of music, had theory classes and was in charge of what was called the Instrumental Ensemble, a group of whatever students had musical instruments. Mr. Earl B. Collins, or "Mr. Earl" as we called him, was a talented organist at the prominent Bellefield Presbyterian Church. He came to teach organ and played the chapel organ for college events.

The Music Department was often given expensive season tickets to concerts at Carnegie Music Hall by wealthy supporters who were away in sunny climes for the winter. These tickets were shared with the students. In those days, formal wear was appropriate for the box seats. We would attire ourselves in long gowns and share the expense of a taxi ride to Oakland. That was a real perk. Other concert-goers may have wondered how these young girls in formal dress could afford such seats.

There was an organ scholarship offered at Pennsylvania College for Women. I had been taking organ lessons in high school, so I filled out an application and was awarded the organ scholarship. It turns out only two students had applied. The only drawback was a required one-credit class in musical theory. This took place at eight-thirty on Saturday mornings and was attended in a daze following Friday night dates that ended at midnight. A one-credit course allowed for only one legal "cut." That meant only one possible weekend each quarter and it was a great deterrent to social life.

Miss Held combed over the freshman applications with eagerness. She zeroed in on any newcomer that played an instrument as a recruit for her ensemble. My resume showed that I played the clarinet in my high school band and unknowingly I come into her clutches. The ensemble consisted of a cello, several violins, a viola, an oboe, a flute and me (though there may have been several others from time to time). The group was not impressive.

Miss Held was a short, prim woman who always wore brown dresses and had a stern countenance. She had a bee-skep hairdo and wore thick glasses. The ensemble was called upon to play at the daily chapel from time to time. Her great pleasure was in conducting this little group, which she did, holding a baton with acrobatic exercise in great swooping motions. I found these performances embarrassing.

There were other more interesting college activities, so I dropped out of the group after the freshman year. The reason I gave was that my younger sister needed the clarinet for lessons. Miss Held could scarcely take this loss lightly. She offered to rent an instrument for me, which I gracefully declined. My place in the ensemble was replaced by a rather dim classmate who had even less to offer in competent playing.

The all-purpose chapel had a stage at one end where plays took place and stage entrances often had to be negotiated by climbing out a window and going in a window at the opposite side of the building. A small platform with a lectern faced the stage. The only organ was there. College dances were also held here.

The college had compulsory chapel for a half hour in the mid-mornings. On Thursday, it was a student government meeting when the seniors all wore black graduation robes. It was worthwhile to buy a cap and gown from a graduating senior as you could be assured of getting a lot of wear from it.

In my senior year, I was president of the YWCA, which had charge of chapel many days. One day, I remember being on the small platform in front of the chapel and introducing the guest speaker, a charismatic Baptist minister. He had the audience's rapt attention and it was interesting to be in front where I could look out and see their expressions.

I was in charge of chapel one fateful day when Miss Held was leading the ensemble. It was not the best performance and the clarinet player who had taken my place punctuated the music with frequent squeaks. I sat on the tall chair on the platform in acute embarrassment, probably with a red face. I knew that I had to hold a completely straight expression. If a smile or giggle escaped, the audience would explode with laughter. It was the best effort I could make for Miss Held.

Many years later, our friends in U.S. Steel, John and Irene Bird, were transferred from Louisville, Ky. to the Pittsburgh law office. They bought a house at 1453 Wightman Street from a family estate sale. It happened to be the house where Miss Held had lived with her bachelor brother, the head of music for Pittsburgh Public Schools, and another sibling.

The square yellow-brick house was in a good neighborhood, Squirrel Hill. It had a wide porch with the main door entering into a front hall and stairs going up at the rear. The house underwent a complete transformation outside when the Birds had the porch removed, replaced by an attractive doorway and small entranceway, and had the brick painted white.

Inside, the wall standing between the front hall and living room was removed. The most daunting change was moving the staircase from the back to the side wall, as that involved moving the stairs to the basement as well. The family had three children and lived in the upstairs amid dust and construction for months. There was even a brief hospitalization for the mother, Irene, who was allergic to dust. At the end of it all, their house was a beautiful home and probably a good investment, though I am not sure Miss Held would have approved of the changes they made.

The Coca-Cola Business

College was an exciting new world of independence, challenging classes, social events, dating, no sororities but many campus clubs vying for members. New friendships were made in the dormitory as I found myself sharing other's lives. Jean Archer, her high school friend Nancy Doerr, and I formed a trio. We sympathized with Nancy when she failed to get a letter from her boyfriend, Dave, and cheered on her romance. I met him briefly at a dance. Nancy danced only with Dave and never exchanged dances, as was the expected custom.

My college career was adequate rather than outstanding. Social life seemed more important than academics. One early venture was the Coca-Cola business that our trio started. Pennsylvania College for Women had no vending machines in 1939. Dorm students walked to Wilkins Avenue near the campus and carried back cartons of Coca-Cola from the drugstore.

We brought Coca-Cola to the college by persuading the Dean that we could manage it. The tall red metal machine was set up in the day students' den in Berry Hall. It had a side door that opened onto a belt that supported the chilled glass bottles and released one at a time when a nickel was deposited. Our job was to keep the machine stocked, collect and roll the nickels, get up early to meet and pay the delivery driver, and store the weekly supply of wooden cases. At inconvenient times we were often visited by annoyed customers telling us that the Coke machine needed refilling.

The business carried on successfully throughout our sophomore year and provided a profit of $15 dollars monthly for each of us. In those days that amount went a long way.

Distance does not always make the heart grow fonder. Dave disappeared from Nancy's life, much to her consternation. To cheer her up, Jean and I arranged a date with a Washington & Jefferson College Delta Tau Delta brother that we knew and liked. Fred Wilson soon took Dave's place in her heart and we never had a chance to dance with him again. In fact, Nancy married Fred.

In our junior year, Nancy left the campus for Allegheny General Hospital where she spent her first year as part of a combined five-year nursing and college degree program. The student government association, of which I was a member, seized upon the Coca-Cola business as a way to enrich its treasury and so it had to be turned over to them. The secretary was Louise Wallace, daughter of the head of the Chemistry Department. Running the business from where she lived adjacent to the campus was not easy. Her records were so poor that it seemed to be a losing proposition for the student government.

The result was that by our senior year, the Coca-Cola concession was returned to Jean and me. Nancy was no longer on campus. We were back to rolling nickels and sleeping with the money under our pillows the night before our weekly early morning rendezvous with the salesman, who by now was an old friend.

Ten years later, I was grocery shopping in Pittsburgh and met our salesman, who was now a sales manager for the area. What would have happened if we had stayed with the Coca-Cola business, even to the extent of buying stock!

Camp Redwing

Camp Redwing was the Girl Scout camp of Allegheny County located in Renfrew, Pa. Summer jobs were hard to find in 1941 and it was an achievement just to get an experience that would look good on some future resume.

Before the local Girl Scout troop broke up for lack of a leader, I had been an enthusiastic scout. In college, I found myself the leader of a Girl Scout troop that met nearby at the Third United Presbyterian Church on Shady Avenue. I was too young to be the legal leader, so the leader of record was a busy housewife who gave me moral support and advice in her kitchen. A Girl Scout board member was appreciative as well. An essential part of scouting is badge work which requires individual attention. I felt guilty that I couldn't do that with such a large group. The only equipment was "sit-up-ons," which were square floor mats we made each year to "sit upon," and there was an American flag to pledge allegiance. We recited the Girl Scout pledge and sang some songs. The girls then split up into patrols for activities before coming together at the end of the meeting to sing Taps. The troop did spend an overnight in May in a log cabin owned by the Girl Scouts in Schenley Park. The only cooking

Me, center, with the Redwing camp counselors

facility was an outdoor fireplace that we managed somehow. A young married woman was co-leader just for this event. We were hard put to feed everyone after the rain came. The scouts were probably glad to get back home on a damp Sunday morning.

The scouting was some recommendation for my position as a counselor at Camp Redwing. We were to arrive at camp early for orientation, which turned out to mean the setting up of cots and the stuffing of ticking mattress covers with straw. There was a handyman who helped erect the tents. He also drove the camp station wagon to bring baggage from the train, get supplies and take food and bedrolls for camp outs.

This was a fairly primitive camp with only two permanent structures, the small house of the camp director and the open-air kitchen, dining hall and activity room combined. The camp was divided into units according to age and the units consisted of tent platforms. I was a camp counselor for two months in Creekside. We all had camp names and mine was Skeeter. At one point during the summer, there was the sobering experience during heavy rains of watching the creek rise hourly just outside our tent. Finally, the sun appeared and the water receded.

Campers arrived from Pittsburgh by train every two weeks and the time between groups was the only time off. Two big events of each session were a square dance and an overnight hike during which they slept under the stars. Before the square dance, it was necessary to practice. Then, the night of the dance, the farmers and workers from the country nearby came to dance with the young campers. They brought families with them who looked on. Then, after the campers went to bed, the music continued and it was their time to square dance. The energy of these men was amazing after a day of hard physical labor.

In the days before the hike, there was practice assembling bedrolls, as this was before sleeping bags. The bedrolls and food supplies were transported by the camp station wagon to the overnight site. The handyman was the only male and so he was very popular for heavy lifting.

The hike was not far and the first big challenge was the building of a latrine. It was supposed to be placed between two trees so that a primitive seat could be lashed to the trees. Not only was it difficult to find a suitable location but there are roots between trees and the digging was not easy. After much labor, the hole was still not very deep and the novelty of the latrine soon made it overused.

On a well-remembered night, we put our beds in a former cornfield. First, all rocks had to be cleared away and then a hip hole dug for greater comfort. It isn't easy to work your way into the blankets without disarranging them. Not long after that, the stones that you had failed to clear away began to dig into you, or perhaps they came up from underground. Returning to camp after breakfast cooked on an open fire, the tent with its cot and the straw-stuffed mattress seemed almost luxurious

Romantic names were given to what was a pleasant but ordinary countryside. A bridge over the creek at Renfrew was called Silver Bridge. A barn on a hillside produced a fine echo and was known as Echo Barn. The campfire ring on the hill above camp was surrounded by tall pines named The Cathedral. Even dishwashing was glamorized by calling it "bubbling."

Eight counselors were in each unit with four to a tent on each end of the line of tents. One of my tent mates was a tall blonde who used an eyelash curler and mascara every morning, to my amazement. We dressed in shorts and jeans except for visiting days and special times when official scout camp uniforms were required. It was necessary to buy our own uniforms, at least two to last through the summer. We were working for room and board, which was our tent!

At the end of the previous year, each counselor had been given $10 as payment. This was widely known and discussed hopefully as the summer drew to a close. As it turned out, there was no cash bonus in any amount. Our recompense was only the experience and memories of Camp Redwing.

Our Gang
1940 – 1941

Two years during summer vacations from college, a group of local young people got together for picnics, swimming and miniature golf outings. These were group parties and no dating was involved. The boys provided the cars and some of the money for food and the girls did the shopping and managed the refreshments. Bread or buns were ten cents and the hamburger was twenty-five cents a pound. Hot dog, pickle and cookie prices have been forgotten.

The gang consisted of Phil Blum, who was home from Muhlenberg College and helping in his dad's shoe store; George Klinefelter, who was home from Heidelburg College and working in his father's barber shop; and Henry Grabman, who was back from Carnegie Tech and working with his father a plumber. Mr. Grabman insisted that his son go through the apprenticeship to become a licensed plumber as a trade to back up his engineering degree.

Driving the gang to a picnic in a convertible

Charles "Bud" White was working as a radio engineer and lived with his parents at the Orphan Home and Farm where his father was the superintendent. He had the keys to give us access to the small swimming pool there and the adjoining open woods of tall, old trees was a great picnic spot. Jeanie Beighley was home from Allegheny College, Hope Mitchell was home from

Muskingum College, Betty Passavant was back from Smith College and I was back from Pennsylvania College for Women. Jim Henderson from Penn State and a few others were added from time to time. Summer jobs were non-existent for the women and the men only had jobs with family businesses. War clouds were looming and those carefree summer days would soon become a thing of the past.

George lived next door and we often played tennis early in the morning on Miss Emma Passavant's clay court. He would wake me up by throwing a tennis ball into my bedroom window, and then would eat breakfast while I dressed. We would walk through the dewy grass past beds of roses through her garden. If Campbell's drugstore was open, afterward we would sometimes stop in for a slushy of frozen Reymer's Lemon Blennd. He went on to open his dad's shop and I went home and had a bowl of cereal.

Only once was I asked on a date by Henry. He was at nearby Carnegie Tech and was a member of the ROTC. There was to be a Military Ball where his attendance was mandatory. He had no extra money for social affairs and no dress clothes. In this instance, he would wear his military uniform and he needed a partner. I was booked for that night and had to decline. His friends found him a blind date and I promptly forgot about the incident.

Some sixty years later, my husband and I were living in a retirement community where Henny's sister, Laura, was a resident. He and his wife came to visit Laura and us. His wife was very friendly and thanked me for declining to go to the dance with him. She said that their marriage was the result of his blind date for the Military Ball and, if I had accepted his invitation, they would never have met. What an amazing story!

The Quadrille

Although PCW was a woman's college, there was no lack of social life on the weekends since the University of Pittsburgh and Carnegie Tech were both just a mile away from campus. Open house mixers were held at our college and there were many opportunities for blind dates, big band dances at both schools, and fraternity parties near at hand. By the spring of my freshman year, Washington & Jefferson, the men's college thirty miles to the South in Washington, Pa. provided more dating opportunities.

The Quadrille of 1940 was an elegant affair held in the beautiful ballroom of the George Washington Hotel in Washington, Pa. The gentlemen wore formal attire and the women, full-skirted evening gowns to twirl under the high ceiling with its huge crystal chandeliers. Tall windows were on one side of the room opposite a balcony. The cream-colored walls had ornate woodwork outlined in gold. Mirrored sconce lights decorated the walls.

The Quadrille was under the joint sponsorship of Washington & Jefferson College and Pennsylvania College for Women, along with automobile magnate, Henry Ford, who wanted to promote old-fashioned dancing. A busload of girls went to three rehearsals before the big event in April. Many of those dancing partners became long-term dates.

Henry Ford was interested in preserving the past through his Dearborn Museum and the collection of historic buildings that he purchased and moved in order to form Greenfield Village in Michigan. He was also interested in preserving customs of the past such as old-time dancing. He hired historic dance authorities Mr. and Mrs. Benjamin Lovett to teach 18th-century dances and published their book of music and instructions. Two undergraduate students at W&J were given summer jobs at his Dearborn plant. Part of their duties was to take dancing lessons from the Lovetts. Then they were required to teach these dances at the college in preparation for a Quadrille Ball.

In March of my freshman year, there was a sign-up sheet at PCW for those willing to go by bus to Washington for three dancing lessons. These were held in the drafty gym in W&J's Old Main. For the third and final lesson, there was a rehearsal where Mr. and Mrs. Lovett supervised the dancing. They presided over the grand finale the next evening.

The jitterbug was the current dance craze. The Quadrille was completely different. It was related to square dancing in form, but was done with graceful slow gliding steps, moving from one partner to another. On the final evening, there was a string orchestra at one end of the hotel ballroom. Spectators sat on the balcony and my mother and a friend came to watch. A select group of sixteen of the best dancers did several special numbers. Following the dancing, a midnight supper was served in a high-ceiling formal dining room.

Pooch O'Donnell, me, Jean Archer and Bob Younkin

My friend and future roommate, Jean, and I were in a set where the four Washington & Jefferson dance partners were members of Delta Tau Delta. That was the start of my long relationship with the college. We began to double date our dancing partners. When Ed "Pooch" O'Donnell left for summer vacation at his home in Glen Ellyn, Ill., he gave me his fraternity pin. His friend, Bob Younkin, bought a sister pin for Jean. When he came back in the fall, I returned his pin to him. He was glad to wear it again and we continued to date. It was a great party time for all of us. The oncoming war was still thousands of miles away. This expanded our social life, although we were still often going to events at Pitt and Carnegie Tech.

86

There was one college mixer when I felt like the "belle of the ball." The dance was in the dormitory dining room and was well attended by men from Pitt, Carnegie Tech and W&J. There was a stag line and constant cut-ins so that I never finished a dance with one person. Some of the partners I knew and with others there was just a brief whirl, scarcely long enough to exchange names, as the stag line seemed to be following each other in quick succession. Many of the college dances were held at the University Club, which had a beautiful long curving staircase. It always made one feel elegant to sweep slowly down the lovely steps in a formal gown. These were our party days.

Our college friend Lucy Cummins lived in Washington. Her parents welcomed us to stay overnight for college dances and fraternity parties there. She was already dating another fraternity brother, Bill Dickey. On a warm May evening, there was a dance at PCW. I had overnight permission to stay with a classmate who lived in Shadyside. I had dinner with her family and then dressed for the dance. Her escort was a Delta Tau Delta member who had a convertible and I have a wonderful memory of driving up the narrow, winding Woodland Road lit with lanterns toward the college.

The Quadrille of 1940 was the last of an era. By 1941 the country was involved in WWII and men were beginning to leave college for the armed services or work for the war effort. Only the memory of that elegant April evening remains.

Four
Wartime

Senior Year
1942 – 1943

My roommate, Jean Archer, and I came up in the world in a big way in our senior year by drawing the best dormitory room on the campus of Pennsylvania College for Women.

Several years before, the tall bamboo fencing that shielded the adjacent Mellon mansion had come down when Paul Mellon donated his Pittsburgh estate, built by his father, Andrew W. Mellon, to the college. Named Mellon Hall, it became the senior dorm, thus doubling the size of the adjacent campus. Dean Mary Helen Marks' residence and quarters for home economics classes were on the first floor.

Jean and I were assigned the late Andrew Mellon's second floor bedroom. After three years of the communal bathrooms, we had a large private bath with a separate shower stall. There was a walk-in closet with built-in drawers. The spacious room was carpeted in a soft green shade and had a marble fireplace. Leaded glass windows overlooked the front terrace toward Woodland Road and lovely landscaping from the bay windows at the side. A wing next to the room had been Paul Mellon's all-aluminum office, now the Alumnae Office, and beyond was a wood-paneled sitting room with crewel drapes. Another bathroom was often used as a passage to the room of our friends on the other side. Close friendships grew up between the second-floor occupants: Martha Jane "Trux" Truxall, Peggy "Suppie" Suppe, Marian "Gussie" Teichmann and Elizabeth "Lib" Esler. Added to our large bedroom was June Hunker, a former day student whose parents were wintering in Florida.

The main entrance was under a porte-cochère and a circle driveway centered with a fountain. A heavy wooden door opened a few steps up and into a large wood-paneled great hall. To the left was a paneled library with needlepoint furniture, to the right was a white-walled dining room that overlooked the front terrace and doors into the kitchens and maids' quarters. There was a music room and sunroom as well. On the lower floor was a small ballroom and further down a bowling alley and a swimming pool.

Sunday morning breakfast was special. It was the one day in the week that we could sleep in and have breakfast an hour later than usual in robes and housecoats. We sixteen seniors of Pennsylvania College for Women that lived in the Mellon Hall dormitory could gather around a long oval table in the beautiful white dining room for a leisurely breakfast time.

One wall was a group of leaded glass windows facing Woodland Road. A small side table sat there. Above a white marble fireplace hung an oil portrait. Along a side wall was a long heavy mahogany buffet. The breakfast menu was simple and never varied: orange juice, crispy bacon, toasted pecan rolls and a choice of coffee, tea or hot chocolate. Some students had ample time to go to an eleven o'clock church service. Some girls went back to bed, others gathered for a cigarette and chat. No one worked on those Sunday mornings.

Physical fitness was emphasized as part of the war effort. At 10 p.m., exercises were held in the large front hall with changing leaders. We wore pajamas for the half hour of exercise and usually wore a bathing suit underneath so we could go directly down to the pool for a relaxing swim. We had no problem sleeping after that.

This was the lap of luxury except for our classes, studying, term papers, blue book exams and concern for the war.

The Start of It All

In late September of my sophomore year, I was at W&J over the weekend for a dance with Ed, or "Pooch," as he was called. He had arranged a ride back to Pittsburgh with a fraternity brother who lived in Mt. Lebanon. Going with us was a recent grad who was attending law school at the University of Pittsburgh, Dan Core. He had been the pledge master the previous year and came to visit his "class" of fraternity brothers. I was seated between the two fellows on the front bench seat of the car and treated to an interesting conversation during the hour-long drive.

A month later, I had my first date with Dan, a first daytime date. It was Nov. 7, 1940, the day after election day. He was co-chair of the Young Republicans and the party had been defeated locally in spite of his efforts. Wednesday afternoon was a day without classes at Pennsylvania College for Women. It was unusual to have a daytime date in the middle of the week. It was lunch at Webster Hotel coffee shop followed by an afternoon at the Carnegie Museum's Biennial International Art Exhibit. This was a new dimension to my social life.

Perhaps that wasn't really the start of it all, for later Dan told me that he really fell in love when he walked down the stairs in the Delt house and saw me sitting on a couch wearing a black dress and little black hat with a veil. It's hard to imagine that attire in a frat house today. He admitted that he tried hard to impress me during our ride back to Pittsburgh later that day.

His pledge brother Ed asked him to look after me, since transportation was hard to arrange in those days. So Dan would stop by campus and escort me around the city. He brought me a poster from an inter-fraternity dance that I had gone to at Pitt and it was a fun decoration for my room. Another day, he left off a book of poetry but didn't come in. Then, he took me out to dinners at Anthon's in East Liberty. That was a bakery with booths to the rear. We would sit over our $1.25 dinners and talk for hours. A kind waitress, also named Amy, seated us at a back booth where we would sit until closing.

Dan and I never went to a movie during our dating years. There was always too much to talk about. We did go to the Savoyards performances of Gilbert and Sullivan at the Twentieth Century Club auditorium. Before long, Dan told Ed that he was acting for himself and not on Ed's behalf. Some of the fraternity brothers took sides at the time.

Young couples dating and falling in love seldom realize they are not alone in their own romantic world. They rarely anticipate that this new relationship is really a package deal. There are parents on both sides, brothers and sisters, aunts and uncles and assorted friends who will all come into their future life. This often comes as a shock.

My mother, Dan Core, me and Ceil holding her cat

Just a month after we had met, Dan attended the Christmas Dance of the Junior Community Club in Zelienople. Unbeknownst to me, while he was sitting out a dance with Mother that evening, he let her know what his intentions were. He wooed her at the same time he was courting me.

I became acquainted with his sister, Jane, when she attended Sunday afternoon symphony concerts with us at the Syria Mosque. She was ten years older and not the motherly type, but since Dan's mother had died when he was eleven years old, she filled that role somewhat. She was warm and witty. Dan's brother was five years older than him and, when we drove to the mining town where he was working, we went out to dinner with him and his fiancée. I was not only impressed with Dan, but liked the family and friends that I met. We had dinner after concerts at the Villa d'Este restaurant on Centre Ave. in Shadyside with two of his W&J professors several times.

I was still seeing Ed, but our dates were sometimes contentious as he was jealous of Dan and anyone else that I went out on a date with. To avoid the draft, he had dropped out of college. He was able to get a job with Westinghouse in Pittsburgh. It provided him with the funds to realize the dream of buying a first car. This was a bright red Chevrolet convertible. There were some fun picnic outings with friends and he often parked it at the college for my use during the day since he was working at night. I don't recall using it much, but it was a flashy car to be seen in.

We drove to visit his family on a spring weekend despite my mother's opposition. His parents were pleasant and his younger sister gave me her room to stay in. We had a day in Chicago and met some of his friends on Sunday. It was not a completely comfortable weekend, however, as I knew my mother didn't approve of the trip. She may have feared that I would elope with Ed. At the time, I thought my mother disapproved of him because he was Catholic.

Dan was drafted for the war almost immediately, and soon became a private in the Army. Although he was not on the scene, he wrote interesting letters to me almost daily. He used Bartlett's Familiar Quotations and included romantic quotations of famous poetry in his letters to me. His letters were constant and compelling.

Meanwhile, Ed and I were not getting along well because of his jealousy. We had a stormy session one night outside the Royal York where he grew physically violent. I exited his car in anger, determined to find my own way home. Reluctantly, I got back in and agreed to be driven back to the dorm. I probably didn't have enough mad money for a cab. But from then on, I refused further dates with him. I saw how easily infuriated he could become and was no longer interested in seeing him, not even casually.

When Dan came home on leave, we went to his Oakmont home and I met his father, Dan Sr. for the first time. He met me with open arms and a kiss and called me "Ahmy," pronouncing my name as he had pronounced his late wife's. Her name was Amarilla, her nickname was "Amy" and it was pronounced with a soft "A" sound. Since I had lost my father at the age of nine, he became "Dad." His first kiss was a warm welcome to the family.

It's hard to remember a first marriage proposal from Dan since there were so many – and never on bended knee. I don't know when Dan proposed for the first time, because he did it so often. On New Year's Eve of my final college year, there was a phone call from Dan in Texas repeating the proposal that he had made many times before and the answer was finally "yes." I could see my goal of graduation in sight in five more months.

Dan had a leave in March on his way to Duke University for Officer Candidate School. Shortly after my June graduation from college and his commissioning as a second lieutenant, there was another leave. It was then that he gave me the engagement ring.

Dan had prepared for his arrival with a series of single gardenias. That was always his flower of choice. I wasn't quite certain when he would arrive and he kept me in suspense by arranging to have a white gardenia delivered each day, for four days in a row, with an accompanying note. Finally, he phoned me from the station to say that he had arrived and was on his way to the dorm. It would be the first time seeing each other after our long-distance engagement. From that moment on, I listened for the doorbell. A maid usually opened the door for us when the bell rang, but that night I was ahead of her. I rushed down the wide steps to open the door myself and flew into his arms.

Our wartime wedding came off as planned on May 13, 1944. Most Cinderella stories end on the wedding day. This was true when I walked down the aisle to the church altar to be wed not to a prince, but to the most charming man I'd ever known. That day can be relived from a brief video converted from the

Dan and I on a picnic during his leave from officer candidate school

short wedding movie taken that day. It was the start of my "happily ever after."

It was the best decision of my life and led to sixty wonderfully happy years with our three children: Gordon, Philip and Amy Jane. Our early dreams of travel came true and we made friends in many far-flung places as we traveled the world.

The Core Family

The past influences the present and on into the future. The Core family history is set primarily in two Southwestern Pennsylvania towns, Washington, Pa. and Kittanning, Pa., along with the smaller adjacent town of Ford City, Pa.

The Rev. Jesse Franklin Core, Jr. was a Methodist minister at the First Methodist Church in Washington, where he and his wife, Sarah, built a home on North Main Street, which was out in the country then, and raised six children, three sons and three daughters. Pictures show him as a tall, robust balding man. He was a veteran of the Civil War who had tried to enlist with his older brother Michael, a member of the famed Ringgold Calvary, when he was underage. He was sent back to his home in Scenery Hill, then called Hillsboro on the historic National Road, but he returned to the army the next year and was accepted.

After his war service, he studied for the ministry at Millersburg Academy in Kentucky. We have the letters that he wrote during his courtship of Sarah

Katherine Heiner of Kittanning, Pa. He called her Sallie or Sadie and there were ups and downs because her parents were Episcopalians and weren't pleased with a Methodist suitor. We also have a fulsome newspaper account of their wedding, which included many fine details, down to the ushers, "Briney, Hancock, Milliron, Copely, Neale and Croll, [who] performed their arduous duties to the satisfaction of all." Because it is so entertaining, the account has been read at all of the family wedding rehearsal dinners.

Frank, as he was called, was a minister of the "fire and brimstone" Methodist church on Smithfield Street in Pittsburgh and lived in the Hill District when his son Daniel was born. Each of the Core children was born in a different town in Western Pennsylvania, as the young preacher was often being moved to new churches being "seeded" in the rapidly growing Methodist denomination, before finally settling in Washington.

Though he was the youngest son, my father-in-law, Dan, was given the longest name, Daniel Brodhead Heiner St. Cyr Core. I remember it by heart as I embroidered his initials on handkerchiefs as a gift once and they took forever! His father enjoyed ostentatious names, as he gave his older sons the names Karl Leopold Wilhelm Core and Paul Albert Agassiz Core. Both were educated at Washington & Jefferson College. Karl became a construction engineer and worked and lived in Ford City, Pa., while Paul was a lawyer who worked in his hometown, living in East Washington.

Rev. Jesse F. Core was known as a forceful preacher, occasionally removing his coat and rolling up his coat sleeves during his sermons, and sometimes remonstrating his six children as they sat in the front row pew. Their home on North Main Street was so rural that they had a milk cow for which the boys were responsible. One day the cow wandered off and was hit by a train, to their delight. Their joy was short-lived, however, when some kindly parishioners replaced the cow with a new one.

Their father kept a fast horse and made his parish calls driving a sulky cart. No card playing was permitted in their home. Family stories go that Dan Sr. and his sister, Bird, were playing cards one day when their father returned home unexpectedly from his calls. Panicked, they threw the cards behind the large bookcase in the living room and had to remember to be on hand when the bookcase was moved for spring cleaning.

The Cores were of German stock and the Reverend's father, Jesse Franklin Core, Sr., briefly owned and managed the Beck-Ringland Stagecoach Inn and Tavern on the National Pike Road during the Civil War, after his farming days were over. But if anyone ever suggested his father was a tavernkeeper, they were quickly corrected and informed he had run a "hotel." The original Core family farm was located next to the National Pike just past a little lane called Needmore Rd., and the value of his real estate in 1850 was $200. Later in life, after Jesse, Sr. had retired and moved the family into town, they lived directly behind the Century Inn, on what is now called Fava Farm Rd., and his real estate was valued at $400, which likely included the tavern.

Frank died at the relatively young age of fifty-two in 1898. Sarah Heiner Core, Dan's grandmother, mourned the love of her life deeply, and lived on in the family's Victorian house on North Main Street until her death in 1930. They had written passionate love letters to each other during their courting days, and my husband Dan preserved and transcribed these.

The oldest girl in the family, Lorena, married a Washington & Jefferson graduate, Robert Murray Gibson, who had a brief career as a professional baseball player before going on to law school and becoming a Federal Court judge in Pittsburgh. Karl and Dan Sr. worked for and with their mother's Heiner brother in Kittanning while Paul was an attorney in Washington. Two of the Core brothers became prominent citizens of Ford City at that time. Karl was superintendent of the Pittsburgh Plate Glass Company, the largest industry in the town. Bird and Sarah Core, the youngest sisters, never married, and had fulfilling careers partially derailed by the Depression.

Rev. Jesse Franklin Core, Jr., D.D.

Daniel had worked as a cashier in banks until he was called to service as the head of the National Guard to fight in the Mexican Border Wars. He returned to the bank until World War I was declared in 1917. He married Amarilla Luella Getze, the daughter of local doctor George Getze, who founded the first hospital in Tarentum, Allegheny Valley General. They had three children: Amarilla Jane, Jesse Franklin III and Daniel Heiner, Jr., born in Ford City in 1917. When visiting his hometown, my husband liked to point to the window of the upstairs bedroom of the house at 1201 Fourth Ave., where his mother gave birth to him and say, "I was born in the bay window." His father was stationed as commander of Company K in Camp Hancock, Ga. and, as a baby, Dan was baptized there by a chaplain with an Army helmet holding the christening water.

The Heiner family history book tells of the battles in which Captain Core fought in France. Returning to Ford City with his fellow soldiers, he was a founder of the American Legion. He returned to banking, where he became the head of the bank. He and his wife, "Ahmy," built a spacious house in Lenape Park, a new upper-class neighborhood on top of the hill in Manor Township, overlooking the town from the south. His older brother Karl, now head of the local glass plant and his wife, Mildred Hoyle Core, built an identical house next door. They had three young daughters, Mildred, Mary and Natalie, who were near to the ages of their boy cousins.

Mildred was an ambitious woman and a would-be actress. She once entertained a company of dancers who were playing in Pittsburgh. Prohibition did not restrict her entertaining, so much so that my husband once joked that he gave up drinking at the age of sixteen after all of the liquor he drank at her parties. Relations between the rival sisters-in-law were not close.

My husband, Dan, was given the title Junior for convenience, but never had his father's full cumbersome name. His sister was ten years older and his brother five years older. When their mother died, sister Jane reluctantly assumed maternal duty of Dan when she was around. She had gone to Miss Sayward's, a finishing school in Philadelphia, now long extinct, and then to the Margaret Morrison Carnegie College at Carnegie Tech, now known as Carnegie Mellon University. Due to lack of funds caused by the Great Depression, she never finished her degree there. She lived with her father in Oakmont and became a stenographer at the YMCA until she met her husband, Dan L. Milling. They married in 1943 and moved to Beaumont, Texas. She was talented in art and music and the family has many of her beautiful paintings and sketches.

Jesse F. Core III, known as Bud to the family and Jesse to his friends, graduated from Ford City High School and then was sent to Culver Military Academy in preparation for entering West Point. With many local political connections, his appointment was assured. But that didn't happen. Bud failed the physical due to flat feet and albumen in his urine. Neither of these things were deterrents in later life, just in entering West Point. Instead, he went to Pennsylvania State University, studied mining engineering and retired from U.S. Steel as Executive Vice President of Coal Operations.

Dan's mother, Amarilla, was a contralto, trained at the Philadelphia Conservatory of Music in her youth. She sang at the Ford Memorial Methodist Church, where she was the choir director, and she often performed at services and was much in demand for other local events. She was the first president of the American Legion's Women's Auxiliary and a social star as the wife of a prominent citizen. Dan's older sister, Jane, was becoming an accomplished pianist. So, surely, young Dan Core would prove to have some musical talent.

His father was not easily convinced and instead of the expense of buying a violin, he insisted that a violin be rented. An instructor was engaged to come to the house for the weekly lessons. Not long into the start of Dan's career as a violinist, the teacher arrived promptly at the house but the reluctant pupil was nowhere to be seen. His mother knew his haunts and where to search. There was a small stream some distance to the rear of their Lenape property where he liked to play. He was called back to the house for the lesson, returning in an untidy state. The music lesson began. There was a strange smell in the room. Then the teacher realized that his pupil had a dead fish in his shirt pocket. He resigned on the spot and never darkened the house again.

Dan grew up as a music lover, not a performer. He liked to whistle. He had an amazing memory for tunes and words that he liked to sing. But it was impossible to harmonize with him since he was wont to change key frequently.

On trips to Ford City, we would drive by Dan's former home. The house was well-maintained by subsequent owners. The only change that could be noted were the small pines on either side of the house, now towering trees. Back then the twin Lenape homes were located on the Kittanning-Leechburg Highway in Manor Township. Today the town has grown to meet them, and their addresses are 728 and 734 Main Street in the Lenape Heights neighborhood. Whenever we visited, there were always old friends to see in Ford City: the Heilman homestead in Manor on the Allegheny River, the Heilman shoe store, Dan's high school teacher and friend, Ted Rupert, who became our dentist, and others.

On one nostalgic trip to Ford City, Dan found a small lane behind the Lenape houses and drove as far as possible to its end. From there it was a short walk to the small stream and the fishing hole that ended his violin career.

Dan's mother passed away from pneumonia in November 1928, when he was eleven years old. Her death was supposedly brought on by singing in a cold church while sick herself at the time. She was well-liked and the community was shocked by her death. The family was fractured by the loss.

Dan Core, Sr. with wife Amarilla, daughter Jane, son Jesse and Dan Jr. as an infant in the cradle in 1917

Daniel Core, Sr. was a struggling widower when President Franklin D. Roosevelt declared the month-long Bank Holiday in 1933 that shut down the banking system. That resulted in the closing of the Ford City Bank and his unemployment during the Depression. He and Dan were alone in the big house. Families helped each other and his wife's cousin, Marge Kennedy Coulter, and her husband, Sam, who was out of work, came to live with the Cores, along with their three little girls. There was ample room and Marge ran a cheerful house. My husband remembered those days fondly.

His father found some solace in his stamp collecting hobby and made a little money in trading sometimes. He also liked to fish and hunt, although he had to cut back on the number of dogs that he kept. There was a fire in the garage where the pump was kept that supplied the house with water. No funds were available to fix the pump and so water had to be carried in for some time.

Karl Core became seriously ill soon after the death of Dan's mother. Dan remembered going with his father to Washington, D.C. where his uncle was staying at the home of the Hammonds, wealthy relatives of his wife, Mildred. He died there in February 1929. His widow stayed in Washington, D.C. His oldest daughter, Mildred, married a man in the foreign service who was sent to South America, and daughter, Mary, married an Army man. Natalie fulfilled her mother's ambitions by becoming an actress. She married a fellow actor and worked in Hollywood. She had a role in the TV soap opera *Dynasty* and guest starred in now-classic shows like *Bewitched, Mama's Family* with Carol Burnett, and the hospital drama *ER*. Most famously, she was the woman in the classic Audrey Hepburn film, *My Fair Lady*, who faints in the Ascot Races scene.

Daniel Brodhead Heiner, Dan's great-uncle, was an attorney, a member of Congress and later a collector of Internal Revenue with strong political connections in Kittanning and the area. Dan took me to his home and introduced me when we made a brief call. Somehow, he managed to introduce me to many friends and relatives when he was courting me. That was a plus for they were all such nice people.

In eighth grade, Dan won an American Legion award as a top student. He has written about all the magazines that came to their home and the many books purchased. He loved the written word. Sometimes he and Bud would crawl into the third-floor attic space under the eaves and read by flashlight.

At Ford City High School, he earned top grades. He was not the class valedictorian in the class of 1935, although he came close. Instead, he was elected as class orator by his peers to give the commencement speech, rather than the valedictorian. He was in all the high school plays and programs. He supported the athletics of the school from the sidelines. Ford City had a winning basketball team at the time. Although Dan was six-feet-tall, he was not fast enough to make the team. The school had an outstanding coach who went on to become a well-known referee that Dan followed for many years. His high school signature was a purple felt hat worn on most occasions.

When Dan graduated from Ford City High School in 1935, it was the middle of the Depression. There were no funds for college. However, his father was determined he would go. He took him to the family's alma mater, Washington & Jefferson College, where his brothers Karl and Paul had graduated, and borrowed $500 from the college to enroll him. He worked multiple jobs to earn his way through college before he finally graduated with the class of 1940.

Dan was always a loyal alumnus of the college and later served two separate terms as an alumni representative on their Board of Trustees. Our two sons later graduated from W&J. Then, our eldest son, Gordon, worked in the development office of the college for seventeen years, so the connection lasted for a long time.

Dan Core, Sr. was finally hired as Clerk of Federal Court near the end of the Depression. Undoubtedly, there was nepotism involved since his brother-in-law Robert Murray Gibson was the judge. The Ford City house, heavily mortgaged by that time, was sold to Frank McNutt, an insurance man. His only son, Frank, Jr., was a classmate of Dan's in high school and at Washington & Jefferson College and became a doctor. Dan Sr. moved to Oakmont, a Pittsburgh suburb, with his daughter, Jane, and then later moved in with Dan and me during the early years of our marriage. He worked in downtown Pittsburgh until his death in 1950.

Bird Foster Core
1890 – 1944

The family story is that when Bird was baptized by the visiting Methodist bishop, he turned to the father, Reverend Jesse Franklin Core, Jr. and said, "Is this a Christian name for the child?" This may be a clue to the typical "birds" that he knew.

Born in Johnstown, Pa., Bird Core spent most of her life in the family home at 620 North Main Street, which was then on the outskirts of Washington, Pa. Her father was a minister and the presiding elder of the Methodist churches in the area and the girls in her family were considered "society misses" in the early days of the 20th century. She was a person of many talents with a quick mind and a warm personality. She was popular with students at Washington & Jefferson College, a men's college in the town. She was engaged eight times and never married, but remained lifelong friends with all of her rejected suitors. Later in life she had a "gentleman caller" who was a local lawyer. They spent a lot of time together and might have married if it had not been for his spinster sister who lived with him and was firmly opposed to Bird.

Aunt Bird sitting on the front stoop of the family home on North Main St.

From her teenage years she was a Washington society girl, and she created and ran the playground system in town. She was the organist at the First Methodist Church where her father preached, starting in her youth. She was enlisted to direct plays at the college and had many friends among the faculty. Some of the favorite gatherings at her home were play readings. She would borrow scripts from the library and pass them out to a cast in advance and then they and others would have an evening of reading and discussing a particular play with mutual enjoyment. She was named the Director of Playgrounds for the city in her twenties and many of the playgrounds standing today were built and tended to by her hands in those "gay old days" of pre-WWI America.

The beginning of the Depression were dark days for the Core family. Dan's grandmother, Sarah Katherine Heiner Core, died in September 1930 at the age of 82. She had outlived three of her children, who had all died in succession during the three prior years. The family home on North Main Street was divided into a downstairs and the upstairs apartment, where Bird lived.

There was originally farmland around the house, but now large Victorians and later model homes grace both sides of the street, and behind the property are small, city-style neighborhoods with houses packed tightly together and cars parked end-to-end on both sides of the road. The Core home is now gone, replaced with a stout white brick office building, but what was originally the driveway of the house remains, named Core Street. Nearby is Coremont Avenue, another street named after the family. It cuts diagonally across Katherine Avenue, which Dan always said was named after his grandmother.

Bird's nephew Daniel Heiner Core, Jr. not only visited his grandmother in Washington, Pa., but during his college years lived with his Aunt Bird. He slept in the round tower room. It was the depth of the Depression in 1935, and college would have been impossible without this place to live. He joined the Delta Tau Delta fraternity and was able to take his meals at the fraternity house in exchange for waiting tables there. Dan had a laundry route at the college thanks to one of Aunt Bird's friends, and also sold corsages for college dances. Somehow, he and Aunt Bird managed to scrape by, pooling their meager resources.

Dan worked for the laundry of Alex Murdoch, running a route through the college during the summers. By his sophomore year, things had not improved and so he dropped out of college and worked in a steel mill, which was headed by a good friend of Aunt Bird, Walter Baker. He commuted there by street car and continued to live with her. By the next year, he had enough money to continue college, though not enough to pay off the student loan. This was finally paid off during WWII.

Bird had friends of all ages and from all walks of life. While living with Aunt Bird, Dan was her assistant host when she frequently entertained "town and gown" friends and he got to know older people well. The years of living with Bird rubbed off on him. He knew how to treat women of all ages and was a great favorite of all. He knew how to brighten a conversation with a good story or a joke that he could adapt to the occasion so that it seemed to be original.

Bird was a wonderful hostess and people loved to be around her. While she played the organ and directed local plays, nothing she did earned much income in this post-Depression era. Her friends knew that she could not afford to entertain and so they all brought the refreshments for the evening. She made everyone feel that they were important to her. Years later, when Dan was in the Army and needed three references to apply to officer candidate school, he had letters from two military generals. They were old Washington friends of Aunt Bird who knew Dan personally from her frequent salons.

I met Aunt Bird on my first big date with Dan. We'd had just a few dates the fall of my sophomore year. She wrote me a very proper invitation to spend the night at her home following the annual Charity Ball in Washington, Pa. at Christmastime in 1940. It was held during the holidays and so meant travel to and from Zelienople. It was my first dance with Dan Core in his newly acquired tuxedo. There was a dinner party before the formal dance held at the home of the Dorseys. Their two sons, close friends of Dan, were home from college and their escorts and Dan and I were the guests. Their teenage sister was also included in the group.

Sitting on Dan's lap in the ballroom of the George Washington Hotel during the 1940 Charity Ball

After the dance in the beautiful ballroom of the George Washington Hotel was over, the group returned to the Dorsey's for breakfast at 2 a.m. It had been a long day, beginning in the afternoon with the drive of fifty miles from Zelienople, so Dan and I returned to the house on Main Street.

There we found Aunt Bird sitting up in bed, reading and waiting to hear all about the party. She was interested in who was in attendance and just what each person was wearing. I was impressed with Dan's ability not only to tell her about her friends who were there, but his total recall of color and fashion details and the description of the evening. All fatigue seemed to drop away in talking with Bird. We sat up until four o'clock in the morning. Then after a long sleep-in, we dressed and went with Bird to the hotel for brunch where she was able to greet and introduce us to many of her friends.

It was late afternoon by the time Dan and I returned to my home. A young married neighbor, Sis White, who was like an older sister to me, was visiting. Upon meeting Dan, she invited us to have potluck supper across the street. I think she and her husband, Herb, were interested in this date of mine. He charmed them just as Aunt Bird would have done and it was the beginning of a wonderful romance.

Aunt Bird was too ill to attend our wedding in 1944. She was staying with her sister, Sarah, in New York City at that point so the trip would have taken too much out of her. We called her from our hotel that evening so she could wish us well. She died of cancer some months later. It may have been lung cancer as she was a heavy smoker – a sign of the independent woman in those days, which she undoubtedly was!

World War II Remembered

The Japanese attack on the United States Naval Base on Pearl Harbor changed lives for the immediate present and years to come. December 7, 1941 was a "day that will live in infamy." That invasion plunged America into a war on two fronts, the Pacific war with the Japanese and the Atlantic front against Hitler's Germany. Congress declared war the following day. The war clouds had been forming for months on both fronts.

The Sunday that Pearl Harbor was bombed, Dan and I were on an afternoon date to see the Pittsburgh Symphony Orchestra at the Syria Mosque. As we left the darkened concert hall and our eyes adjusted to the light, we did not realize we were stepping out into a changed world.

Many young men rushed to join the armed services, some through sheer patriotism and others in order to secure a place of their choice in the service, rather than being drafted. Others dropped out of college for the protection of jobs in the war industry, which turned out to be only temporary.

Dan in uniform visiting me in my hometown

Dan had his draft orders six weeks later. He was able to secure a two-week extension to take his second-year semester law school exams and complete the semester at the end of January. He left from the East Liberty train station the first week in February, just five days later.

The first stop was Fort Cumberland, Md., where there were tests, both physical and mental, and where uniforms were issued. Uniforms were in short supply and most were ill-fitting. One difficulty for Dan was Army boots because he wore a size 13. On the basis of his high aptitude tests scores, he was sent to Fort Benjamin in Harrison, Ind. as a private to train for the finance corps. Following that he was sent on to Texas.

At my woman's college, the college president made classrooms and faculty members available for evening classes for service men. We took Red Cross courses in home nursing to make up for the registered nurses leaving for the war. It consisted of learning how to change a bed with the patient in the bed, how to give a bed bath, take temperatures, handle bed pans, etc. There was special emphasis on physical fitness. The faculty worked overtime and the students were seldom seen there. Some of my classmates dropped out of college to get married to longtime boyfriends leaving for or already in the service. We wrote many letters to everyone we knew in the service.

In my hometown of Zelienople, my mother became an air raid watcher. A small cabin was erected beside the reservoir, which was the highest point in town. Watchers had classes to learn to identify different German aircraft. Women were on duty during the day and men at night. It was important to watch for any enemy plane that might target the important steel mills of Pittsburgh. This was a serious concern because we had all watched the bombings, or The Blitz as it was called, that had occurred overseas against Britain for the last two years. Even as far inland as Southwestern Pennsylvania, it was possible that stealth planes from Germany could fly over to attack the "Arsenal of America," as we were called by President Franklin Delano Roosevelt. Black-out curtains or blinds were closed at night across the region. Rationing of clothing, particularly shoes, food and gasoline was in effect.

Even before gas and tire rationing, there were fewer cars on the road and they usually had more than one passenger, no matter where they were going. There were food shortages, both from imported foods and from difficulties in transporting goods, so rations were instituted so people would not hoard necessary products. Beef and butter were rationed, chicken and fish not as much so. There were coupon books filled with stamps and red and blue points were needed for purchases.

Following graduation, I worked in the office of the Johns-Manville company in Zelienople, usually riding my bicycle to work or walking. The plant was in the war industry, making liners for steel furnaces. At a desk near mine, the man in charge of purchasing materials for the plant had to work with quotas and fill out forms for his orders.

Mother had ordered a walnut corner cupboard, custom built by the Dambach Lumber Company, and modeled after an antique one owned by the Whites. It happened to be the last walnut available to civilians before the war. During the war, walnut was needed for gun stocks. Of course, all production of cars and civilian goods such as stoves, refrigerators, sweepers and other household items was stopped for the duration of the war.

It took many years after the war to convert back to civilian goods. There was no new housing and when housing resumed, the houses were very small. Families doubled up as war brides returned to their family homes, often with small children. Housing was especially scarce near bases where wives tried to live near their soldier husbands, even temporality. Rent controls on housing and price controls on food helped to keep inflation and price gouging in check.

A Blind Date

The year was 1943 and the event was the prom of my senior college year. The United States was at war in earnest. We were no longer sitting on the sidelines watching invasions in Europe. Suddenly the country was attacked from the West, where it was least expected, and we were fighting a war on two fronts.

Despite the war and the scarcity of young men, college events were scheduled. My women's college tried bravely to carry on with its traditions. One of our dormitory friends came up with a solution of sorts. For the annual prom, our friend, Martha, rounded up a group of blind dates from the nearby Pittsburgh Theological Seminary where her cousin was a student. With his recruiting help, she was able to enlist six prom escorts. There were no prerequisites as to dancing ability. It is not clear why these men were spared military service, but they were a pretty uninspiring lot. My date was one of the better-looking and, as a matter of etiquette and a thank you, he took me out again after prom.

He invited me out on a Sunday night some weeks later. Our evening was attendance at the Third Presbyterian Church on Fifth Avenue near the campus. During the service, he made careful notes on the printed program in the pew and asked my opinion of the hymn selections. I think that he was doing his homework and covering two bases at one time.

Me, center, posing with members of the Prom Committee

After the service was over, we walked to a drugstore on Highland Avenue for a milkshake and then back to the college with further discussion of the church service.

A fashion show and bridge tea on Saturday afternoon in Mellon Hall followed the prom. It was to be a benefit for the United Service Organizations. I was chairman and at a loss for an escort. The weather proved to be a mixture of rain and ice, but as a favor to Dan, one of his best friends, Daniel Finkbeiner, taking a graduate year at W&J, came up to escort me. He arrived bearing a record that was a gift Dan had arranged. I've never forgotten his kindness in that hectic time.

Peggy and Ed's Wedding

"Oh, what a beautiful morning, Oh, what a beautiful day," was the popular song from the musical Oklahoma that I was humming that Saturday morning in August 1943 while waiting for an early bus to Pittsburgh. The sun was shining and it was truly a beautiful day. At the Pennsylvania Station, my college roommate June was waiting and we boarded a train to Johnstown for the wedding of Peggy Suppes and Edward Yingling. Peggy had worn her lovely blue star sapphire engagement ring for months before our college graduation. The train windows were open and bits of ash flew into the window on the crowded ride.

Peggy's high school friend Robert met us at the Johnstown station and gave us a lively account of the activities ongoing at the Suppes' home. He said the house was full of Mrs. Suppes' friends, who had all rallied to the occasion by filling the house with flowers. He said Mrs. Suppes would periodically look at the flowers and then burst into tears.

Mr. and Mrs. Suppes had been planning an elegant wedding for their only daughter's wedding to her high school sweetheart. Her grandmother's wedding gown was at the dressmaker being altered for the large church wedding. Dr. and Mrs. Yingling were also pleased with the wedding, but were insistent that their minister son should conduct the service. World War II made a wedding date uncertain since Ed was in the Army and his older brother was an Army chaplain stationed in far-flung Alaska.

A number of things came together to change the wedding plans from the big church wedding that the families wanted to an informal home ceremony. Firstly, Mrs. Suppes was so immersed in wedding plans, which seemed to grow more involved every day, that Peggy was concerned for her mother's health. Then they found out that Ed's brother was coming home for a brief leave from the military and Ed could get home at the same time for the wedding to take place. Everyone rushed into action.

When we arrived, the Suppes' house was ready with a flower-decked mantel above the living room fireplace where the ceremony would take place. The dining room had a table covered with an elaborate lace cloth and the punch bowl and silver serving dishes in place. June and I had a chance to freshen up from the train trip and were taken to the country club for lunch on the terrace. We were both wearing pastel summer suits. Peggy wore a light gray suit and matching hat and her only attendant, a cousin, wore a darker gray suit. I had a chance to show them my newly acquired engagement ring. The formal announcement of my engagement and a tea were planned for later that September at the College Club. A photographer took pictures of Peggy, her cousin and us in her bedroom before the ceremony.

Punch, tea sandwiches and wedding cake was served in the dining room after the ceremony. Mrs. Yingling was a pillar of the Women's Christian Temperance Union, so the punch was non-alcoholic. However, Mr. Suppes had made a special trip to the rear door of the local Elks Club, where he was a member, to secure mixed drinks for the celebration. Downstairs in the game room was where

Ed Yingling and Peggy Suppes together on a picnic while they were dating

wedding gifts were on display. Mr. Suppes quietly pressed some of the guests to go in to see the wedding gifts, and when they arrived, they discovered the secret bar area. Thus, there was a reception on two levels that ne'er the twain did meet.

My college friendship with Peggy and Ed Yingling continued over the years. We visited each other with our growing families whenever we were in the Pittsburgh area. Peggy became a Presbyterian minister, the first woman in the region, and received her doctorate. When we returned to the states and were living in Mt. Lebanon, we celebrated Peggy's ordination with a party. We admired her career in the ministry. We traveled together when she was a widow. She took part in my husband's memorial service and I trusted her to lead my sister's funeral. Now I miss them all.

The Wedding Dress

Dan Core used his winning ways with my mother from the first time they met, so that she was content to be gaining a son, not losing a daughter. Her one condition to our marriage was that she felt that I should work for a year after college to gain business experience. It was wartime and I was able to find a job in Zelienople and live at home rent-free while I planned my wedding.

A groom rarely buys his wedding attire, since rental agencies specialize in supplying the men with their one-time suits. For a 1944 wartime wedding, no decisions had to be made; the groom wore an Army officer's uniform, as did his best man and usher. The bride is the center of attention at weddings while the groom seems merely the necessary accessory. Therefore, the wedding dress is the most important dress of her lifetime.

Formal attire was worn more often in those days and there were degrees of formality. There were dinner dresses with sleeves and straight skirts and ball gowns with wide skirts for dancing, bare shoulders and often long white kid gloves that went above the elbow. The gloves were expensive to buy and to have cleaned.

We shopped first for the wedding dress at Joseph Horne's in Pittsburgh and it was exciting to try on a variety of lovely gowns in their elegant bridal salon. But from childhood most of our family had shopped at the family department store, Boggs and Buhl on the North Side, and our long loyalty meant that we needed to go there as well. The center of shopping had gradually moved to downtown

Pittsburgh, across the river. Though Boggs and Buhl no longer had a fancy salon or a wide selection, there was one ivory satin gown that was a perfect fit, had a long train and came at a bargain price. The decision was made. My mother had set a wedding budget and then left all decisions to me, thus avoiding any dissension.

We then bought ivory tulle and I made the matching headpiece with its fingertip veil, as well as a small hat for my mother to wear. The satin shoes required using valuable wartime clothing coupons.

Most couples go to the courthouse together to get their marriage licenses. The fee at the time was $2 and I was the only single person in a line full of couples, as Dan was off in the Army. That $2 was never repaid to me and it was pointed out at our fiftieth wedding anniversary celebration that with compounding interest, that investment had grown to an impressive sum!

A date could be set for our wartime wedding, but all plans had to be tentative as the Army had priority

My portrait for the newspaper, complete with the faux bouquet of flowers belonging to the studio

over everything else. We were aware that our church wedding could be cancelled at the last minute and I was prepared to pack my trousseau for a simple ceremony elsewhere.

Fortunately, our luck held. The wedding and simple reception was held at the Zelienople Presbyterian Church on Saturday, May 13, 1944. Dan was in his officer's uniform. Two of my college roommates were my bridesmaids and my sister, Ceil, was the maid of honor. They all wore pale blue crepe dinner dresses with short sleeves and draped necklines. They carried purple lilacs for the early May wedding.

At that time, wedding accounts in the newspaper showed only the bride's picture. My dress was carried to a downtown Pittsburgh photography studio for the wedding picture. They offered a small selection of fake bridal bouquets to be held for the photograph. My real wedding bouquet was white lilacs with a center of white gardenias to be removed for the going away corsage. This was discarded at the hotel the next morning so that no one would know we were newlyweds. All the bouquets were put on the tables as centerpieces for the reception tea that followed in the church hall.

There was no close relative to walk me down the aisle. Perhaps it was women's lib: I walked down the aisle by myself and my mother answered the minister's question "who giveth this woman?" from her front pew. It was a standard Presbyterian ceremony and all went well. I was happy and not at all nervous.

Two years later, Dan was overseas and I was in Pittsburgh working for the YWCA. My roommate, Jean Archer, was in the South Pacific with the Red Cross. She was coming home to be married to her fiancé, Dan Rothermel, who had limited Navy leave from the Philadelphia Navy Yard. She had resigned from the Red Cross to get home as soon as possible. Her mother, sister Marian, and I arranged for the wedding to take place just after her return.

Jean and I had worn the same size in our college days, even to our shoe size. As my former bridesmaid, Jean knew what my wedding dress looked like and that it would fit her. Marian and I bought pale blue bridesmaid gowns and made our own hats to match, trimmed with the fabric flowers from the dress. Jean got home two days before the wedding. Her fiancé, Dan, arrived a day ahead of Jean to meet the Archers for the first time on his own. Except for a light snow, the December wedding in Ben Avon went off without a hitch. And both of our weddings were celebrated by fifty-year anniversary parties.

The wedding dress was packed away and neither of our daughters were able to wear the gown again. At Jean's suggestion, it was donated to the wedding gown collection at the Zelienople Historical Society, where it is brought out for special exhibits, since it was purchased at Boggs & Buhl, the store founded by the grandson and grandson-in-law of one of the town pioneers, Christian Buhl.

An Extended Wartime Honeymoon

The day before Dan and I were wed, he got word of orders sending him from the Army Specialized Training Program unit at the University of Illinois where he was paymaster, to the US Army Finance Office in Chicago in two weeks' time. Of course, the wedding would have been on regardless of any transfer, but this was marvelous news, as it meant that we had what turned out to be an extended honeymoon for the next ten months, before the arrival of his overseas assignment to the Pacific and Japan. But first, we had time for our official honeymoon weekend at Turkey Run State Park in Indiana.

We left our wedding gifts behind and set off by train the Sunday morning after our wedding from Pittsburgh to Indianapolis, with all our worldly goods in two suitcases. We were intent on being discreet about our recent wedding because the trains were packed with soldiers heading off to war.

Dan bought the Sunday paper. I left my corsage at the hotel and we behaved with great decorum all day on the train. As we were pulling into the station in

Indianapolis, Ind., Dan reached up to the rack for my topcoat and a pocketful of rice fell down, showering my head. The soldiers whistled and hooted at us and we were glad to be leaving the train. From the Indianapolis train station, we took a bus to Turkey Run State Park where we had reservations for four days. After a few wonderful days at the

Rice being thrown at us as we left on our honeymoon

park, we left for a new temporary home in Illinois. It was a fairly short bus trip to Champaign-Urbana, Ill., where Dan had managed to rent us two rooms in a private home. Housing was tight in wartime so there was only a bedroom and a makeshift kitchen. The one bathroom was shared by the entire household, much like a boarding house. Fortunately, our time in Champaign was brief. We were only there for a fortnight in weather that was still fairly cool. It could have been hell during a Midwestern summer.

Chicago was a wonderful place to be stationed. There was a large USO there with special entertainments. Transportation was free to uniformed service people. There was a post exchange nearby for the best buys. Theatre was inexpensive and second only to Broadway.

The months from June 1944 to April 1945 were a blissful time for us in spite of the war. Then Dan got his orders for overseas service, first going to Camp Pendleton in California and then a 40-day ocean voyage to Hollandia in Indonesia and then on to the Philippines. When the Japanese acknowledged defeat following the atomic bombs, Dan spent six months in war-ravaged Japan helping them rebuild. He was now a captain in the Finance Corps and had been in the Army for four years. He wanted to get back to his life. Those were difficult months as Japan was damp, cold and gray. Soldiers were released by a point system based on their time in the service, number of children, etc. Patience had to be exercised.

Finally, Dan was shipped back to the U.S. in March 1946, just one month too late to return to law school at Pitt. It was a happy day when we met at last in Columbus, Ohio where Dan was discharged. I borrowed Dad Core's car and drove to Columbus, where Dan was expected to arrive by train, making hotel reservations. I spent the night at the hotel so that I could be at the station first thing in the morning.

Dressed in my best silk dress with white gloves, I met that train, and every other train until the evening came, when no more arrivals were scheduled. I was tired and my lovely silk dress and white gloves were limp and wrinkled. I returned to the hotel discouraged and cried myself to sleep.

At midnight, there was a knock on the door. I woke up and opened it cautiously. To my surprise, Dan stumbled in, equally exhausted from the long *bus* ride the army had sent him on.

Chicago
June 1944 – April 1945

Chicago was a wonderful city and assignment for Dan, as everyone made the service people so welcome there during the war. Since it was rated number two as compared to New York, it always seemed to try harder, and it was a warmer and friendlier place to live in spite of the wintry winds off the lake or the Illinois prairie. During WWII, it was the transportation hub of the country. It was the transportation center during the time when there was constant train movement of the armed forces, all being moved from one part of the country to the other. Everyone had to change trains in Chicago. Trains from either coast and from the Southeast and Southwest all converged in Chicago where service men had to change trains and stations. There was a large United Service Organizations in the Loop to provide hospitality and entertainment, and all the transportation in the city, primarily the famed Elevated, was free of charge to those in uniform. There was free admission or reduced tickets for servicemen for all the city's entertainments.

We were babes in the woods when it came to apartment hunting in wartime Chicago. The Finance Office where Dan worked consisted of five officers and almost five hundred civilians, nearly all women. It was in the First National Bank on Lasalle Street downtown. By the greatest stroke of good luck, among those employees were two women who were giving up their hotel efficiency apartment at 1025 North Dearborn on the Near North Side. It was completely furnished, including linen service, and was rent-controlled for $50 a month plus a $1 telephone charge for switchboard service. This was one block from Clark Street to the West and the excitements of Rush Street to the East. Oak Street Beach and Lake Shore Drive were a short four-block walk. On some pleasant days Dan would walk to the office.

The apartment was on the tenth and top floor and consisted of one room with a kitchenette behind folding doors. A double door led into a closet/dressing room and then into the bathroom. A Murphy bed came out from the double door and, when it was down, it blocked the opening of the door into the outside hall. Our outdoors space was the tenth-floor fire escape, where we sometimes sat. We took long walks around the neighborhood. We thought it was wonderful and realized how lucky we were to have this time together.

That summer there was a fire in the basement, with most of the smoke coming up to our floor. The elevator could not be used, so we had to walk down ten flights of stairs. I dressed hastily, tossing on my precious (and expensive) alligator heels and clutching my four plate settings of sterling silver, a gift from my wedding. I was intent on saving them. We met our neighbors for the first time as we stood outside together on the sidewalk. My feet hurt like hell.

Chicago had fewer theatres than New York, but the theatres were small and we could buy seats in the last three or four rows of the house which was the $1.20 section. We would ask for a date when the first row of that section was available. My Christmas gift was antique opera glasses for use at the theatre. We saw *Voice of the Turtle*, *The Glass Menagerie* with the original cast and *Oklahoma* three times. Mother visited us for a week and stayed at the YWCA just two blocks down Dearborn. We took her to see *The Student Prince* and that stands out as one of the worst musicals ever. The male chorus must have been picked up from the street as they only mouthed the words to the songs.

Dan and I clowning around on the streets of Chicago

There were several couples from Pittsburgh living in Chicago at the same time. There was Janet and Lloyd McClelland (he was an attorney and not in the service due to polio) and Mary Jane and Bill Lowe, a W&J alumnus, in Evanston, also in the Army. We had dinners and played bridge with them.

The Reddings were parents of a friend of Dan's from college. They lived in Winnetka and adopted us during our time in Chicago. Their eldest son, George, was Dan's Delta Tau Delta fraternity brother on Navy duty and what they were unable to do for him, they did instead for us. They took us to some elegant Lake Shore Drive restaurants and had us to their lovely North Shore home. Thanks to price controls, it was possible to shop at Oak Street Market several blocks from our studio apartment. It was an upscale shop that catered to the high-rise apartments of Lake Shore Drive and would ordinarily have been out of our price range. One Sunday dinner at their spacious home, we were served an entrée that looked like meat loaf but was actually walnuts, bread crumbs and onions as a substitute. These were wartime sacrifices we all made.

Dan saw many college friends passing through Chicago and we had an active social life as we toured Rush Street bistros with them and made one or two drinks last all evening. When Aunt Lillian and my cousin, Geraldine, from Kansas stayed over one night on their way East to visit relatives, Dan made room for them by going down the street to the nearby YMCA to spend the night there.

Accustomed to volunteering, I took a week-long American Red Cross training course to do social service work. This consisted of home visits in an area North and West of the Loop, calling on the families of service men who requested help. I learned to find my way around that area by bus. However, it soon became evident that the costs of transportation and lunches involved that turned this "job" into an expense we could ill afford.

I then got a job at Marshall Fields, and added some black dresses to my wardrobe. That was the required attire for sales clerks and a twenty-five percent discount was offered for purchasing this work clothing. Other discounts were less generous, but it was difficult to be immune to the enticing displays as you entered the beautiful store each day. As a lowly worker, when you went through the swinging door marked Employees Only, you found yourself in the catacombs, a dark, cramped and dreary world of tiny offices and crowded lockers. It was the "upstairs and the downstairs" of the merchandising world.

After Christmas I took a job with the Chicago Red Cross at their offices on Michigan Avenue in the block next to the Stevens Hotel (thus being able to afford lunch). What went on daily was so interesting that I should have paid the Red Cross for the entertainment! Our section manned the phones in what was called Brief Service. We gave answers to questions and handled wires from chaplains asking for verification of requests for emergency leave based on family illness or similar dire events. Much of the work was helping soldiers get home leave in case of death or an illness in the family. Every day was interesting and different. Anything involving more than phone calls to doctors or funeral homes for confirmation went to case workers for investigation. More complicated matters were referred to Continued Service.

We got some ridiculous questions, too. If anything was to go wrong, it usually happened in Chicago, where service men traveling across the country had to change trains. When the trip went awry, we were there. Travelers Aid and the Chicago Red Cross played an important role in rescuing service people with problems.

There was a certain sense of living on borrowed time with so much happening in the war. It was like living in a tunnel, hoping that someday there would be light at the end and everyone's life could get back to normal. I bought a Pyrex baking dish one day, and that may have been what brought on the overseas orders that Dan got in April. He left for the West Coast and the Pacific. I wanted to apply for overseas duty with the Red Cross, like my roommate, Jean Archer, but we decided that with my mother and his father each living alone, it would be best for me to be nearby them in Pittsburgh. Our extended honeymoon in Chicago was suddenly over.

In mid-April 1945, our final celebration was dinner at one of Chicago's most elegant spots, the Pump Room, where waiters wore knee breeches and served the dinners on flaming swords. Chicago had been such bliss that we dreamed of returning to live there again, but that was not in our future.

Dan and I with two of his fraternity brothers on a night out in Chicago

Republican Convention
Chicago 1944

The GOP convention was held in Chicago in 1944 in the midst of WWII. Franklin D. Roosevelt was the two-term president of the Democratic party. He was running for an unprecedented third term and there was little doubt of the country changing their leader during the war. Thomas Dewey was the GOP nominee.

Dan was a Second Lieutenant in the Army Finance Corps in Chicago. A regular army colonel was in charge with four other officers under him, supervising five hundred civilian workers. Four floors of the First National Bank on LaSalle Street were taken over for offices.

The GOP Convention was the big event in the city that hot July. Only delegates could be accommodated in the huge auditorium. Tickets were free, but very limited to any outsiders. However, Dan was able to procure tickets for every day of the convention for us. The current governor of Pennsylvania, Edward Martin, was originally from Washington, Pa., and was a retired Army general and a close friend of his Aunt Bird. When Dan had lived with his aunt during his college years, he'd had frequent contact with the governor. In fact, as a general, he had provided one of Dan's recommendations for Officer Candidate School.

Dan collected these prized tickets at the hotel room of Gov. Martin. It was a brief, friendly meeting and he was introduced to Joseph Pew, a wealthy "man behind the scenes" Republican who was in the room at the time. Returning to the finance office, he became very popular when he shared tickets with his fellow officers. They were allowed to take a brief time off to attend.

We went twice to the convention and entertained the colonel and his wife. Col. Ayres was short, stout and balding and walked like a duck. I was in awe of the older couple and didn't know quite what to expect. The auditorium was steamy hot. This was before air conditioning. Dan and the colonel could not shed any part of their uniforms. The colonel's wife surprised me when she complained to me about her girdle. Such intimate comments were unexpected.

Down on the convention floor, the delegates were all suffering from the heat. There was a sea of damp shirts. From where we sat, we could see Gov. Martin in the front row. I was impressed with his dignity, as he never shed his coat or tie. Later, President Franklin D. Roosevelt made an electioneering appearance in Soldiers and Sailors Field, and though we can say that we saw him, the crowd was so great and we were so far away that it's hard to be certain who was in that limousine.

The GOP convention was a dull affair, actually, but it was just the thrill of being there. Never again would anyone want to repeat that steam bath.

A Portrait of June

June Hunker was tall and well-built, not thin, but not heavy. Framing her attractive face was thick, dark blonde hair that her hairdresser thinned regularly. June lived with her parents in a spacious brick house in Munhall. Her father was a senior executive at Gulf Oil's Pittsburgh headquarters. He was a self-made man, a generous provider and June was his pride and joy, perhaps more favored than her quieter older brother.

June had a Hammond organ at home and took lessons at the Pennsylvania College for Women from Earl Collins. I first met June in Music Department classes. She was a day student her first three years in college. Her parents were planning a month-long stay in Florida and so arrangements were made for her to move into a dormitory for her senior year.

My roommate, Jean, and I had roomed together for two years and in our senior year when the room drawing was held, by the luck of a draw, Jean and I had snagged the largest bedroom in Mellon Hall. There was ample room for a third bed and desk, so June joined us.

She proved to be a most compatible roommate and we soon became a trio. She was a science major and we learned to tolerate her experiments with fruit flies and another project that took over the bathtub temporarily. I knew her as a fellow organ student. In the spring, June had a student organ recital in the chapel with a goodly attendance of her family's friends. We wore formal gowns and I was her page turner. She also began to play the organ at a small Lutheran church in East

Liberty. She fit into our second-floor circle of friends seamlessly and we soon became the three musketeers.

June had a high school sweetheart named Cyrus "Cy" Poole. He was the son of a widowed mother and could not afford to go to college. He worked at a local gas station before he was drafted into the Army. Now it was graduation time and June's one request was permission to visit Cy. His mother had invited her to go along with her to visit his base in Ohio. Her parents and particularly her father had long opposed their romance. He had objected strongly from the start. She was denied permission to make this brief trip.

As a graduation gift, June was given an expensive white rawhide leather suitcase, which may have been a black-market purchase, as leather goods were severely rationed during the war. It seemed like a slap in the face. We sympathized with June.

The summer after graduation, June and I went by train to Johnstown to the first wedding in our college circle. She was at my engagement party at the College Club in the fall and the next May was a bridesmaid at my wedding together with Jean Archer and my kid sister, Ceil, as the maid of honor.

Our paths parted for a time as Jean was teaching in New Jersey and I was off with my soldier husband in Chicago for almost a year before he was sent overseas. During those months, somehow June was able to persuade her parents to agree to her marriage to Cy, who was stationed in Ohio. They were somewhat mollified by the fact that she would stay at home with them, rather than trying to follow his Army assignments. I got a job back in Pittsburgh in 1945 while Dan was overseas in the war and was eager to renew our friendship.

June was in Mercy Hospital for a surgery and I went to see her in recovery. Her mother was there and, after our visit, she went into the hall with me and said, "They just sewed June up; there was nothing they could do." That seemed incredible to me. I was too young and naïve and couldn't understand what she was saying. The dreaded word cancer was never spoken.

A month or more later, my mother came home from a large luncheon bridge party and told me that one of the women there had told a story about a young bride who was dying of pancreatic cancer, the worst kind. I knew a local Zelienople Lutheran minister, Philip Seiberling, was a friend of the Hunker family and had performed her wedding in Pittsburgh earlier that April. Suddenly, it all came together. I immediately went to the parsonage, interrupting his wife, who was in the middle of her ironing. Mrs. Seiberling admitted that it was my friend, June,

June Hunker's senior portrait

who had the cancer, and consoled me, but she was terribly upset because she felt that she had betrayed a confidence.

June's young husband, Cy, was able to get home on leave from time to time. When June first became ill, she thought that she was pregnant and was thrilled. These hopes were dashed time and time again. This went on as her health kept deteriorating. Her parents took good care of her until the end, but I doubt if they ever told June that she had terminal cancer. They cared for her lovingly as she rapidly went into decline, losing her sight and finally going into a coma before dying at home on Jan. 6, 1947 at the age of twenty-four.

Perhaps only her parents and doctors ever knew the truth. It wasn't until many years later I found out that her death certificate, now available online, showed she'd died of ovarian cancer. The failed surgery in 1945 was actually the second one she'd had, and it been the one that had shown the cancer had metastasized. Should they have told her? That is a question I will always wonder about.

June's funeral was at the fashionable Samson's funeral home in Oakland. At the viewing, June was attired in her wedding gown. It was sad to see the contrast of the white gown against her gray, disease-ravaged face.

Several years after June died, I was in downtown Pittsburgh and saw the back of a woman some distance away who was walking just like she used to. My first instinct was to catch up with her. Then I remembered. June was gone.

Past History

The location and lives of past boyfriends become unimportant years later. We catch bits of information from mutual acquaintances. Bob Younkin and Ed O'Donnell both left Washington & Jefferson College midway through because of WWII. When and where they finished their educations is unknown.

Our eldest son, Gordon, worked for W&J in its development office and made a trip to Texas to visit alumni. He met Bob Younkin, then a doctor and on his second marriage. It was difficult to imagine that he had completed medical school since his undergraduate study was a struggle. Perhaps his second marriage was not too happy for he confided in Gordon, "I should have married Jean Archer." He told him that he realized what a mistake he had made in breaking up with her all those years ago.

We heard that Ed O'Donnell was a schoolteacher in Minneapolis and knew that he attended a number of W&J reunions. When we were living in Minnesota, there was a phone call one day from "Pooch." Dan answered the phone in the kitchen. I was showing out a guest at the time. When I entered the kitchen, I heard the end of a conversation that meant nothing except that my husband's voice was not his usual jovial tone. His replies were cold and brief as though to an annoying solicitor. When he turned from the phone, he said "That was Ed O'Donnell." We don't know if he was calling from in town and planning a visit or calling from Minneapolis. The question that Ed asked was, 'What were we doing in Duluth?' Dan simply said that he was working there. Afterward, I teased him a bit for not being cordial to a fraternity brother. After all, if it had not been for Ed, we would never have met.

Both Bob and Ed retained a loyalty to Washington & Jefferson College. The way that I learned of their deaths some years ago was seeing their names under legacy gifts in the alumni publication.

Going Places

The main goal of childhood is to be grownup and independent, to leave home and see the world. When the train whistle echoed through the valley and passed this small town, it brought dreams of going places.

My mother did take my sister and me to Atlanta, Ga. and Alabama to visit my father's family there. Another summer, we went by train to Boston and visited Uncle Ed Winter's daughter, Jean French, on Cape Cod. There were several car trips to visit relatives in Missouri and Kansas. Mother's cousin, Jo, was with us to share the driving. We stayed in tourist homes along the way, where homeowners opened their homes to allow weary travelers like us to spend the night.

My first trip on my own was my junior year in high school, when I went by bus to visit and tour Hood College in Frederick, Md. A second cousin was a student there and it was a school that I was considering for college.

High school graduation was a landmark occasion. Leaving home for college, even though not far away, brought a degree of separation. Being away from parental restraint and living in a big city brought great freedom. However, there were college rules and curfews. I quickly learned that it was not considered safe to be out after dark alone or in certain parts of the city at any time.

During college days, there was a trip to the University of Vermont for a student conference, by train from Pittsburgh by way of New York. A weekend in Chicago by car and a week at Eagle Lake with Carnegie Tech, Pitt and PCW students. My final departure took place 1944, following marriage to Dan Core. We left by train to Indianapolis for a brief honeymoon and then a transfer to Chicago quickly followed.

A job in Pittsburgh at the Chatham Street YWCA and a furnished apartment with coworker Connie Scott filled the year of Dan's absence. Dan promised me that, if I married him, he'd show me the world. But joint dreams of far-flung travel were put on hold by years of law school, finding a job and raising a family.

Five
After the War

Fairmount and Friendship
1946 –1949

Every object in our first postwar apartment had a history. Everything had been begged, borrowed or bought at Goodwill.

World War II had ended at a certain hour of a particular day as far as hostilities were concerned, but wartime conditions dragged on for years afterwards. Some troops stayed in place and became armies of occupation. Men were released from their services by a point system that took into account months in service, combat duty and family responsibilities.

There was a severe housing shortage. No new houses had been built for years. Many families had doubled up during the war, with wives and children often going back to a family home for the duration. Now that the men were back, more homes were needed. The production of household goods such as washing machines, refrigerators, stoves, etc. had stopped for the production of war materials. The conversion to peacetime manufacturing took months and years. Fortunately, rent controls stayed in place during this difficult time.

I had been sharing a furnished third-floor apartment on Ellsworth Avenue with Connie Scott, a coworker at the YWCA, with the understanding that she would move out when Dan returned from Japan. The owners lived on the first floor of the large brick house on Ellsworth Avenue and the second floor was another apartment. Less than two months after Dan was home, the owners informed us that we would have to move, as the property was to be sold and razed for an apartment building. What a dilemma and where were we to find another place? Ironically, today the house is still standing and my suspicion is that they were looking for tenants who would offer them extra rent money under the table.

Dressed in my best three-piece going away suit, I answered an ad at a square yellow brick residence at the corner of Fairmount and Friendship in Pittsburgh's

East End, now known as the neighborhood of Friendship. It was an elegant private home with a third-floor apartment consisting of two rooms plus a kitchen and bath that had just been converted for rental. It had only a sink in the kitchen. Any tenant would have to provide the stove and refrigerator. We were in luck on that score, for Dad Core's rented house had just been sold and he had the precious appliances to give us, as well as a double bed. He gave us a choice of an antique sewing table, and we had that refinished in Zelienople, together with a balloon-back cherry rocker purchased at a yard auction. He sent the grand piano and some other furniture to Dan's sister Jane in New Mexico. Dad stored his books and several trunks in a storeroom several blocks away in Oakmont in the back of a pharmacy.

Dad took me to the attic to see if there were any picture frames that would be useful and it was there that I saw his grandfather Daniel Brodhead Heiner and grandmother Mary Graham Heiner in handsome wide gold frames. I asked if we could have those portraits. Dusting them carefully, washing them gently and repairing the canvas on the back, we took them to the apartment and hung them side by side over the large couch. The portraits were old and rather severe-looking, but they certainly added an air of distinction to our attic home, and every home where they have traveled with us since then, even to the Bahamas where they barely survived an attack of flying termites. Great-grandmother's inner frame was damaged and had to be replaced with another unmatched frame, but my sister, Ceil, saved the original outer frame by painting it a brighter gold and putting a mirror in it.

From my college days, I had a big wing chair and the material for a slipcover as well as a radio/record player. At a Laughlintown antique shop, I had purchased a walnut drop leaf table and an old oil lamp that had been converted for electricity. A side chair was a wedding gift from our bridesmaid Jean Archer and a bookcase was the gift of our best man Frank Crnic (said to have fallen off a truck!) We had a set of six hand-pegged ladder-back chairs with woven hickory bark seats and a small matching stool. Two were considered captain's chairs, as they had arms. We had ordered them from Adam Schantz of Harmony, while Dan was overseas. Adam, who was then in his seventies, was still making chairs in the same way his father and grandfather had trained him.

We inherited a large couch from Aunt Bird Core in a roundabout way. After she died, Dad Core had sent the couch from her apartment to Bud and Margaret. They really didn't want it as it was crowded into their small dining room. They were delighted to pass it on to us and we arranged to have it reupholstered, with the upholsterer picking it up in Dormont and delivering it to our apartment when the job was finished. A year or so later, an old friend of Aunt Bird's from Washington, Pa. happened to run into Dad and said, "Whatever happened to the couch that I loaned to Bird?" He was shocked, but when he explained that it has been passed on to his son and wife who had just had it reupholstered, he graciously said, "Well, never mind." The couch was long enough for a six-footer to sleep on and opened to make a double bed.

The kitchen at 301 South Fairmount Street was outfitted from Sears with a base cabinet and wall cupboard that we painted white and a plastic-topped wood table that was greatly reduced because of a scar on one corner. All the windows were short and high so white ruffled curtains from Woolworth's fit well.

My teenage dream was to have a skirted dressing table, which is ordinarily one of the most impractical pieces of furniture since there is only one small drawer behind the arms that open. We found a three-drawer nondescript dresser at Goodwill, fitted it with hinged arms and a mirrored top and I had a lovely dressing table that I skirted with floral chintz. Dan's sole wartime trophy was a square trunk that had been a Japanese aerial camera box. Castors added to the bottom and a slipcover of chintz made a matching seat. We found a handsome chest of drawers at Goodwill, our favorite place to shop.

Mother had given us the handsome walnut corner cupboard. I wonder if we could have gotten it up the stairs to the third floor. At any rate, we never tried for there was not a single corner that it would have fit in, since while the rooms were fairly spacious, the walls angled in below the ceiling. That cupboard stayed with Mother until another move.

The apartment had bare wooden floors that had just been finished around the edges. We made our biggest investment in a soft green rug for the bedroom and a gray rug for the living room and they were the ingredients that pulled everything together. They lasted for many years in subsequent moves.

Mrs. Emma White was our widowed landlady whose family home this had been for many years. Three unmarried daughters lived with her and were employed downtown. Her only son had a real estate office and handled the rental. A married daughter lived in Fox Chapel with her husband and two daughters and another married daughter lived nearby. We found out, to our mutual surprise, that this daughter, Katherine, was married to Dan Gibson, a first cousin of Dan's and the son of a federal court judge. He was known as a brilliant attorney and a dedicated drinker. Later in life, he went on an infamous bender and used his dentures as collateral once his cash had run out. The next day he realized he didn't know which bartender in Pittsburgh he had left his teeth with. So he took out an ad in the newspaper asking for the bar where he had pledged his teeth to call him so he could settle his bill. He received four separate replies!

We shared the front hall entrance and stairs with the White ladies and also had laundry privileges. The machinery there was so ancient that we didn't use it often. We lived there for three years and it was all very amicable.

Dan resumed classes at the University of Pittsburgh School of Law with the financial help of the GI bill. His only wardrobe was the indestructible Army clothing and some trousers we had dyed to cover the khaki color. He owned one white shirt given to him by Mrs. Dorsey. Mustering out pay provided funds to have two matching topcoats tailor made by Hemphills in Tarentum. They were covered with placket fronts and wore like iron. Everything was hard to buy then. I was working at the Chatham Street YWCA and often had evening hours. I was never bothered by coming home by streetcar through the Hill District late at night. Dan got a part-time job in the credit department at the East Liberty Sears store, which was evenings and Saturdays and Sundays. Sometimes it seemed as though we had more time together when we were dating then now that we were married and living together. Those weren't the easiest of times. The most painful were several enforced separations – once, when I had to spend two months on the job at Camp Carondowanna, which was three miles west of Zelienople, and the two months when Dan stayed in the YMCA in Philadelphia in order to attend the nearest bar exam cram course.

There was good streetcar transportation a short block away and then we sometimes borrowed Dad's gray Dodge coupe. On one warm day, I washed the car, but since it was parked on the busy street, I only did the curb side. That meant that Dan was forced to do the whole car again later.

We didn't have enough money to have a budget but, instead, kept a daily journal of every cent we spent, even including the odd nickel candy bar or daily newspaper. A pressure cooker was a good investment since it enabled me to cook cheap cuts of meat. We experimented with heart, kidney and tongue. The kidney was revolting because of its smell, but the tongue became a favorite. The heart never became tender.

During the fall hunting season, we appreciated the rabbits that Dad shot, since he presented them cleaned and ready to cook with bay leaf added.

My Cooking

On Saturdays during my childhood, Mother did the baking and cooking for Sunday dinner and for the coming week. Mrs. Brenisen came in from the country and made her weekly delivery of butter, eggs and a pint of cream. She had lengthy conversations with Mother at the back door. Mother was a good listener as Mrs. B. recounted her troubles with her husband and her oldest boy.

The first thing that Mother did was to put the cream in a saucepan over low heat to sterilize it and make it last longer. This was an early form of pasteurization. An abundance of whipped cream could be made from the weekly deliveries. Mother baked cake or cookies and made a molded salad and a dessert. Sometimes she asked me to scrape and grate the carrots for the "Golden Glow" gelatin salad. That involved putting together the heavy meat grinder which was fastened to the edge of the kitchen cabinet. Certain pans and bowls were always used for the familiar preparations.

Stuffed pork chops was my favorite dish and snow pudding, a gelatin-based dessert that used egg whites and sugar, was my favorite dessert. Mother decided that if I wanted to eat these dishes, I should learn how to make them. I started making just those two things and my cooking was limited to that for a long time.

Then in my junior year in high school, Mother slipped on the ice and broke her right wrist. Reluctantly, I learned to do all of the cooking for our family under her guidance. Instead of only the two favorite dishes of the past, I was taught to prepare a complete meal so that everything was ready for the table at the same time. I didn't fall in love with cooking or develop great skill, but this experience was valuable in the days before frozen dinners, prepared mixes and the microwave.

During my teen years, I also helped Mother with her entertaining. This I enjoyed much more. She was happy to have me entertain my friends at a luncheon or dessert party.

My cooking skills were never mentioned during the romantic days of courtship. When Dan and I were first married, he was stationed at the University of Illinois in Champaign-Urbana. The day before our wedding, Dan's orders had come through for a transfer to Chicago in two weeks. We knew that our time at the university would be brief. We usually had cereal for breakfast and ate most of our meals at the university cafeteria It was not worth it to buy the basic kitchen supplies needed to make meals during such a short stay.

So, the first dinner of our married life was in Chicago. I bought Chef Boyardee spaghetti, since all the ingredients were contained in one box. Salad was a head of iceberg lettuce with a simple dressing of lemon juice, salt and pepper. It was as though I had produced a miracle! Dan was surprised, pleased and impressed to find that he had a bride who could cook. He had never inquired about something so basic before.

Dan considered himself well-fed from that point on. Cooking was my department. In later years, he did learn how to fry an egg and a hamburger, but he never took up the popular activity of outside grilling or barbecuing. He declared that cooking should be confined to the kitchen. His conviction was reinforced by a number of disastrous outdoor dinner parties we attended, where the guests had to fill up on potato chips and drinks while waiting for the meat to be done. Once, the host could not get the charcoal to light for a very long time. At another party, the smoke from the grill blew the wrong way and in moving the grill, it tipped over and spilled all the charcoal. What a disaster!

Miss Sarah Katherine Core
1884 – 1948

Any word picture of Sarah K. Core has to be a combination of fact and fiction, for there is no one left to attest to either. This is a quilt of recollections of others' stories of her. She was probably the most exotic member of the Core family; a large woman with a resounding voice, an ample bosom and big ego. She had sandy, dark blonde hair that was aided by the drugstore later in life. She had a fine voice and studied and sang abroad in operas before settling in New York City.

We first met at a family dinner party at the small Dormont home of her nephew, Jesse "Bud" Core, and his wife, Margaret, during the Christmas holidays. She had come down from Manhattan like a homing pigeon to the family home in Washington, Pa. Her spinster sister, Bird, was living on the second floor and renting out the first floor of old Victorian family home. This was in contrast to Sarah's grand Upper West Side third-floor, eight-room apartment in an elegant building that had both a doorman and elevator operator. There were fireplaces in many of the rooms and marble and gold gildings from its heyday of the 1920s.

Sarah had an impressive singing career as a young woman, graduating from Wilson College in 1908, performing at suffragette events all over the Pittsburgh area, and going on an operatic concert tour through Europe. She was one of the last Americans to get away from France at the start of World War I. Her niece Jane Core Milling later had her lengthy passport framed. Jane was also given a silver ring with a blue stone inset that she said had been an engagement ring of Sarah's from a French sweetheart.

Aunt Sarah in her college days at Wilson

Sarah settled in New York City during WWI and volunteered for the war effort as an entertainer with the YMCA. She built her career in Manhattan, singing in concerts, performing on the radio and producing her own work for the stage. She was a charter member of the Schola Cantorum of New York, an acclaimed ensemble. While Sarah was never a star at the Metropolitan Opera, she was in the chorus for three years, and Dan liked to say, "Aunt Sarah carried a spear at the Met."

Of the numerous nieces and nephews, the Gibsons and the Cores, her favorites seemed to be my husband Dan, Jr., his sister, Jane, who had similar musical and artistic abilities, and most of all, Ruth, the eldest Gibson niece. Ruth was a very successful secretary and lived with her father, Judge Robert Murray Gibson, in Pittsburgh's East End. When Ruth was married later in life to widower Lou Hamilton, they converted the third floor into their own apartment, so she really never left home. She was the family member that Sarah called upon when she needed help.

As Sarah grew older, she became more bohemian and eccentric. The Great Depression had made employment difficult for artists, and the effects of years of penny-pinching were apparent. She was to give a concert in Pittsburgh's Schenley Hotel and Ruth, aware of her aunt's precarious finances, gave her money to buy a special ready-made dress for the appearance. Much to her dismay, Sarah ignored her advice and bought material instead. She sewed what she probably thought was a great dress for the occasion, but what was really a frumpy outfit.

As well as occasional vocal roles, Sarah gave voice lessons in her apartment. She had the experience from her days teaching music at Shorter University in Georgia and the Ethel Walker Preparatory School in Connecticut. She also became the landlady for her eight-room apartment on the coveted Upper West Side. Since the start of the Great Depression, she had sublet rooms in the apartment to various artist types that she knew to make ends meet, and complained about her holiday expenses, when all the building people expected generous Christmas tips. She lived in the spacious living room with a marble fireplace and large windows to a balcony. This was her studio, her living room, dining room and bedroom, with a daybed behind a corner screen. The other rooms were rented out to individuals who shared the two-and-a-half baths and the kitchen. Her tenants were typically other musicians, writers and painters.

The maid's room and half-bath were off of the kitchen. The apartment was furnished with antiques, a big comfy sofa and some handsome oil paintings. Most of the large paintings were of Mediterranean courtyards or other foreign settings. The American painter, John Barber, lived in the apartment for some years before his marriage, and perhaps some of these works were painted by him or other artists who lived there in lieu of rent. We know he painted at least one portrait, for it was at Sarah's request. It was a small, unsigned oil portrait of her mother, Sarah Katherine Heiner Core, as a young woman. It was appropriately set in a deep antique frame.

There are many amusing stories about Aunt Sarah. Jane once visited her in New York where Sarah was attempting to grow some tomato plants on her balcony. She kept complaining that the plants showed no signs of growing tomatoes. All she saw blooming were blossoms, which she explained that she had to keep pruning after they wilted. Jane had to carefully explain to her aunt that the blossoms were what the tomatoes grew from, and she shouldn't remove them no matter what!

Aunt Sarah had excellent taste but a beer budget, and so much of her shopping was done at flea markets and street sales on the sidewalks of New York. As a wedding gift, Dan and I received a beautiful 16-inch-tall clear crystal vase with both etched and incised decorations. It had a small chip on the base, so it was probably a bargain. In some sixty years, there have not been many occasions to use it since it needs tall arrangements, such as irises. She also gave us a silver-plated Tiffany card tray which never was used for its intended purpose. One Christmas, we received a small curved-top Victorian frame with crazed glass, which I gilded and had fitted with a mirror and have appreciated ever since. A secondhand store in New Castle had a matching version of the frame in a larger size, so it was added to our collection. Then my own late grandmother's larger frame in the same pattern was acquired to hang above a bedroom dresser. Fortunately, we were antique lovers, but other members of the family sniffed at "second-hand."

We visited Aunt Sarah briefly one weekend when Dan was taking the bar exam cram course in Philadelphia. It may have been then that she promised us three antique Victorian side chairs with curved harp-shaped backs and carved fruit with rich embroidered seats. Later we drove to New York and took Aunt Sarah with us to the wedding of Converse Murdoch and his bride, Petra. The Murdoch family were all old friends from Dan's Washington, Pa. days. Dan and Connie were close friends from his visits there.

Sarah was a strong personality and, as a result, went her own way and didn't always get along with her siblings. Distance makes the heart grow fonder, it is said, and so Sarah would come by train to visit at Christmas bearing gifts and ready to set all of her relatives on what she perceived to be "the right path" all in two weeks' time. At the home of Jesse and Margaret Core, newly married with a toddler daughter, she declared firmly that the first thing they should do was to buy a piano and begin lessons for the child. They had neither the money or the space for a piano and they were some years off before music lessons would be appropriate. She often returned from this mission rather disappointed since no one jumped at her command. She also returned with items from the dwindling family home that she quietly appropriated as part of her heritage.

Dan Sr., Bird and Sarah, the remaining of the six Core siblings, tried to support each other later in life. When Bird was diagnosed with cancer, Sarah took her to New York to stay with her for a brief time. It was a kind gesture and, in the end, Bird died there with her sister by her side.

A few years later, Sarah herself became ill with cancer. At that time, there were few treatments available, but this Methodist minister's daughter became a Christian Scientist. The readers and visitors provided support and comfort in her last years.

When Sarah had to be hospitalized in her final months, she called her niece, Ruth, to come help. Ruth arrived post-haste from Pittsburgh to get Sarah to the hospital as quickly as possible. Sarah refused to budge until she had dictated her will to Ruth, having her type it out and getting some neighbors to witness it. There was little in financial assets, but she wanted to distribute all of her belongings in detail, down to "the cut-glass celery dish." We were given the promised chairs and our choice of the paintings in the apartment.

Some months later, Ruth had the sad task of clearing out the apartment and distributing the bequests. As for the will itself, the state of New York declared that it was invalid and any assets should be subject to state law. So, we drove to New York for the chairs and chose the small Barber painting of Dan's grandmother, Sarah Katherine Heiner Core. It has traveled widely with us since.

Chatham Village
1949 – 1951

Our planned family was postponed for four years by World War II, then law school, and finally job searches. So, after Dan graduated from law school, the Philadelphia cram course, the bar exams and had his first job, it was time to think about starting our family. Much to our dismay, that didn't happen right away as we had expected. However, once underway it was an easy pregnancy without the usual morning sickness. The only nausea was when I over-indulged in something extra sweet or when I ate the prescribed liver, which neither I nor the unborn one liked.

With the advice of college friends, a prominent Pittsburgh obstetrician, Dr. Joseph Eisaman, was chosen. He was strict about diet and did not believe in "eating for two." As a result, I gained only fifteen pounds, all concentrated in the active bowling ball in front. This was supported by a cumbersome corset of lacing and straps to take strain off the back.

During that time, although we were in the city, there was a lot of walking since we shared a car with Dan's father. We had the car during the last month so it would be available to get to the hospital and we did a lot of riding the last few weeks, seeking out the bumpiest roads we could find in the hopes it would induce labor. I remember listening to endless baseball games on the radio. Boring!

Natural childbirth courses were just becoming popular. We read the books, but didn't have time to take any course. Talking to my friends, who by this time had one or two children of their own, the main problem in childbirth seemed to be how to recognize labor signals so that you didn't rush to the hospital early and then had to be sent home, or the alternative case, where you had to get to the hospital with all possible speed.

The pressing problem during this time was the question of where we would live after we became a family of three. Our third-floor apartment was in a private home and would be difficult for both us as well as the family living downstairs. At the same time, Dan's father was asked to give up the rooms he was renting in a private home that was being sold, so we were searching for a place that could accommodate him as well. The wartime housing shortage was still severe and this was a discouraging hunt.

Chatham Village on Mt. Washington was an innovative housing concept when it was planned and built by the Buhl Foundation in 1932, being one of the first planned communities in the United States. By the time it was being built in the early 1930s it was one of the few big city construction projects going on during the Depression. The Bigham estate on Pittsburgh's Mt. Washington had a large parcel of undeveloped land and an old brick mansion which backed onto a wooded hillside with many tall old trees. The brick townhouses were built in groups of two, four and six units with variations in rooflines depending on the terrain. These pristine rentals were maintained inside and out by management. This attracted young professionals, who lived there many years and only moved away when their families outgrew the houses or their children were finished at the Whittier Elementary School.

It was modeled on town houses and developments in Europe. It had been created both as an investment and as a social experiment. It was well-planned, with units ranging from efficiency townhouses to large three bedrooms. The landscaping was outstanding, with large trees that had been preserved and the contours of the natural landscape maintained. Front doors faced courtyards with central grassy shaded courts that had front yards enclosed with low hedges. Integral garages were at the back of the buildings under a tiny balcony and rear basement doors were on the street. There were sandboxes in each courtyard for children and a playground and tennis courts at one end. Community activities took place in the double parlors of the original Bigham Mansion, which served as a clubhouse. There were woods behind and below, making it an intimate, warm community seldom found in city living.

We had put our name on the rental list at Chatham Village three years before, after visiting our friends Ed and Jane Young there. Looking for other accommodations and finding nothing, we were becoming increasingly worried. I would call the Chatham Village office monthly, only to get the same negative response.

I was seven months pregnant and getting nowhere with my calls to Miss Lutz, the manager of Chatham Village. It was time make the connection to my late Uncle Henry Buhl, Jr. I made an appointment to see the president of the Buhl Foundation, Dr. Charles Lewis, whose office was in a downtown bank.

My condition was obvious. I made a personal appeal to Dr. Lewis. I told him that we had been on the waiting list for three years and would soon need housing for ourselves, the coming baby and my father-in-law. Explaining our need and the long wait, I pointed out that Great-Uncle Henry would not want me to live this way. He was sympathetic, but promised nothing. He said that Miss Lutz handled all Village management, including rentals. That was in March.

Two weeks later in April, we had a call from Miss Lutz, who said that she had a three-bedroom townhouse for us to view that would be available July 1, if we would care to come to inspect it on the Saturday that the present tenants had agreed to. It was a rainy day and we had to hold back the shrubbery as we climbed the steps into the courtyard, but it was the happiest rainy day of my life. I thought that I had gone to heaven!

The people in the house had been there for nearly twenty years and were only leaving due to an out-of-state transfer. They asked where we lived in the Village, and were surprised to learn that we were coming from "the outside." Apparently, the usual waiting-list system was for a resident to be moved from smaller to larger quarters. That's when I knew that Uncle Henry had really helped us from beyond the grave.

Dan and I left for Magee Hospital at 10 p.m. on June 1 with my labor pains. After I was "prepped" for delivery, Dan spent the night in the hospital room in a reclining chair timing contractions and sleeping fitfully. By the morning, I was moved to one of the numerous delivery rooms right beside the delivery table. Sounds from other tile-walled rooms told me that I wasn't feeling that badly in comparison to some of the other pregnant women in labor.

My contractions had slowed and so I was moved to an adjacent labor room. Soon that room was needed and I was demoted to the hallway. It was uncomfortable, confusing and discouraging after everything had gone so well up to this point. There was a wheelchair trip to X-ray and a climb onto a cold hard table and then I was returned to the delivery room where amniotic fluid was drained. I was given morphine during the wait for an operating room. It had been fourteen hours of intermittent labor.

Dr. Eisaman had to perform an emergency caesarian because the baby was in the birth canal in a dangerous "face presentation" position, trying to enter the world "chin up." The top of the head is smaller than the full face. Dan had been sent out for a late breakfast and came back to find that he was being paged so that he could sign a legal document authorizing surgery. After months of reassuring him that childbirth was normal, suddenly this was happening. He was panicked.

The doctor was noted for his unique technique of this special surgery so there was an audience of students and interns on hand. I was given a spinal anesthetic and with the end of pain, the effect of the morphine, the oxygen being administered and the knowledge that something was happening, at last I was euphoric. I was flying!

I couldn't see, but I could hear what the doctor was explaining and could carry on a lively conversation with the nurse at my head. She told me when the baby, all of 8 lbs. 12 oz., appeared. It seemed a long time later that the doctor finally spoke to me saying, "It's a fine baby boy." I was able to reply, "I know. His name is Gordon."

Firsts and Lasts

I left the East End apartment one spring night for Magee Hospital and never returned. Before leaving, I had done some of the packing for our moving. Gordon was born on June 2 via caesarian birth and after a two-week hospital stay to recover from the surgery, I went to my mother's home in Zelienople. There I could recuperate further with fewer stairs. That left Dan with the moving, which he managed himself with the help of a friend. This was his first and last Adventure in Moving!

Dan had a wonderful ability to make and keep friends. He formed strong ties with former teachers. One was Ted Rupert, who had been his Ford City high school math teacher. After the war, when Dan was finishing law school, Ted decided to become a dentist. He had a seven-year-old daughter at the time, but with the help of his working wife and his savings, he made it. We were

Gordon and I at Chatham Village in 1949

living in that third-floor apartment in East Liberty and Ted was often there. When time came to leave that apartment, he helped Dan with our move to Chatham Village. After Ted set up practice in Ford City, we went there for all our dental work and could have a visit as well.

We moved into 438 Bigham Street in Chatham Village on July 1, 1949 when Gordon was just one month old. The front door opened into a living room with a fireplace on the left wall. Triple windows looked onto the green court. A stairway went up on the right and a doorway to the kitchen straight ahead had been replaced by a built-in bookcase. A wide doorway led to the dining room where the corner cupboard found its home at last. French doors opened to a small wrought iron balcony where newly purchased heart-shaped metal ice cream chairs were placed. There was just room for lunch for two. Upstairs were three bedrooms, one of which was very small, but ideal for a nursery. Gordon was bedded in the antique crib that my sister and I had both started life in. Several months later, this needed to be replaced by a regular size crib. Betty Doty, my friend from the YWCA, gave us a child's wardrobe and we bought a bassinette changing stand. Our bedroom furniture from the apartment fitted nicely in the front bedroom. The larger back bedroom was reserved for Dad Core, who moved in several months later with his bed, bookcase desk and favorite rocker.

The Village had a drugstore, small grocery and gift shop at the entrance. In good weather a fruit and vegetable truck stopped almost at the back door and parked for several hours. An apartment addition to the Village was across the street from the entrance. This is where buses to downtown stopped. The Village office was back of the shops. Dan would often walk to the incline on Grandview Avenue and then walk across the Smithfield Street Bridge to his downtown office, the U.S. Steel and Mellon Bank building on Fifth Avenue. It was a fun experience to go into the city that way. Dad Core was still working as a clerk of the Federal Court on Grant Street. He took a later bus and had a late breakfast. These were normally bacon and eggs and burnt toast. Our vintage toaster, which was all that could be bought at the time, had to be carefully watched and then flipped to the other side. Dad would forget, but then cheerfully scrape the burnt toast and insist that charcoal was good for people. Dad had his shirts laundered and his noon "meat and potatoes" meal downtown.

Those weren't the easiest days. Dan was working as an attorney with Pittsburgh Limestone Company, a subsidiary of U.S. Steel. Dan had a demanding boss and perhaps that was the reason he developed an ulcer. The doctor put him on a bland, meatless soft diet. Dad, meanwhile was a meat and potato eater, but with false teeth could only eat the most tender meats. I preferred salads and needed to eat often to breastfeed the baby. Meals were difficult to plan.

After the months of pregnancy, I was looking forward to normal activity again. Recovery from the caesarian surgery slowed this down. Then there were the months of sleepless nights with a new baby. The benefits of breast feeding were stressed but it was difficult to know how much milk the baby was getting. It was necessary to stick to a bovine routine of constantly grazing, for if I became tired, the food supply dwindled and feedings became more often and disruptive.

It was a vicious circle in those early days and difficult to know when one could even leave the house. All went well after the first six months.

On Saturday nights, Dad Core would often take me out for dinner at Innocenti's, a little Italian grocery store just up Bigham Street with a restaurant in back. This was a treat. It was nice to have Dad Core with us. He shared in expenses and was great as an occasional babysitter when we went out briefly. As Gordon grew older and was more active, we hired babysitters, as much for Dad as for Gordon. Dad was a heavy smoker and he tended to fall asleep in a chair. We were concerned about a possible fire. Dad was slowing down in his movements. He stayed up late at night reading and had a difficult time getting up and underway in the mornings.

Dad was under the care of his doctor in Oakmont and made no comments about his health other than complaints about the ill fit of his false teeth. His teeth were the greatest entertainment for Gordon. Dad would play a peek-a-boo game with him, popping his teeth in and out of his mouth as the baby laughed.

Dad spent Thanksgiving and Christmas holidays with Dan's brother, Bud, and his family. He continued his fishing vacations at Georgian Bay in Canada. Bud took him on his last fishing trip, and even when he had to be helped in and out of the boat, he was still determined to "get his catch."

Dad Core at his bank teller window

Several weeks after Dad's vacation. he seemed to be very slow in dressing one morning. When I went upstairs to check, I was just in time to catch him, nearly dressed and slumping behind his bedroom door with slurred speech. He'd had a stroke and was taken to Wilkinsburg Hospital, where his Oakmont doctor practiced. Our doctor and neighbor Bob Laughlin had made an immediate house call and counseled us on future possibilities.

Several days later, there were further strokes and Dad went into a coma. Dan's sister, Jane, came from Texas and Bud was on hand for the hospital vigil long enough to realize that death was a merciful solution. Only after his death did we learn that Dad had cancer of the prostate. The doctor never told us and we wonder if the doctor even told him. He was seventy-one. There was a Pittsburgh service at Samson's in Oakland and then a second American Legion service in Ford City. He was buried in Manor Church Cemetery beside his beloved wife, Amarilla. It was so moving when the legion members saluted their captain as they passed by his casket.

Jane stayed on for a week after the funeral and helped sort things out. There wasn't time though to empty the storeroom in Oakmont. That took several months for there were over 2,000 books stored there. We collected boxes and drove to Oakmont on weekends where we packed as many boxes as the Dodge coupe trunk would hold, then unpacked and arranged them in the basement. We filled the basement twice. Each time we had dealers come to make selections and then Lutheran Services would collect the rest. It was intriguing to find a lot of duplicates and particularly, two identical sets of the Encyclopedia of Music – no music, just ten volumes about music. We made a vow then and there to use the library more often, and only buy books that we had first read and felt were worth keeping. After the funeral and Jane's departure back to the Southwest, we had a belated vacation. Mother took care of Gordon and we took the train to Toronto for part of a week.

Life in the Village brought new friends and neighbors: the Balfours, the Livingstons, the Ghents next door and Newstetters, who had a baby girl Gordon's age. Cousin Carrie Gelbach and her daughter Ruth lived nearby and we became reacquainted, since Ruth and I were no longer in rival high schools. Ed and Jane Young, who had first introduced us to the ambiance of the Village, were there, though due to his work schedule as the KDKA program director, they weren't often at Village affairs. Several radio personalities lived in the Village. Christmas brought many small parties and, at New Year's, there was a dance in the double parlors of the clubhouse. This was followed by the January wedding of my sister, Ceil, to her beau, Layton Geddis, in Zelienople.

Spring was beautiful with many flowering trees and the brilliant blooms of rhododendron and azaleas. It also brought word of an impending transfer to New Castle, Pa. We had lived in Chatham Village for just two years, less time than we had been on the waiting list. We left with regret and the hope of returning someday.

Aunt Bessie Geddis
1885 – 1958

We met Bessie Bourne Geddis at a wedding. It was the marriage of her nephew Layton Geddis to my sister, Ceil, on January 13, 1950. Aunt Bessie immediately included us in her family circle from that day on and sent us greeting cards for every occasion. To emphasize her goodwill and the sincerity of the printed greeting, the cards were always sent airmail special delivery, even when we lived in different sections of the same city. As a spinster, she had a high regard for motherhood, and so my mother and I would receive special Mother's Day cards with a pretty handkerchief and a dainty embroidered sachet enclosed.

The wedding was a happy event on a dark winter day. There was only a short time for festivities as Layton had just started a new job and could not ask for time off. The rehearsal was Saturday morning followed by brunch at the Kaufman House. The candlelight ceremony was at the Presbyterian Church with a family dinner reception at the Maples, a mansion turned tea room at the edge of town.

It was lovely and simple. Ceil knew how to plan a wedding as she had been a consultant at the Bridal Shop at Kaufmann's, Pittsburgh's leading department store. She knew that you could order a bridesmaid's gown in white that was less elaborate, less expensive and a dress that could be worn again. Years later, the gown was worn by two of her daughters, Chris and Gail, for their weddings. Then the matron of honor's gown was the same design in dull apricot satin. Extra material was ordered to make stylish helmet caps to which the brides veil was attached. The bride's gown had just the suggestion of a train. The heavy satin had a jacket with three-quarter length sleeves

Ceil's 1950 wedding portrait

and a double folded face-framing neckline going down to the small buttons at the waistline. Underneath was a simple formal gown.

Layton had his brother-in-law, Donald Wright, as best man and two other friends as ushers. I was Ceil's only attendant as matron of honor. My husband, Dan, walked her down the aisle of the church in our father's absence and our mother "gave the bride away" from her seat in the front pew. The dinner reception was confined to out-of-town guests which were mostly the groom's family from Erie. They would be going there to live in their new apartment the next day. Aunt Bessie, however, lived in Pittsburgh's East End and it was our responsibility to drive her home, since we were living in Pittsburgh's Chatham Village at that time.

Layton and Ceil had a one-night honeymoon at Webster Hall Hotel – one double at $8.50 – then went to Zelienople to pick up wedding gifts and drive them to their Erie apartment by Sunday evening so Layton could go to work on Monday morning. There were many Geddis in-laws for Ceil to get to know in those early Erie years.

Aunt Bessie was the only relative on the paternal side of the Layton's side of the family. She had two brothers. Robert, Layton's father, who had died, as well as her other brother, Craig and his wife. They had a son, also named Craig, who was "away at school."

During the one-and-a-half-hour trip, we got to know many things about Aunt Bessie: that she lived alone, the house was too big, she knew she should move, she was thinking about moving, where would she go and how could she manage it? We learned that she was a charter member of College Club in Oakland where she attended the weekly Friday luncheons and lectures; that she wanted to stay near the Third Presbyterian Church on Fifth Avenue where the family had always belonged and attended regularly. She had a full schedule because on Wednesdays she went to the Women's Missionary meetings at the First Presbyterian Church in downtown Pittsburgh. These activities served to keep her too busy to address the matter of moving. She was an active recluse.

She did have help at the house, Miles and Marjorie Manning, a black couple who came in daily. Miles had chauffeured her to the wedding, but she didn't want him to have to wait until the reception was over to take her home in her aging Packard. Miles took care of the car and the yard and Marjorie did the housework. Aunt Bessie didn't mind staying alone at night. She was comfortable in the fine area where she had lived so many years. "It's a lovely neighborhood," she said.

We delivered Aunt Bessie to a substantial brick house at 5870 Aylesboro Avenue just half a block away from Shady Avenue. It was indeed in an upper income neighborhood of similar large four-square brick houses. That was the last time that we saw Aunt Bessie in person, but she continued to keep in touch with us and over the years we learned a great deal more about her.

Her adored father, Robert Hamilton Geddis, came to America from Ireland in 1873 as a teenager in revolt against a widowed father who he felt had remarried hastily and unwisely. To emphasize his break with his family when he emigrated, he changed the spelling of his name from the Scottish Geddes to Geddis. In 1896, he began his employment with Jones and Laughlin Steel Company and was director and full sales manager of the firm at the time of his retirement in 1925. He married Sarah Jane Patterson in 1883. He belonged to all the finest Pittsburgh clubs and the contents of their dining room china closets showed that they must have entertained elegantly at one time

Bessie Geddis was born in 1885 and remained rooted in the turn of the century. Pictures show that she was an attractive young woman. She was bright as well. She attended Vassar College where she was graduated summa cum laude. Her life was privileged and protected. When she took the train to and from college, her mother accompanied her as a chaperone on the trip. She had a strong loyalty to the past. She "kept house" for her father after her mother died in 1935.

When her father died in 1944, she didn't dispose of his clothing or personal effects. Like Queen Victoria, who had her servants care for Prince Albert's room and wardrobe after his death, Bessie simply closed the door. Since her father had a great regard for the Wall Street Journal, she continued to respect his judgment and renewed the subscription, which arrived daily, year after year, and was seldom, if ever, removed from its mailing wrapper. She was also loyal to the ice man who kept her icebox supplied, so that when the icebox rusted out, she sought out and found another icebox so that the nice ice man would keep coming. She had the same loyalty to their Packard car and never considered replacing it. Miles dusted and polished it, since he had little else to do, long after it could be trusted to get around the city safely.

Bessie enjoyed shopping, not for herself, but for gifts to her nieces' and nephews' children. Mansmann's was a small, high quality department store in East Liberty which was convenient to her and her favorite place to shop. She often couldn't decide which color to buy and so would sometimes purchase a child's sweater in three different colors. Since a little one would quickly outgrow a garment, these extra gifts were quietly exchanged for other things. Sometimes Bessie bought things as gifts and never got around to sending them. She spent little on her own clothing, although she did own five fur coats, some of which may have been her mother's and which were kept in storage for years and became terribly out of date. Mansmann's had a dry goods department and there Bessie often found lovely fabrics. Some green satin and red velvet must have caught her eye near the Christmas holidays. She purchased dress lengths of each for garments which existed only in her mind. She put the box away in the attic with the sales slip and tissue wrappings where they stayed undisturbed for years.

In an attempt to control her generosity, Mr. Charles Dodson, the bank officer who managed her trust funds, tried to set up some limits by way of a "spendthrift trust," which she found a great nuisance.

Miles drove Miss Bessie on her rounds in the once-imposing Packard. Eventually, it seemed as though the polish that Miles applied so faithfully was all that kept the vehicle together. When her car could no longer be depended on to make the trip from the city to Pleasant Hills for a holiday meal, Layton would arrange to pick her up. She was always ready and waiting at her front door and he was never invited into the house. The last time he had been inside was during his college days, when necessity forced him to ask to use the bathroom. There was a powder room off the big front hall and he noticed there that every ledge and surface was filled with the small glass insulin vials emptied by his diabetic aunt.

Bessie also managed to keep her bank manager outside the house. Although they were responsible for her well-being and would have made funds available for house repairs, she never reported any leaks in the roof nor would she let the trust people inspect the house. Aunt Bessie was a recluse in the sense that she kept her home off-limits to all except her help. She spent little on her own clothing and appeared regularly at her three weekly outings in old-fashioned attire and a shabby fur coat. Some of her friends, who saw her only at the missionary society, felt sorry for her and would bring her little gifts of homemade jelly or baked goods.

The big house didn't seem lonely to her and it was far from empty. With unopened Wall Street Journals arriving each mail day and being set aside, the boxes from shopping trips, insulin vials and all those cans in the coal cellar, the house was filling up. The attic was filled first and then gradually the bedrooms were filled and those doors were closed just as her father's room had been.

Eventually, there were pathways through the downstairs rooms and of course those cans in the basement. Marjorie came in daily, but it was doubtful what she could do in the way of cleaning under the circumstances. She was growing older, too.

Was it her thrifty ancestry or just eccentricity that kept her from throwing anything away? During World War II everyone was asked to save tin cans for the war effort. Saving was what Bessie did best and she set aside an empty coal cellar for saving cans. She collected cans for years, but never got around to turning in any of her collection. Long after the war was over the pile of cans continued to grow higher and higher in the old coal cellar. It was the can collection that was finally her undoing.

Aunt Bessie had no fear of living alone in the big house at night. She felt safe in such a good section of town, until one fateful night when she was awakened by a tremendous noise coming from the basement. She was badly frightened for the first time, so much so that she called the police, who responded promptly. Burglary was not unknown in this neighborhood by now. At last she was opening the front door and the house for inspection. The officer who appeared politely concealed his amazement at what he was seeing and carefully checked the house from top to bottom. The culprit was found in the coal cellar. Something had caused the small mountain of cans to shift. It was no intruder, but thought to be vibrations from a streetcar, which then ran on Shady Avenue just a half block away. Once started, the pile of cans continued to move and clatter. After the policeman left, he did his duty further by reporting what he had seen to the nearby fire station marshal.

Thus, things began to change. The fire marshal paid a call upon Miss Bessie Geddis and gently but firmly pointed out that her home was a fire hazard and that she must clear things out. She was a good citizen and embarked on this eagerly. She told her relatives that she was very busy cleaning house. Shanahan, the leading local moving and storage company, was ordered to deliver packing boxes. She went to work with great goodwill filling boxes with whatever came to hand, including the unopened Wall Street Journals which her father had valued so highly. Eight large boxes of a great mixture of things were then picked up and put in storage at Shanahan. There were more empty boxes delivered to the house.

It was some months after this that Aunt Bessie had a diabetes attack that put her in the hospital for the last time. She told her visitors that she hoped to get well soon as she had so much to do at home. On October 1, 1958 she died of complications due to a blood clot.

Bessie Geddis' funeral was handled by Samson's, old established undertakers of Pittsburgh. It was said that if you were buried from Samson's you had "arrived – perhaps too late." The service was held at the Third Presbyterian Church on Fifth Avenue, not in the small chapel, but in the great echoing space of the large sanctuary. Her father had been the church treasurer for thirty-five years.

We were at Bessie's funeral out of respect to her and sympathy for my brother-in-law, Layton. There were relatives there that we hadn't seen since their wedding eight years earlier. We were able to add our bit to the sparse attendance.

Ladies from the First Presbyterian Church missionary group were amazed to find that their shabbily dressed friend was from a fine old Pittsburgh family and somewhat of an heiress.

Then there was the big old house on Aylesboro Avenue to be emptied at last. Layton's mother and sister Ruth came from Erie and stayed in a nearby motel to work on the clearing out. Nephew Bob and his wife were at a distant Army post and he got leave to come and help out. Nephew Craig was still "away at school." This turned out to actually be the state mental hospital at Polk. Layton spent weekends and as much time off as he could manage to work with his mother and sister on Bessie's house.

They started in the large, high ceiling attic and soon found that junk and treasures were jumbled together. It was impossible to make so many trips down the stairs and so they began to throw the trash out of the third-floor window into the side yard, where the pile quickly mounted. Brand new things, still with their sales slips, were in boxes among the papers, so everything had to be examined carefully. Then they worked their way through the second-floor bedrooms. There was no dumpster and the trash pile reached to the second floor. A truck made several trips to haul trash. The next-door neighbor looked with alarm at all of this and complained about the fire hazard, not realizing what he had been living beside for many years. The packed boxes were brought back from Shanahan and sorted through and the fur coats were recovered from their years in cold storage. They had not improved with the passage of time.

Finally, the first floor was cleared of its passageways and tables could be set up so that the bank representatives could come in to appraise china, crystal, silver and the valuables that had been uncovered. The family was then allowed to purchase items from the estate at the appraised prices. Layton and Ceil bought the Steinway upright grand piano with a wonderful crisp, clear tone. The bank then took care of the final disposal. Aunt Bessie's story remains within the family as a reminder not to save string and Wall Street Journals and whatever you do, keep cleaning the house!

Risk

Risk is always with us. Life is continually changing and risk comes with every change. Risk may be as minor as trying a new recipe when trying to impress guests. My husband often worried about that when I would tell him what I was planning. Those recipes usually turned out fine as I was careful about following directions. At least there were no complaints.

Risk is involved in travel in these troubled times. There are many protective measures at airports. So many places in the world are no longer deemed safe places to visit. Those risks seem minor when compared with the experiences of our ancestors who came to a new country. Before them came the explorers and soldiers who risked death. Driving a car is a risk that we take for granted except on days when weather makes road conditions hazardous. Even crossing the street can be a risk.

Dan's dream when he started law school was to work in private practice at the county seat in Washington, Pa. He was able to enter law school at the University of Pittsburgh thanks to a modest bequest from the estate of his step-grandmother, Clara Getze. After his four-plus years during WWII, when he returned to Pitt, there was the GI bill plus a part-time job at Sears Roebuck that enabled him to finish school.

The war had made many changes to Dan's prospects for private practice. The fraternity brother who had promised to take him into his practice had been drafted himself and was starting all over. Aunt Bird's attorney friend was winding down his practice and did not have enough business to take on a young lawyer. Dan had no resources to start on his own.

So Dan got a job as a corporate attorney for Pittsburgh Limestone Company, a U.S. Steel subsidiary. It became a permanent one, lasting thirty-four years, spanning two countries and involving nine required moves to different locations. Dan's employment with U.S. Steel Corporation began in July 1948 and ended with mandatory retirement at age sixty-five in 1982. There were transfers to different subsidiaries and time back in Pittsburgh at the main law department.

Being transferred to a new community, buying another home there and moving is one of the more traumatic events of life. When touring a house for the first time and, perhaps the only time, there are so many things to see and questions to ask. More time is usually spent deciding on a major appliance than in buying a new home with a bevy of potential mechanical problems. Time for making this important decision is limited. Attention is focused on the dwelling. Questions about the neighborhood or neighbors are not included.

The greatest risk of all is when you decide to marry and make a lifetime commitment to another person "for richer or poorer, in sickness and health..." No wonder that young people get cold feet and have wedding day jitters. They know little about the whole package they are taking on or what may lie ahead. That is why it is called "taking the plunge." Many more risks are involved in this new relationship. Those fortunate ones find that the future risks are best conquered together.

The First Transfer to New Castle
1951 –1953

The first corporate transfer of the Cores was from the lovely townhouse in Chatham Village on Pittsburgh's Mt. Washington to the first home we owned in New Castle, Pa. U.S. Steel paid for our moving expenses. It was there that our second son, Philip, was born.

The beginning of 1951 found us living at 1107 Delaware Avenue in New Castle. Dan was still with the Pittsburgh Limestone Company, a subsidiary of U.S. Steel and had been transferred to the downtown New Castle office. Hillsville was the limestone plant outside the town. We bought our first house, a square frame home with a porch across the front, three bedrooms, one bath and unfinished attic and basement. Son Gordon was two years old and shortly joined by Philip.

Older employees were welcoming and helpful to us as newcomers. Through one employee who lived nearby, we found a wonderful babysitter in his childless sister-in-law and her husband, Mr. and Mrs. Waite. A retired company man lived around the corner and his driveway and garden bordered our backyard. At his suggestion, he helped Dan to build a fence for the safety of the children and the safety of his garden as well. Dan was a reluctant handyman. Other newcomers to the office had been moved there from Rogers City, Mich., a limestone port on the shore of Lake Michigan.

Dan's job was to obtain leases in Butler and Lawrence and Beaver Counties for limestone exploration and mining. The lease involved holding payments which increased when limestone mining took place. There was some negotiation involved and it was impossible to seal the deal on the spot with a company check, so, he would make out a personal check instead and then get reimbursed when he returned to the office. We had a very modest checking account but it was like a swinging door when those checks went out and the covering checks came in.

There were several underground mines in Butler County that had been mined out. One of them later became a mushroom farm and another was set up to be used as storage for U.S. Steel paper files of all kinds. That was the mine at Boyers, which has a completely different ownership and use now.

One Sunday afternoon, we took a drive to that mine and drove into it – a huge space with many pillar supports left in place. Dan stopped the car and turned off the headlights. It was the first time I had ever been in such complete darkness and it was a suffocating experience. It is difficult to understand how miners can cope with this at times. Gordon and Philip would have been with us, but were too young to remember the experience.

Dan made occasional trips to Boyers and we knew the men in charge there. He and fellow employee, Elder Wallace, also traveled to West Virginia and Maryland to visit the limestone sites there.

The Day Philip was Born

Dan and I were firm believers in family planning, so it was five years before we had a family. There was World War II and then Dan needed to finish at Pitt Law School and find a job to support a family.

We were planning to have a family of three. I had seen my good friend, Sis White, in action with her four young children. She was efficient and energetic and I realized that I probably couldn't cope with four children. When it was time for our second child, we were living in New Castle and Dr. Eisaman had referred us to Dr. Wallace, an obstetrician friend and colleague. Dr. Wallace had his office in a big, older house on the hill in New Castle. He made it clear from the start that he felt that more than two caesarian deliveries were dangerous and he would tie the tubes of any patient after a second delivery – no quarter given or questions asked about religious affiliation. The die was cast.

We were fortunate to have a wonderful babysitter in New Castle (or perhaps babysitters) in Mr. and Mrs. Waite. They fit into a grandparent role and sometimes took Gordon to their home, where he had undivided loving attention. If waiting for a first child was difficult, it was much more so when one had to be prepared and up-to-date on all household chores for a second maternity hospitalization.

Dan and I were awakened at about four o'clock in the morning by the start of my labor pains. The Waites were the first to be alerted. We bundled up a sleeping Gordon and took him to their house where they tucked him into bed between them. It was a short drive to Jameson Hospital. There I was quickly stripped of all clothing and personal possessions, including my wedding rings. These were put into a brown paper bag and handed to Dan. It made me feel like a corpse somehow.

Reading the medical records, the nurses seemed to take a particular interest in the progress of this labor. At 7 a.m. I recall being told that things were proceeding nicely and I was hoping that this would soon be over. Although surgical gauze and sterile gloves were used for each examination, it became painfully irritating to be checked as the time dragged on and on. It was nearly two o'clock in the afternoon and I was left alone in a delivery room in great discomfort. There was an intravenous pole beside the hard table and when that was removed from the room, I felt I was really being deprived.

Finally, it came to push and shove time and I recall being painfully pushed on the abdomen and told to bear down. When I said I was trying, I was told to just be quiet and push. Philip was born at 2:10 p.m. on November 5, 1951. I don't remember any more since I must have been put under anesthesia for vaginal stitches. When I woke up, I was in a bed in the maternity ward and Dan was there with the gift of an antique ring. Although he put it on my hand, I couldn't really focus enough to see the ring for several hours more.

At that time, the usual hospital stay was one week. Many women came from the nearby Amish community near New Wilmington and these mothers just stayed one night and then took their babies home dressed in the handmade, dark-colored clothing of their denomination.

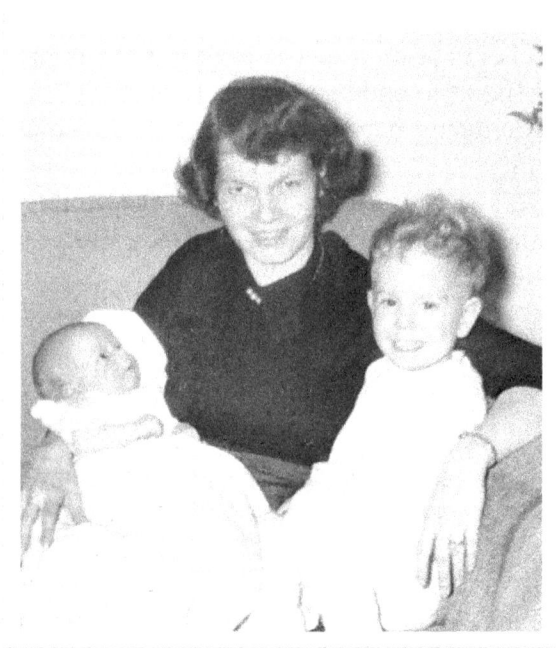

A newborn Philip and a tow-headed Gordon sitting in their sleep-deprived mother's lap

Meanwhile, back at our home, Mrs. Sam Johnson was the maternity housekeeper in charge. She was a large elderly widow who specialized in this kind of home care. By then my mother had suffered a heart attack and could not be on hand to help, so she offered to pay for maternity care. Mrs. Johnson looked after Gordon and did the cooking and housework and, when Philip and I were home from the hospital, I took complete care of him. We had an antique crib at the foot of our bed and nights were not restful as I was up to nurse and change the baby often. If after those ministrations, Philip was still crying and restless, Dan would pat his bottom and count the pats as he tried to get him back to sleep.

Mrs. Johnson was with us for two weeks after I came back from the hospital and she slept in our guest room. She said she could not claim to be a good cook, but I thought that everything she made was wonderful. It was such a treat to have our meals prepared for us.

Great Expectations was a movie showing at the time and we decided that we liked the name Philip since it was not too unusual, nor too common and we thought that Pip might be a nice nickname (of course he never was a Pip). For the second name we chose Kennedy, an old Scots-Irish surname from Dan's maternal family.

We got the impression from the hospital nurses that Philip's delivery was something extra special and of course for us, it was!

The Goldfish Saga

Distant corporate decisions were made to merge Pittsburgh Limestone and Michigan Limestone companies, closing offices in Western Pennsylvania and moving the headquarters to Detroit, Michigan. Hugh Lewis, head of the office and his wife, Gertrude, had been especially kind to us when we first moved in. They had us to their home for bridge and Gertrude took me to an antique auction. With the merger, though, the Lewis' would soon be moving to Detroit.

Hugh and Gertrude had a small pond in their backyard for a pair of goldfish. In the winter, they kept the fish in a large galvanized washtub in their basement. They decided to make a gift of the goldfish to the children.

Quite unprepared for this largesse, we had only a small fish tank for the fairly large fish. It sat on the desk on the living room. Until we could get something larger, the water had to be changed daily. This meant taking the tank to the kitchen sink, filling a white enamel dish pan with fresh water and transferring the fish there until the tank was emptied, scrubbed out and refilled with clean water before replacing the fish.

Days could be hectic with two little children. About two weeks into the custody of the goldfish, I was standing wearily by the steps and getting ready to go up to bed when I looked at the cloudy fish tank and asked Dan to take care of the goldfish. And he did.

He had also had a tiring day and when he came into the bedroom he said, "I cooked the goldfish!" He had absentmindedly filled the dishpan with hot water, put the goldfish in it, emptied the tank, scrubbed it and when he looked around to replace the fish, he found them lifeless in the hot water. How were we going to tell the Lewis', who had not yet moved? They were coming to our house to play bridge the next week and would certainly ask about their goldfish.

Murphy's Five and Ten Cent store carried goldfish, so I hurried there to get replacements as one fish looks much like another. Unfortunately, the store only had small goldfish and the Lewis goldfish were large. Large goldfish could be specially ordered but they could not be available until the next fish delivery – the day after the Lewis were to come to our house. What a predicament!

Then came a phone call from Gertrude Lewis suggesting that we come for a spaghetti dinner and bridge at their home. She had a cleaning lady that day who made a wonderful spaghetti. I breathed a sigh of relief and it looked as if we were saved.

We had a lovely supper and were at the bridge table when Hugh Lewis asked how the goldfish were doing. Dan was unable to prevaricate and so the sad story of the demise came out. It was a relief to make a clean breast with his confession.

Several more weeks went by before Hugh Lewis left the New Castle office. When Dan would go into his office, Hugh would greet him in a low, grave voice saying, "You killed my goldfish!"

Welsh Hymn Festival
Gymanfa Ganu

The Welsh are noted for their love of song. The most exciting singing event ever attended was our first afternoon at a church in New Castle. Our neighbors, the Williams, invited us to accompany them. The church was packed. There was a large choir and everyone was furnished with paperback books of the hymns written in both Welsh and English. The talented director led not only the choir but also the audience in song. The result made the spine tingle. There was such an outpouring of voices raised in song and it filled the sanctuary with a glorious sound.

There was an intermission for a simple 'tea' of bread-and-butter sandwiches and a robust tea. Something learned at the 'tea' was the secret of thin-sliced buttered bread. The end of the unsliced loaf was cut off, then the next slice and then before cutting another slice the bread was buttered while still attached to the loaf. I learned that this was how thin bread buttered sandwiches were made, and I remembered it for future tea parties. The audience returned to their seats refreshed and ready for more song. It was a thrilling afternoon.

Many years later when we were living in Mt. Lebanon, there was an announcement of a Welsh Hymn Festival being held in a small church in Oakland. Remembering that wonderful afternoon in New Castle, we decided to go. We were there early and there was not as large a crowd as before. Some gentlemen were seeking people to be in the choir. One man came down the aisle, looking directly at my husband. Dan doesn't like to refuse anyone, but he definitely was not choir material. To his great relief, the gentleman asked him if he would help take up the collection. He recognized an honest face!

We were on a canal boat trip in Wales in the 1970s and hoped to visit some small-town choir practices along our way to Llangollen. We were assured of a warm welcome. Unfortunately, the national Esttifodd singing contest had just taken place and choirs were taking the month of August off. I have a copy of a paperback Welsh songbook I picked up on that trip that I sometimes play on the organ to remember that day in New Castle.

Country Life in Allison Park
1953 – 1954

Two years after moving to New Castle, the U.S. Steel subsidiary Pittsburgh Limestone was merged with Michigan Limestone and the New Castle office was closed. Some employees relocated to Detroit. Dan Core returned to the law department of the downtown Pittsburgh office of U.S. Steel.

Transfers are immediate. Moving a house and family are not. Dan commuted to Pittsburgh by train from New Castle. That meant bundling up toddler Gordon and baby Philip to drive Dan to the train station in the early morning hours and picking him up in the evening.

Housing was still in short supply at the time of the Korean War. We were directed to a house in Allison Park by older friends from the Fourth Presbyterian Church. After house hunting for several weekends, that house, in what was then a rather rural area, was the most appealing one we had seen.

The little white Cape Cod house with ancient oak trees around it seemed ideal. It was on Cherry Street, a cindered country lane, and had an acre and a quarter of land in which two little boys could safely play. Today the street is more built up and the house number has changed to 4868 Cherry Street. We had confined our house hunting to the Northern suburbs of Pittsburgh to be closer to their grandmother

Dan and I in our Allison Park living room

McKay. Dan's office was in downtown Pittsburgh some fourteen miles away and he commuted by the bus service on nearby Route 8.

Dan always felt homeless and anxious until a new home had been found. He told the owners that he would write up a purchase agreement and bring it to them the following weekend. Then, happy with the decision, he left town for a business trip.

While he was gone, I began to have some doubts about the rural location. He was disappointed when he returned to find that I was not completely pleased. To calm my fears, he called a U.S. Steel employee who lived in this area. This man assured him that the location was fine, even though it meant a hike from Cherry Street to Route 8 to catch the bus to downtown Pittsburgh. So I agreed.

The house had a circular drive at the side for entrance to the basement garage. On the first floor was a living room that was entered from the front door. It had a wood burning fireplace at one end and beside that a French door to the side porch. On the left of the front door an archway opened into the dining room. There was a full bath on the first floor and beside it what was probably intended as a bedroom. We decided to convert that to a family playroom instead.

The second floor had three bedrooms and an unfinished powder room. One of the first things home improvements we had done was to complete that and divide the attic space off the master bedroom into a finished closet and door into storage space. The house had to be painted and, when spring came, we selected a warm barn red with white trim for the exterior. It all looked cozy and comfortable.

But soon flaws developed in this paradise. We moved into the country house in Allison Park shortly before the Christmas season and were nicely settled in by the next summer. There was no city water, which meant our dependence on both a well and cistern system. That is when we discovered that the well had a limited supply of water and one could only guess how much might be in the cistern unless there had been a lot of rain. The well didn't dry up completely, but we had just enough water to drink and enough for one toilet flush per day for most of the summer. We could scarcely invite guests to share our sylvan lifestyle. Fortunately, the upstairs powder room had been connected to the cistern, so we prayed for rain on all counts. Any chance of drilling the well deeper and getting a greater supply was negated when we inquired and found that the house was near if not over the Wildwood Coal mine. There was a chance of piercing an abandoned mine tunnel and losing the meager water we had.

The problems only seemed to increase come winter. There was an electrical pump needed for the well and cistern and it was housed in a little pump house addition that was entered by a low opening from the basement garage. In cold weather, this pump had to be kept from freezing by means of a kerosene burner, a delicate operation to refill and regulate and remember to light. If this wasn't done properly, there were several times when black greasy soot filled the house.

The house was heated by an oil furnace. Our previous home had never had any furnace problems and it came as a shock to find that the beast in the basement was extremely temperamental. The furnace man came often to make repairs, which were more expensive since it involved a trip to the country. That was true of all the services that were needed. When we were without heat, even if just for a day, I sometimes took the boys with me and we visited friends in Chatham Village across the city. For overnight stays, we fled the cold by visiting Grandmother McKay in Zelienople. Everything in the country turned out to be expensive. All phone calls to Pittsburgh were toll calls so I couldn't indulge in long chats with old friends.

With summer came the challenge of planting some groundcover on the acre of arid ground beside the house. The previous owner had managed to level the property by taking the fill from the nearby Pennsylvania Turnpike which consisted of rock and clay. Dan took soil samples to send off to Penn State for testing. It is doubtful if they had many samples of such unpromising soil. Their recommendation included lime and fertilizer and sowing Bird's Foot Trefoil. He acquired a portable spreader and worked on the acreage. He suffered from hay fever in those days and shouldn't have been

Gordon, Dick and Dan Rothermel, and Philip playing in the Allison Park neighborhood

spending so much time outside. He was a willing, but not a happy farmer. By our last summer there, the trefoil was growing so well that Mr. Ahrendt, a would-be farmer who lived nearby, asked if he could pasture his cow there. He brought her daily and staked her each time in a different part of the field. That solved mowing problems and added to the much-needed fertilizing. The cow was a great attraction on the day that she produced not one, but two calves right in the field mid-afternoon.

Allison Park was not a close-knit neighborhood back then. The people all around had large lots and lived in the country because they wanted to do their own thing and keep at a distance from neighborhood relationships. It wasn't easy to get acquainted and, while the boys had plenty of safe room for play, there were no nearby playmates. Playmates for the boys came in the form of visits from my college roommate, Jean Archer Rothermel, and her two boys, Dan and Dick.

To the right of our house and closer than necessary was an almost identical house. The two houses had been built by brothers from a Sears home kit. A couple with a teenage daughter and twelve-year-old son lived there. Her widowed father, not yet retired, also lived with them. We probably would not have found much in common anyways, but she'd had a stroke and her speech was halting. She would visit on our side porch and conversation was tiresome and painful since she seemed in a semi-vegetative state. What little conversation her father offered was in the form of dirty stories.

Beyond our field was a two-acre plot with a driveway leading to simply a rooftop with a chimney. The Duggans, who owned this peculiar-looking building, had taken advantage of the free fill from the turnpike and had their acreage filled in to completely surround the one-story house in which they lived. Their announced intention was to use that house and add another floor above ground. The boys were fascinated by the low-pitched roof and found it a great place to climb on. We never saw Mrs. Duggan, but her husband would rush furiously out of the house and chase the children away. In the three years that we lived there, no progress was made on the building. When we checked out our former house years later, the situation remained the same.

Mrs. Kovachik, the cleaning woman, lived with her miner husband and two schoolboy sons at the dead end of our road. Her husband, Paul, had always worked in the nearby mines and, when they were shut down temporarily, he worked on a highway crew. He liked the mines much better than working outside in all weathers. We bought eggs from them and they were responsible for finding us our first dog, a golden cocker spaniel we called Taffy.

Ladies' Day Out

After one year of country life, we would have looked for another house except that Dan was told that his transfer to a new job out of Pittsburgh was imminent. But the location of the subsidiary's new office had not yet been decided. There was nothing we could afford to do but soldier on where we were. Dan was travelling often and I joined the Richland Civic Club for some community activity. A requirement was so many hours working at their shop and taking part in the annual chicken barbeque, or Country Sociable, where I ended up in charge of a huge amount of melted butter meant for the grilling.

Promoting the Richland Civic Club in faux poke bonnets

My salvation was the Ladies Day Out program of the downtown YWCA. It provided a day-long program of classes, lecture and a delicious ladies' lunch for me with congenial women. This was combined with daycare for the boys which gave them playmates, lunch and naps in a children's program. Gordon was old enough to join me in the swimming pool for a mother and child water babies' class. Noontime programs were stimulating and it was at the YWCA that I heard my first talk about herbs. A tiny garden of herbs was an outlet that developed from that experience.

Mary Shaw Mahronic was the delightful talented art teacher at the Y. On the way to her class, she would often pick up bread and fruit or vegetables as materials with which to set up a still life for the students to paint. We were told to handle this with care as it represented her supper as well. She interlaced the art instruction with her comments on her life and travels as an artist, which were amusing and a far cry from the activities of suburban housewives. I had little success with the still life painting. Instead, I often painted the rooflines of the neighborhood and the background of skyscrapers which were visible from the windows of the YWCA on Chatham Street on the edge of the Pittsburgh's Hill District. I still enjoy painting cityscapes to this day.

Tonsils and Surgeries

Country life and all that fresh air were not as healthy as one might suppose. The boys had a series of colds, sore throats and fevers that they passed back and forth. It was like a seesaw; one boy would be sick and recover and then it was the turn of the other one to repeat the process. An especially low point was the Christmas Day when the two children were both down with fevers at the same time.

Medical thinking had changed by this time from almost automatic tonsillectomies to avoiding surgery, if possible, since children often outgrew early infections. Reluctantly, Dr. Bardonner decided that tonsil removal for Gordon, at the age of five, was the only solution. He scheduled a date for surgery and it was necessary to keep him healthy in preparation.

The other deadline was the impending birth of our third child. We just managed that. Philip went off to stay with his grandmother and Gordon and I went to Children's Hospital where we spent two nights. I was due to go to Magee Women's Hospital the next week for a Caesarian section and asked Gordon's nurse what would happen if I started labor at Children's Hospital. She said, "We'd ship you off to Magee right away!" After the tonsils came out and Gordon was home, it was a wonderfully restful week. Philip was still visiting his grandmother in Zelienople and Gordon was recovering and content to play quietly alone.

Since I was back in Pittsburgh with Dr. Eisaman again, I told him that I would prefer a normal delivery as it has been successful before. I thought he was in agreement until the day of the February checkup, when he informed me he would be away for a week, but had scheduled me for a C-section the Monday of his return. He said that this was a large baby and there were dire consequences if the scar tissue should give way. It would mean the possible loss of the child and the destruction of the uterus and any chance for another child. So it was decreed!

Planned C-sections are half-hour operations compared to the emergency two-hour surgery I had when Gordon was born in 1949. The obstetrician's instructions were to check into Magee Women's Hospital in Pittsburgh the afternoon before the scheduled caesarian section, which was early on Monday morning. On a Sunday, the admitting desk wasn't fully staffed and so we were shuttled to a small sitting room where we sat and sat and sat. Finally, someone came by, and assuming that I was in labor, she took the vital statistics with many apologies and great haste and hurried us to a room. There was nothing to be eaten before surgery. Then the hospital routine began. There was what is delicately called "prepping" which involves shaving the pubic area for labor even though surgery was planned above that area. I objected because that is so prickly when the hair is growing back.

Dan was with me until bedtime and, kissing me goodnight, said he'd return early the next morning to the waiting room near the operating room. The head nurse made an appearance during her royal evening procession and asked if I'd had a boy or girl. Couldn't she see by my shape that there was no baby yet?

I was wheeled to the operating room at 8 a.m. and the surgery was finished by 8:30 a.m. A spinal anesthetic is delightful compared to labor pains and the baby girl arrived so easily, perfect in every way but for a small birth scar on top of her head. She was a mostly bald baby for the first year. There was an hour spent in the recovery room and then I was back in a room and the baby were in the nursery. A woman volunteer wheeled my gurney. Dan presented me with an antique ring for the occasion.

Dan managing two wriggly little boys

Dan had seen the baby and we were ready with a name, so I said he might as well go back to the office. It was a mistake to send him away so blithely, for I realized that I'd had nothing to eat for hours. With the spinal block I could not raise my head for another twenty-four hours or the result would be very severe headache. I was starving and there was no way that I could feed myself the bullion and tea that was allowed. The same volunteer came back and fed me and her kindness has never been forgotten. She said it was her fifty-fifth birthday. Her husband was an executive at Kaufmanns. She was on the board of Montefiore Hospital, but was a hands-on volunteer at Magee. I sent her birthday greetings for several years. I can no longer remember her name, but I've never forgotten that meal.

Doctors don't spend much time on their hospital rounds but residents are much more available and interested in a patient's history. Apparently, I was unusual in having had a face presentation caesarian surgery, then a normal vaginal delivery. The resident had assisted at the surgery and said that this baby had also been in a face position.

Whether she would have changed position before normal labor or, whether Dr. Eisaman's dire predictions might have been correct or not, is difficult to know. Since face presentations occur once in 5,000 births, according to the resident, it would have been against the odds for one person to have two such situations.

Amy Jane was born February 22, 1954 and weighed 8 lbs., 6 oz. Her footprint was stamped on our birth announcement. Our family was complete.

My Fairy Godmother

Sidney Duerr was in her sixties when we first met in the herb garden of her country home. A small woman, simply dressed, with her gray hair worn in a bun, she might have been thought of as plain except for the sparkle in her eye and her bright smile.

Some years before we had a family, I had heard a fascinating talk on herbs and had taken notes for some future time when we might have a house and garden. After her inspiring presentation, I asked the speaker where herbs could be found and she gave me Sidney's name and address. It was some five years later before I could think about a garden and luckily still had my notes and her address. By then we were living on a barren lot in Allison Park, one acre of which was a level field of highway fill, devoid of topsoil. In one corner was the house, surrounded by old oak trees. With three young children under the age of six, I was desperately looking for something to do. I could only manage a very small garden and for that felt that herbs would be ideal, with the most variety in a minimum space. My garden ended up actually being about the size of a dining room table.

Doing some further reading about herbs, I prepared a list of ten plants that would give me a good start and then called and made an appointment with Sidney, who lived in Valencia, about ten miles away.

Sidney lived in a brick ranch house screened from the former highway with tall trees and a woodland. Her more formal front door was seldom used. A brick walkway went up from the side driveway to a covered side porch decorated with a well-worn wooden garden bench, antique tools and gay geraniums in old crocks. Everyone went in by the kitchen door. To the left was an old-fashioned sink. There was tiny sprigged wallpaper, and paneling concealed the modern stove and refrigerator. In the far corner of the spacious room by the front window was a round table under a cranberry glass shaded antique light. There was a comfortable wooden rocker nearby.

She greeted me with warmth on that first visit and we found the plants that were on my list that she dug from her large garden. Along the way, she kept spying other plants and asking if I knew about them. "Do you know lemon balm?" "Do you know sweet woodruff?" She would cite their virtues and urge me to try this or that while adding them to my basket. At the end of my visit, I was loaded down with twenty different plants but, when I went to pay, she would take only money for the plants that had been on the original list. She insisted that the others were gifts that she just wanted me to try out.

It was easy to see that she was not in the herb business to make money, but to share her knowledge and love of the plants. She had been a school teacher and must have been an excellent one, for she continued to teach so many people in so many ways. When Sidney learned of my gardening ignorance, she invited me to join the Piccadilly Garden Club, which was a local group that specialized in herbs, to a certain extent, as well as educational and competitive gardening events. She did not drive so I would pick her up for meetings, and although she considered it a favor, to me it was a great privilege to be able to spend so much time with her. The conversations were true educational sessions and I learned a great deal from the group activities.

Herb gardening was an interest that began when I was a homemaker with three small children and needed an outlet beyond the routine of toilet training and diapering. It was something I could enjoy in our isolated setting. One day two little boys were found in the tiny garden munching on chives and mint, so herbs made the difference in our lives.

Sidney was a guiding light and started what became a lifelong fascination with herb gardening that led to me becoming the President of the National Herb Society of America. In 2005, I was honored to receive the Society's Helen de Conway Little Medal of Honor, a lifetime achievement award my mentor Sidney had received more than thirty years earlier.

The Christmas Tree Party

The Christmas custom of going to the woods and finding and cutting your own tree seemed most appealing. A small advertisement in the newspaper alerted us to a farm in the area where trees could be selected and cut. We put a long sled in the back of the station wagon along with the well-wrapped children. The December temperature was fairly mild and there was just enough snow on the ground to allow the sled to slide easily and carry the children. This small adventure was repeated for two years.

It was in the swimming pool at the Chatham Street YWCA that I made the acquaintance of a friendly older woman. When she found out that I lived in Allison Park, not far from her home, she invited my husband and me to their annual Christmas tree party.

Marion and her husband, a Pittsburgh attorney, had bought a tree farm in the country. They were not interested in the labor of planting, pruning and selling trees, so they hosted a party on a December Sunday afternoon for their friends to come and harvest some of their pine trees.

Dan and I arranged for a babysitter for our young children, dressed in our outdoor clothes and arrived promptly at the farmhouse. It was a cold, gray afternoon. The roads were clear but the snow earlier in the week was still covering the fields. We were only the second couple to arrive. After introductions were made, we set out to find our tree. The only instruction given was to try to thin out where the trees were growing too close together.

It was a slipping, sliding trek over the hilly terrain and it was not easy to find an ideal tree, since the trees had not been groomed for several years. We could hear the other couple some distance away. They were disagreeing loudly over the merits of each tree that the other one selected. Finally, we heard the man say, "Why do we have to come to this party every year and tramp around in the snow and cold? Why can't we just go to a Christmas tree lot in town and buy a tree? We didn't hear her answer, but we knew very well that they had been the first guests on the scene!

Cutting down the tree of our choice, we pulled it back to the car and loaded it into the station wagon. By the time we got back to the house with our Christmas tree, there were more cars in the driveway. Guests in ski attire were having refreshments before they started out. Many had brought food and the women had bags with dress clothes. We found that the tree cutting was just the start of a long party and that women later changed into long skirts for the evening.

Our babysitter would be expecting us back before dinner time, so we had a bit of refreshment and made our apologies for the early departure from what was our most unusual Christmas party.

Finally, the long-anticipated transfer to the new office came. We left country living with great relief. How we managed to sell that house ourselves I can't recall. We didn't lose money, nor did we make a profit on the sale. Our only profit was in what we learned about ourselves and about the perils of country life.

Six
Life in Suburbia

Home in New Albany
1954 – 1958

New Albany, Ind. was a venerable old river town on the northern bank of the Ohio River directly opposite Louisville, Ky. It bordered on the South and mint julep country. Located at the Falls of the Ohio, it was where goods had to be trans-shipped before the river was dammed and the locks were built that would allow for continuous boat passage on the river.

At one time, the majestic stern wheeler paddle boats were built in the town. Large mansions on Main Street, which ran parallel to the river, mirrored those glory days of prosperity. No view of the river remained because of the massive flood wall built by the federal government after years of river damage. Only the sound of the boats remained, but you could go to see the river at the locks.

This was the seat of Floyd County, a mostly agricultural area. Part of the city included Silver Hills which was actually a high river bluff reached by a winding wooded road. We could hear the river boats signaling at night and, when we went to do important shopping, we went "over the river."

We moved to New Albany on December 4, 1954, a day of record cold weather. Reacting from the isolation of country life in Allison Park, we could now be much more social. We joined the Hutchinson Memorial Presbyterian Church and the Silver Street PTA. There was an active Newcomer's Club which met in the high-ceiling parlor of a former mansion now owned by the American Legion. We could accept invitations and one of the earliest was to an open house by our real estate agent.

When we were invited to a country club dance, one of my first questions was "what is it in aid of?" In Pittsburgh, where almost every event was a benefit for one charity or another, it was surprising to learn that things were more relaxed here and this was purely a social event. My first big luncheon invitation was to

153

the country club for lunch and then to the home of the hostess for an afternoon of bridge. I was looking forward to getting acquainted over a light, conversational game. My three other table companions were old friends and avid bridge players. I was terrified to find myself in this silent, intense company and knew I was out of my depth.

Though the shipbuilding industry had long since left the town, lumber was still an important industry in New Albany when we lived there. It had one of the first prefabricated housing plants in the country, Gunnison Home Company. Dan was now an attorney for U.S. Steel Homes Credit Corporation, a different subsidiary of the U.S. Steel Corporation. He worked with the sales team and also was the assistant secretary for the company.

The company had acquired the Gunnison Homes Company, which had thrived under the pent-up demand for housing following WWII. Under the auspice of U.S. Steel, Gunnison began to experiment with housing that would use the maximum amount of steel products possible in housing construction instead of wood. The credit corporation arranged financing for developers who were building large groups of these houses. We soon became acquainted with officials in both companies.

Gordon resumed first grade at Silver Street School, a fairly short walk from home. Philip was enrolled in a private nursery kindergarten school that met in the Episcopal Church Parish House, a Main Street mansion. He went there reluctantly and, after several tearful mornings, finally agreed to sit on a chair outside the open door of the class, answering questions that the teacher asked him from the doorway. It was two or three weeks before he finally moved inside with the others.

On one Thanksgiving holiday, we drove to Indianapolis to see the city and the Christmas decorations. I made a train trip to Indianapolis later with another woman. We were delegates to a statewide PTA convention. It was difficult to know what to report back since it was deadly dull, full of parliamentary rigmarole. Badges had to be worn for admission to the hall. It was hard to imagine that any unauthorized person would want to crash such stuffy deliberations.

In past Christmases, we had made special outings to select and cut our own trees at a tree farm. In Southern Indiana, again we went to the country and bought one of the plentiful evergreen trees we saw growing wild in many fields at a very reasonable price. It was cut for us, so it wasn't until we got home to set up the tree and decorate it that we discovered that this species of juniper was discouragingly sharp and prickly. It almost seemed to reach out and attack us! We never bought a native juniper tree for Christmas again.

It was fun to explore a new part of the country. People from Floyd County came into New Albany to shop and do business and the downtown area served shoppers who came to the great old Victorian courthouse. More shopping was available over the river in Kentucky and New Albany residents usually went to Louisville for shopping, dining out and entertainment, as that was where the best department stores, hotels and restaurants were located. The local expression was "going over the river." There were interesting restaurants, though, with the children, the big cafeteria there was the best choice. We had some friends in

Louisville where we were invited to dinner. There was a fine symphony and outdoor summer theatre and we made good use of the excellent Carnegie Library downtown. One of the attractions along the riverfront was the impressive paddle wheel steamboat that would often dock there.

The Floyd County Historical Society held open meetings in the public library. This was an excellent way to learn about the past of the area. The members of the historical society were most welcoming. They were older and some were descendants of the first families. They were pleased when I, as a newcomer, shared their interests.

Nearby was the quaint small town of Corydon, the original state capital. Jeffersonville, Ind. was an adjoining town and one day we explored under the bridge and found a rock pile of fossilized bones from animals that had watered there centuries before by the river's rapids, the falls of the Ohio River. The river was out of sight but at night we could hear the boat whistles signaling at the lock. We sometimes went to see the riverboats go through the locks and we visited the boats when they were docked in Louisville.

Dr. Baker

Dr. George Baker was an old-fashioned family doctor who worked completely on his own. He had no nurse or receptionist. He had no appointments and dispensed his own pills and medications. His patients' medical records were in his head. There were only rare cases that required prescriptions. He made house calls before and after his afternoon office hours. Dr. Baker's office was on the ground floor of a brick residence downtown. His home was on Glenwood Court, just down the street from where we lived.

The day we moved to New Albany, I caught a cold that turned into a sinus infection. The December day that the moving truck unloaded our things was unusually cold at six degrees above zero. Gordon was just recovering from chicken pox and had passed on mild cases to Philip and Amy Jane. The three children were in Dan's care that day at the Seelbach Hotel in Louisville. For the first time in my life, I understood what a "killing headache" was and so I went to the doctor's.

There was no way to make an appointment with Dr. Baker, who had been recommended. I went to his office before two o'clock and found the waiting room filled with a throng of waiting patients. I despaired of being at the end of such a long line. When white-haired Dr. Baker slid back the-old fashioned pocket doors and made his first appearance, more than half of the patients in the waiting room stood up and moved inside the office. This was surprising. I learned later that these were all regulars needing refills of medication. They soon came back out clutching their refills of pills and tonics. That meant that the line was greatly shortened.

When I got to see the doctor, he was able to treat the sinus infection and brought me instant relief. Treatment involved lying on a gurney with medicated swabs on wires up my nostrils. During the three years that we lived there in the Ohio River Valley, I dreaded getting a cold since a sinus infection always followed. It only happened there and when we moved away they completely disappeared.

Dr. Baker and his wife were wonderful neighbors. He still made house calls. If one of our children was sick at night and you called his home before he left at seven-thirty in the morning, he would make his first stop at our house. If a house call wasn't necessary, there was no need to wait in his crowded downtown waiting room. You simply knocked on the back door of the house where he had the first-floor office and he came and took us inside. This avoided spreading or picking up germs in the patient waiting room or waiting with sick, restless kids.

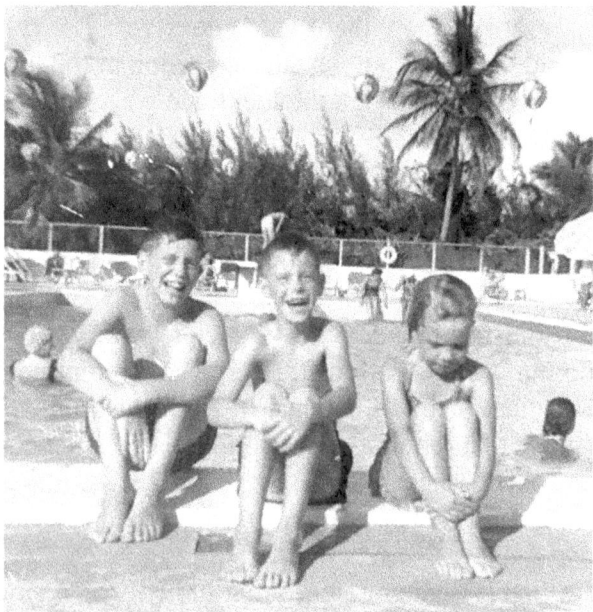

Our vaccinated children happily enjoying a day at the pool.

There was always the worry about the risk of polio, which seemed more prevalent in summertime, and the public pool was the perfect breeding ground for it. The happiest headline in my life was the April 1955 announcement of the Salk polio vaccine. We hurried to get the shots for our three small children. Then we purchased a family membership at the public pool in Jeffersonville.

There was no hospital in New Albany at the time. The nearest hospitals would be across the river in Louisville. Dr. Baker had gone to medical school in his thirties after he was married and had a son. On the basis of age and family, he was not drafted during World War II. As one of the few remaining doctors in town, he carried a heavy workload. He would come home late at night almost too tired to sleep and his relaxation was listening to classical records. Dr. Baker represented everything that a physician stood for in his practice. We were fortunate to have him as our doctor, neighbor and friend.

Meeting the Neighborhood

House hunting is a time of tension. This is especially true when a company transfer mandates a move to a strange new city in another part of the country. Houses are all so different and a quick purchase involves too many factors. A home choice is made many times with less research than when buying a major appliance. It is logical to ask the real estate agent questions about public transportation, location of shops and local schools from elementary through high school. But there is rarely an opportunity to check out or choose neighbors in a strange new city. It is impossible to know who they might be aside from the exteriors of nearby houses. Moving and meeting neighbors is like opening a surprise package. It's astonishing what you may find.

The best way to quickly find out about the neighborhood is to have young children who do a lot of the investigating. This was true when we moved to a tree-lined dead-end street with no sidewalks. The children could usually play safely on the street. There were a majority of older retired residents, but fortunately there was the Kraft family at the corner with three boys who were the same age as our two boys and one girl. Paul, Charles, and Kurt Kraft soon teamed up with Gordon, Philip and Amy Jane Core. Dorothy Kraft and I didn't have time to gossip over coffee, but we were in constant touch by phone as to where the gang was and what was going on.

Paul Kraft Sr. was a handsome, dark-haired man who ran his family's long-established funeral home. As a result, one of the favorite neighborhood children's games was to play funeral director. We had a big red wagon that our kids contributed to the cause, and turns were taken being "the body" lying stiff in the wagon while someone else pulled it. The rest of the children made up the semi-solemn procession down the street.

The milkman was a favorite figure when he made his midmorning deliveries on the dead-end block. The children would gather around his truck and make their choice of chocolate milk or orange juice in small cartons that he was "giving out." As mothers, it was much easier to have the nutritious drinks given as a novelty treat by the milkman and added to our household milk delivery bills instead of having to call them home for snack time. The braided rug in our breakfast room was known as the vitamin rug since so much milk, orange juice and vitamin drops had been spilled on it. A Mrs. Elliot had a tiny shop around the corner with a few basics such as milk and bread. The main attraction there was wonderful homemade ice cream and the children could get there without crossing a street.

Just next door was dear Reba Burton, who wore two hearing aids. The tragedies of her life were not having any children or close family, the passing of a devoted husband and then the loss of her hearing. Before that, she had been a church organist and choir director at First Methodist Church for many years. She had both a piano and an organ in her living room and still could enjoy them with the help of her hearing aids. She took the hearing aids off when she went to bed or took a nap and, during that time, was completely incommunicado. Distant relatives turned up unexpectedly one afternoon. I knew that Mrs. Burton was at home having her usual nap and would be heartbroken to miss this rare visit, but there was no way to reach her by doorbell or phone and the house was securely locked. I had no recourse to help them.

Mrs. Burton was short and somewhat plump, always dressed conservatively in black or navy. She let herself go with color in pert little hats and matching gloves and seemed to have a wardrobe of matching umbrellas. She didn't drive but would be seen at the end of her driveway waiting to be picked up for church by her good friends and nearby neighbors. At home she busied herself with craft projects for the Methodist bazaar and Sunday School decorations. She often shared these with our children.

Her late husband had a long illness and, as an accountant, tried to plan a budget that would allow his widow to stay in their home after his death. But he didn't reckon with inflation and with the health problems that his wife would have. After several lengthy hospitalizations, Mrs. Burton realized that this put an unfair burden on her good friends who collected her mail, drove her to the doctor, and helped pay her regular bills during her illnesses. One problem was that they had no legal status to act in her behalf. Her lovely little home was no longer the affordable safe haven that she needed.

Her minister was a great help in finding a solution. With special dispensation, since she was only fifty-five years old and below the usual admission age, she could be admitted to a Methodist Retirement Home in Franklin, Ind. She would deed her house to the church in exchange for a cottage being built on the grounds of the home and so could take her precious piano and organ with her. We learned from Christmas cards that she was the baby of the retirement center and the darling of her new world. She lived there happily for the next twenty years, until her death in 1976.

Directly across the street lived Miss Maude, a stern spinster with her frail little mother. It was not a place where the children went. When I called upon the ladies, the door would be slowly unlocked and as soon as I stepped inside, it was bolted behind me. Miss Maude was an only child, carefully reared and trained chiefly in music so she inevitably gave music lessons, although she didn't care for children. It might be assumed that Maude and Mrs. Burton would have their love for music as a common bond. Instead, there were bad feelings when Maude complained that Mrs. Burton's loud playing was annoying her.

Maude and her mother had moved from their large frame family home on Jefferson Street to a neat two-story brick house in Glenwood Court with a dignified traditional Federal doorway. There was no place for sitting outside in what were always warm Southern Indiana summers.

Curiosity may have prompted her to call on me soon after we moved in. I learned that she was an only child and that she had taught piano and was now retired. It was the kind of work that a well-brought-up young lady could do. Miss Maude was afraid of men, disliked children and was somewhat suspicious of everyone else.

We also saw her at the church that we joined and noticed that she was afraid of drafts and coughs. As a staunch Presbyterian, she sat alone in church near the back where she could get up and personally adjust the windows. There was no air conditioning. If anyone sneezed or coughed within three pews from her, she would glare at them and then gather up her purse and umbrella and pointedly move to a farther pew.

She was sometimes absent from Presbyterian services when she drove to Louisville across the river and took part in the spiritualist Unity Church there. The high point of her life were the summertime national two-week meetings of these groups that were held in Kansas. Along with spiritual benefits available in Louisville, she was a believer in irrigation treatments that benefited her health. One day she tried to explain to me the great benefits of colonic irrigation treatments that she took in Louisville. That was completely beyond my ken.

We had a station wagon in which I sometimes drove Miss Maude to a local concert series held in the New Albany high school auditorium. She always insisted on checking the rear seats before getting into the car and I'm sure that she looked under her bed each night as well.

Miss Maude sniffed at anything antique, but she bestowed two gifts upon me. One was a white ironstone chamber pot with lid and the other a well-worn brass candlestick. The pot matched an ironstone bowl and pitcher set used in a guest room for many years. I still have the low candleholder. To her it was good riddance. She did nothing graciously.

On the driveway side of our house lived a widow with her grown son. We seldom saw either of them as she went off to work daily in a Louisville department store and the son was rarely seen. He must have mowed the grass. When he did appear, he was a forbidding figure, over six feet tall and very thin. He had a tousled head of dark hair and was often wearing a short robe from which his white legs stuck out. He was only out long enough to pick up the newspaper. We learned that stamp collecting was what he did and that he sometimes submitted articles on stamps to boy's magazines.

In an attractive stone house down the street lived the Schultz family with a teenage daughter and grown son. The daughter was our babysitter. Mrs. Schultz was a lonely soul and terribly crippled with arthritis, but she welcomed the children with candy and treats. Her husband owned a local bar. The Schultzes had "moved up" in the world when they bought their nice house on Glenwood Place. They didn't realize that some of the neighbors would be so cool to people who owned a business that sold alcohol.

Some six months after our move, a new family with children arrived. They had just moved from Louisville, so it was a new neighborhood, city and state for them. Jim Cook was a Buick dealer. His picture was on billboard ads for the new agency in New Albany. There were always two shiny new dealer's cars parked in their driveway. That was impressive compared to our second-hand Ford station wagon. Their three children were a babe in arms, little four-year-old Jimmy and a daughter Jackie, who was the oldest of the children on the block. She not only managed her little brother, but soon directed all the other children. There were often quarrels when Jackie was on the scene. If the trouble was in our yard, my response was to ask Jackie to go home. Her response was to refuse to leave. I couldn't punish someone else's child, but I did escort her to the curb. Life was much more tranquil before Jackie.

Since we were newcomers now feeling settled in the community, I did my best to welcome the Cooks by inviting them over for dessert one night, asking if they played bridge and inviting them for a two-table evening. Each invitation was refused and on the third try, Nancy Cook again refused, but thanked me and said she felt she should explain her situation a bit. She said that she and her husband weren't going out together as they were estranged.

Not too much later, I learned more about their marital difficulties than I really wanted to know. I was ironing at the time she unburdened herself. Her husband was having an affair with his secretary. She was going to file for divorce, but would have to be a resident of Indiana for year in order to start proceedings and have no marital relations with him during that time. She had hired a detective to provide evidence and an attorney for the coming divorce trial. Her husband was furious that she had spent household funds to pay for a detective. He probably shut off all of her allowance because soon her new Buick convertible was no longer in the drive.

One spring evening, she appeared at our door in her housecoat, tears running down her face. She asked to use our phone to call her attorney. The only phone was centrally located in the back hall, but we did have an extra that we could connect to a basement outlet and so could give her privacy if she sat on the steps there.

When summer came, Jim's young sister came to stay with them and worked at his office. Before she left at the end of the summer there was a family vacation. We never knew how it came about, but apparently there was a reconciliation between Jim and Nancy. I was always acutely uncomfortable with her after that. She had confided in me more than I wanted to know, but I was awaiting some word of closure. I didn't dare ask, "what happened?"

We had moved to 2511 Glenwood Court shortly before Christmas and soon learned that the street was noted for its outstanding light displays which had grown competitive over the years. The only solution for us was to decorate the front door and put a pile of gift packages on the deacon's bench and light that with a spotlight. We were the only house on the street with but one light. What had been advertised as a quiet street became a traffic jam in the evenings as cars drove slowly by and then turned in the circle at the end to return.

The next street was Glenwood Place, with much grander homes. The mayor lived there, as well as a wealthy doctor and his in-laws. These were brick homes with tall Southern-style white pillars. These homes also had Easter plantings that the town turned out to view and very lavish Christmas decorations. Louisville florists were hired to entwine the white columns with smilax climbing plants and lights, and there were even lights on the garages. When the festive display was turned on one year, it overloaded the electrical circuits and all power in that part of the city was put out.

One fall, I was assigned to canvass door-to-door in our neighborhood for the Community Fund, as it was then known. I put on a handsome checked suit and knocked on doors equipped with pledge cards, buttons and window stickers to designate annual supporters.

At one of the most elegant homes, I was greeted suspiciously at the door by the lady of the house. Knowing that her husband owned a business in the adjoining town and he would not have made an office contribution to New Albany, I suggested leaving a pledge card that they could discuss together. At this she retreated inside and returned carrying her purse, from which she reluctantly removed one dollar. That would not have paid for one of her fancy spring tulips. Being as polite as possible, I refused her dollar and said that I couldn't give her a window sticker for that. I said I would add a dollar to my family's personal contribution on her behalf. I wonder if she had ever been snubbed that way before. The Community Fund office staff was delighted when I reported the encounter.

Shortly after we moved in, my husband wanted to entertain his office associates who had been most hospitable to us. Our house was nicely carpeted but didn't have any curtains for the many windows. So we measured and I made my first solo shopping trip to downtown Louisville while he watched the children. I bought most of the downstairs curtains in just an hour. There were provincial printed tier curtains in cranberry and white for the two triple dining room windows. Long, beige shantung-like drapes were for the four living room windows. We hung those very satisfactory curtains in different houses for many years.

Silver Creek

Silver Creek was a stream near the Eastern border of New Albany. The highway bridge that crossed the creek led to the outskirts of Jeffersonville, Ind. The name given to the creek was misleading because the stream was a muddy brown rather than silver. It was much feared in spring flood season when it overflowed its banks close to where it joined the Ohio River. Nevertheless, the creek gave its name to the nearby grade school.

The Glenwood Court neighborhood was a dead-end street that stopped at a steep drop to the flood plain that bordered Silver Creek. This was dangerous territory where the children were forbidden to go. Glenwood Place, with a number of elegant homes, was also a dead-end street. Both streets were protected by a massive concrete flood wall near the end on the creek.

Silver Street Elementary School in this part of the Floyd county seat was the elite school of the city. It had the best teachers, the best students and the best parents, who enthusiastically supported an overactive Parent Teacher Association. The school fairs and spring picnics were noteworthy community events as well as fundraisers. Naturally, we became involved in the PTA and I soon found myself an officer.

Another woman and I were sent one September to the state-wide conference for the organization. We traveled by train from New Albany to Indianapolis and spent two nights at a downtown hotel where the large meeting was being held. Some of our expenses were paid by the prosperous Silver Creek School PTA, so we were duty bound to attend all of the meetings. The meetings proved to be boring and political and it was difficult to know what we could report back to our group that would be of interest or help. We wore badges at all times for admittance to the hall. Why anyone would want to crash these dull sessions was beyond imagination. Fortunately, when we returned, no one was actually interested in what happened in Indianapolis.

New Albany also had an active Newcomers Club that met at the American Legion. The Legion had purchased one of the large Victorian mansions on Market Street and shared these gracious quarters with other groups. This was an ideal way to meet other newcomers and get acquainted with the community. The active group had annual fashion shows well-covered by the local newspaper, and I found myself conscripted as a model for their event. They supported the local concert series and the community fund drive.

Modeling in a New Albany fashion show

One spring morning, I hosted a breakfast bridge of three tables for the Newcomers, with reservations to be made in advance. The menu was cantaloupe rings filled with fresh strawberries, pecan rolls, tea and coffee. I had prepared for exactly the twelve guests, myself included. To my surprise an unexpected member arrived. She was an attractive member that I also knew from the church choir who had agreed to take one of our unwanted kittens and seemed blithely unaware of any need to reply to the invitation. I gave up my plate just in time, and lost my place at the bridge table as well.

The leading women's groups in town seemed to be three sororities bearing Greek initials. I had graduated from a woman's college that had no sororities, so these groups were a mystery to me. They all had a rigorous admittance procedure and members were required to spend a required number of hours volunteering at their thrift shop.

I was invited to attend a prospective members event. The groups had rented a movie theatre for a large meeting, which scarcely seemed the best way to vet new members. Some weeks later, a small cream-colored envelope arrived in the mail. The formal message was to the effect that I was to be honored with this invitation to join Alpha Beta Gamma or whatever they were called. The courteous way to invite a new member, in my opinion, would be to say that the group would be honored by my acceptance of membership.

I promptly, but formally declined.

My close neighbor, Dot Kraft, was a native resident and my source for local information. She had served her tedious sorority apprenticeship long since and now enjoyed exemption from all duties as a senior member. She had warned me about what was involved. I felt there was no reason to join such a group since I already knew many of the members.

Hutchison Memorial Presbyterian Church had an outstanding young minister and we met many congenial people there. The Women's Association consisted of circles that met in various members' homes in the evenings. My invitation to a circle meeting came by phone from a Katherine Gentile, who offered to pick me up. The last name seemed familiar to me from our recent house hunting days. A real estate agent had promoted one property saying that a popular Dr. Gentile lived on the same street. "Always good to be near a doctor, when you have small children," he said.

When Katherine Gentile arrived and we were just outside the front door, I made an attempt at friendly conversation by saying that I had heard such nice things about Dr. Gentile, assuming that she was a wife, sister or relation of some kind. She turned to me fiercely and said, "I'm the wrong person to say that to! I was his first wife and he walked out on me!" My supposed compliment had failed miserably and I followed her, speechless, to the car.

The next morning. I called Dot and described my experience, which amused her greatly. She said that the doctor's affair was common knowledge long before his "walk-out." The wife was the last to know and found out that everyone else knew. Her bitterness had spilled over to an innocent newcomer.

After that experience, I learned to consult my friend in advance as to the place I was going, to the hostesses' marital state, number of children, husband's business and any delicate subjects to be avoided.

Dan became acquainted with people through his office associates and the local Bar Association. He was recruited to head the March of Dimes. This involved decorating a downtown store window and visiting tobacco farmers in the area. Since his job as an attorney did not involve any company entertaining, membership in the country club was not one of his perks. As he had no interest in golf, this was of little loss. We were often invited to country club dances by friends. My only regret was that we couldn't afford access to the country club pool for the children.

We ordered from an advertisement in the New York Times one of the earliest small backyard pools. This was a blessing in the hot summer days. The pool killed the grass underneath. The next year, a man was hired to remove the sod, level and spread sand and I laid a brick patio. Free, used brick was transported by our station wagon in multiple loads. The brick had to be cleaned of mortar before being put in place in the area back of the house below the hillside yard. A six-foot maple tree was planted at the edge. I was proud of the weathered look.

Living in New Albany was a happy experience. It was a lively, suburban location and our family thrived being part of a close-knit community again. We learned the importance of the real estate mantra of location, location, location. Some three years later, when Dan was transferred back to Pittsburgh, the house was sold to neighbors on a nearby street who knew the house and wanted to live in the neighborhood.

Cat Tales

Buying gifts for my sister, Ceil, was always easy for we liked the same things. If I found something that I liked, then I felt certain it would appeal to her. Ceil's gifts to me were always appreciated. A cat decoration was a sure thing to buy for her. Not only had she had a succession of live cats but also cat decorations throughout her house. She would ask visiting children to look through all the rooms and see how many cats they could count.

Ceil and one of the "Tinys"

This started in our childhood when the first pet that I had was a cat. Cats came and they seemed to go. For many years each cat had the same name: "Tiny." I was six years older and at first the cats were my pets. As Ceil grew older, she claimed ownership and ownership alternated between us until I became more interested in other teenage activities.

Her cat slept in her bedroom and, in nice weather, would come and go hunting during the night from her open window. The back-porch roof was a few feet below the window and then the attached grape arbor was an easy climb. Sometimes she would wake up to find gifts by her bed such as a dead mouse. One morning, the gift was a live bird that had to be chased out with the help of a tennis racket.

This fascination with cats continued all of her life. The cats that came her way enjoyed a good home and wonderful care and lived to record ages. Unlike the cats of our youth, they had the attention of veterinarians and special foods. Usually there was only one at a time. Her four daughters followed in her footsteps, often with multiple cats that also required the most meticulous care. It would be staggering to count up cat costs!

When my children were small, we had a succession of pets, both cats and dogs. The first cat, given to us by a neighboring young couple, was a sleek elegant seal point Siamese cat named Simba. She was a beauty. Simba didn't care for juvenile company and would not submit to the indignities of being dressed up or playing with little children. She preferred adult company and soon after breakfast would disappear for the day, sometimes under furniture or to the safe haven she found down the street in our New Albany neighborhood. She found more congenial company a few houses away. The neighbors were two sisters, retired schoolteachers that we might not otherwise have met. The sisters admired the beautiful cat and invited her inside. Soon she was a regular visitor there after breakfast, sitting on the outside sill of their kitchen window waiting to be let in for her daylong visit. She returned home at suppertime and after the children went to bed; she was an affectionate, decorative lap-sitter. For the ladies, Simba was the ideal pet. They enjoyed her and had no long-term commitment for her care.

One of our plans for Simba was to breed her with another Siamese and hopefully produce a litter of lovely kittens. There was a breeder in town who agreed to keep her for a week at the appropriate time to mate her for a stated fee and guaranteed success.

But while we had tried to monitor her love life and move her to a breeder, it was all in vain, for a neighborhood swain had gotten there first. Much to our despair, a part-Siamese cat does not resemble its beautiful mother, but has the dominant markings of the very ordinary tabby cat father.

It was not easy to find homes for ordinary kittens. It meant the little ones had to be raised to a suitable age and then be placed in good homes. Unfortunately, it took a lot of persuasion to place those kittens. So much for sex education! We learned that a cat's love life is not easily regulated. Another try with the breeder met with failure again, as she ran away from the breeder's home and was not seen for several months. She turned up nearby in the home of a pair of older adults and we accepted her decision to live there – away from both children and a large Irish Setter.

Later, when we lived in the Bahamas, we would be given a beautiful long-haired gray cat named Misty by friends who had been transferred to New York City, where any pets would not be welcomed. The cat was brought to our house two weeks before their departure. A few days later, it found its way back to them, a distance of several miles. The cat was brought back and we were told to spread a generous amount of butter on its paws. That may have been an old wives' tale, but it worked. By the time the butter was licked off, the cat seemed content to stay with us.

Derby Day

The first Saturday in May is Derby Day in Louisville and marks the beginning of summer for the city and the surrounding area. The week before the Derby is clean-up time. Porches are painted, decks are scrubbed down, and porch furniture is cleaned and put in place. Residents plant geraniums in window boxes and petunias in their front borders. The city of Louisville fills its parks with flowering plants. Parties are planned before and after the Kentucky Derby, as races take place in advance of the final race known as the Run for the Roses.

Across the Ohio River from Louisville, New Albany follows the lead of Louisville in preparing for Derby Day. They accommodate the overflowing crowds that descend on the area then. On that day, the traffic from downtown Louisville is changed in the morning to three lanes in the direction of Churchill Downs with only one lane in the opposite direction. After the race, these lanes are reversed.

Although the Kentucky Derby was a local area event, the attendance from all over the country was so great that it was very difficult to secure tickets. In January, with assistance from the company office, Dan was able to secure two seats for the May event.

We felt fortunate to have seats as there are many people standing on the infield. It was a sunny spring day. I had anticipated a crowd of horse lovers filling the grandstand seats. It was a surprise to find there were a great many empty seats considering the fact that seats had been so difficult to get. The seats were sold, but the ticket holders were lined up at the betting windows careless of whether they saw the race itself, and it's doubtful they did. Those attendees didn't look well-dressed or prosperous at the $20 and $50-dollar windows.

We were completely inexperienced as far as betting was concerned. We made several small bets with little knowledge of what we were doing. Our two-dollar bets came to the grand sun of $10. Fortunately, that was the total of our losses. The horses were beautiful to see and the festive atmosphere made for a lovely day.

Then, as a climax to the big day, we made a visit to a "barn-like workshop" of reconditioned player pianos that we had seen advertised in that part of Louisville. We were trying to avoid the rush of traffic following the Derby, so we decided to investigate the repair shop's advertisement for player pianos. We spent $200 for a restored, upright, pumping, player piano that fateful day. It provided entertainment (and exercise for everyone as it wasn't electrified) for many years to come and was our winning Derby purchase.

Ceil and Layton Geddis with their growing family of girls

The following Derby Day we had Pittsburgh guests. My sister, Ceil, and her husband, Layton, and their two little girls came for the big race. We were going to babysit the girls while their parents went to Churchill Downs equipped with a movie camera. Friday afternoon when they arrived, the weather was warm and sunny and we sat out on our brick patio at the rear of the house. Saturday morning, however, dawned cool with gray skies. The adult guests went off to Derby Day wearing raincoats. The raincoats were needed as the rain came with cold winds. At four o'clock in the afternoon, we turned on the television to watch the Run for the Roses. There was a knock at the front door and two shivering refugees appeared. They came in and removed the newspapers that they had put inside their rain coats for insulation. They told us that the stands selling hot coffee had run out hours before and that there was little demand for the famous mint juleps. My brother-in-law patted his camera and said grimly, "As far as anyone back in Pittsburgh is concerned, these pictures of the earlier races of the day *are* the Derby!"

The Kentucky Derby, like many other sports events, can best be seen on television. Since the race itself only lasts four or five minutes, the time before is filled with interviews of trainers and owners. The jockeys are pictured being weighed in. You can see the horses being saddled and led in to the course. You are in the exclusive section of the grandstand with the latest fashions and the improbable hats of the ladies. Everyone stands as though it were for the National Anthem, when the band opens the ceremonies playing "My Old Kentucky Home" with the crowd singing lustily. Watching the proceedings in the comfort of your home, you are able to see everything and are saved from losing any money on the races. Happy Derby Day!

New Year's Eve at Silver Hills

Names from the past and present float in and out of mind. At breakfast this morning, looking at a ten-inch cut glass pitcher, the names and faces of past friends were as clear as the glass. This pitcher was a prize from a dinner party on a New Year's Eve in 1957, when we celebrated midnight together at Nancy and Dick Stamm's home in New Albany. They were a handsome, young couple who were among others who had befriended us newcomers. They had a son and daughter in school with our two boys and we had met them at church. They had invited us to that first country club dance early on.

Our one-and-a-half story brick house was on a pleasant, newer street in New Albany. We had never looked at any houses on Silver Hills when we were transferred from Pittsburgh as our chosen location was convenient to all the schools and public transportation. Silver Hills was on a bluff above the Ohio River with some lovely older homes and new housing on large lots.

During our years in Indiana, we were part of a group of ten couples, most of whom lived on the hill, for our group parties. It meant that there was little driving involved on what were usually snowy nights. These progressive dinners were well organized by several women who set the menus and assigned the food for each couple to bring. The evening started with cocktails at one home, moved to a second place for the dinner course and then to the final setting for dessert, games and a midnight toast. The men all wore dinner suits and the women were in long gowns.

Dick Stamm ran his family's lumber business. There were a number of lumber companies in New Albany. His company was not the usual building supply outlet. It specialized in veneers that were cut from exotic woods with unusual markings that were imported from all over the world. These woods were cut wafer-thin and matched for beautiful veneers which were designed for fine buildings. Several well-traveled company executives were part of our group, interesting people whose names are lost in memory, but whose faces still remain clear as crystal. The glass pitcher has survived many moves since then and brings back pleasant memories.

Millinery Memories

In my college days, everyone wore hats when going out. Some of the most practical and attractive were made to match a suit or a coat. At the store, I was careful to ask if matching material could be ordered from the manufacturer and had a quarter of a yard added to the purchase. We all knew of a milliner who could make up something individual. This was information that we traded with each other.

Years later, moving to New Albany meant finding a new doctor, a new dentist and a new milliner. I was given the name of Eleanor Wilson, but when I called her about having a hat made, she said that she would have to refuse since she was too busy. Her suggestion was that I sign up for the millinery class she was going to be teaching in the adult education classes at the high school and learn how to make my own hats.

The first session of the class was disappointing, for most of the time she talked about the history and importance of hats and their role in identifying professions and personalities. I was eager to get started on my hands-on projects. In following classes, we purchased a balsam hat block on which to work, learned to shape felt hoods on the block, to wash felt, to reshape older felt hats, iron a grosgrain ribbon in a curve for a hatband and alter shapes. There was felt lining stitched to woolen material that could be shaped. Later, we worked with buckram frames, made and wired our own frames and even stitched and molded woven straw purchased by the yard. Brims were often wired.

Then the bouffant hair-do arrived and started the departure of the millinery. At first there were light veils decorated with flowers that rested on top of the hair, but soon hats completely disappeared.

No education is completely wasted, even though it may go out of fashion. Much of the millinery class has been forgotten, but the first lecture, on how head gear has identified people throughout the years, has stayed with me. Then I moved to a climate where it was only wise to wear a hat in the subzero temperatures in January and February. The most becoming hats were made of fur, but that was a major expense. My old lessons came back to me as I realized that I could easily put together a fur hat from a fur collar. Get out the razor blade to cut the fur from the underside, use a leather needle to stitch ends together, take the excess end and position it for the top, shape the curve for the band, etc. And voila! Suddenly, I was a hatmaker, like my illustrious Buhl ancestors before me.

The Travel Trailer

Sister-in-law Jane and her husband, Dan Milling, lived in Beaumont, Texas near the Gulf. It had been some time since we had seen Jane or she had seen our children: Amy Jane, aged three, Philip, aged five and Gordon, aged seven. I was fond of Jane, but when my husband started to talk about all of us driving to Texas to visit her on his summer vacation, I had serious misgivings about a trip of that length. Our station wagon was not air-conditioned and this was before the time of seat belts.

Since New Albany is across the Ohio River from Louisville, Ky., that was our big city. We had a local paper on weekdays, but always got the Louisville Courier on Sundays. In March, there was a feature article about trailer travel. There was a rental agency near the Louisville airport. Could this possibly be the solution to our travel problem? Now, husband Dan was the one who had misgivings! He was persuaded to visit the rental agency and inspect the travel trailers described in the article. But, before undertaking the long trip to Texas, he wanted to test whether this could work. So, arrangements were made to rent a 13-foot travel trailer for a weekend of travel in nearby Illinois. The station wagon was fitted with a trailer hitch and we purchased a book on state and other trailer parks to plot our weekend.

With children, however, the best laid plans often go awry. We had to cancel our weekend, not once but twice due to illness. The trailer agency was very understanding. Finally, in May, we made a tour of Lincoln country from Abraham Lincoln's early primitive home in Salem to Springfield and the Lincoln Memorial.

The trailer turned out to be the ideal way to travel with children. The state park camping directory became our bible, leading us to many places off the main highways that we would never have found otherwise They had interesting scenery, playgrounds and usually swimming in small lakes. It was easy to have breakfast and lunch in the trailer or at roadside tables as we traveled. Then we usually treated ourselves to dinner out. This was luxury camping and, on a rainy night in the woods, we felt dry and snug compared to people in tents nearby.

The simple trailer had a table with a bench on either side on the right when entering. It converted into a bunk at night. There was a two-burner stove and tiny sink with connection to water below. A double bed was at the rear. There was a small upright closet. Most clothing was packed in cardboard boxes and kept under the bed. A tall white enamel pot with lid was our "loo." The boys could fit into the front bunk and there was a bed roll for Amy Jane on the floor. We all had to bed down at the same time. There was no room to lounge and it was illegal to be in the travel trailer while moving. Dan had to practice backing up and parking. It was important to level the trailer for the night.

The fees were low and accommodations varied at the different parks. Some parks had electric hookups, bath houses and lodges where meals were served. Many of them were located on small lakes with swimming beaches or playgrounds. The most primitive usually had level parking pads and a picnic table.

The day would begin with cereal for breakfast after pushing the bunk back into the table and benches. The children could run around outside before we started back on the road. Wayside parks were indicated on the map and these were good places to stop for lunch. Dan would play with the children while I would get lunch together. If the rest stop had pleasant shaded picnic tables, we would eat outside, otherwise the trailer was available. We would try to find restaurants to have evening dinners. Eating out with children is a challenge if rolls are on the table before the meal is served; they fill up on those or on the sugar packets on the table and don't eat a good meal. Dan and I were often eating their leftovers.

We would stop in the late afternoon, go swimming and then dress for dinner. There was rain on a few nights and it was so cozy to hear the pattering on the roof of the trailer. The trailer experience was so enjoyable and easier than camping.

When we got to Beaumont, we were able to park the trailer in the driveway beside the Milling's house and run an electric extension from the house to the trailer. Jane had borrowed a crib for Amy Jane and the rest of us slept in the trailer. We had our own sheets and towels and as a result, the whole host household was not upset. Before leaving Texas, we made another stop to visit my Gelbach cousin, Stanley Humphrey, and his wife, Dot. He was a doctor in Bay Port. If we did not have the trailer, we would not have been able to make an overnight stop with them. With our own accommodations, we were able to share a barbecue picnic there.

We parked outside the city zoo in Jackson, Mississippi early one day and Dan and the children visited the zoo while I prepared breakfast curbside. Parking the station wagon and attached trailer was tricky and Dan mastered the difficulty of backing up, leveling the trailer, connecting lines and disconnecting the trailer hitch.

Another day, we visited the *U.S.S. Texas*, a huge battleship which looked aground in a meadow. The boys clambered all over the gun turrets of the attraction. Nearby was the San Jacinto Monument containing a very Texas-slanted version of US history. A famous seafood eatery nearby satisfied our shrimp cravings with "all you can eat" for a set price and leftovers to put in the trailer icebox for another great meal.

The homeward journey went so well that I wanted us to buy the same-size travel trailer and plan more travel. But there was a problem of where to store it in off-seasons. When we were transferred from New Albany to Pittsburgh, where we bought a house in Ben Avon, again there would have been the storage problem. A wise decision on Dan's part to stick with a rental. At the time and with the ages of our children, it had proved to be the ideal way to travel and visit.

Company Friends

Ed and Ruth Miller were from Pittsburgh and Tarentum, like us, and we had college friends in common. He was the leading salesman for the U.S. Steel plant. They had four children, older than ours and lived in a spacious frame house on Silver Hills above New Albany. We spent New Year's Eve with them for several years as part of our Silver Hills group. We saw them at church and often chatted after the service.

Ed had a heart attack and was off work for three months, leaving Ruth to cope with four children, paying bills and running the household, as well as trying to keep Ed from bursting at the seams. He was not allowed to do anything, but was full of ideas that he wanted Ruth to carry out. It was a great relief when Ed went back to work. During that time, Dan insisted that I take over the family finances as preparation in case anything like that would happen to us. When the Millers were transferred back to Pittsburgh before us, they built a doubled custom-made prefab U.S. Steel home in Fox Chapel.

Sam Clifford was a salesman for the Credit Corporation and he and Dan traveled together for work. He and his wife, Doris, had just bought a new home in Dormont before their transfer to Indiana and she was so happy with their house there. They bought their new house in Louisville, across the Ohio River from New Albany. Their teenage boy and older daughter were involved in the change. The daughter found a clerical job in the area but the son missed his high school buddies. Doris was going through menopause and very unhappy with the transfer and the changes in her own life. She became a recluse. She did agree to go out on Christmas Day and they came to see us because we were from Pittsburgh.

John C. Bird was a labor attorney from U.S. Steel assigned to the former Gunnison plant. He and his wife, Irene, bought a charming house in Louisville. Irene found it to be a great shopping area for her love of antiques. We got along famously together because we both enjoyed the hunt. She decorated their house beautifully. John was not always aware of her purchases until Christmastime when he might be presented with a chest of drawers. By contrast, my Dan only got neckties or socks or pajamas at gift times.

When the Birds were transferred back to the law offices in Pittsburgh, Irene had a problem. She had to get together the antiques that were being refinished or held for her by several dealers. It was a surprise gifting for John. They entertained often and were among the first to embrace outdoor grilling, which wasn't a popular pastime until the 1950s.

The Credit Corporation subsidiary where Dan worked also included an accountant and his wife and son from Washington D.C. They bought a house near us just inside the Silver Creek flood wall. The head of the corporation first bought a large house in the country with a lovely view. We visited them there and did not envy their choice. We had just moved from country life and learned the lesson of location, location, location! In time, they did the same and bought a house on Glenwood Place beside the town mayor.

After three years in New Albany, the contract documents that had been Dan's responsibility were well-organized and a transfer to Pittsburgh's law office took place. The Millers and the Birds were back, as well, and we kept in touch. It was nice to have friends who were being transferred among the same cities as us, so we rarely had to start from scratch when forming new social circles and friendships.

Our Family: Gordon, Dan, Amy Jane, Amy and Philip

The Ben Avon Year
1958

Ben Avon is a pleasant tree-shaded suburb northwest of Pittsburgh on the Ohio River. The river borders the town, then the railroad beside the river and a steep bluff below the town, so the river is not in view. There are a few houses on top of the bluff, which are rather isolated by Ohio River Boulevard which demarks the actual lower edge of town. Our Dutch colonial brick house was just off the boulevard at 106 Irwin Avenue with maple trees in front and tall oaks in the level rear garden area. It was one of the smaller houses on a street that had several mansions and large older homes. The real estate agent had shown us a larger house next door and we had seen the for-sale sign by the owner. We returned on our own to see the house and found it ready for a luncheon party. While we were greeted warmly by the husband, the wife was anxious that we should take a quick look and get out of the way before her guests arrived. We returned later to buy the house.

Ben Avon had its borough building and all of the few shops in one short block of Church Avenue, along with the streetcar line. There was a drugstore, grocery

172

and beauty shop. Further uphill from Church Avenue, side streets ran up the hill often to dead ends, but there was a winding road that led to Ben Avon Heights with newer homes on larger lots and the Shannopin Country Club. We felt fortunate to be within two blocks of the grade school and the Presbyterian church across from the school. This community was not new to me since I had often visited there with my college roommate, Jean Archer, as she had grown up there, and met some of her friends. It had the advantage of being convenient to the airport, on the same side of the city as Zelienople, and with good public transportation to Dan's downtown office.

The house had a generously-sized covered entry porch. The usual wooden Dutch benches had been moved to the rear patio off the kitchen. Our deacon's bench was right at home there instead. The front hall with the stairway going up from the middle was wider than usual and made for a gracious welcome. A door at the back of the hall opened to a back hall between the kitchen and basement steps which was the only place to hang coats. To the right of the hall was a door to a sun room and another door opened to the living room. To the left was a wider door leading to the dining room which had windows across the front and above the built-in china closets on either side of a non-working gas fireplace.

The house had its good points and its bad points and we set to work with a will to make improvements. The kitchen had been remodeled by the woodworking former owner and painted in hotrod red and yellow enamel. That was the first to be repainted and the built-ins there were not the greatest with rather rough cabinets. There was room to eat in the kitchen. The dining room had wallpaper with huge green leaves that fortunately peeled off very easily and was soon painted a soft gray. The cranberry print double-tiered curtains from New Albany fit nicely on those windows. There were hardwood floors and the rugs from our first apartment found a place there. In the living room there was a wide doorway to the sun porch and a large window at the back overlooked the pleasant back garden. We installed shutters on the high windows on either side of the non-working fireplace and everything was painted a warm beige.

Upstairs were three bedrooms and a bath and a sewing or linen room with built-in cupboards and a single window. The laundry chute was located there, always a great thing to have. The boys shared the back bedroom. The two front bedrooms were connected by a short hall that had high windows above the front entrance and a large walk-in closet opposite the windows. This could connect us with Amy Jane's room. My first dressing table was long gone, but by putting in a wide shelf the length of that area and skirting it with white eyelet material to match the curtains above, it was a nice dressing room

We wanted to put up a dainty flowered paper in Amy Jane's room but there was already wallpaper overpainted with dull green paint. Determined to do the correct thing for the future and not cover paint and paper, we rented a steamer and tried to remove what was there. Unlike the dining room where the paper had come off so easily, this was an inch-by-inch process, very boring and frustrating, but eventually finished.

The bathroom was definitely dated with a clawfoot tub on a black and white tiled floor surrounded by white tile. There was a tub shower and so the look was played up with a shower curtain of white with black sketches of antique bathrooms. Above the pedestal sink (they have now come back again), the medicine cabinet with wooden frame was hidden with an ornate old picture frame and pendant lights on either side were turned up and covered with frosted antique shades Those minor changes made a major difference.

Eventually, we got to the linen room where the brown cupboards were painted Wedgewood blue and an old desk was purchased and divided to support a new long built-in top. That was painted the same color. It was an attractive place to type or sew as well as for storing the linens.

Several improvements that became necessary were not as happy. It was discovered on the day that we moved in, while the telephone man was installing the phone, that there were termites in the basement. Discouraging news! Of course, we had been accustomed to termite control and insurance and regular treatments in New Albany, but never considered such a possibility in Western Pennsylvania. Thus, some of the money set aside for decorating had to go to termite eradication. Fortunately, only a few basement timbers had to be replaced.

We had new neighbors, San and Ned Roudabush, in the larger house on one side, who had bought the house that we were shown. They had three boys, somewhat younger than our children, and were also renovating. We had many things in common and quickly formed a friendship.

We found ourselves doing many things together, from planting pachysandra under the front maples to walking the little ones to Sunday School. A few doors up were the Richardsons with three children and similar interests and between a family with two teenage girls that were available for babysitting. This was a congenial neighborhood. At Christmastime, Joan Richardson had a ladies' cookie tea and we all took cookies and did an exchange so that we each could take home a variety. An older neighbor brought us lemonade when several of us were working in the garden together and there was frequent trading of plants.

To get to the grade school, there was just one street to be crossed in front of the school. Dan and the boys became Indian Guides, a YMCA organization for boys and fathers. They all had Indian names and Dan was known, appropriately, as Bald Eagle. A great deal of time and effort went into the construction of full-feathered headdresses in which I got involved, but other than hosting an occasional meeting, what went on in the meetings was strictly between the males. There was a fall weekend when the group went on a trip to the YMCA's primitive Camp Davis. I saw them off on a chilly wet Saturday morning and was hoping that the weather would improve. The camp was in the foothills of the Alleghenies below Uniontown. A group of women would have chickened out on such a day, but not these macho fathers. I knew that they all were carrying money and credit cards and imagined that they might end up spending the night in a motel, so I didn't worry about them and enjoyed a quiet weekend with Amy Jane.

The "Indians" came back on Sunday afternoon cold and tired. There were no cabins, just lean-to shelters, and Dan had stayed up all night trying to keep a fire burning. It was doubtful if any of the others got much sleep.

Among other Ben Avon adventures, the boys took Dan to see a cave that they had found and dubbed "Indian Caves." It involved crossing the busy Ohio River Boulevard and then there was a twelve-inch path along the edge of the bluff overlooking the railroad tracks and the river far below to a little indentation in the rocks where they had their hide-out. They said they watched the trains go by from their cave (and later confessed they threw rocks at them too). It was a terrifying location and that was immediately banned.

Amy Jane went adventuring on her own one day, after emptying the money from her piggy bank and walking to the drugstore several blocks away on Church Avenue without permission. There our independent four-year-old daughter spent all of her pennies on chewing gum and candy. She was outraged, when upon her return, the candy was taken away from her, placed on the top of the fridge and doled out over a period of time. As she said indignantly, "It was *my* money!"

We had a dinner party for Pittsburgh friends one evening and, as entertainment, we provided a canvas on an easel with brushes and a palette and invited our guests to create an abstract for the evening with each one doing a bit of the composition. Some were very reluctant to take the brush in hand and some guests then could scarcely give up the brush for the next person's turn.

The basement of the house was open and warm and dry and provided good play space for it could accommodate skates and trikes as well as toys. There was an enclosed toilet and sink under the stairs and convenient to the back door which was handy. There was gas heat in the house for the hot water radiators throughout. One winter day there was the smell of gas and a furnace man was called. He turned off the gas and called the gas company. The problem was diagnosed as a break in the gas line between the house and the street which involved digging through the frozen soil with a jack hammer and replacing the line before the gas could be turned on. The water had to be turned off to prevent freezing and we had to retreat to Zelienople until the repairs were made. We returned to a very cold house and went immediately to bed to keep warm until, by the next morning, things were back to normal. Of course, the repair costs in the winter weather were much higher than they would have been otherwise. That also was a low blow to the budget. Any home improvement that isn't visible may be necessary, but is not something that is enjoyed. A generous closet was added in the front hall at the side of the stairs. We were feeling nicely settled.

A summer trip that my mother and I took, was to Pennsylvania Dutch country and the Kutztown Festival which was something that she had long wanted to do. We decided to stay at a bed and breakfast in the country nearby. It was a working farm and rather spare accommodations with a true farm breakfast. On the second night there was a terrific thunderstorm and we woke in the morning to find that a giant tree limb had fallen down on our car, a small station wagon, causing a great dent in the middle of the roof. The front doors still worked and the car was drivable. It looked as though it had been involved in a rollover accident.

There was work to be done in the choked perennial beds in our garden. One of the neighbors had divided her irises and several others were helping to plant them and to divide things on a June day when the phone rang. It was Dan phoning from Chicago where he was on a business trip in connection with the Credit Corporation. He told me to sit down and then asked, "How would you like to move to Nassau in the Bahamas?"

I really didn't know where that was, but it sounded glamorous, exotic and different from Pittsburgh life, so the answer was yes! This was still very hush, hush as nothing had been finalized; it was a possible offer and so could not be mentioned. I went outside to continue with the planting, although practically bursting with the news and feeling like throwing the iris corms to the winds, since I was sure that I wouldn't be there to see the blooms the next year. And, indeed, we weren't. It might have been distressing to be transferred after only a year and after putting in all the work on the house if the transfer had been anywhere else but the Bahamas.

Seven
Life in Paradise

The Corners in Nassau
1959 – 1965

We had a house in Nassau under a tropical sky. Beyond the white picket fence that enclosed the front garden was Dowdeswell Street and on the opposite side was the open space of Eastern Parade. That park was the site of occasional celebrations and rugby games between the Nassau pick-up team and teams from visiting British ships or American colleges for which we had a front seat view. Beyond the Parade was East Bay Street and facing us was the classic pillared front of the Pan American Airlines office. It backed onto the sea and at the side was the ramp which once served the early sea planes. We had a view of the sparkling green-blue water of the channel between the city, located on New Providence Island and off-shore Hog Island, which was renamed Paradise Island by Huntingdon Hartford when he purchased it in 1959.

A stone wall surrounded the remainder of the garden, which extended a block from Dowdeswell Street to Shirley Street at the rear. There the slatted back gate guarded a dilapidated pink garage sheltered by an arching Poinciana tree. Carriage drivers taking tourists on the city tour from St. George's Wharf passed up Shirley Street and we could hear them pointing out the Poinciana, sapodilla, avocado and lime trees. Their route turned on Lover's Lane between St. Matthews Church and its convent onto Dowdeswell and passed the front of the house where the breadfruit trees in the side garden, the croton and hibiscus hedges were featured. Perhaps they assumed our family, sitting outside on the porch, were native Bahamians!

Like houses in England, there were no numbered streets or house numbers in Nassau. Instead, homes had names, usually small signs on the front gate. There was no sign on our house and it was a bit puzzling to give directions. We found that the house had always been called The Corners. We had a new sign installed and resisted the temptation to spell it "The Core-ners." There was a pedestrian alley called Hall's Lane that marked the West side of the property and this connected the two corners of Dowdeswell and Shirley Streets.

We rented this large, white, all-wooden West Indies colonial house which was supported on four-foot stone pillars. Impressive wide concrete steps led up to the front veranda and more modest wooden steps were near the kitchen door in the rear. Latticework and landscaping concealed the base. Wide verandas shaded the house on three sides on both floors. This was a great convenience since no windows had to be closed against frequent tropical rain showers.

The Corners, a tropical hideaway in Nassau, Bahamas

Built in 1917, it was rumored to have been constructed from shipwrecks. We believed it, as there were places in the house where it was nearly impossible to drive a nail into the wood. Piracy was an early Bahamian enterprise; then there was the salvaging of ships that had been lured ashore and these were superseded by rum-running during the Prohibition years in the states. Tax-free liquor was now the current bargain for visitors sturdy enough to lug the bottles home.

Our landlady, Mercedes, Lady Solomon, purchased The Corners from her nephew, Fane Solomon, who had grown up there with his two sisters, widowed father, Cyril Solomon, and spinster aunt, Minette Solomon. Dowdeswell Street was becoming increasingly commercial and Lady Solomon was afraid that he might sell to an unsuitable neighbor or even that an office building might be built next door to her. So to protect her home, Lady Solomon bought it herself. She spent summers in England and had a home on Harbour Island where she spent most of the winter months.

The first thing that was done to the house was that it was "tented" for a gas treatment to kill the ever-present termites. Then it was painted inside and out. The large front room across the front of the house was painted pink, as well as the dining room, while the back hall, pantry and kitchen were pale yellow. The pink living room would not have been my color of choice, but gradually we came to realize that it was appropriate and the pink was leavened by a great deal of white woodwork. There were plaster walls, but a wooden ceiling. In the upstairs, the wooden walls of two bedrooms and one bath were painted pale blue and two other bedrooms and two baths were painted yellow. One of those bedrooms and a bath opened from the back veranda and made a good guest room with its private entrance. It was Gordon's and he moved in with his brother, Philip, when guests were expected. Not as comfortable was the small sewing room at the front of the house where there was a sofa bed.

A local saying was "catch the breeze" and there were seventeen doors to the verandahs and the outside, twelve-foot-high ceilings, wide doorways as well as the verandas to dissipate the heat. The doorways were mainly French doors with shutters which could be bolted at night without cutting off the air. This proved to be very important when it was necessary to batten down during hurricane warnings. Other residents had to rely on solid plywood over windows. When we moved, we brought with us two portable air conditioners. But at the time we arrived on the island, there was a shortage of electricity and no permits for home air conditioning were being issued. By the time the ban was lifted, we realized that it would be impossible to close up the gaps for efficient cooling and also that the wiring system of an old wooden house would make it a risky venture.

Our great fortune in securing this beautiful old house was due to the fact that we were transferred to Nassau by U.S. Steel, who provided moving costs for everything except for our car. Many people who came to the Bahamas were there on two or three-year contracts and there were many more furnished houses available. An unfurnished house was a rarity and rather a drug on the market.

Company people urged us to purchase in the U.S. and bring in addition anything we might need or be planning to purchase in the next five years since prices there were high and the selection was limited. As there were no income or property taxes in the colony, this was made up by a hefty duty imposed on all imports. Nearly everything, including much of the food, had to be brought onto New Providence Island. Therefore, day-to-day living was very expensive. On the other hand, there were concessions made for many luxury items, so that fine china, watches, jewelry, woolens and liquor were bargains for the visiting tourists.

One of Lady Solomon's numerous nephews-in-law, Christopher Plummer, worked for a real estate firm and showed us the house and signed the contract for her ladyship while she was on holiday in England. He was happy to find an American family that wanted an unfurnished home. She was not too happy when she returned to find her next-door neighbors had three children, a dog and a pianola (player piano), as she complained to a friend. She fired that nephew, who was replaced as her agent by another charming nephew-in-law, Trevor Marshall, with a lovely British accent and voice like the Australian actor Cyril Ritchard.

This was a complicated move. Everything had to be inventoried and valued. One of the worst chores prior to moving was preparing that inventory. One list was needed for insurance purposes and it had to be a reasonable figure for replacement. Another list had to be presented for any duty payment in the Bahamas and it was more modest. An inspector came to the house questioning the value of the player piano and the typewriter, until he saw for himself that they were both very old.

A lot of shopping was involved, as company people advised us to buy a freezer and any other appliances we might need for the next five years. Lamps should be of wood or painted metal as the salt air would corrode brass. The car was to be sold after we left since it was needed up to the last day. Our Ben Avon house was advertised for sale in August. Exactly at the time it was put on the market a steel strike began which shut down Pittsburgh's economy. It was the longest strike in the history of the steel industry and it lasted until January. The agent with whom the listing was placed could do little until things returned to normal. We were paying heat bills and making mortgage payments on the Ben Avon house for nearly a year.

Our goods were put into Skyvans containers and trucked from Pittsburgh to Miami. From there everything was flown to Nassau. This was deemed cheaper than the packing against water damage that would be required for shipping by sea. Meanwhile, Dan was in Nassau already working at Navios, a U.S. Steel subsidiary. Any communication with him by mail was slow and by phone was expensive and very difficult to hear. It was like talking into the bottom of a well.

We knew we would arrive before our furniture, so we flew to Newark and spent several nights with our good college friends Jean and Dan Rothermel in Radburn, N.J. Then they put us on the ship headed to Nassau. The *S.S. Nassau* was half-empty. There had just been a hurricane so that many people had cancelled their trips. We were sailing in rough seas in the aftermath. Ropes were strung up as safety hand-holds throughout the ship. The dining table-tops were reversed so that the ledge around the table would keep dishes from sliding off. Fortunately, we had all taken Dramamine from the day we left Ben Avon and no one became seasick.

This was the first time I had ever been on a cruise ship. It was extraordinary. Every night they had a midnight buffet that was set up on the deck, which was as long as a city block. The deck was glass-enclosed so there was no fear of anyone going overboard. There was every imaginable thing on the buffet, including ice sculptures. I had my first-ever shrimp cocktail, and I marveled that my children were trying foods I'd only ever read or heard about growing up.

As it was an end-of-September trip, our three children were the only youngsters on board. The Italian crew watched over them as if they were their own. The ship was on its last trip of a two-year voyage before returning to Italy, where the men would rejoin their children and wives for a month and the ship would be laid up for that time. The deck chairs were wonderful. Terribly tired from the preceding months of harried packing, I sprawled on the padded chair and alternately slept and read.

There was still time to wait before our things would arrive and, during that time, we stayed at the Ft. Montagu Beach Hotel. It was on the shore and there was swimming on its beach and from its dock and also a swimming pool in the new hotel wing with underwater windows for viewing swimmers in the pool from the bar below.

Arrangements had to be made immediately for schooling as we were already well into the fall semester. This was complicated since the recommended private school, St. Andrew's, had very limited spots on their roster available at this time of the year. Our eldest, Gordon, was interviewed and admitted to Class Five.

Meanwhile, Philip was accepted at St. Francis Xaviers, the private Catholic mission school, and Amy Jane went to Mrs. Monroe's Infant School. The hotel packed school lunches for them and my job was to drive to three different locations around the island twice a day.

We, of course, needed a car for this commuting, and providence arrived in the form of a custom-made baby blue 1959 Ford Prefect, a British model. It had been won as a prize by someone on New Providence Island. But after being built and shipped from the UK, when it arrived, the prize winner

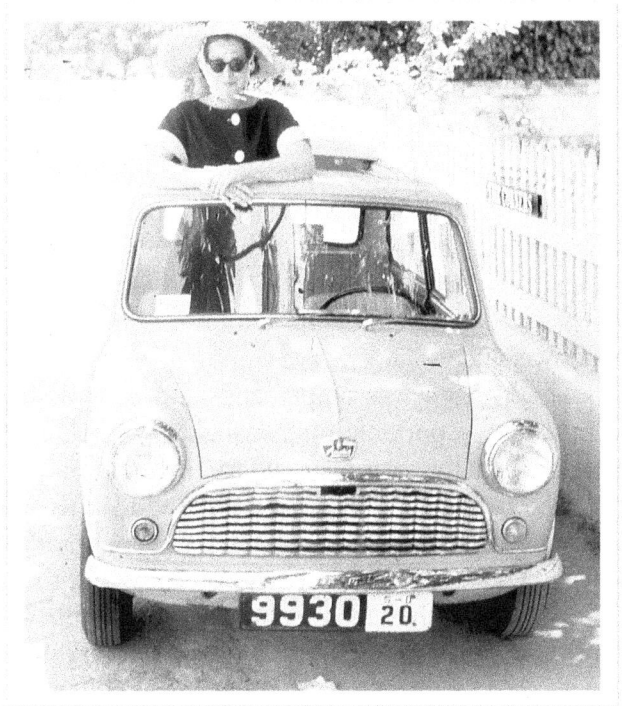

My sister posing in front of The Corners during a visit to see us in Nassau

decided to take the cash value instead. It was sold back to the dealership. So it was we purchased the smallest car we ever owned, perfect for tight island streets but maybe not so perfect for my six-foot, two-inch-tall husband.

Even a beautiful resort hotel with exotic grounds, tennis and swimming can soon become boring. We were anxious to leave for normal living. Our goods finally arrived and our movers turned out to be pick-up labor from the docks.

It was a hectic time, telling the men where things should go. They were also doing a lot of the unpacking. A plumber was on hand to install water lines to the washhouse and the bottled gas for the stove was delivered. Before the plumber left, he took me aside and pointed to one of the movers, telling me to keep my eye on him as he had a bad reputation.

Two large items wouldn't fit in the plane and were left in Miami to be delivered later by boat. One was the tall antique corner cupboard, considered not an essential furniture piece, and the refrigerator, without which we couldn't live in that climate. We had to return to the hotel and, after a few days, a temporary refrigerator was found for us.

All of our worldly goods were at the empty house and in view of the plumber's warning, Dan and Gordon stayed in the house overnight. They had an uneasy rest. It was an eerie experience hearing the creaking noises of a strange old house, the coconut branches brushing against the building with an occasional coconut falling on the roof and rolling off. The huge breadfruit leaves rustled as they fell down through the tall trees and the tree frogs made their own chorus. We kept things tightly secured for the first months, but the expected burglar didn't appear.

A cedar picnic table and benches were on the back veranda for lunch in winter. In the summer it was cooler inside. In time we added a coral pink wrought-iron glass-top table to the porch outside the dining room. Our large cherry dining room table suited the ample room and an antique walnut drop leaf table on the side was opened for breakfast and lunch. Our player piano fitted well in all the space there. The living room had bay windows on both ends and, below one, a padded window seat. We hid Christmas gifts there and it was only after we left the beloved house that the children learned the secret of the space under the window seats.

The kitchen was empty and held only a sink. We brought our own stove, refrigerator, a portable dishwasher and kitchen table. Off of the kitchen was a powder room that was reserved for the maid. Between the kitchen and dining room was a large pantry with a small sink and some built-in shelves. It also had a door into a closet under the stairs where canned goods could be stored and it was kept locked. The room held an upright freezer and the mangle.

Just down the steps from the back porch was our washhouse. It had solid doors and shutters that could be locked at night and housed the washer and dryer and had ample room to store bicycles at one end. A family of five could produce a lot of laundry in that hot climate.

We took good care of The Corners while we lived there. We had the gardener, who came two to three times a week to cut back the endless growing plants, paint the picket fence and the veranda floors. We had a maid, Edith, who came daily to help clean and cook for us. This was a service you were expected to have in the Bahamas. We put up Christmas lights along the veranda and became Bahamian by leaving them up permanently. We'd turn them on for parties. Thanks to some friends in the company, the children soon acquired a substantial wooden playhouse with shingle roof and shuttered door and window. It was ours for the reasonable cost of moving it to a shady spot in the back garden.

We had a wonderful house in Nassau and it lives vividly in memory's eye. It was torn down some years after we left. After Lady Solomon died and her home was destroyed in a fire, it too was leveled. The projected office development was never built and the jungle has now reclaimed the land. When I last visited in 2007 it was still a wild corner of downtown Nassau.

A special memory that I told myself I would always remember was a simple day in The Corners' garden. Near the back of the house between the kitchen and the washhouse was a side-gate into Hall's Lane that was always bolted shut and rarely used. A vine called queen's lace was climbing above the gate with the most beautiful violet-blue blossoms. The sky was a clear bright blue, the sun was warm and I felt a moment of pure bliss, happiness and gratitude for this wonderful time.

Breakfasting in the dappled light of The Corners back garden in 1963

Mercedes, Lady Solomon

It was important to be on good terms with our landlady, Lady Solomon. As she was known for being rather temperamental, we were careful not to become too involved. And we never expected to mingle socially with our landlady, but that all came along in time.

Mercedes, Lady Solomon was born in Nassau of British stock. She was a member of the Lofthouse family, one of the leading white families in the city. She married Sir Kenneth Solomon, a barrister and scion of another old white Bahamian family. They had no children, but had a bevy of nieces and nephews, so it seemed that everyone who was "anyone" was related to them. Her husband was active in Bay Street politics and eventually became the Speaker of the unicameral House of Assembly and President of the Legislative Council. At some point during this time, he received his knighthood. Sir Kenneth was the head of government during World War II when the Duke of Windsor, the abdicated former

King Edward VII, was essentially exiled to serve as the Governor of the Bahamas with his wife, the American divorcée, Wallis Simpson.

Lady Solomon was not only the wife of the Speaker, but, as such, was the leader of local high society. She was chairman of the British Red Cross, founder of the Nassau Garden Club, officer of the Daughters of the British Empire and a host of other activities. When the Windsors arrived in Nassau, they had little experience in hands-on management of community affairs or local government. Thus, the Solomons became their mentors in many ways. The home where Kenneth and Lady Solomon lived was liberally decorated with silver-framed autographed pictures of the Duke and his American duchess.

Our house, The Corners, had been built by Sir Kenneth's brother, Cyril Solomon, and was next door to the home now occupied by Lady Solomon, called The Ark. The Solomon family carried out their biblical surname by giving their homes vaguely religious names, such as The Temple and The Ark.

The Ark was an imposing two-story white wooden West Indies colonial structure with verandas on all sides. It sat fairly close to Dowdeswell Street and the property was surrounded on all sides by a high stone wall, pierced by wooden gates opening into the garage from the front. Inside, it was rather grand with a ballroom on the second floor. The land extended through the block to Shirley Street and on the back corner was a cottage occupied by a young attorney, Geoffrey Johnston, and his wife, who was a niece of Lady Solomon. We learned our house was called The Corners because it abutted Hall's Lane and ran through to a corner of Shirley Street on the next block.

We didn't expect to socialize with Lady Solomon, but when she first returned to the island in October, she did come to call and stayed for tea. Lady Solomon wanted to inspect our family and warn us that the plywood panels in the storeroom off of the upstairs veranda must be kept flat to prevent warping. They were the protective covers to be put over the bay windows of the living room in case of a hurricane. That possibility had never entered the minds of we native Western Pennsylvanians, who had never seen hurricanes except in the form of a dose of heavy rainfall leftover from a storm. The many French doors had screens and shutters, which we thought was all we might need before her warning.

After the departure of the Windsors following the war and the death of her husband, Lady Solomon's position as the social leader of Nassau went somewhat into decline. She then spent the long summers in London, England where she had a circle of friends, and the winters in her house on Harbour Island in the Bahamas.

On the Out Islands, her title gave her prestige among seasonal foreign residents. Her spacious house, The Ark, was her residence for only a few weeks in the spring and fall. She had lost touch with many friends of her youth who resented her autocratic ways. She liked to drink and had alienated her old friends she had grown up with by snubbing or criticizing them, and making cutting remarks when "in her cups." In many ways she became a lonely woman.

She had a house in Harbor Island where she could maintain her status as the social leader and she was happier there in the winter season. As our landlady and next-door neighbor, we treated her with care and a minimum of involvement.

However, she did love to go out to see and be seen by local society. I sometimes took her as my guest to the monthly luncheons of the American Women's Club. These luncheons were an innovation in Nassau, where the men usually came home from work for lunch, so dinner was late in the evening. This made most women's affairs and benefits into an afternoon tea, in the British tradition. There Lady Solomon could socialize with many people and she enjoyed her noontime cocktails. Her Ladyship reciprocated by taking us to the exclusive Lyford Cay Club several times.

By 1973 we were living in Minnesota. This was not considered home as far as our now mostly grown-up children were concerned, so we decided to celebrate Christmas with a return visit to Nassau, where there were many friends and we could "step back in time."

We went to our old church, St. Andrew's Kirk, and were invited for Christmas dinner by the Bartletts at Brandy Hill. Our friends Liz and Derek Parrish had a big Boxing Day party on the terrace of their West Bay Street apartment overlooking the harbor, where the champagne flowed freely and a merry time was had by all. There was a New Year's Eve gathering at Jean and John Chaplins at Camperdown Heights where guests from the kirk choir and the Nassau Operatic Society performed. And, of course, there were the annual Junkanoo parades on Boxing Day and New Year's mornings.

Lady Solomon invited us to The Ark for a New Year's Eve supper and then to accompany her to the celebrations at the Royal Nassau Sailing Club. She was a heavy woman and walked with a cane. We went to the club carrying her shawl and cushion and were seated at a table in a small room just outside the restrooms. There were few, if any, chairs or tables in the main room of the club, since this was a dance and cocktail affair with everyone moving about, which she was not able to do. Many people came in to greet her, or found her ensconced with her party as they passed on their way to the restrooms.

We had been away from Nassau for eight years. I am sure that there were many who were surprised to see us there. They must have wondered how we happened to be Lady Solomon's guests. We wondered a bit ourselves, but had had a delightful time listening to her at supper. We also learned some things that we hadn't known about the children's activities back in the day, such as when they had climbed over the wall from our garden into hers. They had hidden behind the huge shrubbery during some of her large evening garden parties so they could watch the goings on.

Shortly after midnight, like Cinderella, her ladyship was ready to leave the sailing club party. We took her back to The Ark where her maid was waiting for her. There was a small outside elevator that went from the ground to the first and second floors and we tucked her into the seat inside of it, together with her belongings. Then we waved goodbye as she ascended into The Ark. That was the last time that we saw Lady Solomon. She died five years later at the age of eighty-five.

Miss Minette Solomon

Miss Minette Solomon, Lady Solomon's sister-in-law, was our lovely neighbor across from The Corners, our Dowdeswell Street home in Nassau. She had lived in The Corners before us, managing the household for her brother, Cyril, after his wife had died. There were twin girls and a son, Fane. After the girls were married and her brother died, Miss Minette and nephew, Fane, were alone in the big house. Fane was a confirmed bachelor. He built a modern duplex across the street with an apartment for himself and another upstairs for Miss Minette. Their gardener, King, stayed in Fane's employ with much less to do since the grounds of the new place were small. He took care of two large guard dogs and kept the cars polished. The dogs were meant to be fierce, but the children soon made friends with King and the dogs as they sat outside much of the time. On an island where almost all the cars were second-hand, Miss Minette had a real antique. It was a black open-air ancient car that she drove carefully as far as her small business off Bay Street.

Miss Minette's nephew, Garth Duncombe, owned the Ironmongery on Bay Street. He had a little room off the side alley that he gave to Miss Minette, where she operated an antique shop during the tourist season. As a maiden lady of modest means, she partially financed her visits in England by purchasing antiques, which she sold in that tiny shop behind her nephew's Bay Street store. Her wares were china, glassware and decorative ornaments that she bought during her summer stays in England and shipped back to Nassau in what the trade refers to as "smalls." Her shop was open in the mornings at her convenience. She would return home for a late lunch, which was the end of her working day. We talked about antiques and I visited her at the shop several times. She never suggested that I purchase anything because she admitted that she was charging "tourist prices."

When I visited Miss Minette in the evenings, I would knock at the gate below and she would call down asking, "Who's there?" When I answered, I would be invited up to the broad veranda that faced the Eastern Parade. Her flat was simply furnished. In the kitchen, a tall wooden food safe stood on legs that rested in cups of oil to prevent ants from climbing up to the safe. There were no screens on her windows but she did sleep under a mosquito netting at night. She explained when she welcomed me, that if it was Teddy (Lady Solomon's nickname) come to visit, she would say that she was just getting ready for bed. No refreshments were ever offered or expected. We just enjoyed each other's company.

Lady Solomon often invited Minette to accompany her to England on her extended stays as a companion, offering to pay all the expenses. Although Minette had very limited funds, that was a sacrifice that she was unwilling to make. She had acquaintances in England and preferred an inexpensive boarding house to luxurious travel with her sister-in-law who lived at the Dorchester Hotel on Hyde Park.

Miss Minette talked about former days in Nassau and could answer many of my garden questions. She took me to visit her sister Vera Solomon Patterson's garden one afternoon. We were there for tea with several other older ladies. They were all old elite white Bahamians, and, I had been told, as an American newcomer, these were people you might meet, but you would never see the inside of their homes. But my experience was that when there were common interests, where you were from did not matter.

International Garden Club

Moving to the Bahamas opened a whole new world of gardening to me. The garden in the backyard at The Corners had established plantings of many exotic flowers. I started teaching myself about tropical plants. Bougainvillea climbed up to the back of the second story with its purple and scarlet blossoms, and other flowering trees bloomed at the rear of the property. At night there was the scent of the night blooming jasmine, the deafening chorus of tree frogs and the rustle of palm branches sometimes brushing the roof.

We were informed when we came to Nassau that it would be easy to get to know our fellow American expats within the small population on the island. A sizeable number of British colonials were working there on contracts, as well, and we would meet them at social affairs. The third group was white Bahamians, who were born there and were part of the old guard. We were told we would rarely interact with them. The last was the majority black Bahamian society, some of whom were employed by the white Bahamians.

At the time, New Providence Island had few gardening clubs. There was the Nassau Garden Club, founded by Lady Solomon, which was very exclusive. You essentially needed to be born into that elite white Bahamian society to attain any sort of membership. Then there was the Carver Garden Club (named for the famous African-American horticulturist George Washington Carver) that the black Bahamian society ladies joined. The Bahamas remained quietly segregated.

Friendships were quickly formed with other expats from international places like the Netherlands, England, Canada and the U.S. Those of us who shared an interest in gardening decided to form our own gardening group, one designed for expats like ourselves. So, the International Garden Club was born. As its founder, I was nominated to be the first president.

The International Garden Club's largest event of the year was our annual flower show, which was held in the Emerald Beach Hotel and even promoted across the U.S. in newspapers as a tourist attraction. We held tours of area gardens and invited visiting speakers such as Dorothy Elsmith, an herb gardener who visited from Massachusetts. She gave a program on herbs and introduced me to the Herb Society of America, of which she was a member. I had never heard of the Society and upon meeting her after her speech, she invited me to join and promised to send me an application. That never happened since, at the time, membership was restricted to U.S. residents. But years later when I returned to the States, I joined the Herb Society and served a term as national president.

Today the International Garden Club still exists in Nassau, and their flower show continues to impress Bahamians and tourists alike.

Orchid Hunting in the Bahamas

Like orchids, rare and hard to find, so too, was befriending the old guard of white Bahamian society. It is hard to know why we were accepted. When we had moved to the Bahamas, we had been informed that we were not likely to associate with the old Bahamian families. We might meet them but we were unlikely to be invited into their homes, let alone go on excursions with them. Perhaps it was because we moved into one of the older colonial residences and shared the aura of the original Bahamian families. Maybe our cordial relationship with our landlady Lady Solomon and her family paved the way.

For whatever reason, we were able to cultivate friendships, not only within the expat community, but among both white and black society in Nassau.

Vera Solomon Patterson was a Bay Street "boy" in that, as a widow, she owned a shop on Bay Street that specialized in madras Indian cottons. Her only son, Jack, helped in the shop, but his real interest was nature and the ecology of the Bahamas. He was a somewhat reclusive young man. When Vera's sister Minette found that I was interested in gardening in this whole new tropical world, she arranged to take me to tea at Vera's house to see her gardens. There were two other Bahamian ladies there. They joined in telling me how much better life was in the "good old days."

Helen Higgs was the leading garden lady. She wrote a weekly garden column for the *Nassau Guardian* and sketched and illustrated several booklets on the fruits and flora and the bush medicine of the Bahamas. She was the person who organized the orchid hunting trip. Helen invited me to go with her and another friend to search for orchids in the bush west of Nassau. I was honored to be included. Helen was her proper name, but she was known as Nellie to everyone for her warmth and enthusiasm. She went to great lengths to identify native plant material, which she painted in charming watercolors. She served as a judge for flower shows and horticultural exhibits in addition to her own gardening.

Our guide was Jack Patterson and we had a black Bahamian with a large machete employed to clear a path for us to get through the thickets of undergrowth. Walking was difficult over coral rocks that were concealed in greenery. Jack knew where to go, and as a result, we finally found tiny yellow and orange orchids growing on the low branches of trees.

Nellie also edited a Bahamian cookbook "by the ladies of Nassau," which was popular with tourists. She collected recipes for turtle pie, fruit cake, guava pudding, conch chowder, coconut puddings, sea grape jelly, banana bread, hominy griddle cakes, Bahamian Johnny cake, crawfish salad, papaya cocktail, sapodilla pancake, sesame seed candy, fried achee or ackee, and stuffed breadfruit. There were repeated printings of this book with changes made along the way. Instructions for the recipes were printed just as they were collected from the donor, who was listed by name and location. Directions were often vague and varied widely. A few used standard measurements, but others used pounds, knobs, pinches and tea cups.

The recipes were untested. Nellie would never have had time for that. She published a recipe by her married sister living in Lake Forest, Ill. in the book. Her sister had a wealthy husband and did no cooking. Nellie decided to try the gelatin salad listed under her name. It refused to jell, even after being put out in the cold. Anyone with cooking experience would realize that the liquid amounts were incorrect for the amount of gelatin.

When Nellie asked me for a recipe to be included, it marked my acceptance in the community. She regarded the ladies of the cookbook as a kind of social register. Serving with Nellie later as a judge at a flower show, I found that she leaned toward the generous and abundant arrangements, rather than artistic displays. She was a multi-talented woman and a tireless promoter of the Bahamas.

The beautiful tiny orchids that we gathered that day returned to town and were inserted in the branches of an avocado tree in the back garden. They bloomed there for years without needing any tending. They felt at home there and we felt at home there, too.

A Tropical Night

Living in Nassau, we found ourselves in a diverse society where the majority of the population was black. We had the opportunity to meet and befriend some members of this Bahamian community through our church, St. Andrew's Kirk, and other local activities we participated in.

The Carver Garden Club was a group of some twenty black Bahamian ladies. One of the big events of the Club's year was a Christmas tour of their homes and a contest. There were prizes awarded for the best door décor, the nicest Christmas tree, the most attractive centerpiece, the best overall outdoor lighting and the finest interior display. Three judges

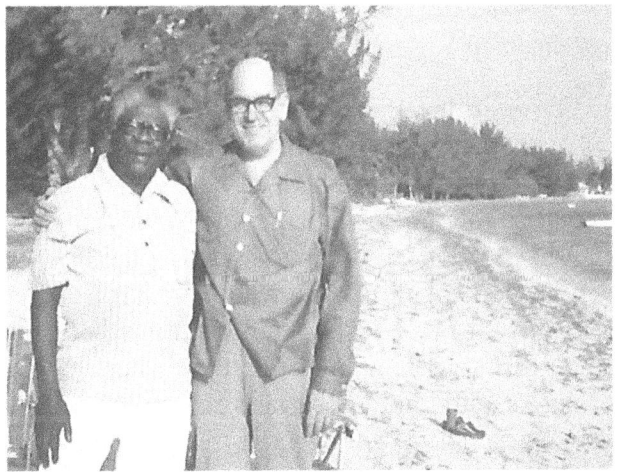

Doc Eneas and Dan Core during a reunion trip to Nassau

preceded the tour guests and the climax of the evening was a supper party on the patio of one of the members.

We were invited to this special evening by our dear friends the Eneases. Dr. Cleveland W. Eneas, Sr., a prominent dentist and Bahamian senator, was known as "Doc" to everyone on the island. Dan taught Sunday school class with him at St. Andrew's Kirk and I sang in the choir with his wife, Muriel, who was the former headmistress of St. Anne's School. I was active in the International Garden Club and Muriel, or Fini, as she was called, was a member of the Carver Garden Club. We had many common intellectual interests and enjoyed spending time together. Our friendship lasted long after we moved away from the Bahamas.

That December evening, Dan and I were the only white guests. Doc did the driving for all of us and we progressed from home to home on Bahamian time – slowly. The houses were very nicely decorated and ranged from simple cottages to one large estate. All of the hosts were warm and welcoming to us, even though we were strangers. All they needed to know was that we were friends of the Eneases. We felt honored to be included.

The weather had turned unusually wet and windy for Nassau. The social hour at the end of the tour had to be moved from out of doors to a barren church hall at the last moment. The hostess was a talented local decorator and she quickly transformed the hall with artifacts from her shop and handsome candle stands. White sheets covered two bleachers for the buffet, lit by a pair of handsome candelabra on top. Since it was the Friday night before Christmas, one side was for fish dishes. Because the tour had moved so slowly, everyone needing time to visit the twelve houses, it was well after midnight when we gathered for the feast. The Catholics in our party could then eat what they pleased.

We got home at two o'clock in the morning. As I was undressing for bed I happened to glance in the mirror. I thought how pale I looked and realized how much at home I had been made to feel on that dark, tropical night.

Indispensable Edith

Living in the Bahamas was like stepping into another world – the waning days of the British colonial system. The homes were large and sprawling and it was de rigueur to have a staff of both a maid and a gardener for your home. This was quite a foreign concept for our American family.

A succession of maids assigned by an agency had preceded Edith. The last one was a tall, silent woman who wore her hair in two pigtails and always had on a white hat. She had her own uniform from her former job in a resort and informed us that she might be going back there when the high season started. One Monday morning, she did not appear and several hours later Edith Rolle walked into our lives.

Edith started each day doing the breakfast dishes, arriving after Dan had gone to work and I had gotten the children off to school, which they walked to every day. The powder room off of the kitchen was considered her territory, and she used it for changing into her uniforms. The family only used the powder room in case of an urgent need, for there were three other bathrooms upstairs.

I did the laundry with the washing machine in the wash house and she hung the clothes outside to dry. In a warm climate, there is a lot of laundry. I used the Ironrite mangle in the pantry to iron sheets, pillowcases, and Dan's shirts. The mangle, or wringer was a large, mechanical piece of laundry equipment consisting of two rollers in a sturdy metal frame. The boys' school shirts and Amy Jane's blouses were too small to fit the machine so Edith did the hand ironing. No clothing was ever thrown away by us, even after it was outgrown or damaged. Items were placed on the low chest in the powder room and disappeared, to be repurposed by Edith.

She came in every day of the week except Sunday, with a half-day on Fridays when the shops closed early on East Bay Street that she made up on Saturdays. When she did

The children in their spring British school uniforms

babysit for us, the extra time was paid or she was given time off. She never stayed overnight because although she had no children at home, she was responsible for her sister's young niece.

Edith was from a large black Bahamian family that all lived close together on the east end of the island, in something of a family compound called Elizabeth Estates. Her family, the Greenes, were originally from Andros, and her husband's family, the Rolles, hailed from the Exumas, and even had a town named after them. But we knew nothing of her spouse until one day she asked for a day off so that she could buy a wreath and attend her ex-husband's funeral. He had tragically died in a cabin fire in a drunken state after knocking over a kerosene lamp. Her aged mother-in-law could not attend the funeral so Edith went to call on her afterward.

She had definite ideas as to what was proper in Bahamian society and never rode in the passenger seat of the car beside me, even though I asked her to. I took her to the pier on East Bay Street when buying seafood, as her skill was essential in choosing the best fish and in bargaining for the best price. Returning with the newspaper-wrapped fish to the kitchen, Edith would filet the fish for our dinner. Fish liver was small but she considered it a real delicacy. Edith kept the head to make a fish stock for herself and the cheek pockets were another delicacy she enjoyed.

Burrows, the gardener, came two days a week. Edith did not like or trust him, but sometimes I needed him to come inside with a ladder to inject wood poison in the flying termite holes that appeared in the wooden ceilings, or little mounds on the wooden floors. Gardeners were and still are a necessity in the Bahamas, where plants seem to sprout up overnight and grow at Jack-and-the-Beanstalk speeds.

Parting with Edith was sad when we were transferred back to the Pittsburgh area. Dan paid her a generous final wage and she gave me the parting gift of a large, beautifully decorated straw basket, which I have kept all of these years.

We found her a job with a couple who had a small deaf girl. The father was a British executive with the Bahamas Electric Company, and it should have been easier for her than dealing with our three growing children. Later, while on a return visit to Nassau, we discovered by chance that Edith was working as a chambermaid in the hotel where we were staying. We were happy to see her but shocked to hear that the little girl had taken out her frustrations on the staff, and the job we had referred Edith for had gone so poorly. Years later I was pleased to hear she'd lived a long life and had many grandchildren and great-grandchildren to be loved and remembered by, just as she was fondly remembered by us.

Holidays in a British Colony

Christmas in Nassau, Bahamas was low-key. There were no Santas on the streets and decorations were minimal. The company employees of Navios had a Christmas Eve party at six o'clock for all their children with simple food and a live Santa who gave out one gift that the parents smuggled in to him. The children went home happy and ready for bed.

We were happy to be able to extend the Christmas holiday on December 26 by the traditional British Boxing Day, the time when, in the past, gifts were given to servants. It was now a day to give gifts to friends and have daytime parties. Our English friends, Liz and Derek Parrish, included all of us on Boxing Day from the beginning of our stay and a final party on our Christmas holiday visit in 1973.

Navios Corporation president Bill Yost was a former naval commander who ran a tight ship, both at the office and in his social life. There was ample help at that beautiful home. He and his wife, Maria, had elegant New Year's Eve dinner parties there. Company executives and wives were guests as well as some of the Yost's personal friends. Dress was formal and guests were expected to arrive promptly. Drinks were served in the large living room and tables were set up for dining in a large sheltered patio garden. It was all most decorous and followed a precise pattern each year. We could be certain that the party would end exactly after midnight. Bill would make a champagne toast and toss his glass in the fireplace. His wife had lost several valuable glasses this way and so she tried to make certain he was handed a cheap glass for his toast. Finally, we would sing Auld Lang Syne and depart.

We appreciated this regimen because it meant that we could go on to later more informal celebrations or even stay up for the Junkanoo parade on Bay Street which started at 2 a.m. and lasted until dawn. We had the children with us for Junkanoo and sometimes ended with early breakfast at the Fort Montagu Hotel and then went home to bed.

In January, there were two Scottish events. The St. Andrew's Society, with membership limited to men, had an annual dinner. Burn's Night was celebrated by the Nassau Burns Society with a dinner dance at the Nassau Beach Resort Hotel at Emerald Beach. Much was made of the featured dish, haggis. Officers of the society were photographed meeting the B.O.A.C. plane that brought the imported haggis from Scotland. The presentation of the haggis was the main dinner feature.

With bagpipe accompaniment, it was brought to the head table with great ceremony, where a dagger was plunged into the sheepskin coating and a toast made to the haggis. (Poor Robbie Burns would have turned in his grave to know of the extravagant and costly proceedings in his honor.) A Scottish friend confided to us that, in his opinion, the farther a Scotsman got from home, the stronger his feelings were for the "auld country" and its celebrations.

Dan and I attending Burn's Night.

The Reverend James MacIan Jack was the bachelor minister of St. Andrew's Kirk of the (Presbyterian) Church of Scotland. He was one of the members of our table. Attire for the men was formal wear or kilts. When St. Bernard's waltz was announced, Mr. Jack invited me to be his partner. The couple dance was easy to learn and everyone on the floor followed the set pattern, which was followed by all the women twirling at the same time. Dan watching the dance said it was one of the loveliest dances to watch and, given another opportunity, he would like to do it himself.

There was no Halloween. On November 5 there was a celebration of Guy Fawke's Day. He had tried to blow up Parliament in the 17th century. Dummies were made of old clothing stuffed with straw and these "guys" were burned together with fireworks at the Royal Nassau Sailing Club party. The substitute for Thanksgiving in the Bahamas was "Harvest Sunday" at the kirk where the altar was decorated with all the foods of the season, which were afterward given away.

Naturally, there were no Fourth of July celebrations. The American Men's Club organized a beach picnic that day and had the Bahamas Police Band seated under the casuarina trees providing music for the occasion. It was delightful to swim to live music nearby.

A Tree Grows in Nassau

The Bahamian bushland was covered with pine trees. They were tall and spindly with most of the growth at the top. They were on Crown Lands but could be harvested by securing a permit from the Crown Lands office for three shillings a tree.

Some Nassau residents bought Christmas trees shipped in from Canada. They had the wonderful pine scent that is associated with Christmas. They soon shed needles due to the length of their journey and the sub-tropical climate and were of necessity quite expensive.

Seeing all the native pines, I wanted to continue our family tradition of going out to the country to select and cut down our own tree, even though this was not the usual snowy setting. We walked to the Crown Lands Office just two blocks away and bought permits for three trees so that the best of the lot would be the living room tree and the others could be cut up for swags. Although there was an abundance of green foliage all around, it was difficult to imagine decorations without the familiar evergreens.

Children are seldom interested in tradition and went with us reluctantly on this outing. They would have preferred spending the afternoon at the country club beach and having tea on the patio with fresh coconut cake. We were equipped with a hatchet and saw and wore sturdy shoes for, though the terrain was carpeted with low ground cover, it actually concealed large coral rock. There are no poisonous snakes in the Bahamas. At that time, we were blissfully ignorant of the danger from poison oak, a small tree more potent than poison ivy. Luckily, we didn't encounter that, since we wouldn't have recognized it.

It was difficult to see the best treetops from below as they were all sparsely branched. Eventually, we found three trees, cut them at ground level and then made a second cut near the top at what we estimated was living room height and bore home our treasures. At the house, we chose the best of the scrawny lot for the bay window and then Dan drilled holes in that tree and inserted extra branches from the other trees. For decorations around the house, the extra-long needles were given a haircut to look more like Scotch pine. In the end, it was not a bad looking tree holding our usual Christmas decorations. The bay window was surrounded by a cushioned window seat and the children never found out that the seats could be opened and that is where Christmas gifts could safely be hidden. They searched closets and the store room in vain for the six years that we lived there.

In time, with the help of my garden club friends, I discovered how best to use the native foliage for decoration. The sapodilla tree in the rear garden had rosette clusters of leaves with the leathery texture of rhododendron. Preparing to use these tips for decorating the table, I went out into the garden and sprayed them with gold paint, leaving them on the tree until they were needed. Dan was puzzled to see the tree's new décor when he passed by on his way home from work.

The Bahamians loved brightly-colored Christmas lights and put them on their houses where they were left in place all year. That seemed odd at first, but eventually, we did the same on our home. They were concealed along the overhang along the veranda. When we had a party at any time of the year, we would turn them on as a welcome.

Parenting is a long learning process. We learned that it is fruitless to stay up Christmas Eve putting toys together by matching slot A to slot B, etc. The children enjoyed taking part in the assembling. But as far as a Christmas tree, the next year we broke down and bought a tree that didn't have to be reassembled.

The Office Christmas Party

The best office Christmas party was held on Christmas Eve at six o'clock in the evening by the Navios Corporation. The sun goes down promptly all year in that part of the globe. This was a family party and the focus was on the children. All of the twenty-five American employees were far from home (and probably snow) and most of them had small children. In this small British colony, there were no department stores, few Christmas decorations and definitely no live Santas interviewing the little ones.

The office Christmas party was the nicest event of the year. The company had a red velvet Santa Claus costume, complete with white beard. His bag was a large white sheet to contain all the gifts that he had ready to pass out. Parents smuggled in one of their children's gifts, wrapped and clearly marked, for Santa to present to them. It really was a splendid costume that was passed around from year to year to each different "Santa."

First the children had a supper of peanut butter and jelly sandwiches and orange squash before Santa appeared on the scene. The parents stayed in the background with drinks and a snack. The excitement of that many children was wonderful with the opening of each special gift. Santa told them all to go home to bed and get to sleep so that he could visit them Christmas morning. The result was that the children were fed, ready to go to bed and some of the tension of Christmas Eve was gone. Parents appreciated that.

Some years the office Christmas party was hosted by a family that had a spacious house and garden and some years it was held at a club. The Nassau Harbour Club was the setting for our party one year, when it was normally empty at that time. Children were running around the club. At the bar was a lone yachtsman, drowning his sorrows and trying to phone stateside. He was heard complaining loudly, "I am tied up here in Nassau and in this bar with a lot of little kids running around. I don't know what's going on!" That was the year that Dan Core was the Santa. When the party ended, he decided to make some calls in his elegant outfit. He went to the homes of two English teacher families with young children. They were truly overwhelmed to meet "Father Christmas!"

Transfer orders had come from corporate headquarters and, on our last Christmas in Nassau, we hosted the office party at our spacious house. With large gardens and a wide veranda around most of the house, there was ample running room. There were the Christmas lights tucked under the top edge of the veranda. There was a Jewish Santa that year and the only unhappy child was his own little girl, who was afraid of the "Santa" and was trying to find her daddy. Would that all office Christmas parties could be as happy occasions as those parties with the children on Christmas Eve.

New Year's Day Open House

Formal printed invitations were mailed for the morning open house of the Howell-Griffiths. Stephen was assistant headmaster of St. Andrew's school and his wife was the principal of the Infant School there. They lived on the second floor of the school itself with a wide-tiled veranda at the side of their rather basic quarters. Even in cramped quarters, they lived in refinement and were famous for their annual New Year's morning parties. Refreshments were simple, a welcome change from the rich food of the holidays. A hearty Scotch broth was served with French bread and cheeses, scones and tea or coffee was served outside as people came and went.

The Howell-Griffiths were colonial refugees in a sense, for they had previously been in Egypt. Stephen had been headmaster of a British school in Egypt when he married Pearl, a fellow Scottish teacher there. They had a daughter and then a son and were comfortably settled in Cairo. They stored antique family furniture in England and loved furnishings more suitable to the hot dry climate. Suddenly, the political scene changed and the British were ousted from the country. Stephen and the family were placed under house arrest and the school was closed. Finally, they were allowed to leave, but given just twenty-four hours' notice and left with little except the clothes on their backs and one suitcase per person. Back in England, their years of teaching experience counted for little and they were relegated to the status of expats. They did have family there and moved into a modest neighborhood. It was not welcoming to newcomers and they found friendship with an American family nearby. They looked for employment outside of the British school system and that is how they came to teach in Nassau.

My first glimpse of Mrs. Pearl Howell-Griffith was as a member of an audience at a concert in the kirk hall. She was wearing a royal blue velvet dress and her young daughter with her was wearing a matching dress. It was rather elaborate attire for the tropics, more in keeping with what one would find for concert-going in England. The family kept up their dignified British way of life in greatly reduced circumstances.

We got to know them well and kept in touch by visiting them when they returned to England. They moved to Budleigh-Salterton. It was a rather small village on the English coast and noted for its large number of expats who settled there, often bringing their servants with them. Stephen had relatives who lived there. As a retirement hobby, he took up pottery-making with a small kiln. He found a ready market for the miniature mugs, pitchers and other tiny objects in the seaside holiday stores. He gave me an assortment and it was easy to carry them home since they were so small. They had a spacious house and had reclaimed their stored furniture and a large collection of blue and white plates that adorned the wall.

After Stephen died, Pearl made a mother-in-law apartment for herself and turned over the rest of the house to son David and his wife. Daughter Margaret had earlier married a farmer at a ceremony at London's prestigious St. Margaret's Church beside Westminster Abbey. It was one of her mother's proudest moments. The family often had holidays at a rustic country place that Pearl owned in Southerland. We had annual Christmas greetings until Pearl passed on. A very proper British family.

The Tomlinsons

The British colony of the Bahama Islands in the sub-tropic Caribbean Sea had many attractions. The prevailing winds made it warmer in winter than Florida and conversely, cooler in the summer. It was a place of sunny skies, crystal clear waters and uncrowded white sandy beaches centered around the quaint capitol of Nassau on New Providence Island.

The Bahamas had the British legal system and before its independence was headed by a governor and officials appointed by the Colonial Office in Great Britain. There were three ancient forts on New Providence that were never needed for protection and now served as tourist attractions.

Nassau attracted many wealthy residents because it had no income tax. The government was financed by a sizeable duty imposed on all imports. The luxuries imported for the tourists were bargain prices, liquor, woolen, fine china, jewelry and watches. Since there was little agriculture and no industry, almost all necessities had to be imported. Rum was cheaper than milk.

Many off-shore companies used the Bahamas as a tax shelter. A majority of these "suitcase companies" were incorporated in Nassau and their names were posted outside Bay Street law offices. Shipping companies also took advantage of lower fees to register ships in the Bahamas. A number of companies actually had offices and operated in Nassau, such as Outboard Marine Corporation and the Navios Corporation.

Sir Oliver Simmonds was an early designer and manufacturer of airplane parts. He was also a member of British Parliament from 1931 to 1945. His aircraft companies were very important in WWII. In 1945, Sir Oliver sold his British interests and moved to the Bahamas. There he started a construction company and developed Balmoral Beach Club and was a leader in the hotel industry. As an inventor and engineer he built a large home called High Tor on Prospect Ridge overlooking the golf course of the Bahamas Country Club and the sea. It had 18-foot gracious high ceiling rooms, imported English oak door panels, an 18th-century carved wooden fireplace surround and imported furnishings. He designed a floating spiral staircase in the entry hall and enormous windows that slid down to disappear completely. He lived in High Tor until 1963 and then lived in Lyford Cay, a newly developed gated community at the Western end of New Providence until 1977. He died ten years later, aged eighty-seven, in Guernsey, Channel Islands, another British tax haven.

A dinner invitation in 1963 to Bank House, the residence of John Adams, the head of the Royal Bank of Canada, came as a surprise. I had only seen him at St. Andrew's School functions and knew his somewhat younger wife as a fellow garden club member. It was even more surprising to find only one other couple present. That is how we met Joe and Elodie Tomlinson. They were an attractive Canadian couple and apparently important customers of the bank (where we had a miniscule account).

The Tomlinsons were about to move from Florida to Nassau. No mention was made as to where they were moving during the dinner. Many people who came to Nassau were employed on contracts of two to five years and therefore rented. Dan had been transferred to a U.S. Steel subsidiary and there were no similar contracts for that.

The dinner table discussion was mainly about moving questions and we were able to make some useful suggestions. There were two questions that were quite beyond our experience. The Tomlinsons asked about moving their orchid collection and their Rolls Royce. We realized that the reason for our invitation was Dan's legal background and our own recent move from the States. We had no idea that the Tomlinsons had bought High Tor.

Some months later, we met again at St. Andrew's Kirk and saw them at St. Andrew's School, where they also had their children enrolled. Elodie was warm and unassuming. I was invited to see their new home. There was nothing boastful about the tour. In fact, she was pleased to point out the furnishings that Sir Oliver had left for them and the fact that her decorator had saved them the expense of replacing the dark embossed wallpaper in the entry by painting it a creamy white that preserved the brocade look. It was rumored that there were thirty-eight rooms. When I asked how many rooms there were, she seemed surprised and said that she didn't know. The beautiful spiral staircase led to spacious living quarters where there was a large lounge done up in shades of white. She was like any woman who was delighted with her new house.

On another day, three or four women were guests for tea at High Tor. A butler served us on the shaded terrace overlooking the grounds. Elodie had made some of the tea sandwiches herself. She explained that these sandwiches were a family favorite. They were peanut butter and bananas. That seemed a far cry from our exotic setting.

The Rolls Royce was indeed moved to the Bahamas and was driven by Joe or Elodie, not by a chauffeur. In fact, she gave me a lift one day from the grocery store. It was my one and only ride in a Rolls. Long after this I learned that the Tomlinsons had shipping interests in Canada as well as shareholders in MGM Studios in Hollywood. They also had a horse that they raced in Canada and the United States. It was sold or left behind when they came to live in the Bahamas. Meeting the Tomlinsons was not an experience that we would not have had in Pittsburgh.

Entertaining Times

Pleasant memories of entertaining times drift through the mind but names and faces have faded over the years. Unfortunately, no diary was kept to record these halcyon days in the Bahamas.

Since Navios was an off-shore subsidiary of U.S. Steel International and located in Nassau, it was a favorite place for the Board of Directors to hold their annual meetings. In the Bahamas, Americans were not allowed to practice law, and so Dan's official title was Secretary of the Corporation. He prepared the meetings for the Board, and funnily enough, was also one of the original directors for Navios. Years earlier, while working at the U.S. Steel headquarters in Pittsburgh, Dan was called into his boss's office, had papers thrust at him, and was told to sign them. When he asked what this was for, they said U.S. Steel was creating a new shipping company. Dan remained a director on paper for six months until an actual Board of Directors could be formed in New York City, the headquarters for U.S. Steel International. When the Board came to the Bahamas for their meetings, they were often accompanied by their wives and their golf clubs. The meetings were largely pro forma in the Navios Corp. office and then the business visit could be extended to savor resort life.

When a small group came in on a corporate plane, the duty of entertaining them was divided up between the officers of Navios. It was a treat all around for us since the dinners at hotels like the Nassau Beach, the Emerald Beach and the British Colonial would be charged to the company. Life in a tropical resort city was expensive and we never dined at those places ourselves. We didn't want our guests to think that we lived in resort style, so we would invite them for drinks at our home before going on to dinner. They would meet the children and it made our evening more personal.

For the most part at home, we kept to American meal hours. Often there were dinner guests who were new company arrivals or men who were spending two or three weeks on special jobs at the office. One evening two young

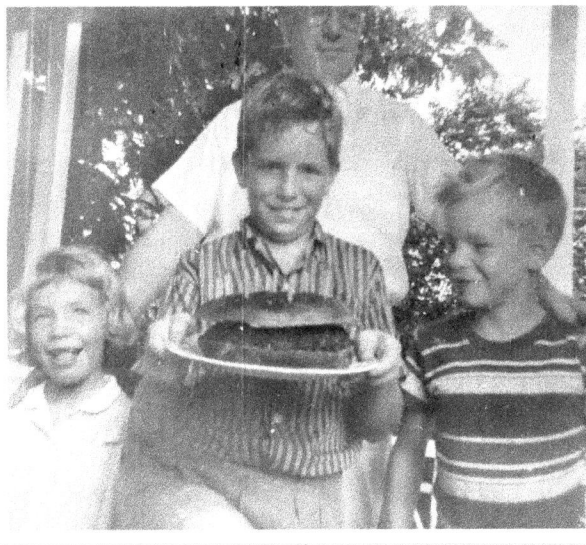

Celebrating Gordon's birthday with a grilled burger "cake" was cooler than baking in the tropics

secretaries came to dinner. These English girls were from the islands of Sumatra and Java and were making their way around the world by working for four to six months at each destination. Their background and travel experiences made for a fascinating evening. Several times there were young auditors as guests. Bill came from Pittsburgh and was known as the "space man" since his job was to design office spaces. He came to dinner one evening and, when he went back to his hotel, he met a Cuban woman in the lobby. In spite of the fact that he spoke no Spanish and she spoke little English, a spark ignited. She was a widow; he was divorced and soon they were married. Bill always remembered dinner with us because it was the night that he met his "senora." We got together with them several years later back in Pittsburgh.

There were some special perks given to employees. Private school tuition fees were partially covered, and the children attended St. Andrew's School, which followed the British school system and was associated with the Presbyterian kirk we attended on Sundays. Because local social life centered around private clubs, the company paid dues for two clubs of the employee's choice. Thus, we belonged to the Bahamas Country Club, which had a nice clubhouse on a beautiful sandy beach, and the adjoining Nassau Golf Club. The children later had memberships at the Royal Nassau Sailing Club where Philip had a sailfish for weekly racing.

With the three children in private school in Nassau, there were calls for parents to volunteer. As a member of the Women's Committee, I was put in charge of a series of dancing classes for the children that was already arranged with a profession instructor hired from Miami. There were trips to the airport to meet her plane and then arrangements for a gala cotillion held at the Emerald Beach Hotel. The teacher gave me a pair of heavy cut-glass perfume bottles as a parting gift that I still own today.

Emerald Beach Hotel Flea Market

There was no publicity for the annual end-of-the-season flea market at Nassau's Emerald Beach Hotel. You wouldn't find out about it by opening the newspaper or turning on the radio. Instead, news about the event seemed to be passed around via word-of-mouth. The sale was a charity event and consisted of things from the hotel's lost and found department and perhaps other Cable Beach hotels contributed to it, as well. Such sales were unusual and looked forward to. A modest admission was charged. The spacious ballroom was filled with tables of used books, sunglasses, beach towels, clothing, costume jewelry and watches. One year there was even a used car. Many bargains were there. Some Bay Street stores may have contributed leftovers.

It was fun just to look around. Then, of course, there was a bar serving soft drinks for a shilling (fifteen cents) and liquor for the same price. The liquor was contributed by local donors. If there was any loss on the drinks, it was made up by the fact that those who had a cocktail began to see everything for sale with a warm, fuzzy glow and made many more purchases than they might have otherwise.

The East Hill Club

The East Hill Club was a members-only restaurant and boutique hotel in a restored mansion owned by a Cleveland entrepreneur. The summer kitchens had been turned into a cool bar and outside was a small pool surrounded by tables for lunching. After seeing the extensive tropical gardens for the first time on the International Garden Club's tour, I was enchanted and wanted to visit the gardens again and again. Thus, we became members of the East Hill Club. I don't recall any special procedure beyond paying the fairly modest dues. Perhaps the president and vice president of the company were references.

On Sundays after church, we would go to the East Hill Club for lunch as a family, as it was just around the corner from the kirk. We would pick up the tissue-thin airmail edition of the New York Times and the Miami Herald at the Lofthouse News Agency. Then we would have a leisurely meal of sandwiches in the shade of the patio and read the Sunday paper while the children took cooling dips in the pool. Rooms at the club were elegant and expensive, as were their dinners. This was an affordable way to enjoy my favorite part of the East Hill Club – the gardens.

In his book, *Nassau's Historic Buildings*, C. Seighbert Russell describes the old house on the ridge of the city as being owned by Henry Adderley in the early 1800s. In 1840, it was sold to a former chief justice, Sir John Lees, and then owned by his son, Sir Charles Cameron Lees, governor of the British colony from 1882 to 1884. In the early 1900s, the Robert Matthews family lived there and they developed the gardens, which stretched from East Hill Street to the Southern Recreation Grounds in Grants Town, "over the hill." After the Matthews family left, seasonal owners took over: first Lord Beaverbrook, the Canadian-British newspaper magnate, and then Lord and Lady Kemsley, whom he later sold it to.

The gardens had been neglected since the time of the Matthews family. The scions of that family were a daughter who'd married and moved away and two spinster daughters and a bachelor son who lived together in semi-seclusion. They gardened passionately and competitively and each undertook long demanding projects in different sections of the gardens. One was a huge banana pit planted for show. There was a long pergola draped with colorful bougainvillea vines which ended with a bench at an overlook. A spooky underground grotto with circular stone steps led into a gloomy room decorated with sea shells. They spent whole days in the garden and had lunch brought out to them. Servants were doing the hard labor as they developed their private paradise. One day a year they held a garden party to show off what they had done.

Lady Solomon, who had known the Matthews, described them as eccentrics. She owned a stunning brass settee purchased from their estate that she'd had reupholstered in red sailcloth. A beautiful piece that I've never seen duplicated.

In 1960, Mr. and Mrs. Samuel K. Wellman of Cleveland bought the East Hill Club property and restored the house as an elegant and expensive bed and breakfast, as well as an exclusive dining spot. No expense was spared in the conversion. The Wellmans engaged the noted English designer, Oliver Messell, to oversee restoration of the grounds. A small swimming pool was built on a terrace below the house beside the thick, stonewalled former servants' quarters, which was converted to a cool rustic bar with changing rooms at the rear. The designer's signature gift (now widely copied) was a pair of tall metal storks presented to the owner and prominently displayed in the garden.

The Nassau social scene was built around clubs and recognizing this, the Navios Corporation included in its perks for employees paid memberships for two clubs of the employee's choice. The usual choices were the Bahamas Country Club, with its pleasant clubhouse and beautiful beach, and the associated Nassau Golf Club. Many executives added other club memberships according to their interests such as the Tennis Club, Nassau Yacht Club and Royal Nassau Sailing Club. We joined the East Hill Club on our own. Since we had a membership there, and none of the other Navios staff belonged, we were asked to entertain at an elegant dinner party for visiting VIPs on one occasion, paid for, of course, by the company.

Walking through the East Hill Club garden on a bright December day in 1963

The East Hill Club gardens were much more attractive than the neglected Botanic Gardens of the island. It was a wonderful place to take visitors for lunch in a gracious setting and then be able to conduct a tropical garden tour of the beautiful grounds. They found it a special treat. Mr. Wellman brought a Cleveland nephew and his family to Nassau as his manager. After some years, they returned to the States and sold some of their things before they left. We have a nest of tables and an antique dough table as reminders of that connection.

A transfer back to the Pittsburgh law office of the corporation ended those entertaining days and nights under the swaying palm trees. Returning to Nassau some years later for a winter week in the sun, we had a cocktail party at the East Hill Club and were able to see many friends at one time. Our guests were given boutonnières of tiny pussy-willows. It was a reminder of Northern spring to the Americans and a puzzle to local Bahamians.

Now the club is no more, taken over by government offices, with the gardens given over to a parking lot. Only a few pictures and our memories remain.

On Stage

The Nassau Players were an amateur group composed primarily of Britons living in the Bahamas. The backbone of the players were the long-term residents working on the island. Much of the spark and vigor came from some of the young bachelor bank employees needing evening entertainments. Terry and Jenny Dunn, an English couple who taught at St. Andrew's School, invited Dan to join them.

Dan had an excellent memory. He had taken part in high school plays. Then, in his college years, he participated in his Aunt Bird's play readings when she entertained college faculty and town friends. For many years after there was neither time, money or opportunity to indulge in theatre. He enjoyed being part of the varied group as a change from his workday world of dealing in legal matters.

Performances were held in a variety of venues, often under quite primitive conditions. A memorable outdoor Shakespearean play was done in Government House gardens with scenes set up on two sides of an open space that served well for the dialogues. Dundas Civic Center had a small stage where Arthur Miller's play, *The Crucible* was performed. When I read the depressing script, I doubted that it would have much appeal. But Dan had the leading role of the "bad guy" and the play was a great success. He was the curtain puller for *Time and The Conways* on the Government High School stage. Not only was this reverse-time play a bomb, but the curtains persisted in sticking. A delightful garden setting for two one-act plays was beside the Green Shutters pub. The lights beneath the shrubbery borders cast lovely shadows against the white walls.

Dan was the only American in the players and was cast in *You Can't Take It With You* as the stuffy New England father of the prospective groom. That accent could well have been done by an Englishman. In a production of *Macbeth*, Dan was one of three soldiers. To represent the military, they had to march on and off the stage repeatedly. This was commented on comically in a newspaper review of the performance.

My part behind the scenes consisted in providing costumes, particularly for the Shakespearean roles. My portable sewing machine came in handy. Son Philip joined one cast as a page. No visible zippers or buttons could be used. It took a bit of research and invention to come up with a "codpiece." I was accustomed to using patterns, but instead, the costume committee had a mass of fabric that was divided with wild abandon. Alarmingly, they cut the forms without any guides. Somehow it all worked out. I also remember sitting at a card table outside a Bay Street store selling tickets for the Nassau Players or the Nassau Operatic Society.

Each year the Players had a picnic party in which spouses were included. There was much teasing and joking about the mishaps of the past. The outstanding player or greatest "ham" of the year was awarded the hambone. It was an actual hambone that had been boiled and scrubbed and tied with a red ribbon.

Dan capped his theatrical career in Nassau by winning the hambone, amid much applause and laughter.

The Breadfruit Business

Breadfruit trees are tall and have multiple sturdy trunks and big glossy leaves that range in size from one to three feet long. The tree is never bare although the leaves fall all during the year. The fruit is as big as a honeydew melon with a pebbled skin like an Osage orange. There is no one season for the fruit and it is available throughout the year. Under the skin a thick white flesh surrounds a firm pod. The flesh is commonly boiled and served like potatoes and seasoned with butter and salt and pepper. It can be fried or made into a salad or even a dessert. The flavor is bland and the texture is similar to a sweet potato.

This was the fruit that was responsible for the famous mutiny on the *H.M.S. Bounty* under the command of Captain William Bligh. He had been sent out from England in 1787 to Tahiti to obtain a shipload of breadfruit which would then be taken to the West Indies where the trees would produce food for the enslaved population. The crew revolted for a number of reasons. After enjoying the good life on the tropical island of Tahiti for more than a year, they were once more on the seas under the stern command of Captain Bligh. In order to keep the breadfruit plants alive during the journey, precious fresh water had to be used for the plants and the sailors were severely rationed. The mutiny set adrift Captain Bligh with eighteen other seamen in an open boat, who succeeded in navigating nearly 3,000 miles of the Pacific Ocean. The mutineers took command of the Bounty and sailed to remote Pitcairn Island where they established a colony. Two years later and again under the sponsorship and with the financial backing of Sir Joseph Banks, Bligh returned to the Marquesas not just to collect seeds, but to propagate thousands of breadfruit plants. These were successfully brought to Navy Island off Port Antonio, Jamaica. Now breadfruit trees grow wild all over Jamaica. In Nassau they were rare as they needed an underground water source, which our garden seemed to have.

The walled garden behind The Corners in Nassau extended a block from front to back. Tall palms and mature breadfruit trees framed the large white house that had verandas on three sides of the two floors.

In the still of the night, a leaf could be heard falling all the way down through the tree. When a fruit became rotten and dropped it made a repulsive round splotch. Our gardener came three days a week and one of his tasks was to pick up leaves and clean up any fallen fruit. He also carefully transplanted crabgrass, which seemed a crime since my previous experience had been that crabgrass was something to be weeded out. On the days the gardener was not there, the children earned their allowances by picking up breadfruit leaves, which did not blow away or disintegrate. As the oldest, Gordon had the largest area, the back garden to police. The next smaller area, the front garden, was Philip's territory and Amy Jane, as the youngest, did the side garden. It was a boring chore, but quite easy to collect the huge leaves and carry them to the compost pile at the side of the garage.

There was much more breadfruit than we could ever use, but no way of picking it. We had no way of sharing it until the day that a small Jamaican man appeared at our gate asking if he could buy breadfruit. He offered to do the picking and said that he wanted fruit for himself and would sell fruit to other Jamaican friends. He had a bicycle with a large wicker basket attached. We arrived at an agreement that he could pick the breadfruit and keep it for no charge if he would also pick an

A back view of The Corners, with the breadfruit trees arching over the back garden

equal amount for us. Thus, the breadfruit business began. It proved to be a welcome supplement to the children's allowances.

Gordon priced the fruit according to size, from one shilling and up, marking each fruit with a black crayon. Put into a wheelbarrow and taken to the wide back gate on busy Shirley Street, the children would take turns selling and calling out to passersby on the opposite sidewalk. Sometimes tourists would stop by and ask about the breadfruit.

Business was good since breadfruit was a scarce item in the Bahamas. Profits were divided simply – the person who made the sale got the money. If the breadfruit was held over to the next day, it could be kept fresh in a washtub of water. The little man became a regular visitor and told us to call him Uncle Joe. He was agile and fearlessly climbed up the big trees.

Nassau had certain exclusive neighborhoods, such as the mansions facing the sea on Montagu Foreshore, and the seaside villas on the waterfront along Eastern Road. On West Bay Street were seaside estates past the country club and large hotels along the road to exclusive Lyford Cay. Blue Hill Road led to the native section "over the hill" away from the sea. The highest point on the island was only sixty feet above sea level.

Our house was in town with Lady Solomon's large mansion next door, but a rundown bungalow was on the other side. There were a garage and gas station two doors away and the Model Bakery a half block away. We did most of our grocery shopping at East Bay City Meat Market about four blocks away. From our garage we entered the one-way Shirley Street and went East for two blocks and then left through a narrow alley past a section of small, wooden shacks of just one or two rooms.

Amy Jane was in the back seat as we were making our way slowly along the sandy road when she pointed to a turquoise-painted shanty and said, "There's a nice lady who lives there. She bought one of my breadfruit." Apparently, business had been slow on Shirley Street one day and so she had put breadfruit in the wicker basket on the front of her bike and set off to sell like the Bahamian women who sold fruit and vegetables from old baby carriages. They wheeled their merchandise along the street and called out what they had for sale. Amy Jane rode along and called out "Breadfruit for sale."

She and her friend, Valerie Witmer, often explored outside of our neighborhood by bike. One day she came home and announced to the family, "I saw a dead man today." She and Valerie had stumbled upon a small funeral home with its door wide open earlier that day. There weren't many people about, so they slipped in and peered down into the open casket, where a black Bahamian man lay in repose. Amy Jane recounted to us that a man approached the girls and asked, "Did you know him?" After she shook her head no, he solemnly pronounced, in his thick Bahamian accent, "He was a great mon."

My friends in the States would have been shocked to think that my eight-year-old daughter was on her own in a strange part of town. Actually, people were very kind, especially to children, and she was really quite safe on our small island.

Breadfruit was only an occasional item on our menu. You were supposed to be able to do the whole range of potato preparations with it. We weren't adventurous and just boiled it. House guests, of which there were many, were usually served breadfruit at least once during their visit. When the Rothermels came from New Jersey with their three children, they were served breadfruit early on in their visit and seemed to enjoy it boiled in chunks and seasoned with butter, salt and pepper. A few nights later, a starch was needed for dinner and I decided to repeat and vary the breadfruit as mashed "potatoes." The grownups ate in the dining room and the children were on the veranda, just outside at a picnic table. Suddenly, there was a cry from outside. "Mother, what did you do to the breadfruit?" We all discovered at the same time that breadfruit doesn't mash, but quickly becomes like wallpaper glue, thicker and thicker until it doesn't leave the serving spoon. The family still considers this my greatest cooking disaster of all time.

On the South Embankment of the Thames in London there is a deconsecrated church that was once St. Mary's of Lambeth and is now the home of the Museum of Garden History founded by the Tradescant Trust. Captain William Bligh belonged to that parish and his tomb is in the churchyard. One of its permanent exhibits is about breadfruit. This charming small museum has a lovely gift shop and tea room and seems largely manned by friendly volunteers. We have made visits there over a period of years, photographed Bligh's tomb and paid our homage to this remarkable man. It was our sentimental remembrance of the breadfruit business.

The Hudsons

John Chaplin, headmaster of St. Andrew's School in Nassau, made a trip every two years to London to interview and hire teachers for the school. An advertisement would be placed in an educational journal asking for applications. These would be examined and prospective candidates would be asked to come to London for an interview. One year it seemed like an ideal hire to find an attractive teaching couple, the Hudsons. They had a school-age son and daughter.

Teaching contracts were usually made for a two-year period. Travel expenses to the Bahamas were paid and return fares were covered at the end of the contract. Often the contracts were renewed for another two-year period and the transportation costs allowed for a holiday in the UK.

St. Andrew's School was housed in a large old mansion. The assistant headmaster, Stephen Howell-Griffith, his wife, Pearl, and their two children lived in an apartment on one wing of the second floor. They both were teachers and she was in charge of the Infant School. There were just a few rooms on the third floor to provide temporary quarters for new teachers until they could find housing.

The headmaster and his family were on leave in Scotland when the Hudson family was due to arrive. He and his wife rounded up basic furnishings. We had donated an air conditioner for the apartment. As I was on the School Committee, Dan and I were asked if we would welcome the Hudsons and help them to get settled in. We looked forward to helping the newcomers, as we had been new residents ourselves.

The Hudson family arrived in August, several weeks in advance of school opening and in the heat of a tropical summer. It is difficult to know what their expectations were. Their reaction to their new situation was decidedly negative even before their teaching jobs began.

School parents, who also had been alerted to befriend them, issued invitations which were coldly received or refused. We took them to the Bahamas Country Club for a Sunday afternoon of swimming and tea on the terrace with our children. Mr. and Mrs. Hudson were not interested in swimming and allowed their children to go into the sea reluctantly. The country club had a lovely white sand beach with shallow water and no surf. The beach sloped gradually until it was possible to swim to a float anchored not far out from the tide line. A friendly barracuda was often seen enjoying the shade under the float, but we would not be going that far.

Bahamian waters are a clear light turquoise, so clear that the sandy bottom is visible. I was encouraging the children to paddle in the shallow water which they did timidly. For the first and last time in my life, I saw a twelve-inch slim snake emerging from the sandy bottom and quickly moved the children in a different direction. There would have been a ghastly scene if they had seen what I saw. Some fifty years later, reading a book about the Bahamian fish, I now know that what I saw was called a snake eel with a snake-like head and a tail that fastened it in the sand. We were well-informed by others of things to avoid in the water.

The Hudsons could have been anti-American and perhaps we were the wrong people to greet them. They could have made their minds up immediately that

Nassau was not what they had expected. At any event, they made no attempt to find more congenial housing. Living in the sketchy quarters was free, but certainly not desirable. They seemed ill at ease. The two children were not allowed to go downstairs and play in the spacious school grounds on their own. Were they intimidated by the largely black population? We never knew.

The headmaster and his family returned and school began with both of the Hudsons teaching and their children attending classes. The boy and girl were attractive but shy. Less than two months into the school year, Mr. Hudson met with the headmaster and indicated that he and his wife wanted to be released from their contracts to return to England at the end of the first half of the year. This left the school in a bind as far as replacement for two teachers was concerned. No return fare would be provided in the terms of their contracts. The Hudsons were most insistent and finally a compromise was reached that return fare would be paid for all of them at the end of one year rather than the contracted two years.

They were adequate but not enthusiastic teachers as they reluctantly served what they regarded as imprisonment on a primitive island. What tales did they have to tell on their return to England?

A Cloudy Afternoon

The sun shines brightly nearly every day of the year in sub-tropical Nassau, Bahamas. Even in the rainy season the sun disappears only briefly for a sudden downpour and quickly reappears. A rare cloudy Sunday afternoon was a treat. For Jean Chaplin it was a reminder of her Scottish homeland; for me it was the memory of Western Pennsylvania skies. We decided to take our children to the beach. The weather was cool enough to build a driftwood fire and to toast marshmallows. We even took hot chocolate that day.

Jean taught English classes at St. Andrew's School, where her husband John was headmaster. There had recently been a house built for them on the school grounds. It included a rarely needed fireplace, which they were excited to take advantage of. Jean and the children were gathering driftwood for the fireplace.

I was building a small pond at the base of a breadfruit tree in the side garden and needed rocks to circle the shallow basin. Our station wagon had ample room for the children and our collecting of both rocks and woods.

The cool breeze was an invigorating change from the usual sultry air. Jean strode off briskly along the beach just above the tide line. We had this part of Cable Beach almost completely to ourselves. As Jean got close to one of the big hotels, she saw a man with a young daughter. He was looking very glum. She greeted him cheerily. His reply was, "How long will this terrible weather last? We are only here for a few days!"

Jean quickly covered her exuberance and, on behalf of the Bahamas Office of Tourism, offered apologies for the cloudy weather.

House Guests

House guests can be a delight or a disaster. There were some of both when we lived in the Bahamas. Nassau was the capitol city and a popular resort. We learned how to cope by issuing specific invitations when we found that friends were planning to visit and so the balance fell on the side of delightful times.

Nassau is a small island measuring just seven by twenty-one miles. The old forts, the straw market, Government House, Flamingo Gardens, The Queen's Staircase, the beaches and wharves became tiresome when we were the tour guides repeatedly. Therefore, we replied to letters saying that we would be happy to be a bed and breakfast for their visit. We had a small room that opened off the back veranda that had its own bath and private entrance by way of the back outside staircase. Guests could come and go at their own schedule, and we arranged activities together in advance.

Our days were busy with the children in school; Dan was at the office and with all of my charity and volunteer duties, it was impossible to drop everything to host our guests. By extending definite hospitality, our visitors would be free to make their own plans. Over breakfast, we could make suggestions about what they might like to see

Our "guests" my sister Ceil and brother-in-law Layton visiting us in 1963

and to provide information about the town. At our convenience, we sometimes asked our guests join us for dinner. The usual practice, however, was to see them in the evening, have a drink together while we heard about their day and have a pleasant visit together before bed. Then, on weekends, we often planned boating outings or beach picnics.

This worked well for the most part. However, a young secretary from Dan's former office in Indiana came to stay with her husband. We didn't know them well and I remember them sitting in the living room and looking at us blankly, seeming to expect that we had a full program planned for them. They didn't seem to have a clue as to what they wanted to do.

Besides family, one exception was made for an older couple, Herb and Florence Canardy, from my hometown of Zelienople. They were noted for their hospitality and I had been the beneficiary of their kindness for many years. She had a bridal tea for me, among other things. It was a real privilege to be able to repay them in this small way by guiding them around the Bahamas.

We have had the pleasure of being house guests over the years. We always try to be as helpful as possible and take them to dinner and the theater. Our friend, Jean Chaplin, at the Harbour Mews Club in Nassau, put a note on the chest in our room with a schedule of the week that showed the things we would be doing together and when they had engagements and we would be on our own. Taking reading material for quiet times was appreciated.

Our hostess, Liz Parrish, in Grand Cayman would set up a breakfast bar with trays that could be taken to the dining room table or outside by the pool or wherever we wished. She appreciated table setting and kitchen help. She said her visiting sister in-law had never volunteered.

When I was back in Nassau and visited Peggy and Roger Jones, I had a downstairs guest room and bath back of their library and a door that opened to the pool. They had breakfast by themselves upstairs and told me to help myself in the kitchen. I might not see them until the cocktail hour in the library. When I went with friends to a potluck supper at the kirk, I was able to prepare a simple dish to take. They entertained many visitors, so I was pleased when Peggy said that I was one of the nicest guests they'd ever had.

We were privileged to be house guests. We were also delighted to be able to host so many house guests by providing accommodations and mutual freedom.

Edith Fair's Budgies

The Fair family lived in a spacious house on a tree-lined cul-de-sac off Village Road. There were three boys and the family pets were a dog, a cat and a pair of tame blue budgerigars. The birds were caged in the screened lanai. When it was time to clean the cage, the birds were allowed to fly free in the lanai, after the house door was closed to protect them from the house cat.

Early one morning, attired in a cool housecoat, Edith was cleaning the birds' cage. Somehow one of the blue budgies escaped. Feeling certain that her pet was somewhere nearby and would respond to her call, Edith set off, first in their garden and then down the street. She kept her eyes up in the trees and called, "Pretty Boy, Pretty Boy, Pretty Boy" as she walked along. She was oblivious to the curious stares of the maids coming to work that morning.

With no results from her morning search, Edith put an advertisement in the local newspaper. The paper was not noted for its accuracy and so under the Lost and Found Section, Edith's ad read, "Lost, off Village Road, a blue baby buggy. Contact Edith Fair at 72345. Reward." Edith's friends who read this were puzzled as to why she would have a baby carriage, since her children were all of school age. They also wanted to know how she had lost an entire buggy.

Pet Portrait

Snooks was a silly name for a serious black dachshund. He didn't have any American Kennel Club papers because he was born in Beirut, Lebanon. There were papers attesting to his inoculations in Chicago, Ill. He was a well-traveled creature when he came to live with us in Nassau; a sedate, housebroken, intelligent dog.

Snooks' former owner was a handsome young bachelor who worked for the international department of the Parker Pen Company. He had just married a local woman and was soon to be transferred to Switzerland. Due to quarantine regulations and housing considerations, he reluctantly decided that it would be wise to find a good home for his pet. It was through mutual friends that Snooks came to live with us soon after we moved to Nassau.

Our home was on a block-long walled lot with ample running room. Snooks soon learned his way around. The home had seventeen screened single French doors in the house. All except the kitchen door

Snooks in front making himself at home with the Core family

opened outward and could be pushed out from the inside unless bolted as they were at night. The kitchen door opened inward and that was the way that Snooks could come back into the house. Visitors were sometimes puzzled by hearing a screen door slam when no person appeared.

Snooks came equipped with a green-cushioned metal bed and a plaid car rug as his blanket. This was installed in Amy Jane's bedroom. He never laid claim to other beds or couches.

Strange as it seemed in the tropical climate, he liked to cover himself in his bed and would pull the blanket out of the bed, get into the bed, and with his teeth would pull the blanket back over himself. At times his tail might be left out. One morning there was a scream by our maid Edith from Amy Jane's bedroom where she was cleaning. She had seen the blanket in the dog bed begin to move mysteriously, not realizing he was under it!

He liked his bed and, in the evening, when we said "bed" he would go upstairs obediently. Some evenings it was not even necessary to send him to bed for he went on his own. What a delightful contrast to our three children, who resisted bedtimes.

Snooks was the perfect gentleman on almost all occasions. He didn't jump on visitors or bark immoderately. Amy Jane had some friends who were afraid of all dogs. One day they were at the house to meet and pet Snooks and perhaps overcome their fears. She went into the back garden to find him since he was not coming at her call. She spied him digging under the hibiscus hedge and pulled him out by his back legs. Interrupted in digging up a bone, he resented this and turned to nip her arm, much to the horror of the visiting children, who were now doubly confirmed in their fear of dogs.

Dog licenses were issued by the only veterinarian on the island. He often gave heartworm shots at the same time, as dogs there were very susceptible.

One day a small woman with a French accent came to see us. She was from Haiti and lived just up the block in back of us on Shirley Street. She had a female dachshund that she wanted to breed and had seen our dog and thought he might be a good match. We were quite willing to have Snooks visit her cottage on the appropriate week. There was no talk of fee; it would just be a neighborly favor as we explained that we had no proof of pedigree. She did offer us one of the litter when the puppies were born, but we explained that we were not interested in a second dog.

Shortly before the puppies were born, we lost Snooks when he succumbed to heartworm. Amy Jane went to see the puppies and chose one of the smallest from the litter. So Snooks was followed by his son, who was named Oscar Heiner Core by Phil, who thought a dachshund should have a German family name. I joked that he was the Oscar Mayer Weiner Dog, though we simply called him "Oscar."

Hamster Travels

Some couples have dogs before they have children. Other couples have children and then acquire dogs or other pets. They feel that this is the way to teach children the facts of life, birth, growth and death. In Allison Park, on a sunny afternoon, we watched a cow giving birth in the nearby field. In New Albany, Ind. we saw kittens being born to a beautiful Siamese cat.

During St. Andrew's school days in Nassau, hamsters enjoyed popularity. As parents, we were implored to set up a happy hamster home. It could even make money when the hamster babies were sold to school mates, the children said. There were no pet stores in Nassau. A hamster couple had to be purchased on our next trip to Miami, along with a cage and accessories. Bahamas Air was much more accommodating in those days. There were no restrictions on the importation of hamsters. Three hamsters were bought, one male and two females that went back to Nassau with Dan and the three children. Meanwhile, I flew on to Pennsylvania to visit my mother and then from there to New York, with the plan to take in a few plays and return to Nassau several weeks later.

The hamster cage was put in the outdoor shelter of the upstairs veranda which surrounded the house. I don't know just what went on from that point. But I had a message before leaving Pennsylvania that one hamster had died. "Bring a female replacement on your way back!"

There was a pet store in New York just a few blocks away from my hotel. On the day of my return flight, I went to the store before noon and purchased one hamster and a tiny cage to transport it in. I had checked out of the hotel and, with my bags and the hamster, went to the central terminal in the city. At that time, one could check bags there and take a bus to the airport. At the check-in I had to purchase a $3 ticket for the hamster. It was weighed in and the bag containing the cage was duly tagged.

Then, to my horror, I was told that my plane had already taken off for Nassau because the schedule had been changed in the time

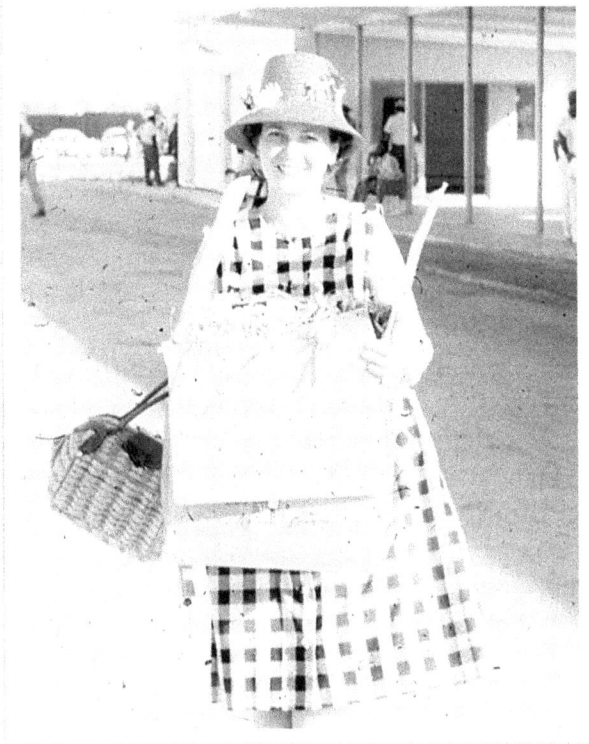

Going to the Nassau airport became a regular occurrence, both to greet travelers, as well as travel ourselves

since my return ticket had been purchased some three weeks earlier. This was before confirmations were required. There was nothing to be done except to spend another night in New York and get the flight the next day.

I returned to the hotel and was back in the same small room. My bags were already checked in at the terminal, so the only thing I took back to the hotel was the hamster. I had to sleep in my slip. That was an uneasy night. Hamsters are nocturnal and the cage was in the tub in the bathroom where it made a lot of noise.

The change in plans required a phone call to Nassau. In addition to telling my family what plane I would be on, I was told there had been another hamster passing, so please bring two hamsters with you.

I got up early and was at the pet store when it opened to buy another hamster. This one was put in a separate box with ample air holes and set in the same bag on top of the cage. Back at the airport terminal, the only thing I was carrying was the hamsters. The bag was weighed again but the clerk did not look inside. He merely said, "this hamster weighs more than it did yesterday." I couldn't face the thought of buying another hamster ticket, so I simply said, "He ate a lot."

Back in Nassau, it didn't take the hamsters long to reproduce. Soon there were tiny pink babies that looked like wads of bubble gum. The assumption was that the parents, and perhaps particularly a loving mother, would take care of them. Wrong! Not only did they not take care of them, they ate them! This cycle was repeated several times with no solution to the cannibalism. It was a lesson in life and death that put an end to the hamsters that had traveled so far and even had their own airline ticket.

Pony Club

The Nassau Pony Club was having its annual Spring Gymkhana on Paradise Island. A small ring offered a few shaded bleachers for parents and friends summoned to the occasion to watch the competitive horseback events taking place. The riders were mostly young girls aged eight to fourteen, which included Amy Jane. A card table was set up to collect modest admission fees and I was manning this entry point.

When the wealthy American businessman, Huntington Hartford II, bought the majority of Hog Island in 1959, he renamed it Paradise Island. Then he proceeded at full speed to develop it into a fashionable resort called the Ocean Club, complete with a golf course, tennis courts, casino and the famous restaurant Café Martinique, seen in the James Bond film *Thunderball*. He was married to his third wife, Diane, at the time. She was a former model interested in horses and so stables were built to house them and other horses that would be available for guests at the resort. A long row of wooden stables painted a soft gray were erected. Red painted buckets hung outside each stall's half-door, as well as some of the tack. All was beautifully organized and maintained.

Since the Hartfords were often traveling or staying at their other homes, exercising of the horses fell to their grooms. Thus, it was that the Nassau Pony Club was invited to have its weekly meetings and riding classes using the horses on Paradise Island. This was a vastly improved setting from their rustic former riding ring on the Eastern side of Nassau.

Huntington Hartford had bought and refurbished a restaurant on Bay Street. From the restaurant there was a fleet of luxurious boats to carry people from Nassau to Paradise Island, as there was no bridge yet to get to the island. Previous transportation had been by basic "bum" boats. The Pony Club members enjoyed this free transportation for their weekly meetings…a posh way to travel!

The pony show was well underway and all of the admissions had been collected when a tall man ambled down the dusty lane in the direction of the riding ring. I was just about to leave my post when I recognized in the nick of time that the latecomer was the millionaire Huntington Hartford himself. What a big mistake it would have been to ask him for an admission fee to his own benefit!

Tropical Fish

A large library table sat in the middle of Grandmother's living room in Zelienople with a family Bible and a small encyclopedia. Among the small number of colored plates there were pictures of colorful tropical fish. The only fish in this part of the country were shades of gray or brown, so, these photos seemed unreal and unbelievable. Any fish was a menu rarity. The local butcher shop had fish available only on Fridays for its Catholic customers.

Thirty-some years later those tropical fish turned out to really exist off the pier of the Fort Montague Beach Hotel in Nassau, Bahamas. Small and delightful to watch, the names did not matter. For fish dinners, larger fish, such as grouper and turbot, were purchased from local fishermen at the East Bay Street docks.

More experienced residents of Nassau enlivened dinner parties with warnings about the perils of the beautiful sea. One had to be wary of the lovely coral since some of it was stinging coral. Floating jellyfish also had stinging tentacles that were hard to see. The spiny black sea urchins often found in colonies on the sandy bottom were not to be stepped on. The sting ray with its big wings had a poisonous barb in its tail with which it defended itself. In deeper waters were sharks and barracuda. Luckily, these dangers could be seen and avoided. No streams brought soil into the ocean, so, the sea was crystal clear to twenty or thirty feet.

The Bahamas Country Club had a wide sandy beach as well as locker rooms for changing and an open patio beside the beach where bathers could enjoy tea with fresh coconut cake, or fruitcake for the British. The Nassau Golf Club was next door to the country club. The first hole of the golf course ran from the clubhouse tee eastwards off along the

Amy Jane and Philip swimming in the ocean

sea. A low hedge separated the fairway from a narrow beach. The shallow water was a fun place to go snorkeling and collect lost golf balls. On a sunny Sunday afternoon of drifting along the shore, I found myself feeling part of the marine world. A large school of eight-inch, almost transparent, fish, was moving below me. The group swam one way and then turned and moved in another direction. I have no idea how long I was part of that underwater world.

A wooden float was anchored off the country club beach in water ten feet deep. One could swim to it and then climb on the float for a brief rest and perhaps a chat with other swimmers. A friendly barracuda liked the shade underneath the float and never bothered anyone.

Some of our house guests went deep-sea fishing on chartered boats. Most tourists were living in hotels and gave away anything caught to the boat captain. We asked them to bring the catch home to provide a fresh meal and often add more to our freezer. Pictures taken on the dock proved the catch at the end of an outing.

Then there was the day in Nassau when Gordon, Philip and I went out for a half-day on the tourist boat that promised "Underwater Diving" and a chance to pat and feed "Harry the Grouper." A husband-and-wife team, the Hartleys, came to the Bahamas annually, living on their boat and sending people down in diving bells to the sea bottom, a depth of about thirty feet, probably. Instructions were first given on the hand signals that would be used by the leader to tell us what we saw and what to do. Only three people went down at a time with the guide. For an additional fee, he also took pictures underwater and thus we have a picture of Philip with the famous fish. It was amazing that touching that fish underwater didn't give the slippery feeling that one would have on touching it out of the water. It was a fun experience!

Living in the subtropics was a brand-new world. There were so many things to be learned. Most of my learning was in the plants of the spacious gardens surrounding our house. The colorful tropical fish were enjoyed but seldom named.

A Dark Night's Ride

Spending two weeks in Jamaica for our summer vacation might seem like a strange idea when the Core family was living in Nassau and could be expected to get away to the U.S. or England to escape the tropical heat. Jamaica, however, has higher elevations and can be quite comfortable. It is also decidedly cheaper off-season. We planned our own tour and rented a car for our family of five. Actually, it turned out to be three cars in all, since the first two died.

The trip seemed to be ill-fated. We booked our flight and made some reservations through a Nassau travel agent. The agent didn't provide the best service, for during the trip we discovered that one of the hotels that had been reserved for us had been closed for a year. We flew to Montego Bay and stayed at a small bed and breakfast, which was a refreshing change of pace from most tourist hotels. One of the nearby attractions was a natural wonder, where the water was highly phosphorescent.

There was an inn nearby where dinner was advertised with an included boat ride on the bay after dark. There we found that we were the only diners and there was no printed menu. The waiter gave us a somewhat vague suggestion that there might be a chicken dinner. We sat by flickering kerosene lanterns for what seemed hours growing hungrier and bored.

One of the children took a peek into the kitchen and reported that potatoes were being peeled. Perhaps the chicken was being caught at the same time, we speculated. As the evening wore on, the mosquitoes appeared. When we finally were served dinner, the hour had become late and we were in no mood for a boat ride with more mosquitoes. So we went to the end of the dock and saw the florescence by dipping a pole into the water and stirring it around. Not the best night of the trip.

We drove along the Eastern coast of Jamaica and saw a very English-looking town square in the small town of Falmouth. We found a cliff-hugging small hotel, the 'Falcon-Dip,' overlooking the sea. It had a small pool the children enjoyed, which was the replacement for the non-existent hotel booked by the travel agent in Nassau. While everyone else had breakfast in the dining room, I enjoyed the luxury of eating alone on a balcony above the sea and trying the fish on the menu.

Piracy and Murder

The large courtroom was filled to capacity on this May morning. All the doors and windows were open in the Supreme Court of the Bahamas. Spectators even filled the windows. It was the only time I had ever been in a courthouse in the Bahamas.

The slow-moving ceiling fans did little to dissipate the tropical heat of Nassau. At the time of the trial in 1961, the Bahama Islands were a British colony and the legal system followed British law. The attorneys were educated in London and dressed in the traditional black robes and short white wigs. The chief justice wore crimson and a long white wig. This attire added to the warmth of the day and must have been painful.

The case under consideration was the most sensational in many years. It involved not only murder but piracy. Piracy was an even more heinous crime in a seafaring country like the Bahamas.

The facts were roughly as follows: A trio of men from the U.S. had chartered a motor cruiser for a deep-sea fishing outing, manned by a licensed captain and a mate. At some distance from Nassau, they had responded to a call for help from two men, also U.S. citizens, who appeared stranded in an abandoned lighthouse by a tiny cay. The Good Samaritans brought one of the men on board while the other man swam out to meet the boat.

Then the man drew a gun and announced that they were taking over the boat. When the captain resisted, he was killed. The others were forced to swim to shore and abandoned on the small cay from which they were rescued by the Coast Guard several days later.

Meanwhile, the culprits could find many hiding places among the 3,000 mostly uninhabited cays of the islands. But the boat would soon need refueling and this meant they would have to go to larger ports. An international search went on. Seven months later, the two pirates were found in Cuba and extradited to prison in Nassau until trial.

On this steamy morning, the defense attorneys had the victims on the stand. These men were from the Pittsburgh area and had returned to Nassau at their own expense to see justice served. The defense was questioning them so aggressively that it seemed unfair to subject the victims to such grilling. The criminals were given a fair trial. In the end, they were convicted of both murder and piracy. There were no postponements or lengthy appeals. Two weeks later, they were hanged in the swift execution of Bahamian justice.

Our Friend Fitz

The verdict was suicide. That was the decision reached by the police magistrate in Nassau, Bahamas. The local officials were not noted for thorough investigations. Even less attention would be given to an American resident with a work permit in the Bahamas.

Lloyd Fitzsimmons and his wife, Ruth, had moved from New Jersey. They were of Irish Catholic backgrounds. He had a very responsible position as Treasurer of Navios. They had a teenage son and a younger daughter around Gordon's age. It is always difficult to assess a marriage from the outside. Ruth was somewhat domineering, while Fitz was friendly and easy-going. They didn't seem affectionate in public and people speculated about their relationship.

Dan worked closely with Fitz both in the office and on a number of business trips that they made together. He enjoyed his company and working with him. We were living back in Pittsburgh when we were shocked to learn of his death.

The account that we received was that the Fitzsimmons had been at a dinner party and he left early. He had had a lot to drink and also was on medication. It was said he took more pills and drank more. When Ruth returned home, he was in a coma. The strange circumstance is that she did not call for any medical help from a local doctor or a hospital, but called a doctor friend in New Jersey, who owned a private plane. She begged him to fly down and he arrived in Nassau to sign the death certificate. The body was taken to New Jersey for the funeral and burial.

Dan was so saddened by the loss of a good friend that he and our older son, Gordon, set out immediately from Pittsburgh to New Jersey to support the family during the funeral. They arrived at the address there. When his widow opened the door, her sharp response was, "What are you doing here?" They didn't feel that it was very warm or welcoming.

Volunteering with the British Red Cross

When the Bahama Islands were a British colony, the British Red Cross was the most prominent charity there. The wife of the acting governor was the honorary president of the organization. There was a small building for headquarters in Nassau and a paid director. The largest fundraising event of the year was the Red Cross Fair that took place in the spacious gardens of Government House in March. This event attracted a huge crowd since this was the only day of the year the gardens were open to the general public. Every other organization in the city took part with a stall of some kind and there were additional committees set up to handle special stalls such as the white elephant sale, the food stalls and the sewing booth. Besides the food stalls, there were plant stalls and needlework stalls. The American Women's Club had a large booth called Serendipity and we offered many enticing imported gift items at attractive prices. The Bahamian government gave unusual dispensation and waived duties for any goods imported for the Red Cross benefit.

You never knew what would appear at the white elephant booth. One friend said that was her favorite charity. She would buy with gay abandon as the prices were right. She'd use the items for a time and often give them back to that booth another year so she could repeat the process all over again with new-to-her items.

During the year, one of the groups recruited for duty was of volunteers for the Children's Ward of Princess Margaret Hospital. The large pink buildings of the hospital were on Shirley Street with a spacious lawn along the side separated from the side walk by a tall iron fence. A number of Poinciana trees provided shade. Under one of the sprawling trees was a playhouse with a fenced-in yard. This was for the children who were well enough to go outside for fresh air and sunshine and a chance for exercise.

There was a small front porch and toys were stored inside. The children were between two and four years of age. They were unaccustomed to organized play and were content to be on their own. Stuffed toys were not an attraction to the children, being either too tired or ill to care much about them, and the shapes were not of any familiar animals found in the Bahamas, where pot-cake dogs hung around but were not pets. Cars, trucks, and planes were accepted play objects, but since there were no trains, the children did not understand their purpose.

Hospital volunteers provided their own uniforms, which were blue maid's uniforms with white trim, purchased at Sweetings Dry Goods Store on Bay Street. A red and white Red Cross patch was sewn on the left sleeve for identification. Two volunteers were on duty for each morning's play time. Thus, I had the pleasure of becoming friends with two women with whom I shared these days. One was Edith Fair, a slim witty English woman whose three sons attended St. Andrew's School with our children. Her husband was with Barclay's Bank and they were a fun couple. When he was transferred to New York, my next companion was Hope Mackenzie, the wife of a colonial government official. They were originally from Scotland, but had had assignments in many other colonies, some in Africa. We knew them from St. Andrew's Kirk and had dinner parties together. When they returned to the UK, we visited them in Lochearnhead, Scotland and later Hope and her relatives in the village of Sixpenny Handley, near Salisbury, on each return visit we took to England.

The Children's Ward was one large room filled with high-sided cribs. There was little extra space in the room and so it was difficult to add any decorations by the volunteers. This problem was solved by creating mobiles made from Christmas cards to hang over each bed.

Polio had largely been eradicated in the United States following the Salk vaccine inoculations. It was no longer the dreaded disease for our children. But the Bahamas had not had the benefit of this protection and there was an outbreak in Nassau. Suddenly, vaccination was mobilized, now in the form of medication on a sugar cube. Stations were set up in different parts of the city and people were urged to get the free help.

Edith Fair and I tending to our Red Cross duties at the Princess Margaret Hospital

Some of the polio patients were in the children's ward. This presented a huge problem for the volunteers who had children and were afraid to be exposed and possibly carry polio to them. The morning playtime outings were suspended. One of the most dedicated volunteers was the wife of the American Consul. She was a young woman who used crutches as a result of polio, and over time she came to help, since she explained that there was no longer any danger there for her. She was a real angel.

Being a hospital volunteer was a real role reversal for many, since we were the white women wearing maid's uniforms and looking after little black children. In most white Bahamian homes, there were black servants responsible for little white children. A legitimate excuse for Bahamians not keeping an engagement was not your child's illness, but being without a maid that day. Coming from our middle-class American background, my daughter had only known local teenage babysitters before we moved to Nassau. One day Amy Jane innocently asked me, "Why do those white children have a black mother?"

With Bahamian independence in the 1970s, the role of the British Red Cross diminished. Local hospital volunteers were organized as "Yellow Birds" to help in many departments of Princess Margaret Hospital.

Meeting Prince Philip, the Duke of Edinburgh

While the annual Red Cross Fair was the only time Nassau's Government House Gardens were open to the public, there were occasionally opportunities to attend other events at Government House. Garden parties were by invitation only. These affairs were a much more modest version of the royal garden receptions found at Buckingham Palace, and was held from time to time when the resident colonial governor and his wife entertained. The invitations were on cream-colored cards and specified formal dress for the ladies and for men, that decorations (such as military medals) could be worn.

How did one get an invitation to these special occasions? It seemed a bit presumptuous, but the procedure was to go to the guard house at the gate of Government House on the hill overlooking the harbor. There at the gate you would sign the guestbook, indicating your residency on the island. In due time, we received our first invitation.

The Governor and Lady Stapledon held their receiving line attended to by his aide-de-camp and her secretary, and in this case, their twenty-year-old daughter, arrayed along the walk at the base of the steep terrace below Government House. The police band provided music and the refreshment was a vile-tasting rum punch, which was definitely not thirst-quenching on a warm evening.

Lady Stapledon was an independent soul and original thinker and began the custom of serving ice cream cones as the dessert of the evening. It seemed a bit incongruous to see all these men and women in formal attire strolling around with ice cream cones in hand.

One of the most memorable garden receptions at Government House was held to honor Prince Philip on the occasion of a visit to the Bahamas in October 1964. Prince Philip was flying himself to Mexico for a nine-day state visit before taking a tour of various South American countries over the course of the first two weeks of November. His itinerary had only allotted one day for visiting the crown colony of the Bahamas.

The prince arrived in Nassau by Royal Yacht with so much pomp and circumstance it felt like it was Commonwealth Day. The entire island seemed to be on hand to welcome him, and this included a presentation from St. Andrew's school children, which Philip and Amy Jane participated in.

In the evening, there was an opportunity to view a "royal progress" firsthand. At the reception, certain people were to be presented to his Highness, such as the Colonial Treasurer, an elder and fellow kirk choir member; the Chief Justice and his wife, whom we also knew; the chairman of the public works board, the head of the schools, etc. The aide-de-camp had asked these guests to stay in place on the grounds until the Prince was brought over to meet them.

The Bahamas was a small colony with British, Bahamian, Canadian and American residents forming a microcosm in the capital of Nassau. We knew many of the people who were to be presented at the formal reception, so it was a simple thing to make our way over to them, chat with them, then to step back when the prince appeared in order to overhear the conversation.

Prince Philip was impressive, with intelligent small talk. He would be told what the person did and would ask a short, pertinent question, listen attentively, make a brief comment and then move on. It was all gracefully and pleasantly done. In a way, the repartee was like a ping-pong game at which he was a master. It was a special royal skill, which the Queen did not have, according to biographies.

On The Occasion of The Visit of

H.R.H. The Duke of Edinburgh

His Excellency the Governor and Lady Grey

request the pleasure of your company at a

Reception

to be held in the grounds of Government House

on Tuesday, 20th October, 1964, from

9.30 p.m. to 11 p.m.

Dinner Jacket with decorations: or Dark Suit

An answer is requested to the Aide-de-Camp Government House

The invitation we received from the new Governor, Sir Ralph Grey,
when Queen Elizabeth's husband, Prince Philip, visited in 1964

The end of the garden party was signaled when the police band played the national anthem and everyone stood at attention. Our English friends, Liz and Derek Parrish, came back to The Corners with us for a nightcap. We asked Derek why he hadn't worn the WWII medals to which he was entitled. In reply, he slyly lifted the lapel of his dinner jacket to show us his medals hidden underneath.

There were less-exotic events at Government House during those years and I joined the Queen Mary's Needlework Society that met monthly on the wide verandas there. Little actual sewing was done during those meetings except for labels on completed garments. Some cutting was done for layettes and children's garments for Princess Margaret Hospital. These items were distributed to be taken away for assembling and finishing and to be returned at the next meeting. Hot tea and biscuits were served no matter how warm the day.

All strata of local ladies were there in attendance. One lady had come from working in the Straw Market, propelling herself by wheelchair. I offered to take her home as the wheelchair could be loaded in the back of our station wagon. This was an uncomfortable ride back since in the enclosed space of our non-air-conditioned car on a tropical afternoon, my guest proved to smell badly.

Lady Stapledon was a musician and greatly interested in The Nassau Operatic Society. Despite the grand name, it only mounted semi-annual performances of light opera, musicals and Gilbert and Sullivan works. She directed many of these productions and conducted the singers, one or two piano players and co-opted several members of the police band for percussion on concert nights. Her daughter, Carolyn, took part in the chorus and was also on the costume committee.

One afternoon, that committee gathered in an upstairs wing of Government House to work on costumes. I recall entering the wide front hall with spacious high ceiling rooms on either side. I had a glimpse of the formal drawing rooms as I went to the second floor. I went up the stairs and down a long hallway, painted white with many closed doorways and a long strip of woven straw carpet, or sisal, on the floor. It was like an old-fashioned summer resort hotel. This didn't seem to be a section that had been redecorated. I could understand why the Duchess of Windsor reportedly had not been impressed by her quarters when she had visited.

Close Encounters in the Bahamas

Living on a small sub-tropical Caribbean island provided opportunities for celebrity sightings at unexpected times and places. Cocooned by the surrounding seas, the Bahamian islanders are remarkably indifferent to world affairs, and, as a tourist destination, they are accustomed to celebrity visits and pay them little attention. The only exception to this was the British Royal Family, since the Bahamas were a British Crown colony and later a member of the Commonwealth before finally being given full independence in 1973.

President John F. Kennedy, British Prime Minister Harold McMillan and Canadian Prime Minister John Diffenbacher had a mini-summit meeting at a secluded Lyford Cay estate west of Nassau in December 1962. There was just one public appearance scheduled for the "Nassau Agreement" but, to mark the occasion of the meeting, each of the government heads planted a tree on a broad triangular traffic island that was on the main road to the airport.

There was a small note in the newspaper about the proposed tree planting appearance and that seemed the best place to avoid any large crowds. I packed a picnic lunch and we wore bathing suits under cover-ups and drove out West Bay Street along the sea until we arrived at the traffic island, which was opposite a sandy beach. It was obvious that this was the right place, since there were two newly planted trees and a third hole that had been prepared for President Kennedy to plant a tree ceremoniously. No one else was around but there was some equipment, including a truck on the side of the road.

Gordon, Amy Jane and I investigated the truck and then went for a swim and ate our picnic lunch. We were alerted by the arrival of the police that the motorcade was not far behind. We took our places just behind the rope, which was two yards from the waiting tree. Suddenly, a group of press photographers arrived ahead of the President's car and we found ourselves pushed in back of them. I got a grainy picture of President Kennedy, but it mostly contained the ear of the photographer that was blocking me. There were also several rather dim pictures of McMillan and Diffenbacher, who remained in the back of the limousine. The primary lingering memory of that day, besides our pleasant picnic lunch, is the rudeness of the photographers.

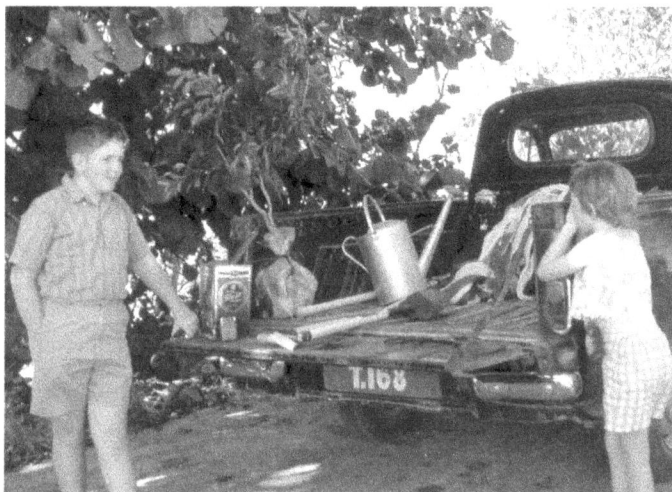

Gordon and Amy Jane checking out the gardening truck and tree to be planted by President Kennedy

One day Dan was driving the children in Nassau while former Prime Minister Winston Churchill was in town. Churchill was out being given a tour of the island, and Dan just happened to pass him by on the road. He instructed the children to look out the windows and drove by very slowly so they could get a glimpse of the great man. Then he quickly went up the street and turned around, and they drove very slowly back, all peering out the other side of the car as they passed by Churchill for a second time.

We chartered a motor cruiser together with our English friends, the Parrishs, during a Thanksgiving weekend to go from Nassau to some of the Out Islands. Our first overnight stop was in the quaint village of Spanish Wells with its small, pastel houses. We walked around the little town and stopped in a small store where we overheard two of the locals complaining about the millionaires that were blocking the dock and often interfering with space needed by the mailboat. Were we some of those "millionaires," we wondered? On a sailboat that was moored further out, using its dinghy to reach the dock, we heard that Walter Cronkite was the owner of that particular "millionaire" boat. We had no set destination and the captain decreed that the sea was too rough to go to Harbour Island, and so we went in the shelter of Eleuthera Island and stopped to see the dairy farm at Hatchet Bay. There was sunny weather and we each had a turn at deep-sea fishing.

Hollywood Comes to the Bahamas

Arthur Godfrey was one of America's longtime radio and TV stars and a name that everyone knew in the 1950s and 1960s. His radio show was called the Arthur Godfrey Time and his television show, the Arthur Godfrey Show, created the standard all late-night talk shows follow to this day. He was on holiday in Nassau with a group of friends that had chartered a daysailer moored off the Bahamas Country Club. We were taking sailing lessons at the club together with some English friends. Thirteen-year-old Gordon was doing a racing course in a small sailboat that had capsized, so the instructor, in his motorboat, towed him to the beach where he could bail out the boat.

Godfrey's party on the daysailer returned to tie up at their buoy and wait for a lift to the dock. It was taking a long time for the lift to shore to come and Godfrey grew impatient. He decided to swim ashore and when he encountered Gordon dutifully scooping water out of his boat, he offered to help him with the bailing. We thought it was a treat that he'd met Godfrey.

But the enterprising sailing teacher made the most of this brush with fame and the next day the Nassau Guardian headline blared, "Arthur Godfrey Rescues Young Sailor." Included in the article was a dramatic tale of Godfrey saving Gordon's life. Gordon was terribly embarrassed, not only because they reported his age incorrectly, but also to be described as such an inept sailor in the island paper. He knew that Godfrey was only on the beach assisting as a lark and no "rescuing" had been needed. Our English friends lightened the moment when they innocently asked, "Who is Arthur Godfrey?"

These occurrences happened more often than not as the Bahamas was, and still is, a sought-after destination. The "Have A Holly Jolly Christmas" singer, Burl Ives, was a regular visitor to the Bahamas, as he owned a home on Elbow Cay. Once while in the Nassau airport, Dan spied him arriving and pointed him out to Amy Jane. She had a broken arm at the time from jumping off a wall at a friend's house. "That's Burl Ives," he told her. "Go ask him to sign your cast." Amy Jane ran up to him and he kindly did just that. Another time, Bob Hope was seen coming out of customs, and Amy Jane got to shake his hand. A celebrity signature was acquired by Philip while visiting a friend at Doctors Hospital, then known as the Rassin Clinic. Film star Jayne Mansfield was staying there after she and her husband at the time, bodybuilder Mickey Hargitay, had gone missing while water skiing. Their boat had been found capsized and they and their press agent had been feared drowned. It became a national news story. Eventually, they were found, suffering from sun exposure and sand fly bites, after swimming to Rose Island and spending the night on a deserted strip of sand.

In the winter of 1965, the Beatles were in town filming their comedy-musical *Help!* This was at the height of Beatlemania in the U.S., which we were rather oblivious to in this Caribbean country. They stayed at the Balmoral Beach Club, an exclusive private resort designed by Sir Oliver Simmonds. It had just ten villas surrounding a main building near Cable Beach, and because the beach wasn't very much, they would ferry people over to the small island they owned about a mile offshore. The island gave the resort some cachet.

The Beatles flew in on February 22, which was Amy Jane's eleventh birthday. Amy Jane had received permission to take care of someone's pony in our backyard for three days and three nights while the owners were out of town. She and her friend, Valerie, were a bit horse-mad, so they were over the moon about having a real-life pony in their care. They brought him in through the back gate so they could brush and pet him and get him settled into our garden.

Just then all four of the Beatles drove by in a sporty little red convertible, John Lennon in the front seat. They stopped to talk with the girls over the back gate and asked about the breadfruit trees. That was a thrill for them.

This wasn't our only encounter with British "royalty."

Brushes with British Royalty

Besides getting to see Prince Philip when he made a visit to Nassau, the Queen Mother Elizabeth also came for a visit to the Bahamas while we lived there. She was making a tour of the Caribbean and had a daytime trip to Nassau, consisting of an afternoon drive around in a big black limousine with a police motorcycle escort. From her vehicle, she could wave graciously to the crowds lined up to see her along Bay Street. Then there were intervals where there were no crowds and she could relax and enjoy the island scenery. When she came down Shirley Street at the back of our home, The Corners, there was no one around. Our Philip was perched on the high stone wall for a good view. I remember taking a blurry picture of the Queen Mum waving to a lone young boy.

The Core family had a chance to see the Queen herself when we were in London in 1962 and attended the Royal Tournament. That was a wonderful show put on by all of the armed forces. We were among the crowd packed into the lobby to see the Queen and Prince Philip go into the tournament. Amy Jane was on Dan's shoulders for the best view. Seeing the Queen from four feet away, I was surprised to find how attractive she was.

Our Nassau friends also experienced some of these "brushes" with the royals. In Scotland, Jean Chaplin had a friend who was the daughter of the gatekeeper at Balmoral Castle. That girl played with Princess Elizabeth and Princess Margaret as children. She said Elizabeth bossed them around and was "queening" even as a little girl. She reminded her playmates that she had precedence: "She who must be obeyed!" Years later, Jean Chaplin entertained Queen Elizabeth's daughter, Princess Ann, when she stayed at the Kamuzu Academy in Malawi traveling for Save the Children Fund. The press gave the princess a reputation for being sour and nasty. But, when she was in the headmaster's home, she was warm and down-to-earth, according to the Chaplins.

Jean and John Chaplin had another "royal experience" when the President of Malawi made a state visit to London. He was entertained by the Queen and, in return, hosted a state dinner attended by all of the royal family. The Chaplins were living back in Scotland by this time, but were invited to attend the formal affair at Claridges. Jean described the evening and what the women wore. She owned a long, shocking pink formal dress to wear and borrowed an evening velvet wrap from a neighbor. John did not have formal wear, but since the invitation said formal wear or native dress, he borrowed a full Scottish evening kilt attire from a friend and was the only person so dressed. A Malawian cook had been flown in, as well as fresh fish from Lake Malawi. Princess Michael of Kent was present (this was at the time when the papers were blaring the news that her father had been an elite Nazi SS officer during WWII), as was Margaret Thatcher, the prime minister. Jean said it was unreal when the Queen caught her eye and smiled at her – the British signal to give a full royal curtesy!

Our friend Liz Parrish lived in Enfield, the next to last stop on the Piccadilly tube line. She regularly volunteered at a home for the aged. When the Queen made a visit for tea with the residents, Liz was helping in the kitchen and knew she would miss the great event. She was thrilled when the Queen took time to come back into the kitchen to meet and thank the helpers there.

In 1982, Dan and I were vacationing in Governor's Harbour, Eleuthera Island, Bahamas. Our old landlord back home in the states had suggested that for a special evening out we could use his name to make reservations at the Windemere Club on Windemere Island. It was a short distance from our small village and connected to Eleuthera by a causeway. When we called to make a reservation, we were told that no outsiders were permitted at the club at that time. A reason was not given, but we learned that Prince Charles and Princess Diana were there living in Lord Mountbatten's house. The press was camped just outside. It was then that the famous picture of Princess Diana, five months pregnant with Prince William and wearing a bathing suit, was taken by a long-range lens and published in the London tabloids, much to the Queen's displeasure.

How terrible it must be to have every movement viewed, discussed and criticized. The royals are more to be pitied than envied.

The Highland Bus

Our friend, Ann Lorenz, was a corporate secretary at U.S. Steel in Pittsburgh. She was dark haired and petite. She was also enterprising.

It was a sunny spring morning when Ann caught the usual Highland bus to her secretarial job downtown. She did not know the two young women seated in front of her, but she recognized them as frequent bus riders going to the same destination, the U.S. Steel headquarters in downtown Pittsburgh.

The women were discussing a job offer that one had received. It would be a transfer out of the country. It would mean giving up her comfortable apartment, leaving her present roommate and breaking up their household. They shared the iron and ironing board and many of the furnishings. She would have to buy a coffee maker and toaster and make so many changes in her life. This would be stepping into the unknown and she was having many misgivings.

Ann couldn't help hearing this. She began listening intently. Her present job was becoming boring and this was exactly the kind of opportunity that she wished that she had been offered. She quickly decided to find out the name of the woman and in what department she worked. On the bus the next morning, she introduced herself and asked what decision she made about the job offer. She discovered that this prize opportunity had been turned down. Ann immediately made her way to the personnel department and offered her resume for the opening. That is how she became secretary to the president of Navios, the off-shore subsidiary of U.S. Steel where Dan worked. She was a welcome addition to the company group there.

After four years in sun and sand, Ann, who had spent her working life in the corporate world, was finding business dull. With no romantic ties, she resigned her job in the Bahamas and set off for New York to find a place in the more glamorous world of fashion. With her high position at Navios, she was an experienced secretary and got a coveted job as one of two secretaries to Diane Vreeland, the famous editor of Vogue magazine, who is celebrated in posterity as a fashion icon. As many young women would think: "It was a job to kill for!"

The salary was not great and Ann's New York apartment, which was small, cramped and expensive, was a far cry from the sunny tropical apartment she had enjoyed in Nassau. The office staff did not wear the high fashions shown on the runways. Black sweaters and skirts were the office uniform and everyone wore big black sunglasses outdoors and hunched over their desks indoors. They all addressed each other as "dahling."

The magazine made its money with articles supposedly written by celebrities and wealthy socialites, who were given but a token payment and ghostwritten by low-paid staff writers. The photographers were better paid, Ann confessed to us.

Some of the avant-garde fashions were actually impromptu creations. Ann described standing by with a supply of pins as a hat designer wound yards of tulle into a frothy hat for a spring cover while the photographer waited. There were several windings and various takes and the hat would not have survived in a breeze.

The pay did not equal corporate rates and the hours were erratic. Ann was required to carry a bulging black briefcase with her at all times. It was filled with Ms. Vreeland's office materials and she was never to let it out of her sight. That extended beyond the normal nine to five hours. Ann was often called to the editor's home on a Saturday or a Sunday to work. She began to feel chained to the big black bag and on a gray, slushy New York day, she realized that she had no life to call her own.

Ann resigned her "dream job" and found another job writing publicity at the Cotton Institute. She was much happier and this job gave her time to enjoy New York City life – theatre, museums and winter ice skating at Rockefeller Center. It was there that she met a young Canadian man of Dutch ancestry. Their friendship grew and they were soon married. Like in the movies, there was a romantic ending for Ann. All because of an overheard conversation on the Highland bus.

The Lighthouse

Fane Solomon was our neighbor across Dowdeswell Street in Nassau and Lady Solomon's nephew. We were invited to dinner by Fane and returned the hospitality, though our activities as a family with youngsters meant we were in a different circle. Fane was a successful Bay Street businessman and spent his spare time at the tennis club or sailing. He was considered the most eligible and elusive bachelor in the city, as he was old family, handsome, wealthy and unpretentious.

Fane was a romantic and a man who loved the sea and being near the shore. He had sailed a small boat alone, the fifty-two miles from Nassau to Hatchet Bay, Eleuthera, a small adventure that he enjoyed telling us about. He had always loved lighthouses and wanted to live in one. Being a bachelor with ample means, he decided to build his own lighthouse on a small piece of land on the New Providence shore along Eastern Road in Nassau. Since it wouldn't be an operating light and shouldn't confuse sailors, there were numerous restrictions and permissions to be obtained, which took several years. It had a larger than usual top since that was the glass enclosed living room. Small bedrooms, baths, kitchen, etc. were on lower levels. There were the usual circular steps, but also an elevator. Furniture was minimal but designed for the space with a bed built to fit the curved wall. Sheets were nautical and a mural of boat rigging was on the wall behind the bed.

Shortly after the lighthouse was finished, to the surprise of all his friends and family, particularly his aunt, Miss Minette, Fane became a married man. It came as a great shock when he married a young American expat named Diane. Miss Minette was not only hurt, she was angry. She was so indignant that she refused to have his new bride under the same roof as her, and so the new couple went to live in the lighthouse.

The new Mrs. Fane Solomon was young, perhaps fifteen to eighteen years younger than Fane. She had come to Nassau from Millvale, a small town near Pittsburgh, and was working in the office of Outboard Marine's headquarters on Bay Street. We never really saw them together, so we could not comment on any chemistry between the two. Compared to all the women he had squired in the past, this choice puzzled everyone. Perhaps he was doing the honorable thing, perhaps he wanted an heir, the gossips suggested. At any rate, the couple moved to the lighthouse and the bride was pregnant. It may have been a difficult pregnancy. Some young women seem to bloom when pregnant. This was not the case for Diane. We saw her when she brought their laundry to use the equipment at Fane's old duplex. She seemed overheated, with a full and puffy face and blotchy skin. I sympathized with her; being pregnant in a hot climate is no fun. Fane was never with her at these times and soon resumed his routine at the tennis club.

Electric power in Nassau is often erratic. One night we were having our friends, Liz and Derek Parrish, to dinner when the lights went out and we finished by candlelight. There was much chiding of Derek who was an executive of Bahamas Electricity Corp.

Daytime outages also took place and caught Diane in the elevator in the lighthouse, where she was captive for some time. At that point, she refused to stay in the lighthouse and they found accommodations elsewhere. They had a son and then a daughter. Years later, we heard she was living in Florida and that they were divorced.

Apparently, Fane did return to live a bachelor life again in his lighthouse. In February 1982, the "Nassau Guardian" newspaper reported on a break-in there. The burglars first shot his two guard dogs and then, when Fane was aroused by the noise and looked about, he was shot from below and seriously wounded. He was armed and able to return fire before the intruders fled. He survived and lived for twenty more years. Fane was living in Treasure Cay, Abaco at the time of his death in August 2003. His son Martin still owns the lighthouse.

Out Islands

There are said to be as many as 3,000 islands making up the country of the Bahamas, ranging from tiny rocky outcroppings to sizeable land masses. Some islands are small and privately owned while others have a number of settlements. Communication between the islands for many years was solely by mailboats, which transport people, mail and shipping. The mailboats make weekly trips and their arrival at the dock is the big event of the day for the population. They are there to greet passengers, to receive packages and mail and all sorts of merchandise ordered from Nassau.

Nassau was always a tourist destination, from its early days when wealthy people came by ship for winter stays and when the super-rich sometimes had one or even two winter homes. Nassau also made a reputation as a tax haven and many foreign corporations had what were known as "suitcase companies" registered in local law offices. Other companies maintained actual offices there, like my husband's company, Navios, with a large office on Village Road. From our rented house in the center of town we spent Sunday afternoons exploring the rest of the island. Much of the southern side at that time was bush and the sea was shallow with mangrove swamps. Then, we began to hear about the Out Islands and wanted to visit them.

Other company employees could tell us little about the Out Islands, as most of their travels away from Nassau were to Miami for shopping. The office cleaning woman, Mrs. Johnson, was a native of Rock Sound on the far end of Eleuthera.

Only Mrs. Albury, the office coffee lady, could provide any information. She, too, was from Rock Sound, Eleuthera. She had family there and her brother worked for the two priests at the Catholic Mission. The mailboat made weekly trips to Rock Sound, traveling the length of Eleuthera, making stops at the small settlements along the way. The Mission had a guest house and Mrs. Johnson said that she would contact her brother and make arrangements for an overnight stay there. With her encouragement, and after a message to her brother requesting an overnight stay at the Catholic guest house, we packed baskets from the straw market, including some food and overnight supplies, and bought roundtrip tickets on the mailboat.

Thus, it was that the five Cores set forth early one morning to the dock where we boarded the MV *Air Swift*. Rock Sound would be reached in the late afternoon and the boat would unload and reload overnight to leave early the next morning for its return trip. During the week, the boat went along the West coast of Eleuthera and on the weekend went to Spanish Wells and Harbour Island off northern Eleuthera where the crew lived.

We did not go ashore on any of the brief stops along the way when mail and cargo were delivered. The small clusters of houses could be seen at a glance. The largest town was Governor's Harbour where from a distance, the white houses on the hillside resembled a New England village.

On reaching Rock Sound, we left the dock and walked up a dusty road to the Catholic Church, which was a prominent landmark. At one side sat a small rectory and another white building which was the guest house. We found no one about. Backtracking to the center of the village, we found a small eating place, had some ice cream and inquired about the priests. In these small places, everyone knows everything about everyone. Father Charles was at French Leave and would soon be back. The village "grapevine" works quickly and soon the priest appeared having been alerted as soon as he "reached."

After introductions, we were embarrassed to find that Mrs. Johnson's message about our arrival plans had not preceded us. Father Charles was most cordial and said we were most welcome to use the guest house. He invited us to have dinner at the rectory with his associate, Father Damien, and him. He said that there was always frozen food on hand for just such occasions as they were in a lonely post and visitors were a pleasant diversion. We did not want to impose further and had made arrangements to have dinner at the little shop. We promised that, after the children were settled in bed, we would join them at the Rectory.

For two Presbyterians, this visit with two Canadian Catholic priests was a most unusual experience. The two priests had been sent as missionaries to China. During the Revolution, they were imprisoned for over ten years wondering if they would ever be freed. During that time an occasional letter from family or a friend did get through to them. They had learned to endure imprisonment and these letters from home intruded into this life and were very painful since they were reminded of what they had lost.

When they were finally freed and returned to Canada, they had brief assignments there before they were assigned to this mission outpost in the Bahamas. Father Charles did most of the parish work as Father Damien has been sent there for his health and had few duties. They were training a native Bahamian as a novitiate to assist them. Petitions had been sent to Canada asking for teaching nuns so that a school could be started. The two men were glad to have visitors. They spoke of the ages and variety of guests they had had.

Only four white men lived in Rock Sound, all single. That made just enough for their weekly bridge game. In addition to the priests, there was a doctor and an Episcopal priest. They said that the latter was more Roman than they were in his ministry and that he read the pronouncements of the Pope. He practiced a voluntary celibacy and renewed his vow annually. The priests did not understand this. They felt it was an additional hardship to make such a decision each year as he could be open to temptation almost constantly.

Our fascinating conversation lasted until late at night as they were so eager to talk. Finally, Father Damien retired and we stayed on even longer. The conversation of that night had transported us into new and completely different worlds. The magic of that experience has never been forgotten.

Since the mailboat would be leaving early the next morning, Father Charles suggested that he drive us after breakfast to Gregory Town where we could catch the boat. He said that he had business farther on. This gave us time and a chance to see more of Eleuthera. He drove us into French Leave for a peek at that resort. We learned later that Mrs. Johnson's message arrived the day after we had left Rock Sound.

Amy Jane and Claire Parrish in front of our charter cruiser at Spanish Wells

During a Thanksgiving holiday, we chartered a 37-foot motor cruiser, with a captain and mate, together with the Parrishs, our British friends. The first stop was at the Current Marina where the crew got gas. Overnight, we anchored in the harbor at Spanish Wells, a picturesque settlement of small pastel-colored houses on St. George's Cay. The dock was crowded with other boats and our captain tied up to another boat, over which we stepped our way to shore. We walked around the town looking for thyme plants for my garden. It was a Thursday evening and, from the boat, we heard the sounds of a church choir practicing drift over the

232

docks. There was time for some deep-sea fishing and a stop at Hatchet Bay to look at dairy farm cows. The weather was too rough to go around into the Atlantic and stop at Harbour Island.

Several years later, we spent a weekend at the Little Boarding House on Harbour Island run by two retired teachers, who provided wonderful meals of local fish and produce. Our rooms were in a two-story house across the street. On the veranda was a Barwa chair, which was the relaxing high point for me. The Bahamian home cooking was wonderful, for their former students brought them the choicest fruits and vegetables and the freshest fish. On this holiday, there was nothing to do except walk around the tiny village streets and spend time at the beach.

All the beaches in the Bahamas are public and the best swimming and the famous pink sands colored by crushed coral are on the ocean side of the island. We went there to swim and followed the path through tall grasses to the beach and used a simple shack as a changing room. The waves were gentle and no one attempted to swim far from shore. It all seemed so idyllic then.

A year later we met a charming American couple at a dinner party hosted by the president of Navios. After a two-week stay in Nassau, they planned to go to the famous Pink Sands resort for another two-week holiday. We learned some time later that they both drowned there. One of them had been caught in an undertow and the other had gone to the rescue and they both perished. There are no lifeguards in the Bahamas and probably no other people on the beach. Deserted beaches of white sands are part of the charm of the islands.

Recently on the real estate TV program, House Hunters International, the teachers' Little Boarding House was sold for a million US dollars because of its prime view of the harbor.

Our Pittsburgh house guest, U.S. Steel law department manager Louise Bowman and I flew to Harbour Island for lunch at the Pink Sands resort, landing on Northern Eleuthera and taking a small boat to Harbour Island. The locals were so friendly, particularly to visitors in the off-season. We admired a garden and were invited into a cottage home.

Louise was intent on soaking up the charm of the Bahamas and carried a large camera slung over her shoulder and a big floppy hat; she looked like the quintessential tourist as she roamed Nassau. One day, when she came back to The Corners, a visitor looked at her astonished before turning to me and saying, "Do tourists just walk in like this?" I quickly had to explain that she was a house guest.

Rose Island was close to Nassau and hardly qualified as an out island since there were only a few isolated houses there and it was a good place to find a deserted beach to anchor and swim. Mr. Wells and his sailboat were often chartered on a Sunday afternoon.

One winter, when we were living in Duluth, Minn., we met a woman named Linda Hutchison who managed a house and cottage in Governor's Harbour that she owned with a local attorney, Horace Hershburger. We rented the cottage for a week's holiday. The property was up a steep hill and we developed strong leg muscles from trips to the few stores on the one side of the island. There was a gradual hill down to the beach where we swam at the Club Mediteranee. We missed having dinner at Windermere Island nearby since Prince Charles and Princess Di were having a holiday at Lord Mountbatten's residence. There were paparazzi on our returning plane.

Nassau has become built up, choked with traffic and plagued by crime, so the Out Islands are now the places to go for a relaxing holiday.

Eight
A European Tour

Traveling Dreams

Travel dreams were put on hold for many years. When Dan was transferred to the Bahamas, our world opened up. First was our flight from New York to Nassau for his confirming interview with executives at Navios Corporation, a U.S. Steel subsidiary. Then there was my first cruise ship experience with the children when we left Ben Avon for our new home abroad.

Nassau was a British crown colony and Americans found it very British in its form of government, currency and customs. British residents found it very American with its many tourists and proximity to the United States, some 200 miles off the coast of Florida.

Navios was an off-shore tax-exile, a 'runaway flag' shipping company. It had liberal employee vacation benefits to avoid island fever, which is akin to cabin fever. Vacation for one year was three weeks with family transportation paid to Miami. The alternate year provided four weeks' vacation with family transportation paid to New York. These leaves were mandatory. You could not simply elect to collect your travel funds.

The first year we did a house exchange with the Johnsons in Sewickley, Pa. to visit Mother and our siblings' families and to see to the sale of the Ben Avon house nearby, which was still on the market. On the three-week holiday of 1961, we went to Jamaica and found respite from the tropical heat in the hills there.

In 1962, we realized our dream of going to England. We had a number of English friends who helped us plan the trip – from a small inexpensive London hotel to introductions to their families. We met our friend Derek Parrish's sisters near Stratford and the McKenzies' brother, who had us to dinner in Edinburgh. We were advised on many of the accommodations along the way and got as far as the Kyle of Lochalsh and Skye.

In 1963, we spent three weeks in Fairlawn, N.J. on another house exchange with the Shapiros. Gordon was already in the U.S. taking a summer course at Philips Exeter Academy in New Hampshire. This was to get him up to speed for his first year in the American school system. He took the train down to New York City to meet us and then we toured American prep schools before deciding he would attend Westtown, a Quaker school near West Chester, Pa., in the fall. We took a leisurely cruise ship aboard the *M.S. Italia* on our return trip to Nassau.

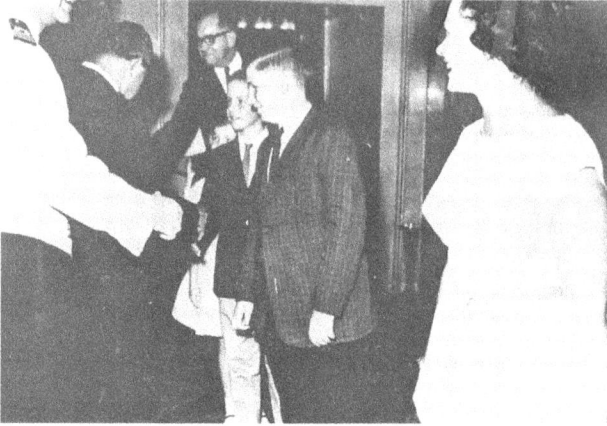

Gordon, Philip, Amy Jane, Dan and I welcomed to the Captain's Dinner by the captain and officers of the M.S. Italia in 1963

In 1964, we went to London, where we picked up a new Vauxhall station wagon we had ordered sight unseen from a Nassau dealer and had it delivered to us in London. Thus, it could be used for our travels rather than renting cars. When it was shipped to Nassau at the end of the trip, it had become a used car and the duty was somewhat less. Europe was much cheaper than the Bahamas then.

Dan joined us for his month of leave with the company but the rest of us enjoyed an extended stay, two weeks before and three weeks after he left. We used our new car to drive all over Europe together, and, at the end of the trip, it was returned to the London dealer and shipped to us in Nassau.

These were the start of our travels. Later, they extended in our retirement years with guided tours in Europe and the Mediterranean or to visit friends living in far-flung locales like Malawi and Egypt. Then there were several very exclusive trips on Great Lakes ore boats during our time living along Lake Superior.

Dan and I never owned a vacation home or even second car. Instead, there were trips all over the world and the wonderful memories we created together.

Anne Hathaway's Cottage

Everyone knows that William Shakespeare's sweetheart and wife, Anne Hathaway, lived in a cottage in Stratford-upon-Avon. The historic cottage is pictured on postcards, biscuit tins and every imaginable English souvenir. It seemed a simple matter for the five of us, two parents and three youngsters on our first trip to the United Kingdom, to find our way there.

We had visited the birthplace of Shakespeare, passed the Trinity Church – which claimed him as its most distinguished parishioner – and asked a passerby we encountered along the way which direction it was to Anne Hathaway's cottage.

The helpful man pointed our way through the small town and said there was a public footpath that would take us there.

We walked and walked and walked and the cottage seemed no closer. Interest was rapidly fading. I wished someone had told us how far this really was. The cottage is actually two miles from town. After all these centuries, the town had grown no closer. At last, the cottage appeared in the distance, and my husband decided that he was too tired to go inside and would wait under a tree until the end of the tour. I scarcely recall what the cottage was like inside, as only that interminable walk was memorable.

Later, while hiking in Switzerland with the family, we came to a signpost that we couldn't make heads nor tails of, so we asked a passerby how far it was to our planned destination. We may not have understood his French correctly. It was either fifteen or fifty minutes, and we simply said, "Merci!" and kept going. It turned out that it definitely was not the former and we plodded on and on. The children groaned and reminded me of a similar folly by moaning, "Anne Hathaway's Cottage!"

If only we had known!

Hitchhikers

Long ago, when the world seemed safer, hitchhiking was how the fresh-faced youth of this country managed to travel. It was ungenerous not to share your car if you were fortunate enough to have one during the Depression. Later, during wartime gas rationing, it was unpatriotic not to fill a car with as many passengers as could be fitted in. For many years, after hitchhiking became dangerous for both the driver and the hiker in the United States, the custom continued in Europe.

There the hitchhikers carried signs with their destination and often their nationality and sometimes they dressed in national costumes such as lederhosen and kilts. When Amy Jane was a student at the University of Dijon in France in 1975, she made a number of trips during holiday breaks. The students would go in pairs, and it was a safety measure to travel with a male friend. Additional protection was to have a Swiss Army knife at the ready. The tenor of a driver's conversation soon indicated if this was a "safe" ride.

Our experiences with hitchhikers in Europe in 1964 were mixed. I was driving in France with our three children: Gordon, aged fourteen, Philip, aged twelve and Amy Jane, aged ten. They had become bored with famous sights and lovely scenery. We were in the "puy" country of central France. Puys are small, bare mountain-like eruptions. We were driving up the steep curving road to see the prehistoric ruins and the view from the top of the famous Puy de Dome, the largest at 4,805 feet.

We were flagged down by a young man. I stopped, thinking that he was collecting a toll, only to find that he needed a ride because hikers were forbidden on that road. He was a Danish schoolteacher with excellent English and American slang polished by his devotion to MAD Magazine. We were the first Americans that he had ever met and he was thrilled. We were equally charmed, particularly the boys. After we had explored the ruins, we were reluctant to lose such a good companion and invited him to continue with us to Clermont-Ferrand where he joined us in our usual picnic lunch in a leafy park. We parted company there since he was meeting a friend in another direction.

Remembering this pleasant experience as we were driving in Germany several weeks later, the backseat bunch urged me to stop for two girl hitchhikers. The children were eager to talk with them, but one of the pair spoke no English and the other girl, with some English, had little to say. Their presence was oppressive and boring.

Philip, with a few German lessons that taught him pronunciation, was carrying a small German phrase book. He read out of it to them for a while in order to carry on a stilted conversation. The hikers' destination was the next large town, but as we came to a small village, they suddenly changed their minds and asked to get out there. We said "auf wiedersehen" with some relief.

We asked Philip what he had said from the German phrase book that caused them to make an early exit. He told us it was, "I think I'm going to be sick." What a diplomatic solution to our problem! We laughed with relief.

Amsterdam

Amsterdam was the next-to-last city visit of our 1964 European travel. Our last brief stop would be in Rotterdam where we would stay overnight and then take the car ferry overnight to England. The final week of the nine-week holiday would be in England before returning the car to London.

The only reservations made were for London at 157 George Street, a small hotel where we had stayed in 1962. An advance deposit was made for the car ferry plane that would take just three cars and those passengers across the English Channel to France. We had also made reservations for a two-week stay at Le Porteau Blanc (White Gates), a pension outside Vevey, Switzerland.

The flat country opened up as we drove into Holland and saw the windmills that we had expected, even if we didn't know exactly what they were doing. In Amsterdam, we found a bed and breakfast hotel in a tall, narrow building overlooking the Singel Canal. The exception was the Saturday night in Aix en Provence that happened to be the final night of a famous music festival.

Amsterdam with its canals was a cooler, greener version of Venice. Streets ran beside both sides of the canals with leafy trees providing shade. Narrow buildings of three and four stories lined the canals. They had differing decorative rooftops like bonnets distinguishing the buildings.

Our hotel on the Singel Canal had an all-purpose room that was both lobby and breakfast room combined. Oriental rugs draped the tables, to be replaced by crisp, checked tablecloths for breakfast. These oriental table covers were reminiscent of old Dutch paintings. Breakfast was bread and butter, cheese, ham and hard-boiled egg with a beverage. Our bedroom looked out on the canal over a window box filled with bright red geraniums.

No rain fell during our Amsterdam stay. The weather alternated between bright sunshine and dark clouds. Now Vincent van Gogh's early paintings of dark skies could be understood in context. Our car was parked nearby but we mostly explored the city on foot.

One sunny day, we had a boat tour of the city's canals that included a visit to a wooden shoe factory. Philip found shoes to fit him, which he wore briefly. The large church that we visited was distinctly different from the ornate cathedrals of France and Italy. There were no stained-glass windows and so it was airy, spacious, simple and filled with sunlight. It stood in stark contrast to the dark medieval churches elsewhere in Europe.

A bus tour took us to The Hague, the site of the United Nations' World Court. We saw the tulip fields, a flower market and the Delft factory in the city there. On the highway, we had the unusual experience of passing under an aqueduct just as a sailboat passed us overhead. We saw the famous paintings at the Rijksmuseum.

With the recommendations of the guidebook, there were interesting places to dine. One tiny restaurant was built like a ship's interior with a steep ladder to tables on a second floor. Another memorable meal involved a reistafel, or rice table, which the Dutch had adapted from Indonesian cuisine. Rice was the base on which many ingredients were heaped – curried meats, coconut, chopped onions, eggs, raisins, peanuts and chutney. It was a seemingly endless variety of toppings and the mixture was surprisingly delicious.

Sunday was an overcast day when we set out for the city tour office. We must have overslept for, when we arrived, we found that the tour we had planned had already left. However, there was space in a group that was leaving in a few minutes. I decided we would go on the other day tour that was suggested, without knowing just what we would see. Throwing caution to the wind, we set off for a day of suspense and surprises. It turned out to be an exciting adventure, because we never knew what to expect next.

A bus took us to the pier where we boarded a boat to cross the Zuiderzee. We learned how the Dutch reclaimed much of their land from the North Sea and the dikes that protected the land. Passing by the seaside resort with the unpronounceable name of Scheveningen, there was no one on the beach on this cool, gray day. The hotel had been taken over by the Nazis in WWII.

Disembarking in the village of Volendam, there were people coming back from church in traditional Dutch costumes. Small, quaint brick houses filled the neat village. A small antique shop was open with some of its wares displayed outside. Its fascinating collection caught my eye. Although committed to traveling light, I selected an antique wooden cookie mold that has been in my kitchen ever since, as well as a small brass warming stand for a tea kettle.

There must have been a box lunch on the boat when our time of wandering through the town was over. Then there was more sailing on the broad expanse of water to a stop at a cheese factory in Edam. Cheesemaking was demonstrated and there was an opportunity to buy. That was easily resisted since we were traveling.

The cheese samples were enjoyed. Instead, I spotted an aged, lightweight wooden cheese mold that I arranged to buy. A brief glimmer of sunlight appeared over the water as the boat made its way back to Amsterdam. The mystery tour was one of our best days in Europe.

Visiting Rotterdam

By 1964, the city of Rotterdam was completely modern. The city had risen from the ashes of WWII and rebuilt. As an important shipping port, it had been a strategic target during the war and literally bombed to the ground. Now, it was once again a busy waterfront. Rotterdam had none of the quaint charm of Amsterdam, where ancient churches, tall houses and tree-lined canals retained their antique charm. Rotterdam had been bombed so badly during the war that everything was new.

From Amsterdam we drove to Rotterdam for two nights before taking the car ferry back to England. Rotterdam was the last overnight stop of our six weeks in Europe. Here we would board the car ferry and have an overnight cabin to return to England's port of Tilbury. The three children and I were on our own again. Husband Dan's monthlong vacation was over and he had left us in Paris to return to Nassau. The shipping and port service company, Van Ommeren Shipping, was port agent for Navios Corporation, Dan's employer. Van Ommeren had made reservations for us in a modern high-rise hotel.

Thus, we had accommodations in a high-rise hotel, an escorted morning tour of the harbor, and then lunch at the revolving restaurant at the top of the Euromast. Two pleasant gentlemen in business suits from Van Ommeren called for us at the hotel in chauffeur-driven Mercedes sedan. They spoke excellent English, as many of the Dutch do.

Our hosts had arranged a boat tour especially for us, but the water was too rough for the company's boat. As a result, we navigated the busy harbor in a floating bus-ferry they had chartered exclusively for us. It was used to shuttle crew members ashore from anchored ships and we rattled in seating meant for forty or fifty people. We saw many big ships and a forest of loading cranes along the shore. We didn't see a Navios ship, but a ship registered in Nassau was in dry-dock.

The Euromast was an elegant setting for lunch with all the waiters in tail coats. I asked our hosts for guidance in ordering. Was there a special dish of the Netherlands? They said, "Of course, you must taste our smoked eel." I was stuck.

It would not have been as bad if I had simply been presented with a few slices on a small plate. However, the waiter wheeled up a cart beside the table, on which a whole eel was artistically displayed on a wooden carving board, and proceeded to carve my portion in front of us. The children regarded it with horror, while I stoically tackled this national delicacy. When we talked about it afterward, they admired my bravery.

On parting with our Rotterdam friends, we were given a copy of an ancient view of the harbor which was four feet long, but rolled up neatly. It was framed and hung above doorways in our subsequent homes.

During our travels, we had stayed at quaint and cheap inns, usually complete with a bidet, which turned out to be useful for washing socks. Rotterdam was our first truly modern hotel. After seeing cathedrals, castles in England, chateaux in France and staying in rustic inns, my daughter reveled in the modern hotel in Rotterdam. Amy Jane looked around at our accommodations with satisfaction. She said, "If I were a princess, this is the kind of place I would want to live." So much for history!

The Vauxhall station wagon was to be returned to the dealer in London for its shipment to Nassau. We enjoyed an overnight in a cabin on the car ferry and then we were back in England with friends for the last three weeks of our holiday.

Photo taken of Gordon, Amy Jane and Phil at the Nassau airport in April 1963 by our good friend, John Kingsley, who had been visiting with us

Nine
Back in the U.S.A.

Mount Lebanon
1965 – 1972

We went back to Pittsburgh again somewhat reluctantly, although the transfer came at a time when it was important to move the children from the British school system to an American college track. Gordon was already in his first year at Westtown School, a Quaker co-ed boarding school near Philadelphia in West Chester, Pa.

House-hunting was easier in a familiar city. We first looked at Ben Avon, which we remembered fondly, and finding nothing available there, turned our attention to Mt. Lebanon, a larger suburb with what was reputed to have the best schools in the area. Dan's older brother, Bud, his wife, Margaret, and their two girls were living in Mt. Lebanon at 278 Kenforest Drive, where they had moved in 1958, so, undoubtedly, this helped with our decision-making process.

Dan started back to work in the law department of U.S. Steel in January and stayed at the William Penn across the street from the downtown office. He made preliminary contacts with real estate agents in Mt. Lebanon.

My trip to Pittsburgh several weeks later was in the company plane. Such luxury! There were lounge chairs, an invitation to the cockpit to see the lights of cities that we were passing over and great refreshments served, with many apologies because the full menu dinners had been used up. A radio phone call was made to Dan at the office alerting him to our arrival at the private landing area. Fred Pate, also of Navios, was on the plane with me.

The first house I looked at was 633 Arden Road, where George and Mary Skinner had lived. He was Dan's replacement in Nassau. The three-bedroom, ivy-covered brick house on a hillside lot seemed terribly small after the sweeping vistas of The Corners, but it did have two baths, a powder room and study on the first floor with a two-car tandem garage. But there was much more on the market and the mating dance with real estate agents began.

That weekend we drove by different possibilities in the Pittsburgh area and Sunday had an appointment with a different agent and made a bid on another brick house. Monday morning, however, while I was keeping another appointment, reality set in. I felt that our bid on the other house had been a mistake and the Skinner's house in Mt. Lebanon that we'd first inspected was probably our very best bet. There was no chance for Dan to see the inside, but he took my word for it and we phoned Nassau and arranged to buy it from George and Mary. The house was on a dead-end street convenient to the junior and senior high schools and just a block from the bus stop. There were other youngsters of the same age as Phil and Amy Jane in the neighborhood and it just felt right.

Our new home in Mt. Lebanon at 633 Arden Road, pictured here in March 1965

The house was a center-hall colonial with a projection in front of the dining room that had a French door opening onto a small balcony over the door of the integral garage. The living room on the left had a wood-burning fireplace with classic white mantle. The Italian builder had embellished the hearth with a highly vari-colored marble, which I painted a flat black immediately. A glass door at the back end of the living room led to an awning-covered patio. At the end of the center hall was a powder room and to the right of that the door to a generously sized eat-in kitchen. From the kitchen a door opened to a maid's room, which had built-in bookshelves, making it a cozy library-cum-study. With our sofa sleeper it gave additional sleeping space. There was a door from the kitchen to the outside of the house.

Upstairs over the living room was the master bedroom, with a walk-in closet and a tiled bath with shower stall. Another full bath was at the top of the stairs and there were two more bedrooms. The hall was spacious enough to accommodate an armoire (purchased at the St. Vincent de Paul Thrift Shop and refinished in antique blue). This matched the double chest in the room that the boys shared. Phil had this to himself when Gordon was at Westtown.

The basement steps were open until we had them enclosed. They led to the laundry area. At the foot of the stairs was the door to a family room that had a brick fireplace and asphalt-tiled floor. We had the room paneled and the furnace in the corner enclosed by shutter doors. The room was almost completely filled by the large pool table left by the Skinners. From the other side of the stairs, a door opened into the garage. On a trip to England in 1969, I found an antique lion's head door knocker, which we added to the front door. On a return trip to visit the house forty-seven years later, my daughter found the door knocker still in place!

The wisdom of having a home with a first-floor powder room and bed space was confirmed almost immediately when Gordon came home from school that first summer with a broken foot. He was soon proving his agility by hopping up the steps. Later, Philip had knee surgery, performed by the Pittsburgh Pirates' orthopedic surgeon, and there were enough times when someone was ill that the room served as an extra bedroom. This was a well-built house with junior steel beam construction and hardwood floors throughout.

We visited various Presbyterian churches in hopes of finding a new church home. There were five large congregations in Mt. Lebanon and we joined the Bower Hill Presbyterian Church, which was almost within sight of Arden Road, across from the empty field at the end of our cul-de-sac and diagonal from the junior high school. It was a highly-organized church with many activities for various age groups, though it was never our favorite congregation. On Sunday mornings, even the people that we had known in the past when we had previously lived in Pittsburgh didn't take the time to seek us out and speak with us. Still, Amy Jane went to confirmation class there and to Jefferson Elementary School, while Philip was at Jefferson Junior High School nearby.

We had moved to Mt. Lebanon for the schools and were firm believers in the public school system, which had provided our own educations. But it soon became clear that Phil and Amy Jane, having grown used to the British education system in the Bahamas, were not at home in the Mt. Lebanon school district. Thus, they each followed Gordon to Westtown School for their high school careers. We made many trips across the state, taking them to and from school, and making visits to that beautiful part of the country.

It was good to be back in the United States among longtime friends that we had missed while we were living out of the country, like my college roommate, Jean Rothermel, and my sister, Ceil, who lived nearby in the Pittsburgh suburb of Pleasant Hills with her husband and four daughters. And of course, Dan's brother and his family, who lived in Mt. Lebanon, were within a mile of our new home.

Best friends: Jean Archer Rothermel and me

It was reassuring to have a support network again after being out of the region for over a decade.

My activities in Pittsburgh included sitting on the Chatham College alumni board and serving a two-year term as an alumnae trustee of the college. I was also on the women's auxiliary board at Dan's alma mater, Washington & Jefferson, where he would become an alumni trustee for two terms. I was on the board of the area YWCA in Carnegie and attended classes there as well as being a representative at downtown meetings, where I knew many people.

I never joined the Mt. Lebanon Woman's League, which was very popular at the time, but became an active member of the Western Pennsylvania Unit of the Herb Society of America and was chairman of the unit. Later, I became National President of the Herb Society of America. That was a lot of work and correspondence in pre-computer and pre-Xerox days, but it provided the wonderful duty of visiting all the then-thirteen herb groups from Boston to California over a two-year period, plus travel to quarterly board meetings. I've retained an active membership in the organization since then and in 2005 was bestowed the Helen de Conway Little Medal of Honor for my contributions to the world of horticulture.

My expertise with herbs and gardening had taken root and soon I was serving on the speakers' bureau for the Pittsburgh Garden Center, giving lectures and demonstrations all over the Pittsburgh region for garden clubs and community groups, as well as, occasionally writing guest columns in the local newspapers.

Dan and I had some interesting evenings after we joined the Pittsburgh Branch of the English-Speaking Union at the invitation of our neighbors, Judge Walter Koegler and his wife, Jean, who lived at 620 Arden Lane. One night we were featured in the local newspaper meeting the Ambassador to the United States from New Zealand, Frank H. Corner and his wife, who were being hosted at the Pittsburgh Golf Club. I joined the annual Heart Fund campaign for the Western Pennsylvania Heart Association and became the chairman in 1966. These activities were reminiscent of our time spent in Nassau and in New Albany.

We were back in U.S. Steel's corporate headquarters, but I seldom felt the constraints of being a corporate wife. There were so many company people living all over the city. Dan's boss and his wife, Bob and Olive Wertz, were a friendly, but erratic couple who lived nearby and they were the source of some strange adventures. Dan was slated to succeed him on his retirement and we did manage to stay on amiable terms. However, corporations evolve and the "mills of the gods" had other plans. The retirement of a railroad attorney in Duluth, Minn., who wanted Dan to succeed him, took us away from Pittsburgh again.

The move in June 1972 coincided with the end of my term as president of the Herb Society and almost the end of my term as a college trustee at Chatham College. It was also a graceful exit from nomination to the citywide YWCA board, where I was involved as a booth chairman in educating about herbs as part of their annual Festival of Nations.

President of the Herb Society of America

The Herb Society of America was founded by thirteen future-minded ladies in the Boston area in 1935. They must have envisioned the growth of the present-day number of units. The Society grew slowly and, in order for all members to have input, the executive officers were rotated every two years between the units and members at large. This was democracy by rotation. It had its advantages and disadvantages.

The chapter I joined, the Western Pennsylvania Unit of the Herb Society of America, was fairly young and felt removed from knowing much about the national organization's plans. The unit supplied all officers with the exception of the second vice president, who was from the nearest Western Reserve Unit and the third vice president from Northern California, who would be the next president. The incoming president was to attend board meetings to acquire national experience. May Ashcraft had stepped down and I was nominated in her place. Katie Wilbert was on the National Board but had never attended a meeting. She agreed to go to New York with me for a January meeting, but bowed out at the last minute. So I went to my first board meeting alone.

The New York Unit hosted the gathering at the Republican Women's Club in downtown Manhattan and I was housed there in somewhat austere surroundings. The third vice president was always noted on the meeting's agenda opposite no report. During a break in the meeting, I was conducted (presented!) to a dowager member of the New York Unit, Noreen Capen. At the time, I didn't realize that I was being interviewed by the financial angel of the Herb Society of America. She was a wealthy woman who had hired its lone employee. She also paid a stated portion of the monthly office expenses. The Easterners were somewhat apprehensive about this new group from the far side of the mountains in Western Pennsylvania. Mrs. Capen seemed rather cool to my youthful age, in comparison to the majority of past presidents.

I had never heard of the Herb Society of America until the International Garden Club in Nassau, Bahamas had a program on herbs given by a visiting Massachusetts club member. When I mentioned this woman's name to Mrs. Capen, it proved to be an "open sesame" for us and she warmed considerably.

The headquarters' office of the Society was at a prestigious address, 300 Massachusetts Avenue, Boston. This was the headquarters of the Massachusetts Horticultural Society and just across from Symphony Hall. Founder Mrs. Anne Burrage had a nephew on the board of the society and surely had a hand in arranging the monthly rental of $15. There was one employee, the executive secretary. She was accustomed to running the Society since she represented the continuity of the organization and also its benefactor. She was seated beside the president at board meetings, who often deferred to her. The office consisted of two attic rooms. Equipment in the sixties was limited to a typewriter, desks, phone and mimeograph machine. There were a few books and the rare books were housed in the Horticultural Society library a flight below. B.C.M. (before copying machines), correspondence involved carbon paper and tissue copies as far as could be stretched. Long distance phone service was more expensive then and conference calls were unknown. Each annual meeting was special with the shared enthusiasm of new herbal ideas, the unusual events and the tours of outstanding gardens.

In 1969, the Potomac Unit of the Herb Society of America hosted what were known then as annual meetings for select Society members from around the country. I had the honor of attending a special early morning event – a private tour of the White House, which had been recently refurbished by First Lady Jackie Kennedy during her historical restoration. This was followed by a tour in the Rose Garden, which had been redesigned by her friend, philanthropist and horticulturalist Mrs. Paul "Bunny" Mellon, an honorary Herb Society member. In the Rose Garden, we had the special privilege of holding our short annual business meeting for the Society.

Mrs. Mellon's interest in gardening and membership in the Herb Society came through her friend and mentor, Mrs. Florence Bratenahl, one of the founders of the Society, who had been responsible for the herb gardens at Washington's National Cathedral, where her husband George was the dean. Her gardens are still an important part of the Cathedral today.

Our Rose Garden experience was topped by a visit to the Mellon estate "Oak Spring" in Upperville, Virginia. On that misty summer morning, Paul and Bunny Mellon greeted each guest in the stone-floored entrance hall of their sprawling French-style house. She was wearing a comfortable full skirt of lightweight tweed and a long-sleeved turtleneck top with a floppy gardening hat. A week later, there was an account in the New York Times which described the skirt as a Balenciaga design, which we would never have guessed. Paul and Bunny graciously shook everyone's hands and then guided us out into the gardens.

From the front hall, a doorway led directly into a beautifully designed French country garden with all the vegetables neatly aligned. Everything was just perfect. If a cabbage died, one of the many gardeners just put another one in its place. Luncheon was served to two hundred guests under a huge white tent. The New York Horticultural Society had been entertained there several weeks before, so the tent had remained in place in preparation for this event as well. Mr. Mellon hosted one table; other members of the family split up to head other tables. As incoming president of the society, I was fortunate to be seated at the same table as Bunny. One of the hosts was the head gardener for the estate. He gave a short speech and said that Mrs. Mellon was good to work for because she accepted his suggestions and respected his expertise even when he rejected any of her ideas. One of the many greenhouses on the property was devoted to topiary rosemary. These plants took time and skill to develop. They were given as gifts to attendees with the request that, after blooming, they would be returned to the Mellons for the skilled care that they required.

A small welcoming card designed by Bunny Mellon and a tiny pot of a curry plant were gifts at each person's place. Round tables were covered in a green burlap-like material. Bunny confessed to us that the curry plants had been cultivated from a plant she had smuggled in from England. Now these attractive, curry-smelling but non-culinary plants are widely available at nurseries here in the United States, but back then they were not. She requested that no pictures be taken that day because she hoped to write a book about her garden in the future. After lunch, we were allowed to explore the gardens on our own. The weather was foggy with a light drizzle falling as we wandered along, happily absorbed in enjoyment of the Mellon gardens.

I always regretted not sending Paul Mellon a thank you note for gifting my alma mater, Chatham, his father's mansion. It seemed unfathomable to me that nearly thirty years after sleeping in Andrew Mellon's bedroom as a mere college student I would be invited to a luncheon by his son and daughter-in-law on their private estate.

For several years, I met with two other members of the Western Pennsylvania Unit of the Herb Society of America each Wednesday morning at the Hunt Institute of Botanical Documentation in the penthouse atop the Hunt Library at Carnegie Mellon University. We were scanning herbal publications and summing up information on file cards for a future publication. The greatest challenge was finding a parking place in Oakland. After that, the setting was ideal as we worked on a green baize-covered table that was set up in the middle of the long-paneled room, elegantly furnished and walled with wire-fronted bookcases.

The periodical articles that we were dealing with were stimulating and sometimes, when something was particularly interesting, we would interrupt our work to share the new discovery. Using index cards, the title, author, publication, date and page numbers were put on each card along with a brief one sentence describing the content. We began at 9 a.m. and at 10:30 a.m. a maid would bring us a tea tray. We stopped at noon and never lunched afterward.

The Curator of Art, John Brindle, sometimes shared with us some of the rare incunabula in the Hunt collection and stories of how these were obtained. He was the first curator the Institute had hired, and his goal was to have at least two botanical drawings from every country in the world. As abstract art was big at the time, he was accepting that, as long as the plant was identifiable.

In the present digital age, those cards seem very primitive. All of that information would be on a computer now, but I have it on good authority that those file cards still exist in basement storage.

The presentations and lectures I have given about herbs and plants over the years have blurred together in my memory. There were many illustrious events held at museums and botanical gardens, but one still stands out clearly to this day.

I was asked to give a garden talk in Sewickley to a group of gardening enthusiasts. The mansion where the talk was being held was a large old Victorian in a wealthy area not very far from the main boulevard. Inside, there was a wide back hall and in the center of the hall, a rough wooden coffin filled the space. It was startling.

I couldn't help asking the hostess what that coffin was for. She paused before sheepishly admitting that her twelve-year-old son was a fan of The Addams Family. He had insisted that a coffin just like the one in the TV show was what he wanted for his birthday. Luckily, the Sewickley theater troupe had recently given a performance of Arsenic and Old Lace. They'd had that coffin stored in someone's attic and were happy to pass it on!

Posing with an aloe plant for a feature about my expertise in herbs and plants

The Great Grande Dame

The late Mrs. Henry H. Hood, Sr. of Washington, Pa., nee Dorothea Hildebrandt Blume, was a grande dame. Her family and friends knew her as Dottie, a person with a warm, bubbling personality. The Hoods had two married sons and a daughter, Nancy, all living out of state. Not long before her father Henry died, Nancy returned to Washington, found local employment and was able to share the large house with her mother.

Nancy joined the Western Pennsylvania Unit of the Herb Society of America, where her mother was an active member. She shared her mother's interest in herbs, entertaining and travel. They made a great team in the kitchen. They took the Society's tour of Japan together.

Lovely gardens surrounded their home at 172 Lemoyne Avenue in Washington with a small herb garden near the kitchen. Long before he died, Henry had a greenhouse built for Dottie, complete with its own furnace. Then it was necessary to expand the herb plot to a property across the road. Fortunately, they had good garden help. One ambitious picnic was held in the immaculate shelter of the two-car garage, which looked like it had never held a car.

Dottie's signature was the fresh flower nosegay in a tiny silver vase pin that she wore every day. She was a delight to travel with during Herb Society trips. She would reject a hotel room if it didn't have a pleasing view. Once settled, she would set out fresh flowers, either from home or the nearest florist, rearrange the furniture and put out her knitting and reading materials. She made certain that there were snacks on hand. She even carried a number of colorful scarves to drape over hotel pictures if she didn't like them. Everything was homey.

Her daughter, Nancy, had a fine pedigreed standard poodle that she took to dog shows. She and Dottie traveled in a van that could accommodate the large dog cage and show equipment. They had great fun "going to the dogs." Nancy was very active in the Herb Society. When she died after a brief illness, it was a great loss to fellow members, as well as to Dottie.

Dottie cut back on driving alone to Pittsburgh. A local friend drove Dottie and several widowed friends to the Sunday afternoon concerts at the Pittsburgh Symphony. Dottie was noted for her promptness until the Sunday when her friends stopped by for her and got no answer. The neighbor who kept her key was called. He went in to find that Dottie had passed as she was getting ready for the concert. A gracious exit for a gracious lady!

Antics on Arden

We made friends and acquaintances along our block of Arden Road and joined together to go to the town council meetings where we petitioned to have the street name changed to Arden Lane. That accomplished two things. It emphasized the dead-end nature of the street, and kept the large trucks that liked using Arden Road from getting stuck at the end of the lane and having to awkwardly turn around. It also reinforced our determination to remain a closed street, since a housing development was going to be built in the field beyond us where the children went sledding in the winter. This was an education in local government when we found how much time and effort was involved in making such a minor change. But we were successful!

My neighbor, Eva Strutzel, at 637 Arden Lane, was a devout Catholic and when the women's auxiliary to the Sisters of St. Joseph at St. Bernard's Parish were having a benefit house tour, she encouraged me to participate. I was busy with my responsibilities as President of the Herb Society and serving on Chatham's Board of Trustees, but I acquiesced and agreed to be part of the event since our houses were right next door to each other. My husband's niece had joined the Order sponsoring the tour and that may have had some impact on my decision.

Nine homes were featured on the tour, including some with indoor or outdoor pools. The chairwoman, Mrs. Robert P. Murray, was intent on showing off the very modern house her architect husband had just designed and built at the corner of Midway Road and Neulon Avenue. Eva's home was an English Tudor that had been professionally decorated, while my house, filled with a hodge-podge of antiques I'd found and refurbished over the years, was marketed to tour-goers as having an "Early American" kitchen with an "authentic" backyard herb garden, which was beside the back door. I prepared homemade herb butter on toast and crackers to serve along with an herbed tomato juice for visitors to sip on as they wandered through the property.

The date of the tour ended up being on my birthday in April. Our houses were open from 10 a.m. to 3 p.m. and you could expect to have visitors at any time. Unfortunately, I had a trustee meeting at Chatham I could not miss right in the middle of the event. Eva assured me she was happy to welcome guests in my stead. I prepped the food and drinks, made sure my house was straightened up, and left for the city, letting my neighbor act as hostess. Perhaps the co-chair of the event, Mrs. Jacob (Jean) Banks, was impressed with my gardening prowess, as she and I ended up being featured prominently in the newspaper article that was published as a promotion for the tour. Then I ended up not being in attendance for part of the event at my own home!

Our dining room was over the garage on the right side of the house. The Smiths, who had a daughter named Sydney close in age to Amy Jane, lived across the road at 634 Arden Lane. Because we were on the high side of the street, you could look down through the windows of their house and see into their dining room. When we ate dinner, we could watch them eating theirs. Sometimes the Smiths would leave the room, leaving their unfinished meals on the plates. When this happened, their little schnauzer dog would hop up on the table and start to eat the leftovers, to Amy Jane's delight.

The house to the right of the Smith's was between the Stahls, who lived at 629 Arden Lane, and our house on the opposite side of the street. The couple who lived there had no landscaping and the house, at 630 Arden Lane, was very plain with square corners and a tight, cropped front lawn. The husband looked like one of the Pep Boys. He was squat with a mustache and always smoked a cigar. His wife was taller and blonde. One summer, they had a house guest who had a little English car, like the ones we'd grown used to seeing in the Bahamas. We only found out much later what prank happened to it.

The neighbor boys, including my sons, who were home for on summer break from Westtown, spent time admiring the compact sportscar parked on the street. Knowing from experience how small and light it was, and because there was no real curb on Arden to make it difficult to move, the boys enacted a grand plan. That evening while no one was around, they carefully rolled the car off of the street and up over the non-existent curb. The group quietly pushed it onto the neighbor's grass, where it sat there decoratively the next morning. The neighbors must have been baffled when they came out the to find the car in the middle of their front lawn!

Once a month was 'Trash Night' in Mt. Lebanon. Things that weren't normally allowed in the garbage could be put out on the curb for free pick-up by the municipality. We lived on a cul-de-sac off Cochran Road. It was interesting to stroll down the street those evenings to see what treasures might be rescued from other's discards. After all, this was an upscale neighborhood. It was best to go early, for outsiders also came from all around the nearby neighborhoods to troll for trash. I found a nice stool one night.

One month, our neighbor Morris "Moshe" Stahl decided to clean out their attic. A large pile of nice art supplies, including an easel, appeared on the curb. Knowing my penchant for gently used items, his wife, Phyllis, hurried over to our house. She begged me to go out to the curb and take in all of the art supplies. "He's in the shower now and if he comes out and sees you, just tell him you can use them," she said. "Please keep them for me overnight until I can come over tomorrow and put them back in the attic. It will be another year before he will clean the attic again!"

Recycling as Fashion

In these modern days, I find that I am once again in style since recycling has become the current fashion. Recycling is what I have been doing all of my life for one reason or another.

As a child of the Great (and long) Depression I remember that all gifts were practical and they were wrapped in plain white tissue paper. This was long before Scotch tape and printed gift wrap papers for every occasion. The tissue paper was carefully saved and ironed for use again. I don't recall that we had any paper towels. Crushed newspaper was used to wipe out greasy skillets and to polish windows that were cleaned with water and vinegar.

Ready-made clothes were the exception. Materials and patterns were purchased. The patterns were saved, reused and adapted many times. The scraps from the sewing were saved for quilts. Clothes were remodeled and passed down in the family or among friends. Shoes were always repaired. Every shoe store had a repair section in the rear where half soles and new heels were added to prolong the life of your shoe investment. It was possible to do your own shoe repair with kits sold at the five-and-ten-cent store. These were usually rubber soles to be glued on.

After the country was catapulted into World War II, in a sense, it was the end of the Depression. It was not the end of scarcity, as all resources were poured into the war effort. Civilian goods such as cars and appliances were not being manufactured. Gasoline was rationed. Everyone was issued ration books for purchases of shoes, clothing, food and meat. Fish was not restricted and chicken took fewer points than beef and pork. Recycling was imperative for everyone. To prevent gouging, there was also rent control.

When Dan and I married, we received low sterling silver candle holders monogrammed with "M" as a wedding gift from Dan's close friend Converse "Connie" Murdoch. His family were long-time friends of the Core family going back several generations. An unusual feature on the candle holders was a top that moved slightly to grip any sized tapers that were inserted. I kept them for over sixty-five years and used them regularly.

Both Connie and my husband were in the Army during the war, so the gift of the pair of candle holders was sent by his mother, Maude, from his New Jersey home. Therein lays the recycling story: she quite frankly told us that this was one of Connie's wedding gifts that was being passed on, since it was suitably engraved with my maiden name.

Connie had graduated from Westtown School and then Bowdoin College where he graduated in time to be drafted into the Army. He was stationed at a base in South Carolina where he met and married, after a brief acquaintance, a young woman from the area. It was probably a quiet and quick wedding, as many wartime ceremonies were. Almost immediately, Connie was sent overseas. It didn't take many months to discover that the bride was preying on vulnerable soldiers and had other alliances. She managed to clean him out financially and the marriage was dissolved, much to his hurt and disillusionment. Some of the wedding gifts had been sent to his parents and they couldn't bear to keep them around.

Connie managed to return from his wartime service physically intact, but it took him a long time to recover from this disappointing experience. It was quite a few years later that we went to New York to attend his wedding to a young woman named Petra. Her nickname was Pete and his nickname Connie. The combination was amusingly confusing. We were in touch for many years until he died. Our children all followed Connie at Westtown School when more non-Quakers were admitted.

When the war had ended, it took several years for the economy to recover and manufacturing to go back to normal. My husband went back to law school, thanks to the GI bill. He had his officer's uniform pants and shirts dyed since they were sturdier than anything that could be bought. He was the proud owner of one white shirt, which a friend's mother had given him.

We were able to rent that unfurnished apartment that the White family had created on their third floor because we were able to provide a stove and refrigerator of Dan father's. We were able to borrow his father's 1939 Dodge coupe from time to time and my mother's prewar Plymouth to get around town.

When we had our first child, there was a small family crib which I had slept in. A friend gave us a baby chest and we purchased a bassinette/changing table. A larger crib was a second-hand purchase.

As a family grows, expenses grow. We began on a succession of houses and mortgages. The company transfers paid for moving expenses but we never stayed in one place long enough to profit from the sales of the houses. One advantage was that we never outgrew the houses either. The country home in Allison Park, beyond the city water lines, taught us to ration water. There was a well and a cistern and, in a dry summer, we had only enough water for one flush a day from the well and held our breath that the cistern reserve would not give out.

In Nassau, my sewing machine came in handy to make the school uniform jumpers that my daughter wore. I made madras skirts and was able to create the costumes required for the school plays. Any shoes or clothing that had to be discarded were put in the maid's powder room and Edith recycled it for us. Dan was surprised one day to see a black Bahamian child walking by wearing the name of his small college on a t-shirt, until he realized where it had come from.

When living in the Mt. Lebanon area near my sister, I often exchanged clothing, books and household items with her. Her girls were happy to have my sons' outgrown jeans and shirts, as they were not available in girl's sizes back then. My daughter found this embarrassing, as all teenagers find their parents. This was her first experience with the recycling between families that had always been done.

I fondly remember a beige ultra-suede dress that was inherited from my sister-in-law, Margaret. Dan's brother, Bud, was a vice president of U.S. Steel and she had a generous allowance. Her clothes were purchased at a small exclusive shop on Highland Avenue in Shadyside, which often ordered things especially for her. Margaret said that ultra-suede dresses were cost saving, since they could be washed and didn't need to be dry cleaned.

The dress was a perfect fit for me and I enjoyed it until hemlines went down. It was cut off and made into a nice jacket since it was a button-down shirtwaist style dress. When the elbows began to wear thin, which ultra-suede eventually does, the extra skirt material provided elbow patches that looked quite smart. A tear finally emerged on the front placket that meant the end of wearing it. I was about to throw away the belt and a tie when I took a second look at the tan shade and thought of the plain beige pillows on my couch. Each one was the right length to make package-like ties around the two pillows, and I dressed them up with ultra-suede trim. I was so pleased!

Recently, global warming has drawn attention to the need for us to recycle. I bundle newspapers and plastic for pickup. When a shopping urge comes upon me, I go to a garage sale, flea market or head to the gently-used shop in my community.

I know how to recycle for I have been doing it all my life. Now I am fashionable at last.

Blessed by the Pope

My black lace scarf has a secret history. The material is cotton and quite sturdy, but looks very elegant. It was purchased at the W.T. Grant store in Pittsburgh prior to a planned trip to Rome in 1969.

The fall and winter before our trip, we took Italian lessons in the South Hills. The evening class was sponsored by the local Italian-American Society. Many of the fellow classmates were adults of Italian background who knew a smattering of the language and wanted to learn more. The volunteer teacher was a middle-aged Jewish man. He was a dedicated member of the Italian-American Society. At the start of the classes, he explained how he had learned Italian. He was an only child and lived with his parents in a tenement in New York City. His mother died when he was a small boy. His father had to work and had no one to take care of him. So the Italian mothers who lived in the same apartment building volunteered to watch him every day when his father left for work. They did so in such a wonderfully loving way that he almost felt like he was Italian, too. He grew up immersed in Italian-American culture. That was why he was so interested in continuing to spread Italian speech and culture.

My husband and I went to London first and spent time there going to the theatre. Then we bought a one week's tour from a London travel agency to Rome. It included air fare, hotel and breakfasts and dinners. There were no optional excursions during the week, so we were on our own. The bit of Italian that we had learned was useful.

Reading travel books provided guidance to the sights of the city and we went as far afield as Ostia Antiqua, the ruins of the old city, where we had the place to ourselves and could imagine how closely together the people lived there in stone dwellings. We took a bus to the amazing gardens of the Villa d'Est and saw the nearby Hadrian's palace ruins.

Dan and I seated on a column in front of the Parthenon

Early one morning, we began a daytrip by bus to Naples. With only a brief glimpse of the city, we went aboard the shop to the enchanted island of Capri, which stands high and rocky above the sea.

Landing in the harbor there, we disembarked and then went to a small boat for a visit to the famed Blue Grotto, a cave under the sea. Only when the weather and tide are right is it possible to enter the cave entrance, so, this was our lucky day. Outside the cave were small flat-bottomed wooden boats each with a boatman. Ours was the first boat. The cave entrance was low and we had to lie down while the boatman pulled us inside. The sparkling aqua light was dazzling and we were alone in that beautiful place for a precious five minutes before being joined by other boats. An experience of a lifetime.

On returning to the harbor, we took a small taxi up the winding road to the village of Anna Capri to browse the markets there and have lunch in a small hotel. We examined the facilities and the rates and vowed to return. Back to the harbor we went, onto another boat to Sorrento, with a young girl playing Italian songs on an accordion while many people sang along.

From Sorrento there was a bus drive along the Amalfi Coast with lovely sea views below. We stopped for dinner opposite Pompeii. We saw only the outside walls and it seemed a waste to be spending time just eating and missing a peek at the inside of that ruined city.

But the high point of any visit to Rome is an audience with the Pope at St. Peters Basilica. To get a ticket to an audience with the Pope required a visit to the American cathedral near our hotel. The black, lace scarf I had brought with me was useful to have on hand when visiting any churches in Rome, as they required a covering for my head and shoulders. The presence of Michelangelo's statues was reason enough to seek out those places.

We set out early the day of the audience and presented our tickets at a side-entrance to an imposing Swiss guard in colorful uniform. Our seats were far in the front, at the side of the tall marble columns that made up the high altar. We had a side view. When Pope Paul VI was carried in, down the distant main aisle, the flash bulbs going off made it seem like Fourth of July fireworks. This was not an intimate audience. St. Peter's was packed with people. A priest acted as the master of ceremonies and welcomed a long list of groups that were present, such as, the Gold Star Mothers of Arkansas, the Little Sisters of the Poor, the French nuns, the German monks, the British sailors, etc. After each announcement, there was clapping and cheering. This was akin to a Pittsburgh baseball game where fans were announced and applauded.

The Pope gave a short address in Italian and repeated the address in English, French, and German. Most of the Catholic audience had come prepared with many objects to be blessed by the Pope. My scarf was the only thing that I happened to have on me to offer up for a blessing. There was a brief prayer and everything was blessed for everyone with one sweeping pronouncement. And that is how the black lace scarf from Grants came to be blessed by the Pope.

A Sailing Adventure

This seafaring tale began many miles from the sea on a quiet street in Mt. Lebanon, outside of Pittsburgh, and the story ends in the same place.

My husband, Dan, and I were intrigued by the advertisements for sailing weekends on the Chesapeake Bay. We signed up for a three-day weekend as a mini vacation and drove to Annapolis, Maryland to board the boat. We arrived at five o'clock in time to stow our few things below deck and meet our fellow passengers. Space is at a premium on a sailboat. There were eighteen passengers but just two tiny cabins. The other sleeping quarters were curtained bunks that surrounded the all-purpose saloon where meals were taken. There was a picnic supper before the overnight at the dock. We would sail the next morning after a simple breakfast. The itinerary was governed by the prevailing winds. This was early September and the weather was sunny and warm. The trip would be within the bay in somewhat protected waters and within sight of land on either side, most of the time.

There was a wide choice of quaint seaside villages where the boat tied up for dinner and passengers went ashore for evening walks. One evening we had dinner ashore at a seafood restaurant. This was not a luxury cruise with deck chairs. Passengers sat on the deck watching the sails and the water. Sometimes, the men helped to work the sheets under the captain's direction. Hearing only the sound of the water and the wind in the sails was quiet and relaxing.

We returned home refreshed and enthusiastic, planning to do such a trip again. We realized that our experience could have been very different if the weather had been wet and we had been confined below deck most of the weekend.

Our neighbor at 642 Arden Lane, Mary Ann McGunagle, was suddenly widowed. She had a recently married daughter, another daughter in college and a son finishing high school. Her husband, George, had died unexpectedly while attending a downtown Pittsburgh AA meeting. He had owned a small remodeling company, G-M Industries, that sold storm windows and patio enclosures. There were twelve employees. His wife not only had to deal with the emotional funeral, but had to cope with the business that was the source of the family income. If she sold the business hastily, it would have been at a "distressed price." There were also the employees to consider. She suddenly found herself the "de facto" president of the company.

Mary Ann met with the employees two days after the funeral. She told them that, with their help and support, she planned to carry on the business. She was a trained artist and award-winning photographer, with a degree in Business Administration, but she had no experience in running the window and patio business. So she decided she would learn from the ground up. She went to work as the mail girl, making the coffee and doing other jobs subject to the instructions of the other employees. She was quiet and modest and for the next two years was too busy to indulge in mourning.

We told our friend, Mary Ann, about our wonderful Chesapeake sailing trip. The next summer she and her son, Pat, took the first of what would be many such trips sailing. They made the acquaintance of other repeat travelers from the area, including a businessman named John Tenos, who was an efficiency consultant. As a result, they were invited to sail with a few new friends on Lake Erie.

Eventually, Mary Ann was asked to accompany a group of four sailing friends who were to deliver a large sailboat from the U.S.A. to Bermuda. Her son by now was in college, so she went alone. The crew were businessmen who had long experience sailing together. It was to be a fateful trip.

Many stories are told of the dangers and mysteries of the legendary Bermuda Triangle. The details of the storm that Mary Ann's crew encountered are impossible to repeat in their entirety. But the final damage to the sailboat came with a rogue wave that broke off the mast and left them completely helpless. Mary

Ann was below deck at the time and tossed about. Even well-secured items were thrown around. One of the men on deck suffered a concussion. The other men tried to protect her from the sight of blood, but she protested. She used a first aid kit to bandage his wounds, and tried to provide comfort and food as they waited desperately for rescue.

Eventually, they were sighted by a foreign freighter which picked them up. They were taken to Hamilton, Bermuda. There they were housed and given clothing and food in the Bermuda Seaman's Rescue house where they spent a week. It was necessary to contact the owner of the sailboat, supply information to insurance agents, government agencies and contact their families. Surprisingly, this did not end Mary Ann's love of the sea.

Back home in Mt. Lebanon, after keeping the business afloat for two years, she had learned much from her position as the "mail girl." She could see places where changes should be made. Mary Ann did not institute any changes herself but hired her sailing friend, John, to join the company as her vice president. Not only did the company flourish, but Mary Ann and John's relationship evolved into a second marriage for both of them.

They bought a boat that they kept moored in Annapolis for many years. The sailing adventure ended happily back on the same street in her Mt. Lebanon home.

The Famous Bridge Evening

The famous bridge evening needs to be recorded since it happened far enough in the past that the actual names of the parties involved can be revealed. The host and hostess, Bob and Olive Wertz, were a brilliant, hospitable, casual and erratic couple. They played an excellent game of bridge and it was their favorite way of entertaining. The Wertzes were legendary in the law department of U.S. Steel, and we soon learned why.

The Wertzes lived at 394 Jefferson Drive, a spacious stone home in Mt. Lebanon's Mission Hills neighborhood. The house was set back from the street with mature trees and lawns surrounding it. The interior was a bit crowded with handsome antique furniture inherited from Olive's recently deceased mother in Boston. They had four children: three daughters and the youngest, a son, Robert, named for his father.

When my husband and I first moved to Mt. Lebanon, we were welcomed to Pittsburgh at a dinner party in the home of longtime friends, John and Irene Bird. The other couple was the Wertzes. Bob was Dan's immediate superior in U.S. Steel's law department. Bob was a Johnstown native who had graduated from Harvard, which obliged him to be kind and condescending to lesser mortals, and Olive was his match since she went to Radcliffe and was Boston-born. We had a pleasant evening together and all of us were invited to visit the Wertz summer home on Big Moose Lake in the New York Adirondacks. This was Olive's family place where they had spent summers for years. They had inherited it from her mother, along with a live-in cook.

Our first bridge evening with them took place shortly after this introduction. At the Wertzes' house there were two bridge tables set up for us and other guests from the law department. The play was routine but was frequently interrupted by Olive, who kept asking Dan to tell her the time on his watch as she wanted to check on the special Indian pudding that was in the oven. After several trips to the kitchen, she returned announcing that she had some doubts about the pudding and had put another dessert in the oven, which then involved more timing on behalf of Dan and his watch.

When the card play was finished, I offered to help Olive with the refreshments and followed her into the back of the house. She first had to unearth a silver chest from under an antique chest of drawers so that the table could be set. In the kitchen, she climbed a stool to a top cupboard and brought down four amber glass dessert dishes and plates. She asked me to dish the warm Indian pudding into the glasses and top that with a scoop of ice cream. There were four more dishes of the set somewhere in the basement and she disappeared to find them.

This gave me a chance to have my first taste of Indian pudding, which is when I promptly decided on the alternative dessert still in the oven, whatever it might be. When Olive emerged from the basement, the new dishes had to be washed. Meanwhile, the ice cream was melting on the first four servings sitting on the counter. Finally, we were seated around the lace-covered dining table, with somewhat warm and drippy ice cream, when Olive suddenly jumped up. She had just remembered that she had forgotten to make the coffee.

At the end of the evening, we were standing in the front hall saying our farewells when Olive asked Bob who had the high score. It was George who was the winner and Olive hurried up the stairs to get his prize. We stood a long time in our coats waiting for the presentation until Olive appeared empty-handed, saying she couldn't find the prize, but would deliver it to George in a few days.

This was our introduction to modern casual entertaining in the 1960s, and it was in sharp contrast to the previous British entertaining style in Nassau, which was formal and regimented.

Then there was the Infamous Bridge Evening. Dan's colleagues all liked to recount the story, which had happened just before we had returned to the States. However, it was described at length and in great detail by those who attended, and became a favorite story told and retold in the law department.

On a spring evening, the first couple arrived and rang the doorbell at the Wertzes. They stood outside for several minutes before checking the time and date. Confident they were on time, they then tried the front door, which was unlocked, so they went in. As they were standing in the foyer and trying to ascertain if anyone was at home, the doorbell rang again. The second couple had arrived. There was still no sign of the Wertzes. Just then the phone rang, which one of the men answered.

It was Bob on the line, asking for Olive. He was told that she wasn't there. Bob didn't seem upset. He said he had been held up at the office but was about to leave. In the meantime, he suggested, "You fix drinks for everyone. Go into the sunroom and tell me what's in the liquor cabinet under the window. I'll hold the phone in case I need to pick up anything on the way home." When the liquor cabinet was searched, it seemed that there was little on hand to make drinks with. Bob pondered this and then suggested, "There's a bottle of scotch in a crate behind the furnace in the cellar, so open that until I get there." By this time the third couple had arrived and everyone was involved in making themselves at home in the living room with a drink.

Just then Olive breezed in the front door, plucked some dresses that had been hanging down from the front hall chandelier and said, "Good, Faith has been ironing. I'm glad you are all here. Where's Bob?" About then the last couple, who were seated on the sofa, discovered that the Wertz's teenage daughter, Faith, was waking up behind them from a nap she had taken under the back cushions! Bob arrived home and the two tables of bridge finally began.

After just a few hands, Bob stood up and told everyone to carry on without him, as he had to pick up his brother at the airport (this was at least a 20-mile round trip). Play went on. Bob came back, introduced his brother, refreshed the drinks and he played a few more hands. Then it was time to take his brother downtown to catch the bus to Johnstown. Again, play resumed without him. Bob returned for a third time, taking up his hand. Play must have ended at a late hour. No mention of a prize was made when the tale of this strange evening was told, and perhaps one could not be found again. Participants in that famous bridge evening would shake their heads as they recounted the story.

Several couples had tales to tell of spending a weekend at Big Moose Lake, the Wertz's summer place in the Adirondacks. They'd leave Pittsburgh on a Friday afternoon, ride for eight hours non-stop with Bob, arrive at a lakeside dock after dark and reach their destination by boat, then repeat the process by return on Sunday afternoon, getting home at a late hour.

Bob had a devoted secretary, Dorothy, who, besides managing his workload competently for him, also balanced his personal checkbook, paid the household bills and wrote the Wertz's Christmas cards (even after he retired). She once went to Big Moose and sat in the bow of a canoe paddled by Olive. It was a dark and windy night of terror. Dorothy couldn't swim and had never been in a canoe before or after that night.

Dan learned not to accept a ride home from the office with Bob as it often meant that there were errands and stops involved and he would be home sooner if he'd just used public transportation. I declined an invitation to go ice sailing with Olive on Little Lake in Peters Township, just down the road from Mt. Lebanon, as I was aware of the uncertainties of wind and steering and the possibilities of open water in the lake. Dorothy's tale of woe undoubtedly sat heavily in my mind. I did once find myself trailing Olive through six floors of a downtown parking garage looking for a car that I couldn't recognize. Olive had forgotten on what floor she had parked. At least we were on dry land on that occasion.

It was a delicate balancing act to remain on genial terms in the face of such generous and overwhelming hospitality. Somehow, we managed not to get too involved. Then Bob retired and we were transferred and moved from Mt. Lebanon to Duluth, Minn. with a profound "Amen."

The news of our transfer to such a cold climate evoked sympathy from most friends. However, people who had actually been to Duluth took us aside and assured us that it was really a beautiful city and that we would love it.

Ten
By the Lake

The Last Transfer: Duluth, Minnesota
1972 – 1998

After seven years in Mt. Lebanon, when a transfer to Duluth, Minn. was mandated by U.S. Steel, I was to sell the house and Dan was to find a two-story colonial with a lovely center hallway in Duluth, just like our home in Pittsburgh. He spent time with real estate agents and then called me to fly up and make a final choice. I arrived in the middle of a blizzard, but that did not deter the agents from driving me around.

The route we took, in order to tour different homes, had me completely confused as to their locations in the city. Also, the house styles found in the Upper Midwest were very different than the ones built in an older Rust Belt city like Pittsburgh. Nothing seemed quite right. Then we heard about one more house that might appeal to us.

Our friends from U.S. Steel, who had entertained us in the past, told us a house in their neighborhood might be for sale, as the owners were divorcing. Conveniently, the house was located next door to them. So we called the day before my week was up and saw 3646 East Third Street for the first time.

Situated near the top of a large hill, the home was more modern than anything we'd lived in before, with a split-level entryway and a beautiful view of the lake from the second-floor deck that jutted out over the backyard. The wife did not know how much she would be asking for the house, so we agreed to return the next day to learn the price.

We agreed on the asking price without bargaining with her, since by this time we had seen enough other houses in Duluth for comparison. Dan called her attorney to inform him of our agreement and make certain that there would be no complications from the divorce. There we lived for twenty-five years with a wonderful view of Lake Superior and many new experiences with new friends.

Duluth Friendships

Franklin B. Stevens, known as Pat, was the resident general counsel for the Duluth, Missabe & Iron Range Railroad. When he retired in 1971, he requested Dan as his replacement. He was an excellent tour guide to Duluth – he found temporary lodging for Dan in the venerable Kitchi Gammi Club, took him around the railroad and docks, introduced him in the office and even drove him down to St. Paul to meet people at the Minnesota Department of Transportation. Though he and his wife, Portia, stayed in town and were part of our social circle, he never dropped in at his old office after his retirement, or even asked Dan any questions about what was going on at the railroad.

A sketch of 3646 East Third Street done by our daughter-in-law, Lois

We ended up purchasing the house next door to the Stevens. They kindly introduced us to the neighbors and to their wide circle of friends. As a result, we had many social invitations as soon as we moved, and made a near seamless transition to Duluth. The head of the railroad, Don Shank, and his wife Millie, also had a small dinner part for the executive staff and their wives as a welcome.

I was just ending my term as president of the Herb Society of America, which I had joined on our return from Nassau. While living in the Bahamas, I'd met Dorothy Elsmith when she had given an herb talk to the International Garden Club. It was she who had introduced me to the Herb Society of America. After coming to Duluth, I found out that this was her hometown and that both her father and father-in-law had been presidents of the railroad in the past. What a small world. She owned a cabin in Wisconsin and vacationed there in the summer. While visiting the city, she stayed at Hotel Duluth and got in touch with me. I was happy to drive her around for visits with her friends and to meet the "old guard," the truly elite ladies of the town.

On the day that we moved in, our new neighbor Sally Birk appeared with a plate of brownies. Her husband, Jack, was head of the railroad's engineering department and they lived just two short blocks away on Valley Drive with their three daughters. Sally took me under her wing and guided me through all the local women's groups. She was a wonderful cook and entertained generously. It was at a birthday dinner that she hosted for me that we met Bill Buhrmann, a work colleague who had just been transferred from Pittsburgh to the Great Lakes Fleet of U.S. Steel. He remarked that April 22, my birthday, was also his wife Lurene's birthday.

When the Buhrmanns ended up finding a home two blocks away from us on East Superior Street, I followed Sally's lead by greeting the new family with a chocolate cake. That proved to be a happy choice on my part, for it was their daughter's birthday and in the press of moving, her special day had been overlooked. Lurene became a good friend. I encouraged her to finish her college education at the University of Minnesota-Duluth, and she ended up getting better grades than her own college-age children.

Dan was a "people person" and, as a result, we enjoyed many wonderful experiences during our Duluth years. When a mandatory retirement arrived for him ten years later, we found no reason to flee to warmer climes and leave our many friends. We loved our lovely home with its view of Lake Superior from the back deck. Duluth had much to offer with a college and university, the Duluth Superior Symphony, the St. Louis County Heritage Center and Transportation Museum, known locally as The Depot, and a fine library. Just across the bay was the University of Wisconsin-Superior, which featured many plays and concerts. Thus, we stayed happily for fifteen more years.

Almost A Real Estate Agent

The lovely Tudor style house across from us on East Third Street was occupied by Maureen Pulver, who had been a widow for forty years. The outside was white stucco with dark wood beam trim. It was narrow but long, so it was quite impressive. There was a den off the living room, a dining room and kitchen on the first floor. Upstairs were two bedrooms and a shared bath and a master bedroom with a charming dressing room leading into the master bath. Tall trees shaded the front and back yards.

When Maureen, at age eighty-nine, could no longer live there alone, her only son, John, put the home up for sale. He was a banker in St. Paul and wanted to handle the sale himself. He asked me if I would be willing to show the house to prospective buyers. He set the price, composed the ad and ran it in the local paper with my phone number for appointments and information. Since I would be interested in what was going on across the street and who my new neighbors might be, this was an ideal arrangement. My responsibility was to show the house and keep a record of the names and addresses of the viewers. That was in case some realtors claimed the first showing. Some showings took little time and others were lengthier. A younger couple with two school-age children came back repeatedly and ended up buying the house. I never knew what they paid as the negotiations were handled by the son.

John had three adult children by a first marriage and two teenage daughters by his second marriage. They came and took most of the furnishings. Other things were put in the garage in two piles…one that they felt were throw away and the other that might be useful for St. Paul's church rummage sale or the Duluth

Woman's Club sale. Maureen had been an active and longtime member of both. I was responsible for contacting committee women from both organizations to come and take away what they could use. Another responsibility was arranging to have the house cleaned in advance of the sale closing and for the trash disposal. I paid those expenses and charged $25 for each showing (nothing for phone calls). He paid me $800, which was a great savings for him and an interesting experience for me.

A month later, there was a phone call from Maureen at her retirement home. She wanted to know if the boots were still in a box in the upstairs sleeping porch. I told her that the house was cleared out but I would try to find the boots. A phone call to the church woman solved the problem. Everything was stored for the future rummage sale and she knew exactly what box the boots were in and arranged to mail them to her.

Dan standing with a coworker on the observation platform of Car Northland

Trains Around Lake Superior

The Duluth, Missabe & Iron Range Railroad, where Dan was resident general consul, was a shortline railroad, bringing ore and later taconite from the Minnesota Iron Range to the docks in Duluth. There, ore boats were loaded to transport the raw materials to mills in Gary, Ill. and Pittsburgh, Pa. The railroad was a subsidiary of U.S. Steel Corporation.

Trains Around North America was a television program on Pittsburgh's PBS station WQED that I found just by chance. The long program opened with a look at the rolling stock of the Lake Superior Railroad Museum at the historical Union Depot in Duluth, Minn. As a volunteer docent there, the trains featured were very familiar to me. Then, between the segments of trains in different parts of the country, the interviews and commentary were also recorded there, for the setting was recognizable.

For so many employees of the railroad, this was much more than a job. Many of them were also railroad buffs. Some of them worked in the roundhouse, others inspected the rails and ties using inspection cars and the office staff relished the opportunities to ride on the railroad.

During the annual visit of the managing board, there was a special tour of the railway system. For this special trip, there was a restored car, the Northland, moved out from storage. The business car, built in 1916 by the Pullman Company, was an all-steel construction that comprised a salon, dining room, several bunkbeds, a private state room with a bath, porter's room, galley kitchenette and an observation deck. Up to twenty-seven people could be seated in the car and it slept up to ten. A catered meal was served during this day-long tour.

The car was air-conditioned in the old-fashioned way, by huge blocks of ice that were carried below the car in its ice bunker, with evaporation providing the cooling. Ice in this large quantity could only be bought and brought in from Minneapolis, some 150 miles away. It was added to the National Register of Historic Places in 1978.

Our First "Saltie" Ore Boat Adventure

Living on a hillside overlooking Lake Superior meant that, during the shipping season, we would often see ore boats, or salties, sailing below. The salties were ships that came from the sea by way of the St. Lawrence seaway through the Great Lakes to this inland port. We could hear a ship's loud horn signaling its approach to the ship canal where the harbor bridge would be opened admitting them to St. Louis Bay. We enjoyed being even closer to the ships when we were downtown and could see them passing under the lift bridge.

On a rainy morning in October, I drove Dan to his downtown office and we saw two ships entering the harbor. I drove to the bridge just after the last one had passed through and could see that the ore boats, the *Philip Clarke* and the *Cason J. Calloway,* were both ahead of schedule at 8 a.m. This was important news, for we were to have our first trip on an ore boat that day from Duluth to Conneaut, Oh. where we were renting a car to travel the rest of the way into Pennsylvania to visit family. Then we would fly back to Duluth.

There was a phone call telling us to be at the Duluth, Missabe & Iron Railroad dock at 10:30 a.m. Our bags were already in the car. We picked up our daughter,

Amy Jane, who drove us to the West End. The gateman at the dock was expecting us. The dock supervisor, George Downs, waved us to a parking space and escorted us to the far end of the dock with two men carrying our luggage. It was tricky walking alongside the ship for there were marble-size taconite pellets underfoot. Slacks were the appropriate wear.

When we came to the ship's ladder, it took both hands for a climb that was straight up and two stories high. I just grabbed on and started climbing without looking around. In fact, I almost went past the step off to the deck. Baggage was brought up by rope and delivered to our room. Captain Klempf was in a meeting, so, we waited on deck and watched the loading, which is a back and forward affair, more complicated than one would imagine. A man on deck was keeping a tally of what went into each hatch and directing the workers.

We met Mrs. Klempf, the captain's wife, who was on board for this trip, a privilege that spouses have at times. She and the captain escorted us to lunch at 11:30 a.m. I was afraid that I might miss leaving the dock and going through the ship canal, but it was 1:35 p.m. before we passed under the lift bridge and into Lake Superior. It was a dull day with rain in the air.

Taconite loading was not as dusty as expected. Some loads had dust; others had steam coming off. There was noticeable dust on the deck which was quickly washed off after the heavy steel hatch covers had been lifted into place with a moveable crane and then secured by dog clamps every 18-inches. Half of the covers were in place before pulling away from the dock and the remainder before passing the railroad bridge on St. Louis Bay.

Captain Klempf invited us to the bridge and, from that grand elevation, we waved to people on shore as we passed by the Canal Park Marine Museum. When there was nothing more to see, we went to our stateroom to unpack. The guest quarters on the *Cason J. Calloway* were two adjoining rooms with dark orange carpeting, beige drapes and twin beds.

Each stateroom had its own large-tiled bath with square tub and shower. There was an armchair, an upholstered side chair and a heavy floor lamp fastened to the floor against rough weather. A blond built-in chest with mirror and pictures completed the rooms. These were in the bow section of the boat. There was a door leading to the observation room furnished with a couch, armchairs, bookcase and TV. It was so much like a living room that it was difficult to believe we were on a boat. The captain's quarters were off this with an inner stairway that led to the bridge. There were only three of us as passengers on this ore boat that was the length of a football field.

It was soon time for dinner at 4:30 p.m. in the captain's mess. Food was the same as the crew and it was excellent. The seamen are the best fed workers anywhere.

There was little to see when we were on the lake out of sight of shore. The exciting experience was watching the captain steer the boat slowly and carefully through the St. Mary's locks with barely a foot on either side of the huge vessel. This was where food supplies were loaded on by a derrick. There were summer homes to be seen going down the St. Clair River and then through downtown Detroit.

When we got to Lake Erie, the weather was rough and it was necessary to stand offshore in sight of the harbor most of the day. Lake Erie is shallow and when there are waves there is danger of grounding a ship, hence the need to keep our distance from the shore. When we finally made it to land, we were met by a company car that drove us to the rental agency for the last leg of our journey. Due to the cool, overcast weather it was a quiet, restful trip.

Volunteering

A lengthy residence in Duluth led to board membership in many organizations in a wide assortment of good causes. The Friends of Tweed board members led tours of shows at the Tweed Art Museum at the University of Minnesota-Duluth and helped with shows and in its shop. We dressed in historical Victorian costumes for these in-depth exhibitions at the museum.

I was a tour guide at the public television station WDSE and took part in their fundraising drives. I was a docent at The Depot which housed the Children's Museum, the Duluth Art Institute, the St. Louis County Historical Society, the Duluth Playhouse and the Minnesota Ballet, as well as the train museum. Later I became a docent for the Glensheen estate after it was gifted to the University of Minnesota-Duluth and turned into a museum.

The Northwood Children's Home held a fundraising Charity Ball each winter. In addition to frequent board meetings, I was assigned to be chairman of their ball a year in advance. It took that long to arrange for the hotel, the menu, the orchestra and the publicity. It also involved getting people to host pre-ball cocktail

Dan and I on the grounds of the Duluth Art Institute in 1983

parties to increase attendance. We hosted one where I didn't take a single drink and left early to check in at the hotel. What a relief when that night was over. The cost of the event itself meant that not that much money was raised. Dan and I supported many causes in the twenty-six years we spent in Duluth.

A Will to Murder

While flipping the TV remote one night, I found the Court TV channel and sat up in surprise when I realized that the program was based on the book, *Will To Murder* by Gail Feichtinger, about the Glensheen murders that took place in Duluth, Minn. while we lived there. It brought back memories of that turbulent time in the quiet community of Duluth.

On an ordinary weekday morning in the summer of 1977, Dan called me from his office to say that on his way to work he had seen police cars congregated on London Road, which sat just at the foot of our street. It was rumored that there had been a murder at the Congdon mansion, Glensheen, on the lakefront. That seemed incredible in our neighborhood, in the city itself, and at a somewhat sequestered property.

Radio programs soon trumpeted the news that elderly heiress Elisabeth Congdon and her night nurse, Velma Pietila, had both been murdered in what appeared to be a bungled burglary attempt. A wave of fear swept over the East End and little old ladies were asking where they could buy a gun to protect themselves. Before very long, the crime was revealed not to be a random affair, but suspected of being planned by her adopted daughter, Marjorie, and carried out by her second, recently-wed husband, Roger Caldwell.

Two elderly ladies, Caroline and Julia Marshall, who lived on the lake further along London Road, were good friends of mine. They also were wealthy spinsters, but lived rather simply and devoted themselves to hands-on philanthropy and civic projects in Duluth. They were lifelong friends of the late Elisabeth Congdon. In the months that followed, they had many stories to share of the elder daughter, Marjorie, for they had watched her and her sister grow up at Glensheen.

She had been adopted as a baby by Elisabeth, who was a wealthy maiden lady in her late thirties at the time. She gave her new daughter many advantages, which included advanced schooling and trips around the world. As a girl, Marjorie was animated and charming. She could manipulate her mother for anything that she wanted. When shopping for sweaters, she would come home with a half-dozen cashmeres. If she was refused anything or asked to curb her spending, her response to her mother was, "you don't love me." Unfortunately, her mother rarely disciplined her. She showed a streak of cruelty at the time of her first marriage in 1951. When she learned that she could not take her horse with her to their new home, she'd had it shot and killed rather than selling it or giving it to someone else. Years later it would come out that Marjorie had been diagnosed as a sociopath as a teenager.

The Marshall sisters said that, by contrast, the younger daughter, Jennifer, who was adopted several years after Marjorie, had a sweet temperament and spent much of her time in the care of the married couple, Eugene and Prudence Rennquist, who served as cook and butler in the household. She married at the age of twenty and moved to Wisconsin with her husband, where they raised six children and she owned several needlepoint and gift shops.

Only family members, the many nieces and nephews, and a few friends attended Elisabeth Congdon's funeral by invitation. This included the Marshalls. Julia noticed a number of dark-suited young men in attendance that she didn't know. She asked one of the men if he was an undertaker with the funeral home or a detective and he admitted to her that he was an undercover policeman.

The Glensheen mansion was donated to the University of Minnesota-Duluth by the Congdon family, with the gardener staying on in his house and continuing the care of the grounds and Vera Dunbar, Elisabeth's manager, retained as an administrator. The cook, Prudence, went to work for Julia and Caroline. They had small appetites and ate little, so, Prudence spent a lot of her time baking bread and pastries, which were frozen and saved for the Pilgrim Church bazaar. Everyone who came for a visit went into the Marshall house by way of the driveway and the kitchen door.

Prudence often recounted the story of how Marjorie, while visiting her mother, had fed her marmalade that she had brought with her, even though she knew that her mother was diabetic and the cook warned her that she shouldn't be eating it. After Marjorie left, her mother was in a coma. Her blood was tested and it was found that she had been drugged. Every effort was made to keep Marjorie away from her mother from that time on. Most of her contacts with her mother were to wheedle substantial sums of money out of her. Millions of dollars were at stake in Marjorie's inheritance from her mother.

We knew friends and family that testified at the two trials, but legally they could say little about it. We heard how Marjorie appeared in court, smiling at the jury and looking domestic with knitting or needlepoint during the proceedings. She was a mother of seven children, and with her slightly plump figure and wearing the large, round glasses that were popular then, could appear quite demure when she wanted to.

We also knew a lot of the Congdon family members, particularly Mary and Bill Van Evera. Therefore, the subject of the ongoing investigation and trials were not mentioned socially. When our son, Philip, was home for Christmas, I warned him about the Congdon affair before we went to a party at the Van Evera's house. During the cocktail time, Bill Van Evera, Tom Congdon, Mary's brother and Salisbury Adams, a cousin, were standing in a group. They were all trustees of the Congdon estate and had spent the day in court. Their discussion about the events of day continued. As the hostess offered Philip an appetizer, she said, "They are talking about my cousin, the murderess." He swallowed his surprise and was suddenly glad he'd been given advance notice.

Another time, we were at the airport coffee shop waiting for a departure and had a bite with Clara Congdon Spencer, another of Elisabeth's nieces. She spent many months in Arizona and told us about sitting beside Tom Hagen on a flight West. Tom Hagen was the adult stepson from Marjorie's third and bigamous marriage. That wedding, to her longtime friend, Wally Hagen, took place in North Dakota while second husband, Roger Caldwell was imprisoned for the Congdon murders. Tom told Clara that he was sure that Marjorie had hastened his mother's death, which came after a visit with her at the assisted care home where she was living. During that visit, Marjorie had fed her, which was chillingly reminiscent of the marmalade incident.

The sensational events which had taken place at the Glensheen mansion were like something out of an Agatha Christie novel. I came to know the floor plan of the mansion well when I served as a tour docent after it was opened to the public as a historic museum. The docents confined themselves strictly to the property's ties to Duluth's railway and iron mining history and other Congdon family history. If anyone in the tour group asked which room was the "murder room" we were instructed to say, "I don't know." Yet, if anyone had read the newspapers carefully, they would certainly know that the first murder, that of the night nurse, had taken place on the broad stair landing, where she had been bludgeoned with a heavy brass candlestick. Elisabeth had been partially paralyzed and was smothered in her sleep. However, she had not died in her childhood bedroom, which you could see on the tour, but in a larger bedroom that used to belong to her elder sister, Helen.

During Roger Caldwell's long murder trial, one of Marjorie's sons was engaged to be married and the couple had planned a large church wedding. The bride didn't want to give up the wedding plans, and the groom acceded to her wishes. Marjorie made her appearance at the ceremony amid much whispering. She had the good grace not to go on to the reception, to the relief of the couple. After a private legal struggle with Marjorie over their grandmother's estate, her children had little to do with her.

Marjorie was acquitted of the conspiracy charges in her mother's murder case, which shocked the public. But in light of the evidence from her conspiracy trial, Roger was granted a new trial. In the middle of these legal proceedings, she was charged for bigamy by the state of North Dakota, with the threat that, if she returned, she would be arrested. By now the legal cases surrounding the Congdon murders had been dragging on for over five years. Finally, in 1983 Roger pled guilty to second-degree murder in a plea deal for time served. He returned to his hometown of Latrobe, Pa., where a few years later he committed suicide. The events that Marjorie had set in motion had ruined his life.

Marjorie did eventually go to prison, though not for her mother's death. Instead, it was for arson and insurance fraud, after being convicted in 1984 of setting fire to the home she and her third husband, Wally, were in the process of selling in Mound, Minn. There were also suspicions that she was responsible for a string of arsons in the area. She spent twenty-two months in prison and after being released, fled to Arizona with husband Wally.

Caroline Marshall had a house in Tucson, Ariz., close to Elisabeth Congdon's former winter place there. Elisabeth had owned a large tract of land several blocks long and several blocks wide, which was originally open country. She had sold a small tract to Caroline, who had designed a simple adobe-type house herself and was very proud of it. She spent time there alone or sometimes with her sister, Julia. It had an outside stairway to a flat rooftop for sleeping under the stars on hot nights. When they were not in residence, they had a young bachelor librarian who acted as caretaker tenant and would move out when they wanted the use of the residence.

She arranged for us to see the house when we were vacationing in Tucson. We were asked to note a primitive Hippolyte painting over the fireplace which they had purchased many years ago in Haiti that had become quite collectible. They spent a lot of time discussing whether it would be better to sell the painting or donate it to a museum for a tax deduction. Its rustic style would have been quite out of place in their Duluth home. We were told that Marjorie was living in nearby Ajo, where the Congdon family once owned vast tracts of land.

It was there where Marjorie was arrested for a second time in 1991, first for trying to burn down her neighbor's home, for which she was found guilty, and then for the death of her third husband, Wally, who was found dead a day before she was instructed to report to prison. The homicide charges in the case of her third husband's death were dropped, but after spending ten years in prison for arson she found herself embroiled in further legal trouble. In 2007, she was charged with fraud after being caught siphoning funds from the bank account of a man who had given her his power of attorney before he died. She'd had him cremated before his cause of death could be determined.

It is amazing that Marjorie, who tried and succeeded in so many evil and murderous schemes, was finally caught and sentenced to prison for arson. Many people are nervous now that she is back on the streets, for she is completely unpredictable. Her story may still go on.

Remembering Ginny

Virginia Wright, known as Ginny, was a pretty, curly-haired blonde when I met her in the late '40s in Pittsburgh. She was a vivacious recent music graduate from Carnegie Tech (now Carnegie Mellon University). We worked together at the Pittsburgh YWCA while Dan was overseas for the war effort. I had always envied Ginny's skill at leading YWCA singing with the help of a small accordion, which I thought was ideal for outdoor gatherings.

I remember many of the details of her wedding plans. The wedding took place in Johnstown with her three sisters as bridesmaids. Their dresses were all different-colored pale pastel gowns. The music was an important part of the planning and Ginny knew it must include Amazing Grace. The groom, Ed Schatz, was a fellow classmate of hers with a degree in electrical engineering. He worked as an instructor at his alma mater. After the war ended, my husband and I had a picnic with Ginny and Ed while I was expecting our first child. They lived in an apartment complex on Negley Avenue that had a shady picnic area.

Many miles and many years later, I thought of her as I answered a newspaper ad for a small accordion. I knew nothing about it, and neither did the seller. When I asked the seller how it worked, he said that he didn't know how to play it and that was why he was selling it! I bought it for $50.

I took the accordion home and hid it in a closet until I could figure it out. When I finally learned to play "How Much is That Doggy in the Window," I decided to bring it out of the closet. This was early in the morning and my husband was doing his back exercises on the bathroom floor. He was really amazed.

Strolling and playing my accordion al fresco

Then I learned to play "Happy Birthday" and phoned our eldest son, Gordon, in Pennsylvania. He asked, "What is this?" My daughter-in-law, Lois, retorted, "Well, it isn't Lawrence Welk!" My repertoire has improved since then and I have even played for an audience of thousands during the Duluth-Two Harbors marathons. For many years I called my friends and family, including my grandchildren, to serenade them over the phone with my accordion for their birthdays.

When Ginny died, there was a lengthy obituary in the Pittsburgh Post-Gazette about her life. She had an outstanding career teaching music in various schools and finding a way to teach music to those with hearing disabilities that she developed at the School for the Deaf.

Each time my accordion comes out, I remember Ginny, my inspiration.

Grandma's Marathon

Grandma's Marathon in Duluth, Minn., is an officially sanctioned race that begins in Two Harbors and finishes on Park Point in Duluth. The somewhat misleading name is that of the bar and restaurant, Grandma's, which originated the event. The route for most of the way lies along Lake Superior. It is fairly level and cooled by lake breezes. In fact, at the start, the temperatures can be quite chilly and layers of clothing are shed along the way. That makes for a popular course.

The marathon is well organized and over the years, as the prizes grew, it has attracted runners from everywhere, including other continents like Europe and Africa. Those are the serious competitors and they forge ahead leaving thousands behind. There are half marathons also that day.

Julia and Caroline Marshall, who lived on the lakeside of London Road along the route of the race, were the first friends who invited me to bring my accordion and play for the runners. That was a fun place to be for several years. Another year, I played in front of the Kitchi Gammi Club closer to the end of the race.

274

Our friends, Bill and Lurene Buhrmann, who bought a house on the lake, began to have Marathon parties each year on the third Saturday of June. They sat up a table and chairs along London Road just before the last uphill. Friends brought casseroles to the house for a picnic lunch afterward, while drinks and snacks were served at the end of their driveway.

By this time, the organizers had recruited entertainment for all along the course and rewarded participants with special tee shirts. Now some eight thousand people were taking part in the race each year. The hotels were full and many residents had family and weekend guests staying with them.

So, I can truthfully say that I have played for an audience of thousands (though they all kept running past)! Runners were a most appreciative audience. They would wave and say' thank you' and sometimes do a little dance. The music was lively, football fight songs, marches, Army, Navy, Airforce and Marine songs. There was no point in starting to play at the start of the race for the professionals could care less. The prize was their goal. It was the slower runners who needed the encouragement. When I would pause between groups briefly, they would say, "Keep it going!" Fingers would get numb and it would begin to seem that the same people were going past again. Thankfully, there was a stool to sit on.

Over the years, I acquired quite a collection of tee shirts from the races. On a sister city trip to Ohara, Japan, some of the large size tee shirts were taken along and proved to be popular gifts for the male hosts there. My last shirt is dated from the year 2000. That was the year that we returned to Duluth for a fiftieth anniversary dinner. We stayed with the Buhrmanns at their lakeside home and were there for the annual marathon party and I made my final performance for an enthusiastic audience.

Cross Country Skiing

Winters are long in Minnesota. The snow stays on the ground and builds up to impressive depths. The weather provides many opportunities for winter sports. Snowmobiling is a big industry. Hockey for all ages from grade school to university is both an active and a spectator sport. The city extends along the shore of Lake Superior with a great deal of land so there is a large ski resort, Spirit Mountain, within the city limits. Chester Bowl is a park with three wooden ski jumps jutting up against the sky that strike terror in the heart even viewing them in the summer. A small ski hill is there and a cross-country trail. Hartley Field, Hawk's Ridge, Lester River and Point Park beyond the airport, all had cross-country trails. You could ski on public golf courses, as well as Northland Country Club.

The downhill facilities at Spirit Mountain frightened me. The thought of going downhill at great speed, or even coping with skis and poles to get on and off the swinging lift seats, terrified me. I settled for cross-country instead. Spirit Mountain did have cross-country trails for a more modest charge than downhill skiing. At a small warming cabin, you paid your fee and received a ticket on a string that you fastened onto a button or zipper pull. You consulted the map and decided on the circular trail according to the rated difficulty. Afterward, there was the treat of lunching by a window in the main lodge and watching the downhill crowd go past.

When I settled for cross-country skiing, I took some adult classes at a local high school where we were told about the best skis to purchase and introduced to the mysteries of waxing for the different temperatures and snow conditions. The first time the class met outdoors was at Hartley Field. We all put on our skis in the parking lot and shuffled awkwardly to where the trail began. There lay an insurmountable obstacle in the form of a ditch with a two-foot rise on the opposite side. Somehow, I was helped over that. As time went on, I learned to pole and glide and place the skis at outward angles for climbing and how to control speed descending. Gradually, skiing became easier and the marked trails at Hartley became a favorite place to go. Parking was convenient on some of the side streets, which dead-ended on the field.

Friends met for skiing together, usually couples on the weekends and groups of women during the week. The parks had trails and the golf courses offered wide-open spaces where you broke trail or followed snowmobile paths. It was challenging to crunch down and drag both poles to slow down. The bright white landscape contours were often deceiving.

Cross-country skiing in style with friends

The upper nine holes of Northland Country Club were easy to access from our house and some days it was possible to ski home to the garage. If I went alone, Dan would know where I was if I didn't return in a reasonable time. Even a familiar golf course looked like another world underneath its white cover. With no crowds or lift lines, it was peaceful and quiet with only the swishing sounds of the skis through the snow.

There were some occasional falls into the soft snow. You had to learn how to use your poles to get back up again. The Minnesota snow was deep and putting an arm down would only sink you further. It was a strange feeling to realize that you had been floating on top of so much snow.

My friend and I were the only cross-country skiers on a bus trip to the famous Lutsen Resort one February day. We had a guide that day who took us on the cross-country trail on a beautiful sunny day and helped us with our technique. Dates were usually made in advance and one day four of us were to go to Point Park.

That morning the weather was gray and foggy and there was thought of canceling. We decided to risk the outing. In our backpacks we had sandwiches and thermoses of hot beverages. We parked at the airport and the narrow trail began back of the building and went through woods (now safe from the summertime poison ivy.) There was no wind. After a time, we cut through the woods and skied along the frozen beach with Lake Superior on our left. We went as far as an old abandoned lighthouse before turning back. There was a large downed tree where we brushed off the snow and sat down for our picnic lunch. From there we were facing St. Louis Bay and the giant gray grain towers of Superior, Wis. The mist gave them a mysterious castle-like beauty.

Hawk Ridge Road was closed in winter and gave a good place to park. There were snowmobile trails along a stream there. Lester Park at the far Eastern end of the city had many marked trails and was the end point of the three-day John Beargrease Sled Dog Race held annually. My favorite place to ski by myself was Northland. My first skis were later replaced with the newer fishtail bottoms that gripped the snow going uphill and folded back going down. This eliminated the business of waxing.

When the time came to leave Duluth, I realized that there would no longer be the amount of snowy weather for cross-country or the proximity to a club like Northland to which I could walk from our house. The skis and poles were donated to Northwood Children's Home. I still have the comfortable boots for bad weather. There were some regrets later when I saw snow cover on the gently sloping four-acre field back of our retirement cottage. I thought how lovely it would be to glide across the field. Time takes its toll and I realize that, if I would lose my balance, there would be no way that I could disentangle myself and get back on my feet again.

Gliding silently in a sparkling world on a cold, sunny day is a lovely memory to relive in the winter.

Dancing in Red Flannels

The Red Flannels was an exclusive dance club in Duluth, Minn. It meets three times a year: fall, Christmas and spring with dinner dances at the venerable Kitchi Gammi Club. Membership is by invitation only. Dress for gentlemen was black tie, with the only exception being young family members who could be guests at the Christmas party.

A revolving committee sent out the invitations, set the menu, hired the orchestra, took reservations and arranges the table seating for each event. The soaring paneled great hall where dinner was served was always decorated with a huge red flannel petticoat draped over the minstrels' gallery railing at one end of the room.

Dinner tables of eight were filled according to names given when reservations were made. If no names were submitted, the committee put together the guests. It took some local knowledge to know that two brothers and their wives should *never* be seated together. Also, there were divorced couples with new partners that should not be combined, or even their relatives. I learned a great deal by being on the Red Flannels' planning committee and concluded that a lot of diplomacy was involved.

The Red Flannels had been in existence for many years. It took its name from the red flannel petticoats that the ladies once wore under their long gowns to keep them warm on the way to the club in Minnesota weather. The petticoats could then be removed in the ladies' room and left and donned again when time to go home. Perhaps the gentlemen also had red flannels under their trousers, though there was no similar decoration of long johns.

The Red Flannels parties were always elegant affairs, despite the inelegant, oversized petticoat decorating each event.

Duluth Polo

The weather was always perfect for Duluth Polo, never too hot or too cool. Rain never fell on those August Sunday afternoons of the polo tournament match between the Duluth team and the Twin Cities visiting team.

The playing field was eight miles north of Duluth on the property of Royal Alworth's horse farm. The road into the barn was filled with the cars of the teams and with horses, so the spectators used an improvised road over a lawn and meadow. Admission was free and open to all. As one of the city's wealthiest citizens, he would have been embarrassed to charge. His three sons all played. The Daugherty family also had sons that played and their daughter served as a knowledgeable announcer from an improvised stand on the back of a truck. She explained the rules of the game, the referees' decisions and the name of the player who had control of the ball. Two young boys manned the large scoreboard at the end of the field. There were four 15-minute periods and ponies were usually changed. At half-time the spectators were invited to go out onto the field and stamp down the divots made by the mallets and the horses.

Some years there was a small refreshment tent. Most people tailgated or spread blankets on the ground with their refreshments.

The Alworths had five children, three sons and two daughters. Mrs. Martha Alworth had many civic interests and never appeared at the polo games. After her husband died, however, the annual tournament was named the Royal Alworth Memorial and admissions were collected from each car for a worthy cause. She was always present to award the tall silver trophy.

Polo was under-advertised and attendance was not large in those days. I hope that those wonderful afternoons are still taking place in Duluth.

Fourth of July

In the 1930s, the Fourth of July was a time for family reunions. The families were large and often took place in a park picnic shelter. Each family spread a cloth on the table and set out dishes and cutlery. The women unwrapped dishes of baked beans wrapped in layers of newspaper to keep them warm, ham, fried chicken, potato salad, coleslaw and deviled eggs. There were a multitude of deliciously tempting pies and cakes. All the food was shared and passed up and down the tables. This feast was the culmination of hours spent in family kitchens. The men tossed horseshoes and visited amongst themselves, and children played tag. After the huge meal, the women did the packing up. No paper plates or plastics were available then.

No public fireworks display took place in our small Pennsylvania town. My father liked to buy and set off one or two 'silver fountains,' a Catherine Wheel attached to the backyard clothes post, or a few aerial rockets. The children had boxes of sparklers. In the early morning of the Fourth, the neighborhood boys set off strings of little red firecrackers. They pounded cap gun tape with hammers. Exploding balls were thrown down hard on the sidewalk. Little gray cones expanded silently when lighted to form tiny crumpled snakes. These were lit by a glowing piece of punk that had been found in the woods and dried for this day.

Many years later and many miles away from Western Pennsylvania, we celebrated the Fourth of July on a Bahamian beach in Nassau. The American Men's Club sponsored a picnic where families brought hampers to the beach and spread towels on the sand. A few tables had beverages for all. The Nassau Police Band sat on chairs in the shade of the casuarina trees and entertained with familiar songs. Floating in the warm gentle waves to the sound of music was delightful.

In Duluth, a much different climate, we were invited to our first large Fourth of July party less than a month after moving in. We had arrived there in mid-June. Two couples hosted this annual event, alternating between their summer places on Schultz Lake and Sunshine Lake. Many people had cabins on small shallow lakes near the city as Lake Superior was too cold for water sports. One host managed a local meat plant and the other couple were co-owners, ensuring that the picnic ham was superb. Grilled hot dogs were available for the children. Guests all brought desserts, salads, or casseroles for the long buffet table set under the trees. It was bewildering to meet so many new faccs at once. In time we became part of that social circle and could count on that party as the main event of the holiday every year.

As years passed, our first hostess, Dixie Smith, died, then Mel Bayley, and finally the original hosts were gone. Their grown children carried on the Fourth of July event in their stead and the crowd grew larger and younger. Softball games, skeet shooting and sailing were added to the usual swimming from the dock. People brought their folding chairs. Cars were parked solidly on the long pine-shaded lane from the house to Normanna Road. During the buffet time, I became a strolling musician with my small accordion.

Back in Duluth after dark, impressive fireworks were set off on St. Louis Bay front near the aerial bridge that is the symbol of the city. It spans the ship's canal that links Lake Superior to the bay and gives access to grain elevators and coal docks. Much of Duluth is built on a hill. The hilltop parking lot of the Methodist Church gave a wonderful view of the firework display.

Full of good food, fresh air and conviviality, we usually returned from the lake picnic about six o'clock. After one happy party, it took some persuading for husband Dan to go out again after dark to see the fireworks. We joined some friends that year on the unopened bridge of a freeway bypass that was under construction near the bayfront where the fireworks were set off. People with boats were anchored in the bay for a good view.

That night the skyward display was dazzling and rapid fire. For the first eight minutes of the show, there was scarcely a pause between the rockets. Suddenly, the pace grew even faster. What seemed like a grand finale erupted on the ground and in the air. We were surprised to have this spectacular ending coming so soon. Then there were fire trucks, police cars and ambulance sirens sounding as they speeded to the scene. We realized that something had gone wrong. This was all captured on the film of the late evening news. We learned that an unexploded rocket had fallen on the setup of the next display set, igniting it and then all the other display groups in rapid succession, with an awesome burst of color, light and explosive sound. That was a very special Fourth of July. The fireworks were shown on the local TV station for many years after.

On the holiday weekend, but not necessarily on the Fourth of July, a Parade of Small Ships mimicked the 1976 Bicentennial parade of tall ships in New York harbor. Canoes were the small ships on the Brule River in Northwest Wisconsin. The procession of canoes, some decorated and with occupants in costume, started up river and people from other river houses joined the parade as it drifted slowly downstream. I was invited to bring my small accordion and sat in the middle of the canoe, while our friend Biz Spencer paddled in the front and her husband, George, handled the stern. The acoustics on the water were wonderful and my friends suggested old songs for me to play. We all made certain to keep a good distance from the canoe that had "canned music" on board.

The final destination was outside the rustic fishing building of the Winneboujou Club. This building was the start of what became a summer colony for future generations. The families not in the canoes brought drinks and snacks. Cars with roof racks were there to return the canoes to upstream docks.

Strawberry Morning

Along the Brule River in Northern Wisconsin is a longtime exclusive summer colony known as the Winneboujou Club. The Brule River flows north from the interior of the state into Lake Superior. The river has a reputation as a famous fishing stream and became a part of history when Presidents Calvin Coolidge and Herbert Hoover came there to fish. Long before that time were the French explorers who named the river, and before them were the Native Americans, who used the river as a waterway trail linking small lakes along the way.

The Winneboujou Club began as a men's fishing club with a long no-frills bunk house. Over time members bought land along the stream and built spacious homes where their families came to spend the summer amid the shade of the tall white pine trees. Succeeding generations followed so that ownership often was shared and summer usage was split up. These properties were never sold to outsiders. The Club property itself consists only of the large original bunk house where canoes are now stored and the year-round residence of the caretaker and his family, who provided security and maintenance for the homes of the Club. Those large homes are set apart from each other by deep woods. Most of them include a guide house from the days when there were resident fishing guides. Now those small places and other cottages have been built for summer use. These make up family compounds.

One summer, Julia and Caroline Marshall invited us to use their expansive family summer home. It had been built by their father, who founded Marshall-Wells Hardware, which was once the largest hardware distribution company in North America, and now they shared the summer time schedule with a married brother and his family. For health reasons, they could not use their precious time. It was a great privilege to be offered the use of this wonderful place.

There were wild blueberries on the nearby sand barrens. Longtime residents knew where the best picking was and kept their spot secret from even their nearest and dearest. The Van Evera's cook even had a special place. However, she was finally tracked down because she wore a bell around her waist to frighten away any bears that were also blueberry pickers. Wild blackberries grew along the country road to nearby Lake Nebagamon. That tiny town had a camp, a few stores and houses and a swimming beach behind the town hall.

There were three commercial strawberry farms in the area. We were staying there one summer during strawberry season. Arrangements could be made to pick there by reservation only. Only a certain number of outsiders could come each day and had to be there at eight o'clock in the morning. That was the time when we usually had breakfast. There were four of us going together: my friend Julia, aged seventy-eight; her niece Muffy, aged thirty-eight; and Muffy's ten-year-old daughter. I told husband Dan that I would breakfast entirely on freshly picked strawberries.

A ten-minute drive brought us to the strawberry farm. We were each given a flat and shown into the field. Each picker was given part of a row that was marked by small flags and told to work between the flags. The berries were big and a glowing red, glistening with the morning dew. With such an abundance, the picking was easy. Eating along the way was another matter.

Thoughts of feasting on the delicious-looking fruit soon disappeared. The soil near Lake Superior was sandy and no strawberry was free of sand. They had to be washed before they could be eaten. We filled our trays, paid for what we had gathered and left the farm before the heat of the day. It was a very hungry Strawberry Morning.

It's So Quiet in the Country

Brule, Wis. was only forty miles from Duluth, Minn. where many of the summer owners lived. The town was so small that if you passed through it on the highway so quickly you scarcely knew it existed. A small motel nestled in the shade of tall pines. Next to it was the Crow Bar and on the corner was a highway restaurant. The train track ran along the highway there and on the other side of the tracks was a canoe rental office, a basic grocery and a bank open a few days of the week. We knew a teenager who waited in the restaurant during the summer, but earned more money and had more fun as a fishing guide on the river.

One of our friends, the Van Everas, owned extended family property along the Brule River and we rented their cabin, the Bridge House, from them for weeklong mini-vacations for a number of years. The rental included a canoe. Since the cabin had no dock and sat on a steep hill above the river between two sets of rapids, we had the canoe delivered to the Spencers. These friends lived one quarter of a mile away and had a dock.

The days were serene with walking, reading and berry picking. The daylight sounds were occasional rumbles from the nearby bridge and the rippling of the river rapids below the cabin. At night, the frogs and the crickets made a cacophony of noise. One night, we heard the distant sound of a siren.

On one of our walks, we had seen an old weathered gate post missing its mate that I coveted. It was at the entrance to Cecily Angleton's place. Our friend Mary, a cousin of hers on the Congdon side, took us there to inquire about the post and, thus, we had a brief encounter with the famous James Jesu Angleton.

Angleton had been top member of the CIA during the time when Allen Dulles was the director, back during the Kennedy administration and earlier. Angleton became convinced that there was a "mole" in the agency and was thought by some of bringing the work of the organization to a standstill because of what was deemed his personal obsession. His other obsession was apparently fishing, which was ironic given his surname, and so he spent time in the summers on the Brule River, where Cecily had a house that was part of the Congdon family properties.

The day we met him, he told us he had been up before dawn on the river. He described his catches of the day, even though a catch and release program was in effect at that time. Was he right or wrong about the mole? We may never know, though recent information that has come to light post-9/11 indicates he may have been more right than people at the time gave him credit for. On the day we met, he only talked about fishing.

Back in the city after that peaceful week, we discovered that we had been oblivious to current events in the quiet of the country. There had been a fight at the Crow Bar between some inebriated patrons. There was a train derailment right in the middle of town that fortunately had missed the large shed where the rental canoes were stored. On one of the bank's open days, there had been a robbery. The siren that we heard one night was for an accident in which a twenty-year-old driving fast had missed a curve in the road and been killed. We hoped all quiet country weeks were not that eventful.

Secret Gardens

Secret and fantasy gardens are most often found on old estates in Europe. My secret garden was a modest Minnesota version created on a wooded hillside city lot overlooking Lake Superior.

The 'Woodland Walk' at the front of the house wound through a small shady area made up of birch, red dogwood and pine trees, where transplanted wildflowers – bluebells, bloodroot, violets, trillium, wild ginger, and forget-me-nots – showed their secrets in spring flowers. One of the pine trees became an outdoor Christmas tree and, in the summer, ferns, wild aster and honeysuckle filled the area. Placed to be seen from the house was the driftwood flower in the woodland border and the weather witch, whose arms raised upwards for good weather, was mounted on the white pine tree.

My herb garden was in the center of the sunny space at the back of the house. Herbs have many secrets to be known only to those who touch, smell or taste their leaves. Sage marked the four corners; thyme made the long borders and curly chive edged the end of the plot. Chives and garlic chives were dividers with tarragon, winter savory, salad burnet and marjoram as other sturdy perennials. Tender plants such as lemon grass, lemon verbena, rosemary, and basil were shielded in the center. The wonder window hanging at the rear of the house gave an unusual view of the sky, trees and garden. The patron saint of gardens is St. Fiacre and he watched over it all from a small shrine at the end of the creeping thyme stepping stone path.

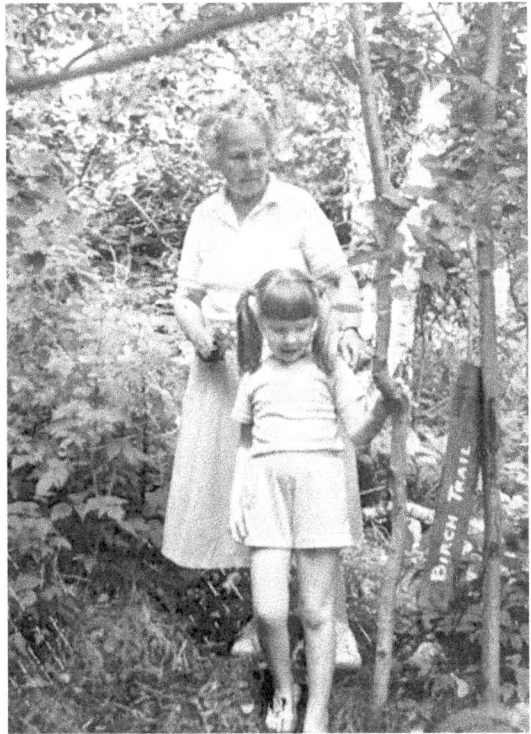

My granddaughter, Sarah, and I exploring the birch trail during a summer visit

The 'Fun Forest', with the 'Birch Trail' marking the way, was a fantasyland for all youngsters-at-heart. Low budget creatures of driftwood stood in for statuary and several dead trees were costumed. Sunbeams danced on the foliage, helped along by a mobile of mirrors and the breeze. It took an observant eye to find all of the ideas, tricks and jokes gathered from many places and friends. Wild roses, thimbleberry and bracken made this a Northern jungle. The secret backwoods path made a retreat where city life seemed far away, except for the occasional sounds of a train or lake-boat whistle or siren.

The Kuypers

Dorothy and Bill Kuyper went to a yard sale and bought a house! On a Florida vacation trip, they followed their usual custom of going to yard sales. This yard sale led them to a house for sale on the next block with a screened-in swimming pool that they bought on the spot.

Bill and Dorothy Kuyper were recent retirees who moved from the East to her hometown of Duluth. She grew up as one of the children of a local judge and former U.S. congressman, Oscar Larson. Bill and Dorothy had no children; their only relatives were the son and daughter of her late twin sister, Ruth. Bill was a nuclear engineer for General Electric and Dorothy was an interior decorator. They had spent the war years being part of the small group doing top secret work at the Los Alamos Proving Grounds in New Mexico, a division of the Manhattan Project. Pictures they showed us were of a young crowd living in primitive conditions.

We met at an evening art class at the University of Minnesota-Duluth and found we had many common interests. Dorothy was a decorator and went by the nickname "Dick." I was invited to go yard "sale-ing" with them. This was always an exciting experience, for Dick was so outgoing. She would find out the life story of the sellers everywhere that we went – were they moving, were they selling their grandmother's things, or whatever. She was a knowledgeable collector and could often use the purchases in her business.

The Kuypers lived in the most unusual house in the city at 5802 London Road. Heiress Elisabeth Congdon had seen the possibilities of an abandoned water intake pumping station on the edge of Lake Superior and had the financial resources to restore it for a residence in the 1930s. Now owned by our friend Julia Marshall, she would only rent it to someone she knew. The property fronted on London Road where there was a garage at one side on the street level. Then steps led down to the front door. A tiny kitchen had space for a small table for two. There was one bedroom and a bath. The all-purpose library faced the lake with extra-heavy stormproof plate glass. Even with that, one storm still tossed a rock into the room. This room had space for a table for dinner guests with unusual chairs that had half backs which could slide under the table and supported people well. The professionally decorated powerhouse was a big attraction on the Duluth Women's Club annual house tour.

Dick did not find it easy to renew connections with her childhood friends in Duluth. So their unexpected yard sale find of an entire house while on vacation in Florida, and the purchase of their Bellaire home, was the result.

Mandatory retirement was facing my husband in two years. We decided to explore the possibilities of moving from Minnesota to Florida. We visited Ruth and Ed Miller living in a high-rise apartment between two waterways; Bill and Elizabeth Johnston in a village setting of one-story homes arranged around a central pool; and the small town of Mt. Dora at a higher elevation in the middle of the state. We also visited Dick and Bill and saw the nearby apartment complex built by U.S. Steel and occupied by many retired employees.

Being with the Kuypers meant shopping again. Many treasures at bargain prices could be found at secondhand, antique or consignment shops. These things came from people downsizing and moving to Florida. At one shop Dick admired a pair of pot metal birds with long swirling tails. This was a stylish table decoration from the 1920s. That would be the ideal gift for our hostess. Dan also remembered that décor from his own youth. As we went on to other shops, he returned quietly to make the purchase.

Some years later, the Kuypers returned to Duluth. This time, they purchased a larger one-story home on the lake at the end of a cul-de-sac off London Road. We had many nice times together there. Then Dick began to have health problems with a multitude of medications fighting each other in her body. The day came when, in despair, she finally flushed them all down the toilet. She passed away not long after that. I felt privileged to 'pour' at one end of the reception table following her funeral at Pilgrim Congregational Church.

After the funeral, Bill asked us if we would choose something from their home as a gift. That presented a problem since a small dish could be something rare and very valuable. The answer was to ask for the pair of birds we had gifted them, since they were not of great value and it was something we and Dick had liked.

The Kuypers had a winter home in Tucson, Ariz. where we had dinner with them after a trip to New Mexico. A few years after Dick died, Bill went to Arizona to sell their place. While there he met and married the real estate agent, a pleasant woman named Sally Allison. I met her the next year when she came to Duluth for Bill's memorial service. Again, I served at the reception. The Kuypers enriched our lives with wonderful memories.

On the (Iron) Range

In our dating days, Dan and I dreamed of travelling, particularly to England (we were both English majors). Then came WWII, finishing law school, getting a job and starting a family. Twenty years later, we finally got to go to England, and then to Europe as a family, due to the generous vacation policies of Navios Corporation where Dan worked. Now that Dan was an attorney for the Duluth, Missabe & Iron Range Railroad, one of his responsibilities was to notify the State Department of Transportation on any changes to the rail lines. The engineers reported these changes to Dan. He needed to doublecheck these for himself, but did not want to leave the office during the week.

So, on some Saturdays, we would make a day of it and I went with him while he inspected the track, or "walked the lines" as we called it. We would drive out to the Iron Range, which is a sparsely populated region in St. Louis County, north of Duluth. It was the "boonies." The town of McKinley, for example was a booming metropolis with barely 300 residents. We would walk the track together as Dan inspected the lines. One time, there was track still there where the engineers had reported it removed.

Dan had a three by six-foot map of St. Louis County (not to scale) as his guide. All the buildings were noted and there were many miles of vacant land. One day we were at a rail crossing marked only with the sign McKinley, and nothing else in sight. I turned to Dan and joked, "You said, 'Marry me and we'll see the world,' and here we are in McKinley!"

Dan and I in the 1990s seeing the world by sleigh - this time guided by reindeer!

Dan always enticed me to go with him by the offer of a nice lunch. Well, not only was there not a place to have a nice lunch, there was no place for eating out at all. I learned to pack a picnic. On one Saturday outing, I packed a picnic lunch after reading an article about, "Cooking on the Manifold." According to this piece, the heat of the engine's manifold would cook a hamburger in a distance of 80 miles. Conveniently, that was about the distance from Duluth to the Iron Range. So I wrapped up two raw hamburgers with onions in aluminum packets and opened the car hood. I didn't know where the manifold was (I still don't) but I tried to find a space where they would fit and not fall out. Buns and beverages went in the picnic basket.

Dan stopped at an intersection to consult his big map. We had been driving for miles with no habitations in sight for the last hour. He rolled down the window, then said, "I smell onions?" in a puzzled voice. I said, "That is our lunch!" Then I confessed to him my idea about the manifold cooking. We decided to have our picnic shortly thereafter. The onions were cooked and the meat was warm…but more like steak tartare. It could have used a few more miles, but it was edible. I never really mastered that mode of cooking nor tried it again.

Through the Great Lakes

Being a guest on a Great Lakes ore boat is an experience reserved for a favored few. There are only two or, at the most, four staterooms for guests on these large football-field-length ships. The ships that enter the Great Lakes from the sea by way of the Welland Canal can be identified by their high sides and top rigging.

Invitations for travel on an ore boat are limited to corporate customers or executives. We were privileged to be 'given' a trip for four as Dan's retirement gift from the Great Lakes Fleet of U.S. Steel. Our New Jersey friends, my college roommate, Jean Rothermel, and her husband, Dan, were thrilled to share our trip. Jean's parents had been on an ore boat many years ago and she remembered their glowing descriptions of their trip. They drove up from New Jersey to join us.

The *Philip Clarke* loaded its cargo of taconite at Two Harbors, Minn., where we boarded. Our destination for unloading was the steel works at Gary, Ind. A weeklong round trip was planned. We did not go ashore in Gary as it was not an appealing neighborhood, but simply enjoyed the view of the shoreline.

The two staterooms, each with a private bath, were warm and comfortable. Chests and lamps were secured to the floor as a protection against rough weather. A heavy door opened up to the deck. A spacious lounge was at the forepart of the ship underneath the bridge. We spent a lot of our leisure time there socializing and enjoying our vacation together.

We were welcomed on the bridge of the ship. The view of the open lake on a clear night was soothing. It was exciting to be on the bridge when the boat went through the locks at the Soo. The language of the pilots and Captain Vendren was formal and courteous. The clearance from the ship-side to the wall of the canal were incredible, and slowly decreased as the huge boat crept slowly through the restricted space.

The officer's mess was where we had wonderful meals with the captain, first mate and engineer. The engineer's position on the boat was on a par with the captain. He extended the courtesy of a guided tour of his engine room. Dan Rothermel had been a Navy officer in the Pacific during WWII and for him this was the high point of the trip. Although we were in awe of the huge turbines and machinery, it was hot and noisy and we were more than ready to leave.

The weather was sunny but always cool on the lake. We spent a lot of time daily walking the length of the boat and toting up our mileage. An antidote to all the delicious food was needed. I had my small accordion and played it on deck and the crew seemed to enjoy the diversion.

An unexpected bonus was added to our travel. After the boat was unloaded in Gary, the captain was instructed to go to Alpena, Mich. and load limestone for delivery to the Canadian side of Lake Huron. Although Alpena is a very small town, I had always been curious about it. When my husband was with the Michigan Limestone Company, we knew fellow employees who had lived there and spoken of it. This time, we did go ashore and a car was put at our disposal to drive around town. We found the only visible activities on a Saturday were several garage sales. We had lunch ashore. That evening, Jean and I dressed for dinner. We had an evening of bridge in the lounge to the sound of the limestone clattering into the holds.

Our ore boat trip was several days longer than planned, which we didn't mind at all. We returned to Duluth, entering by way of the ship's canal where there are always a crowd of tourists at the nearby Maritime Museum and along the sides of the canal watching for the boats. We assured our friends that all of those people who were waving to us had come especially for us. When we reached the docks, there were colored flags displayed that we attributed to our arrival. Actually, we later learned they were warning flags for some dock repairs. At any rate, it was a glorious ending.

Jean and Dan moved with a much-traveled crowd who would often tell stories of their exotic trips. They would sit quietly and listen to these tales. Then they would say, "Well, have you ever taken a trip on an ore boat in the Great Lakes?" and could top those stories with one no one else could match.

True Halloween Tales

Weather in Northeastern Minnesota at the end of October can have a big effect on Halloween celebrations. One year, it was surprisingly mild and we arranged a trick for young visitors. Our split-entry house sat back from the street, partially obscured by a small patch of evergreen and birch woods.

A small trail started close to the street and led through the woods to return to the lawn near the from door entrance. In order to receive their treats, they had to follow the short woodland trail, which had been decorated with ghosts hanging from trees that were made of balloons covered with white sheeting. There were two wide wooden planks to cross and candles set in sand in plastic gallon milk cartons provided a spooky amount of light along the way. I dressed as a fierce-looking witch and handed out the candy from a black iron kettle, saying sternly, "No treats until you take a walk through the enchanted woodland path!" There were giggled and screams as the little visitors delighted in the scary trip.

In costume as a fierce-looking witch

Another year, after the outdoors had been decorated already, the weather turned suddenly cold. The evening started with rain that rapidly turned to snow. Our little visitors rang the doorbell, collected their candy and quickly turned toward warm homes. The snow grew in intensity into a storm that continued all night and the following day, becoming the first heavy storm of the winter season with a deep, lasting snow cover.

One Halloween year, when most of the children had come and gone, two of our neighbors appeared at the door. George Spencer was attired in khaki shorts, a bush jacket and Australian hat, looking like the geologist that he was. His wife, Biz, was much more fancifully attired as a man in drag, wearing a flapper-style dress over a tee shirt. She wore men's socks and high heels. Her face was stippled with black for an unshaven look and a dark velvet headband crossed her forehead with an ostrich feather at the back. We laughed at the absurd get-up and welcomed them into the living room for a visit and drink.

I was assembling snacks in the kitchen when the doorbell rang again, so, Biz offered to answer the door. Standing at the door was a teenage girl, who was not in costume but simply carrying a pillowcase to collect Halloween loot. Biz looked at her closely and putting a candy bar in the bag said to her sternly, "Aren't you a little too old for this?" She had completely forgotten about her own outrageous attire. We all heard her scolding remark and dissolved with laughter as she returned to the living room.

Ripples into Waves

Small pebbles cast into a still pond will create ripples. Huge rocks can cause big waves. Things that others say and do are often the small pebbles that affect others. Larger events cause long-range life tragedies.

Melvin "Mel" Alderink was the general superintendent at the Duluth, Missabe & Iron Range Railway Company. Tall and friendly, he was capable both in and out of his office. The men who worked for him both respected and liked him. Mel wore business clothes on the tracks because he was the supervisor and this was what the workers expected of him. His attire was a sign of his position.

Out of the office, he was active at the Glen Avon Presbyterian Church, where he taught Sunday School and was a trustee. He and his wife, Lorraine, had three daughters. The oldest daughter was married and lived in the Twin Cities. The second daughter was in college and the youngest girl was in junior high school. They had an attractive Tudor-style stucco house in a pleasant neighborhood.

At an introductory company dinner party, Mel and Lorraine were the first to leave because he was very tired. It was explained that he had lupus. It was something that he had lived with for some time. He continued to carry on his career capably for many years. He had the loyalty of the men who worked for him.

Some years later, there were changes in his health and personality. The couple built a modern one-floor home in a wooded plot and began to landscape the surroundings. Their teenage daughter had problems and went to live with her married sister. Mel became less open with his workers and made a fateful decision to promote two men to head the plant without any notice to Red Lewis, the man in charge.

Red Lewis was a capable manager but not a warm personality. He had moved from Alabama to Minnesota to this position and brought with him many strong opinions. He was a real "redneck," but accepted for his skills. The tensions of his job and then the developing work situation went on for some time and spilled over into his home life. As a result, his wife had a nervous breakdown and attempted suicide. She survived, but it had a lasting effect on their family.

As his health deteriorated, Mel retired and left the company. For a time, he was named senior fellow at the University of Minnesota-Duluth School of Business and Economics. Then the couple moved to the Twin Cities and later divorced. His behavior had become more and more erratic, unlike his former sunny self. There were occasional return visits by both of them. It was sad to see what life changes had come to them all. The big event in the still pond had made huge waves in many lives.

Laura Lee: A Portrait from Life

The divorce came at a good time for Printha Markert, if there is ever a good time for such a thing. Nothing was said about the reasons for the divorce. She had been an Army officer's wife for twenty-some years and her two sons were now in college. She came home to live with her widowed mother, Laura Lee, at a fortunate time, much to the relief of those of us in her mother's circle of friends.

Laura Lee Winn had always been eccentric, but she was now even more so. She had a keen mind at the bridge table and never missed the twice-weekly bridge luncheons at the Duluth Woman's Club or her other bridge club. It was thought that those were the most substantial meals that she had. She hated cooking and ate cornflakes a great deal of the time.

Laura Lee had grown up in the Twin Cities as the only child of wealthy parents. She was the center of their universe, and her own, from birth. She married George Winn, a quiet, kind man, and they had two daughters named Jorge (pronounced Georgia) and Printha (sounding like princess with a lisp). George had a management position at the steel plant before it closed and left him looking at an early retirement. Well, it wasn't exactly retirement for he did the cooking, shopping, gardening, walking the dog and everything else in the Winn household.

The Winn home was a large brick Italian Renaissance-style mansion in the best part of the city, Congdon Park, and it had ample grounds attached to it. It had been built prior to World War I by a renowned Chicago architect for a local furniture storeowner and his family before being sold to the Winns in the 1950s. Laura Lee deigned to allow the house to be toured as part of Duluth's annual circuit. The home was filled with lovely elegant furniture, silver and an abundance of fine china ornaments. This beauty was everywhere, covered in clear plastic protection, which kept it clean but did destroy its dignity a bit.

Seeing Laura Lee in the supermarket one day, I said, "Hello, how are you?" She answered, "I never ask people how they are, for then they tell me and I never get the shopping done!" So then I asked, "How is George?" She answered, "He's in the hospital." That is probably why she was reluctantly doing the shopping. George passed on shortly thereafter and was laid to rest with only his widow and two daughters in attendance.

Laura Lee had to take her turn at entertaining her bridge group from time to time. Without George to set up for the entertaining, she found she needed to plan ahead. For this, she would order a sandwich loaf from the deli and ask a friend if she would run by and pick it up for her…and, while she was there, would she select some cookies for dessert and would she please come early. When the friend arrived with the lunch, Laura Lee would then ask her to make the coffee and set it up for everyone.

She had a talent for getting what she wanted. Knowing her fear of the spiraling entrance to the bank parking garage, a friend offered to take her to the bank after George died. But Laura Lee waved her off, as she had already persuaded the bank to come to her.

She was very fond of jewelry ads and was often showing off new rings that she had purchased at JC Penney. She would wear jewelry for a short period of time and then would appear with something new. She had returned the previous purchase and persuaded them to exchange it.

Printha was the daughter who came home after so many years to a demanding mother and a neglected household. She soon realized that there was a lot of maintenance that needed to be done on the grand old home. Wisely, she began in a low-key way – working by herself, long and hard in the garden, pruning the overgrown shrubbery. She quietly arranged for roofing and gutter repairs and, finally, outside painting and repair work. Her mother would not tolerate any intrusion of inside painters.

An attractive, slim dark-haired woman, Printha took time to reconnect with the community. She renewed some old acquaintances with whom she had gone to school, and began volunteering in several organizations. It must have been a way to preserve her own sanity. Several years later, her mother went from merely eccentric into full-blown Alzheimer's and had to spend her last months in a nearby care facility. Printha then lived alone in the spacious restored house and traveled to spend holidays with her two distant sons.

Frank and Janet

Frank and Janet Sklaris married each other three times. The first time was the most romantic. There was a lull between tour groups when they knelt together below the beautiful stained-glass windows of St. Chappell in Paris and made their vows to each other. When they returned from their travels, the second marriage was legalized by a judge friend with no witnesses. A reception was held afterward in the East Lounge of the Kitchi Gammi Club to announce it to their friends. Janet wore a smart, dark gray silk suit. No bridal bouquets were in evidence. The third marriage was some six months later and held before the altar of the Catholic Cathedral with only the priest and the couple.

The third marriage was the most difficult to arrange. Frank was Catholic and he had been divorced years before. He had married a woman with a young daughter and there were no children from that marriage. In the time that followed, he had been a man-about-town and eligible bachelor. He wanted the Catholic ceremony.

Janet Hartman was not a Catholic. She and her ex-husband, Tom, had both been professors at the University of Wisconsin–Superior. They were a popular and attractive young couple. The marriage broke up when Tom developed wandering ways. Janet was heartbroken and left her position and spent a year in England, taking some courses and doing research and writing on English gardens. When she returned to a nearby city, she found a job as the sole employee of a local foundation. The foundation office was in the local hospital that was the recipient of the bulk of the foundation funding. Her divorce was the stumbling block as far as the Catholic church was concerned. She was required to convert and take lessons and, finally, a dispensation was granted to allow the marriage.

Frank's career was in advertising and, for a brief time, he worked in a bank. Here he found the idea which made him wealthy. Bank bills were bundled in plain paper bands. This was an ideal place to put advertising. A copyright was obtained for his "Bankad.'" He bought a building on East Superior Street for his advertising office and rented part of the building to a small radio station. He found a beautiful modern house on a cul-de-sac. It had a stunning view overlooking Lake Superior. It was professionally decorated. The home was entered on the main level adjacent to a two-car garage. The master bedroom was on this floor as well as the living room, dining room and kitchen. The lower floor had a large library, two guest bedrooms and a bath.

Janet owned a tiny partially-finished house with several levels on a small lot on the hillside that overlooked a sweeping view of St. Louis Bay. It was charmingly furnished with flea market finds. She had a busy life beyond her job. As the chairperson of the local ballet, during her term in office, she managed to turn the declining organization around and put it on a sound footing. She had not been dating Frank very long at the time that she had serious surgery that made it impossible to manage the steps in her house. Frank gallantly offered her his master bedroom for her recovery and he moved to the lower floor guest room. Perhaps this was when the casual dating became serious.

After marriage there were four cars for the couple. Janet had her small blue older car. Frank had an all-weather four-wheel drive Jeep and two vintage cars, which were housed in the two-car attached garage. One was the last Cadillac convertible made and the other was a large black Lincoln. The Lincoln was used on trips to spend holidays with his older sister and her husband 150 miles away. The everyday cars sat outside and when snows came, they were down to only one car, Frank's Jeep.

Frank's business was not time-consuming. He amassed a large collection of taped TV programs. It would have taken ages to see them all. Janet made good use of the grand piano that the decorator had placed in a corner of the large living room. She used her gardening expertise in the garden. They had a small roofed platform built in the corner of the garden overlooking the lake. It was a pleasant spot to have a drink together. Both sides of the garden were fenced. On one side was a family with noisy three children. Relations with that neighbor were not friendly. There was nothing to disturb them on the other side.

We knew Janet from her time with the ballet. After she married Frank, they lived around the corner and we began to get together alternating hosting on Sunday evenings. At Frank and Janet's house, there was a wood burning fireplace between two loveseats. Janet served cheese and crackers and stuffed mushrooms.

Frank made gin and tonic with his favorite Calvert gin. He often brought this gin to our house, spurning the more expensive gin that we had. Since we only drank on social occasions, Dan always bought the best for guests. At our house, we invited another couple to join us, but it was apparent that Frank did not want to enlarge our get-togethers. They took us to dinner several times at Northwood Country Club, where they had social memberships. Frank had lunch regularly with a close friend at the Kitchi Gammi Club. Once Janet used her membership in the Royal Horticultural Society to get me a ticket in her name for the first member's day at the Chelsea Flower Show in London.

After twenty-five happy years in Duluth, we were considering moving closer to our family in the Pittsburgh area. Our three children and my only sister lived there. On a semi-annual trip there, Dan was hospitalized for six weeks following brain surgery. This showed us the importance of nearby family support. Most of our friends understood this decision. For some reason, Frank was offended at our leaving and took it personally.

We heard from our former neighbors through Christmas cards and an occasional letter from Janet about her garden. Then, news from friends told us that Frank and Janet were no longer seen at events or dining at the country club. Frank no longer had lunch with his friend and had become a recluse. He was jealous of Janet's friends and monitored her phone calls. Janet worried that she had made a mistake in marrying Frank. She had given up her job, her house and her active life. We wondered whether this was a health issue that had changed Frank's personality. Eventually, Frank's health put him in hospice care at their home. When he finally died, there was a one-inch obituary and no services listed.

Virginia Sellwood

A tiny lady sat beside me on the small plane's brief flight from the Twin Cities to Duluth, Minn. I was glad to be returning home, but feeling a bit proud of recent travels. She asked where I had been and the question was returned. She was coming back from a trip to India where she had visited a friend in Kashmir and had a houseboat holiday. Whether we exchanged names, I don't recall. I was impressed!

It was some months later when I met Virginia Sellwood again at the Duluth Woman's Club. We made friends and she invited me to play at her bridge table at their weekly luncheons. My bridge game was not that good, so it was really the sociability that we enjoyed together. Virginia had a sparkling personality with an interest in people, travel and local events. When she met my husband, our friendship was further strengthened. Dan knew how to treat older women from having lived with his maiden Aunt Bird and knowing her friends for many years.

Virginia had been a widow for many years. Her late husband had been a wealthy man who built a tall downtown building, which bears the Sellwood name. They had a sprawling Tudor mansion on Vermillion Road. They had adopted a boy and a girl, both now adults in the community. Virginia disposed of the large empty house, first selling off the gate house, which the new owners converted into a charming place. A new drive was added before the wooded lot and main house were sold to a doctor with a large family. Virginia then bought the penthouse on the top floor of a nearby apartment building. It had its own elevator and a spacious deck, according to reports. There was some disagreement with the building owners. When we knew her, she had bought a modest ranch style house several blocks from where we lived. The wonderful feature of that house was the view from the side living room window into a beautiful wooded ravine.

Anna was her live-in housekeeper who had been with her for years. She had a downstairs apartment. As Anna was nearly the same age as Virginia, it became a question as to who was looking after whom. Virginia employed additional cleaning help and other assistance when she entertained.

Her two children were not particularly attentive and she rarely mentioned them in conversation. Virginia was from a prominent Duluth family and had several attorney brothers-in-law and nephews and nieces that were closer to her. Her son did accompany her on a trip to Australia. She was ninety years old and that was a daunting flight, except that the plane was not full and she managed to get a center row, where she could stretch out and sleep.

Virginia Sellwood and me at her 93rd birthday party

At ninety-one, she celebrated her birthday by giving herself a hot air balloon flight. This didn't happen exactly on her birthday since weather conditions would dictate when it was safe to fly. Early one morning, she had a call that the flight would take place some twenty miles away. She had to arouse her driver, Jeff, to take her to the starting point. Then, it was his job to follow the balloon and be there to pick her up, wherever they happened to land. That was a challenging task since the balloons do not follow roads. The landing was in a pasture and the only danger was avoiding cow patties on the way to the car.

Jeff took her to bridge often and they picked me up as well. As her cook, Anna was not up to serving, so Jeff often was called upon to help with her entertaining. He was an unemployed graphic artist who was self-employed. He was a congenial escort to the symphony concerts she enjoyed.

Virginia lived to the ripe old age of 94, although her final birthdays were much more sedate than flying to Australia or taking a hot air balloon flight.

Our Friend Sib

Dr. Collins and his wife had only one daughter and named her Elizabeth. As a youngster, she could not pronounce that long name and only got as far as Sib, which she was called all of her life, with the exception of formal and legal documents.

Sib married a local young man who was an Amherst graduate, John Adams. It is hard to know what they had in common. John loved shooting from early morning, cold, marshy duck blinds and hunting, fishing, and poker. She loved the theater and ballet in particular. She did join John once on a duck hunt and swore never again. Any group planning camping trips knew not to invite Sib. With such diverse interests, any romance seemed long gone but their marriage persisted.

John had a job as manager of the city water and electricity department. He lived frugally. They had four children – oldest daughter, Jane, who went to nursing school, two sons and another daughter. Son number one was destined for Amherst, and so Sib went back to teaching English in the junior high school to pay for his tuition.

They began to resemble the odd couple as Sib increased in size and weight and John seemed to shrink smaller and wider. They entertained at two tables of bridge. She served frozen daiquiris and mixed nuts, no fancy snacks. She could be fierce at the bridge table and her comments could reduce an erring partner to tears. At the same time, she was extremely sensitive herself. She was a member of the Marketeers, a women's investing club where stock recommendations were discussed at length and then voted on. Often votes were changed easily. Once, when her recommendation was not accepted, she got up and walked out of the meeting without any formal resignation from the group.

John was a skinflint. One snowy Minnesota night, they were driving perilously from Duluth to the Twin Cities. John was determined to finish the trip without stopping until Sib finally insisted that they stop in a motel for the night, rather than risk an accident.

John's grandfather had founded the Tennant Company, which made machines that did commercial sweeping for factories, malls, city sidewalks, etc. When the company went on the stock exchange, it was revealed that John's share in the company was very large. Sib felt betrayed in light of all the sacrifices she had made over the years. She was furious!

Their resources enabled her to take care of John in their home until his death. She became a wealthy widow. Her funds enabled her to set up, together with another friend, the Marsi Foundation to support the Minnesota Ballet. Later, she financed the practice studio that now bears her name in the former Duluth Grain Exchange.

Is there love at first sight? It happened to Sib when she was eighty. She saw tall, handsome Robert Brownlee after a Duluth Superior Symphony concert.

The venerable Kitchi Gammi Club is situated in a long, elegant Tudor brick building facing Lake Superior. The name comes from Longfellow's Hiawatha, as Gitchi Gummi is the Ojibwe People's word for the lake, meaning "Big Water."

The club is said to be the equivalent of Pittsburgh's Duquesne Club. Andrew Carnegie was once expelled for nonpayment of dues. How could he forget? The club had special dinners on the nights of the symphony with a bus to take the diners from the club to the Arena Auditorium. The bus would return us to the club parking lot. One day, a group was chatting while waiting for the bus. A vivacious widow was talking to Bob Brownlee. Later, she complained loudly to all her friends that Sib simply moved in on their conversation and scooped him up. That was quite true. Sib saw what she wanted. He was good-looking and twice widowed.

Since Sib was a wealthy widow, we, her friends, watched the progress of this romance with some concern. Was he interested in her money? He was largely unknown in our circle. He had no children. He lived on the edge of the lake off London Road.

All the tensions of teenage years were repeated. On their first date, Bob took her to a bright, new, organic food restaurant where they had a soup and salad. The soup was so good that Sib ordered a take-out portion. Then she was embarrassed when she realized that she was a guest of Bob's, and he insisted on paying.

Bob had worked in Brazil and had given his late wife a large emerald ring that he wanted Sib to have as an engagement ring. She demurred, saying that she might accept the ring later, but just a modest ring and something personal was what she wanted. They both got health clearances before the wedding. It would be strictly a family affair, held in the small chapel of Glen Avon Presbyterian church. A date was set for the first Saturday in January so that it would not interfere with the Christmas celebrations of Sib's families in Boston, New Jersey and the Twin Cities.

The Kitchi Gammi Club and Northwood Country Club had many of the same members. Therefore, a reciprocal agreement had been worked out. The Kitchi Gammi Club would have the Thanksgiving dinner for all and Northwood would have the Christmas buffet. Sib and Bob and her daughter, Jane, had Christmas dinner with us. We left the club shortly before they did on what was a snowy day. A few hours later, Jane Adams called to say that Sib had slipped on a ramp and broken her ankle. But there was no thought of postponing the wedding for which so many travel plans were in place.

On the wedding day, Sib had stars in her eyes and romantic thoughts from her wheelchair. Her daughter Jane was rushing around to finalize prenuptial agreements. Sib asked me to arrange the flowers and, at age seventy-five, at last, I was a flower girl at a wedding. A green garland was ordered for the back of the wheelchair with small bouquets at each handle. There was a matching flower arrangement for the altar table, corsages for Sib and Jane, her maid of honor and boutonnières for the groom and best man. I had to be present to make certain that everything from the florist was in place. As the only outsider at this family wedding, I sat in the rear with my husband. Sib's cousin, lovely dowager Virginia Sellwood, hosted the reception at the Kitchi Gammi Club. She was a friend of ours and urged us to attend. We thanked her, but realized that Sib's many other friends might be offended by that, so we declined. Later that evening, Jane brought us a beautiful floral centerpiece from the dinner.

Bob moved only his extra-long bed to Sib's spacious house. The contents of his house were sold. He invited me to take my choice of a collection of large amethyst rocks from Thunder Bay, Ontario, which still graces my garden.

Almost a year later, Bob had a recurrence of a previous cancer and Sib lost her love. Bob was not the fortune hunter that friends had feared. He'd left a $50,000 legacy to the University Minnesota-Duluth senior program in his will.

We left Duluth in 1998 and Sib moved to Friendship Village in St. Paul to be closer to her daughter and a son. When we flew back to Duluth for the Birks' fiftieth anniversary dinner, we changed planes on our return. Jane picked us up and took us for a lovely, but brief, visit with Sib in her comfortable apartment. She passed away a year later.

A Delegation to Japan

It was an unexpected September trip to Ohara, Japan in 1995. I received a phone call from a friend, Norma Bittner, who was going with the Sister City group to Japan. When I said that was something I would like to do during a future interchange, she said that there might be room on the upcoming trip, if I could call the travel agent immediately. After consulting with Dan, I did just that about thirty minutes later. He had spent six postwar months in Japan during a cold, damp winter, just marking time to get out of the Army and home after years of being away. He said that he never wanted to go back there, but if there was a chance for me to go with the local group, he was definitely in favor of it.

Duluth's Sister City Commission was managed out of a City Hall employee's office, in addition to other responsibilities. There was a monthly meeting of participants composed of previous travelers, exchange teachers and interested parties. Some Japanese women were volunteer translators as well as others who helped in the office. There were four very different Sister City affiliations. The Sister City with Thunderbay in Ontario, Canada consisted of sports meetings in each location in alternating years. There was a Sister City relationship with Petrozavodsk, Russia that consisted of a teacher exchange and a small group which went to Sweden. Our group had a young attorney, who was a City Council member. Our leader, Isobel, was head of a city department and active politically in Morgan Park. There were also several teachers, a supervisor of the public schools and some city employees. My Japan-trip roommate, Mary, was a close friend of Duluth's mayor and his family and active politically where she lived on Park Point.

I flew from Duluth, on Northwest to Los Angeles. Arrival in Tokyo's Narita Airport was at 5:45 p.m., a half-hour late. I had already lost track of what time that would be back home. There was just time to go to the restroom, where there were low seats and sinks, before we were whisked off to our destination.

A delegation of men from Ohara, in the Chiba province, was there to meet us and took us on a two-hour bus ride to our destination. It was dark during the ride, but a tourism video was shown enroute. We were to spend a week in Ohara, but would have a one-day trip to Tokyo. That would give me a chance to get together with Miss Ikuko Mori, who had been Dan's secretary after the war at the Army Finance Office in Asaka, housed in a former military academy. She was very competent in English and in stenotype. We had kept in touch with her over the years and had hoped to have her visit us in the U.S. As time went on, that possibility evaporated due to the poor health of one of the two sisters with whom she lived, and then her own age and health. Shortly after our arrival, one of the welcoming men helped me make a telephone call so we could arrange our meeting at the restaurant where we would be having lunch.

Our delegation was split between two small hotels, one in the heart of the town and the other in a more suburban location, which was where my roommate, Mary, and I were. There was dinner at the hotel of a salad, clear soup, and meat patty with squash and a carrot and turnip garnish. We had a private bath and balcony with the room. I stepped out on the balcony to a full moon. The beds were great. There was fresh fruit in the room, a TV, slippers and robe. With our inner time clocks off, we both woke up in the middle of the night and had a snack.

There was an American breakfast at 8 a.m. of an omelet, croissants, pineapple, a half slice of ham and a small bowl of coleslaw. We walked around the nice neighborhood and took some pictures of the varied and lovely houses and gardens. There was neat shrubbery and trimmed hedges and one house had a small golf green in the front yard.

At 10 a.m., we were off and picked up the rest of the group at the Marine Terrace Hotel. We had dressed up for the welcome at City Hall. It was an impressive event with first graders in blue uniforms and yellow hats waving U.S. and Japanese flags vigorously on both sides of the entrance. A band was playing and city officials were lined up to greet us. The band played the U.S. national anthem, which we sang; and then we stood at attention as the Japanese anthem was played, slowly and in a minor key. Flowers were presented to all, so we stood, holding them like bridesmaids. This was followed by welcoming speeches. Isobel gave a response as the Duluth city group leader. The Ohara mayor was a handsome, poised man. Naturally, there were translators.

We moved inside City Hall, a new modern building, and up a wide staircase to the mayor's office, which was decorated with orchid plants and had a smart upholstered seating area. After a brief wait, we went up two flights to see the council chambers. This town is described as a fishing village, but it actually has a population of 25,000 people, which is much larger than our concept of a village. There was a tour of the building and we then went back down to the mayor's conference room where officials were introduced and gifts were handed out to all. Tea was served on lacquer saucers in thin handle-less porcelain cups with small plates of pastries.

We were seated at tables in a rectangle, with officials on one side facing the visitors around the other sides. Covered lacquered bento boxes were brought to each place that opened to reveal separate compartments holding rice, meat and noodles, shrimp and pork with pasta and vegetables. More tea was served. The formality of the occasion dissolved when the Japanese saw our struggles with the chopsticks. Everyone laughed and then forks and spoons were brought out.

Following lunch was a sightseeing tour of the town, the seaport and the Shinto shrine, the bell of which had been returned to Ohara from Duluth, where it had been taken from a scrapyard following WWII. The shrine was housed in a small, open structure with a mossy roof and we all took turns having our pictures taken while striking the bell. That was not an easy feat for the striker was a two-foot piece of timber suspended from the roof by a rope and had to be pulled back and directed to the bell, which responded with a deep booming sound. They say that the Japanese are always known for taking pictures of each other, but we were definitely doing the same.

The next day, we were invited to visit an outstanding garden outside the home of a local Rotarian official. We fed the large koi in the pond near the entrance, in an area of artfully trimmed shrubs. We were invited to tour the home and shown a room filled with dolls in glass cases and then another room where we saw the family shrine and the son of the house explained the family history book in the shrine. We were invited to tea, seated on the floor, and gifts were passed out to the ladies, which were ingeniously folded cloth bags with a drawstring. (It was obvious that they were prepared for our visit, but it was contrived to look very impromptu.)

Some members of the delegation wearing traditional Japanese happis we were gifted by our hosts

This was the week of the annual Hadaka Matsuri celebration, a holiday held only in this city and meant as a thanksgiving for the rice harvest and the fish, the fruits of the sea. The lampposts along the streets were decorated with dried stalks of rice. The morning of the festival, we went to the mayor's home where marchers from his home ward were gathering. He had a very lovely garden where we spread out and, inside, his wife and helpers had put out a buffet lunch. I took the best picture of the trip in the garden of children playing on a bridge overlooking a little stream. The children were dressed in white costumes for this day. Each section of the town has its own Shinto shrine. Men were dressed in white calf-length cotton pants and short-sleeved white tops wearing a headband of their district's color. The heavy ornate shrines were mounted on two long logs and carried on the shoulders of many men on each side. They were taken to the sea in the afternoon and at a beach, each was ceremonially dipped into the sea. A ceremony was held on a large dock overlooking the sea with a Shinto priest making a speech and a dignitary shooting an arrow into the sea to ensure continued success of fishing.

In the evening, there was a parade through town which we joined. Mary said that she had to fend off some saké-happy men who were attempting to touch a very tall stout young woman of our delegation. We ended at the school athletic field where the shrines were paraded around the field and then there were fireworks. We were taken through the school and to a bridge that was a vantage point to watch the activities. It was a long, emotional day for one member of our group. This man's wife had been a popular exchange teacher in Ohara when he was there before. Now, he was returning for the first time since her death from cancer and meeting some of her fellow teachers and friends.

After the fireworks, we were introduced to our host of the home stay. This was something that had been worked out over previous reciprocal visits for the Japanese, who were at first reluctant to stay in Duluth homes or to have visitors in their homes, since most Japanese entertaining is done in restaurants. It was a rare privilege and one of the most interesting parts of our visit. Mr. Shengpei was accompanied by his son, a dentist, and the son's wife, Mia, who both spoke English and could translate for us.

We were driven to an older part of town where the houses were closer together and the son somewhat apologetically said that we would be staying in a 200-year-old house. To me that sounded even more appealing. To my surprise, they had an unusually large back garden in a nation where space is so valuable. In a tiled entryway, we sat on the steps and removed our shoes, by now quite familiar with Japanese custom. There was a small room to the left of the hall that held a couch, several upholstered chairs and a desk, but it never seemed to be used during our visit. We had tea in the dining room just off the well-equipped kitchen where I noticed a counter-top dishwasher and an electric hot water container that had a constant supply of hot water. There was a chair for Mary, who had specified that she had a bad back. Previous to our trip, our ages and needs had been sent to Ohara and the names, ages, genders and interests of the host families had been supplied for the guests. This was so that we could be prepared with appropriate gifts in a society where gift-giving is of great importance. They have to be presented with both hands and received the same way. There were no gifts for the son since he was in another household.

On advice, I had purchased a $45 bottle of scotch called Old Hall at the duty-free shop in Minneapolis for the host and had a simple white French porcelain flower vase for our hostess. We presented our gifts that night and received a variety of scarves. One generous square was meant to be knotted together from the corners to carry books or bundles. One was a blue-and-white printed cotton scarf to be tied around the head. We were also given cotton kimonos for our use during the visit and as gifts. We slept on tatami mats on the floor of the large-sized tea room. It had sliding doors on one side that opened to a tiny, secluded garden. One side of the room had niches on each side, one for the wife with a flower hanging and a flower arrangement, and one for the host on the opposite side that had a sword and helmet. Outside the tea room was the family shrine that was pointed out to us. I noticed later that the bottle of scotch and a large can of peaches were set on the shrine as offerings to the ancestors. I don't know what length of time they have to stay there before being consumed by the descendants.

The bathroom arrangements were truly impressive. There was a large tile-floored bathroom with a large tub and shower. There was a man's lavatory with a urinal and small sink. Beside that room was a lavatory with a most ingenious toilet that had a heated seat, a radio and also a bidet, which had a pipe in the back that funneled water into shallow bowl with a small hole on the top of the tank for rinsing hands and conserving water. It may have had other features incorporated in the control panel on the side of the seat that I failed to understand.

We slept well and had breakfast in the dining room where there was also a TV and where most of the living seemed to be done. At this meal, we were seated at a table and chairs of regular height. The table converted at dinnertime by lowering, to be surrounded by floor cushions. After breakfast, we accompanied our host to a Shinto shrine that was just about a block away, around the corner from the house in a pine-surrounded glade. We followed his example in bowing and in ringing a small bell three times to call the god's attention to our prayers.

When the son and his wife came in, there was a chance to learn something about marriage customs, as we were shown the big book with their recent wedding pictures. The bride had a busy time during the ceremonies as she dressed in three different outfits. The first was a rather plain white Japanese dress; the second was a bright red Japanese dress and with this she wore a black wig with hair ornaments; and then, finally, there was a white satin bouffant European-style gown without a veil. The groom wore formal attire throughout. He was an only child and it was evident that this was a very prosperous family. The amount of land they owned was also testimony to that. We also had a tour of the son's dental office when it was closed. It was quite impressive, as he managed five dental chairs in five different cubicles with no other dentist in the practice, only his assistants. It was a new building that included his own office with a shower room and a separate lunchroom and restroom for his technicians.

A special treat for us was a trip, at least an hour or more away, to a famous amusement water park our host had not been to before. There was an extensive aquarium and most popular of all, a water show with dolphins, probably much like those that are seen in Florida. Our hostess did not go with us. We were surprised when she asked us if she could do our laundry. We politely refused and thanked her as we had been washing small things in the hotel (evidently this is a common duty of a good hostess). It was most unexpected to us.

At dinnertime back at our host's home, we were seated at the lowered table. The young people joined us and we had a lovely meal with a clear soup served at the end. A neighbor man stopped in for a brief visit. Mrs. Shengpei prepared tea in a mini-ceremony. Fortunately, I had done some reading and recognized it as such, so I was able to accept the cup with both hands, raise it up and turn it around three times in the traditional way, before drinking it and she smiled in appreciation. The tea itself was a rather thick, green matcha, but there was mercifully not much of it.

I learned to drink beer at the picnic party held in the recently-built Camellia Park. There was a beautiful slim, red bridge over the ravine in which the park was situated and we walked down a broad path with newly-planted camellias on the hillsides. It was a warm, overcast day. The food on the buffet was new and different but very tasty. The only beverages available to quench the thirst were beer and saké. The latter would have quickly put me out before doing anything for the thirst, so the only alternative was the beer.

We all had interesting experiences during our home stays and were able to compare notes afterward. In one case, the two visitors were not only entertained in a family home, but also felt that they had provided the entertainment for the extended family and friends, who all came to look them over. One young man was by himself at the home of an older widow, who drove him around sightseeing in a manner that he described as terrifying.

One afternoon, the women were taken shopping by several of our hostesses. We went to a bridal shop where we were encouraged to try on traditional bridal outfits. The way in which they were constructed and worn meant that one size could be adjusted to fit all. At a dishware shop, many women bought lacquerware bowls and trays. I found an inexpensive blue and white oblong relish dish as my souvenir of the trip. As we were crossing the town square at 5 p.m., there were chimes playing a familiar tune: "Home on the Range!" I wondered if that could possibly be planned for us, as we were from the Iron Range of Minnesota. When I asked, I was told that the same tune was played nearly every evening as people were going home.

Our day trip to Tokyo started early by train and was accompanied by guides. We went to the main shopping area in the city, which was located in the area near a big historic shrine. My son, Philip, had asked for a fan and it was surprising to find several shops that sold nothing else but fans, in a great variety of shapes and prices. For Dan I bought a small framed reproduction of a Hiroshige rain scene, as well as trinkets for my granddaughters and the neighbor girls. I can't recall the other purchases made, but there were a bewildering number of temptations in the crowded shopping streets.

When our group arrived at the designated restaurant for lunch, Dan's former secretary, Miss Mori, was already there. She had hired a driver to bring her into the city. She was a short, dark-haired woman and we greeted each other affectionately.

I had a letter from Dan to give her and pictures of our family to pass on. Since she had arrived early, she had already lunched. We sat somewhat apart from the group and were able to talk. She had brought me a handsome gift, a brocade evening purse with an explanation inside of the traditional patterned fabric from which it was made. She offered to do the translation of any correspondence with our new Sister City friends. Most of our contacts with her were annual letters at Christmas time. As we said our farewells she said, "I am eighty years old and will keep in touch, but if you do not hear from me, you will know that I am gone." It was a sad thought. Eight years later, we finally failed to get anything from her in the mail.

Our friend, Miss Ikuko Mori, at the Shuzenji Onsen

There was a final official dinner in Ohara with many speeches, great warmth and, of course, picture taking. We were given gifts by many individuals and I was given a set of three bowls by three young women.

It was interesting to me to find the Japanese so friendly with us after the events of World War II. One of the older men told me how grateful they were to the United States following the war. He said that they would have starved without U.S. aid. I was familiar with the Marshall Plan in Europe but hadn't fully realized what Americans had done for Japan. The rebuilding effort that the United States had invested in Japan had turned enemies into allies.

Our delegation was accompanied to the airport for our return trip. While there, I had a chance to do some final shopping as the kiosks were very tempting. It was a chance for me to check out the cost of scotch at the duty-free shop at Narita and it was surprising to find that my $45 purchase in Minneapolis would have cost $75 in Tokyo. I was as impressed as the host and his ancestors must have been!

The return trip was by way of San Francisco and there was a brief layover between planes and a chance to stretch our legs. We all got back to Duluth healthy, but jet-lagged, after an amazing experience in international friendship.

Mr. Nakamura

Tsuneo Nakamura was the principal of a junior high school in Ohara, Chiba Province, Japan. Ohara is on the East coast connected to Tokyo by both train and bus service. Described as a fishing village, it actually has a population of 25,000 with very modern schools and civic buildings. Ohara was a sister city of Duluth, as a result of an amazing connection. A WWII warship named Duluth was given a huge brass bell from a Japanese scrapyard destined for munitions, immediately following the war. It was displayed in the front lobby of Duluth's City Hall.

Years after the peace, a chance visitor identified the bell as coming from a Shinto shrine in Ohara. Arrangements were made to return the bell to Japan. In return, Ohara sent a reproduction replacement and the Sister City relationship was started. Every other year, a group of ten or more adult visitors come from Japan to Duluth, and in the alternate years, Duluth adults visit Ohara, which I did one year. Teenagers from both towns exchange visits every summer.

Mr. Nakamura led the teenage visitors. The students stayed in private homes where their peers lived. This was a real opportunity for them to experience American life. Mr. Nakamura was our house guest. His duties as chaperone were to be present for all the group events planned for the week, the bus tour of the city and official welcome, a picnic in Enger Park and a pizza party at a local sports garden. Otherwise, he had a free schedule. We took him to these events, out to dinner and to local shopping malls. He had a long shopping list. It is a Japanese custom to make a gift of money to a traveling friend and then a gift from the trip is expected in return. In all the stores, he would examine the merchandise carefully to determine where it was made. He would not buy anything that was made in China.

We took him to dinner in the elegant high ceiling dining room of the exclusive Kitchi Gammi Club overlooking Lake Superior. Another night, it was a spaghetti joint tucked away in the West End. There the owner and waitress were thrilled to have a visitor from Japan and pressed souvenir bar mats on him. On the night of the pizza party, we made the obligatory appearance at the sports garden. It was evident that the loud music, pinball games and meal of pizza and soft drinks was not to his taste. Fortunately, there was a Vietnamese restaurant nearby where he had his happiest meal of the trip. The Asian cooking and rice dishes were exactly to his taste and he even bought a second take-away dinner. He was puzzled that the Vietnamese-American waitress did not understand Japanese.

On my visit to Japan during the two-night home stay, my hostess offered to do my laundry. With this in mind, Mr. Nakamura had brought his own towel and laundry soap and asked to use the laundry. Of course, I did his laundry as a courtesy. He was a small man and the size of his underwear reminded me of when my sons were young.

He noticed that our grass needed to be mowed and offered to help in the garden. We assured him that the neighbor boy was engaged to do the mowing and would soon come to take care of it. However, I had been working on a small oval dry pond filled with pebbles and surrounded by a few large rocks at the base of some transplanted larch trees. The dry pond would sometimes be a destination for water coming down a slope from a driveway drain. Black plastic had been put down to kill the grass and form a channel to the pond. Pebbles would be the base for the stream and a few rocks and plants would edge it to create a Japanese rock garden. I asked for Mr. Nakamura's help in placing the rocks. He was really skilled in grouping the rocks, putting them in artistic groups rather than simply lining the channel. We pegged the rocks in place so that they would not move. His help gave an authentic Japanese look to the back rock garden.

Tsuneo was a wonderful guest. We heard from him for many years before he retired, with letters and pictures of his school and students.

A Deluxe Cruise on the Roger Blough

In the early 1980s, there was a marked downturn in the economy and in the steel industry. The railroad that carried the refined ore pellets (taconite) was only running two trains a day from Minnesota's Iron Range to the ore docks in Duluth for shipment to Gary and Pittsburgh mills. As a result, many boats of the Great Lakes Fleet, a U.S. Steel subsidiary, were laid up for years.

By the summer of 1995, business was back to normal and one of the smaller, but finest boats, the *Roger Blough*, had been newly refurbished and returned to service. Our friend Bill Buhrmann was president of the Fleet. He was contemplating retirement and a possible management change, so, for the first time, he planned a recreational lake trip. All of his previous trips on the boats had been for work.

The boat had four deluxe staterooms for a maximum of eight guests and we were fortunate to be included in the party. Bill and his wife, Lurene, Sally and Jack Birk from Duluth, and Norma and Ben, friends of the host, came from Steubenville, Oh. for a week in July, to cruise the Great Lakes. The trip was completely free and not even tipping was allowed.

Passengers all boarded by a graduated side gangplank at Two Harbors, Minn., which was much easier than a ship's ladder. Caution had to be exercised on the ore docks as there was inevitable spill of some taconite, which was like walking on marbles. On the boat itself, the decks were flushed immediately of any spill. There may have been a heat wave in the upper Midwest that week, but on the usually cool lake, the weather was absolutely perfect. Every day was sunny. Inside the ship, our staterooms, the saloon, the Captain's mess and the bridge were air-conditioned.

During the shipping season, the boat crews are away from their families for months at a time working long, monotonous hours. One of the perks of the job, aside from excellent pay, was the fine food they enjoyed. With the president of the Fleet and his guests on board, the food was even more sumptuous and the service was superb. Mid-morning, when we had barely recovered from breakfast, a tray of freshly baked pastries, coffee and juices was delivered to the saloon.

Liquor is not allowed to the crew, but, as guests, there was a cocktail hour before dinner with special delicacies.

When the crew went ashore to fasten the lines or to load supplies at the Sault St. Marie, there was a crane with a swing attached to lower them over the side. That looked like fun but would need a certain skill to maneuver.

The seven-day trip was from Duluth to Conneaut, Oh. and a return. Time passed quickly with the congenial group. We had the run of the boat and were welcomed on the bridge. The only exception to this was the engine room, which was hot, noisy and could be dangerous. The engineer conducted a tour there. One day we flew kites. Another day we hit old golf balls off the deck into the lake. We were out of sight of land for only part of the trip. Sailing under the towering span of the Mackinaw Bridge, we could see the noted Grand Hotel on Mackinac Island. Going down St. Clair River, we could see attractive cottages with green lawns stretching to the river. Several retired boat captains lived there and were usually given a salute by the ship's horn in the daytime or a beam of the powerful searchlight at night.

Air-conditioning did not extend to the galley. One evening, the cook suggested he would like to grill on the foredeck. We were seated at two round tables with red and white checked table covers, watching our steaks being cooked to order as we sailed majestically through downtown Detroit. The streets seemed deserted at that hour, so there was no one to see our royal progress.

During the noisy unloading in Conneaut, we went shore where there were several cars put at our disposal. It is a small Lake Erie town. We had lunch there, but it could not compare with the wonderful meals we had on the boat. The cruise was over too quickly, but memories linger on.

The Train Party

Few people can host a traveling train party. Our host, Mr. Rutherford N. McGiffert, called Turk, was known for his unusual parties. He and his wife, Francie, had a number of outdoor picnics at their home, at which two Greek men would show up with a special spit and spend the day roasting a whole lamb for us to enjoy. They hosted dinners at their club with unusual imported foods or game for their guests to enjoy. There were fishing parties on a Canadian island and houseboat parties for many guests on Rainy Lake.

Every year on New Year's Eve, the McGifferts had an open house featuring oyster stew and a candlelight buffet with much gleaming silver. Even after the Duluth Superior Symphony began having New Year's Eve concerts and the Kitchi Gammi Club offered a special New Year's dinner, a stop was still expected at the McGifferts.

Turk was not only a generous and genial host, but he was also a train buff and big supporter of the Lake Superior Transportation Museum. He was the head of a large company, Hallett Companies, that shipped material from a dock on St. Louis Bay across Lake Superior. But when he organized the train party, he really outdid his former affairs, for there was a great deal of planning and even construction involved.

He chartered a railroad car and engine from the local Duluth, Missabe & Iron Range Railroad. The trip had to be planned for a time when the Two Harbors line was not being used for shipping. The destination for the ride was his house, *Picaroon*, on the North Shore area of Lake Superior. A special stop was built, along with a platform on which to disembark, and sturdy lumber steps to lead down the hill from the railroad tracks to the highway.

Motorists driving along the road on the day of the party must have wondered at the large group of people of "a certain age" that were walking down the highway to the lane that led to the lakeside party site.

Dan and I getting off the McGiffert train

Turk's good friend and retired head of the railroad, Don Shank, was in on the planning and, dressed in a proper traditional uniform, acted as the conductor for the trip. It was the thrill to enjoy a chartered train ride on a sunny fall day in Minnesota.

McGiffert Point
Rainy Lake, Ontario, Canada

A house party for twenty-five to thirty guests is not easy to organize. Much advance planning is needed. The challenge is even greater when the three-day event is located at a fishing camp on a Canadian lake that can only be reached by a two-hour trip from the nearest marina. There are no neighboring cabins within miles, and the marina is the only source for supplies. This is not the luxurious log cabin retreat with massive stone fireplace, as pictured in Architectural Digest, one might imagine to find.

Turk McGiffert, our host, loved to entertain whether it was at his Canadian camp, their place *Piccaroon* on the North Shore of Lake Superior, or at home in Duluth. Turk had bought the land he named McGiffert Point from the Canadian government. A boat needed to be purchased to reach this peninsula and the construction had to start with a dock. Then a simple two-room structure with a large deck was the first building. It had a large eat-in kitchen with walk-in pantry

307

and a smaller room with a potbellied stove, as well as a big window that looked out to the water. Two bunk houses were added, as well as tent platforms. Jean and Howard Clark liked a tent accommodation. Some years later, a plain structure was added to the side and called the Banquet Hall. It was converted to sleeping at night. On the other side of the narrow point was a storage shed for fishing gear, tools, a generator, boat motors and a second dock.

The camp was both a business and a personal venture for Turk. He entertained male business associates, both local and out of state, for fishing visits at his place. He sometimes made the camp available to other executive groups. The summer house parties were for his personal friends. These friends had held a house-warming for him with gifts of equipment when he was first setting up.

Two of the marina's largest houseboats, sleeping twelve each, were rented to transport everyone with their gear to McGiffert Point. These became the dormitories for most of the women. The men used the bunkhouses on shore. Two or more teenage boys, usually sons of friends, were hired to act as kitchen help and fishing guides and they stayed in tents. In time, Turk's two grandsons, Hugh and Scott, became old enough to do this.

Turk's firm owned large commercial docks in Duluth. His management skills were used in the ways that he entertained. A guest, Sally Birk, was enlisted to help plan the menus. She was no ordinary cook, as she had her master's degree in food management from Columbia University and had run an executive dining room for the Stouffer food company. Guests were asked to bring prepared food for the first meals. A roster was set up so that four people were responsible for each meal. The boys took care of clean up and dishes.

Most guests carpooled for the three-hour trip from Duluth, across Minnesota, to cross the border into Canada at International Falls. The marina on Rainy Lake was four miles beyond the border. We were all greeted warmly there as Turk's friends, since he was a valued customer. Anyone planning to fish had to purchase a fishing license at the marina. Turk went ahead with the helpers in a small boat and the houseboats were boarded with all the guests and the supplies. The boats each had pilots that were returned to the marina by the small boat. Good-natured confusion reigned at the dock when disembarking as the baggage was sorted out.

Everyone gathered on the benches around the large camp deck for Happy Hour before dinner. Millie B. and Caroline McMillan, usually two demure widows, acted as cocktail waitresses, dressed in short black skirts and mesh stockings. Petite Millie demonstrated that she still could do the Charleston. I provided familiar songs with my small accordion.

A schedule was passed around to organize the fishing times so that all who wanted to fish could have a turn. There were three boats available. With good luck, the fishermen's catch would be pooled for a dinner of fish. I caught a great big fish and was very pleased with myself. It was the first time I'd caught one since that long-ago day when my mother had told me I was getting too old for shorts. It was the most delicate and delicious fish I have ever eaten, and probably the most expensive considering the $12 license, travel time and equipment involved.

The wild blueberries were in season and enough berries were gathered to make a dessert of blueberry slump. Lunch was usually soup and sandwiches. Turk was a genius at combining restaurant-sized cans of different types of soups that turned out wonderfully. Dudley Smith, owner of a meat-packing company brought ham and steaks. We ate well.

Everyone seemed involved in seeing the fishing boats off. This was not a matter of casting a line from the dock. It was necessary to travel up the Rainy River for what seemed like a long time to a dam. Beyond the dam was another lake. It was necessary to portage fishing gear to three other boats tied up beyond the dam, up a steep rocky path. "Fishermen" were carrying fishing gear, bait buckets and life preserver cushions. The boys and men carried the outboard motors to the other boats, fitted the motors and loaded gear and boaters. We were off again to different spots on the sizeable lake. Fortunately, we were blessed with wonderful weather. On our return, everyone rushed to see what the catch was and to take pictures of their upcoming dinner.

Holding up the catch of my "last" fish!

People who stayed in camp read, played cards and backgammon. Gertrude Jacobson, our resident artist, had a sketch pad and did views of nearby islands. Some of us followed her lead. One evening after dinner, we were surprised by a large boat from the marina with bagpipers on board giving Turk a birthday serenade. Every year Auld Lang Syne was played at the end of the party as our houseboats pulled away from McGiffert Point dock. Those were golden days and golden years.

There have been a number of funerals I have attended where Auld Lang Syne was played. It has always seemed very appropriate and poignant. So why shouldn't we drop a few tears at the passing of the years!

Eleven
A World Away

A Slow Boat to Llangollen
Wales – 1977

The Llangollen Canal, in Wales was just right for a week's trip by canal boat from Crewe in England to Llangollen and return. It had two tunnels to go through, two locks to be managed and two aqueducts that traversed deep ravines. Our canal boat accommodated four passengers. Our travel companions were John and Jean Chaplin, our good friends from Scotland who we'd first met in the Bahamas. Their daughter had made a canal boat trip previously and, on her recommendation, they made the arrangements for the boat charter. It does take very good friends to travel comfortably in such a small space and, in what equals camping conditions.

There were small decks forward and aft. The captain operated from a wheel on the rear deck. The snug saloon held a table and benches, a small sink, fridge and stove that included a warming rack. Midship in the boat was the head, aka the bathroom. Ingenious double doors enclosed a tiny shower on one side and a toilet and sink on the opposite, but with open passage through to the forward deck during the day. At night, the doors opened in another direction and provided privacy. Further forward from that was a bedroom with two bunkbeds and the door to the foredeck.

A network of canals once provided the cheapest and most efficient transportation in Great Britain until they were made redundant by the coming of railways. Many of the canals fell into disuse, though some of them have been restored for recreational boating.

We took a train from London to Crewe where John and Jean met us by car to drive to the boat hire place in the country. My husband and I covered the cost of the boat charter and John and Jean took care of provisioning all of the supplies. After loading the food and our belongings, we set off immediately, with an employee of the charter staying with us for an hour of instruction on all details of managing the boat. There were ropes at the ends of the boat and a sledge hammer and large stake to drive into the bank and tie-up to at night or during stops. There was a long wooden pole that rested on top of the cabin and was used to push the boat if it got stuck in the bank. This could happen often when two boats passed on the narrow canal. John was the captain as he was naturally handy. A well-worn tow path ran along one side where the horses once did the pulling, now provided by a diesel engine onboard. The speed limit was four miles per hour and we were advised it was best to keep at three miles, which is a walking pace. Thus, we drifted dreamily through beautiful rural countryside.

Dan and I in Great Britain with Jean Chaplin

The weather was cool and John and Jean wore their anoraks often. My sleeveless tops and shorts were never unpacked. We all had a turn at the wheel and there were cups of hot tea handed up from the salon. Dan enjoyed piloting during a light rain in solitude. When an overhead bridge came in sight, one person would walk ahead to see if there was a boat coming in the opposite direction, since the canal was one way under the rural bridges. The tow path was a good place to exercise from time to time. We all had a wonderful sense of freedom from the outside world.

There was breakfast and lunch aboard and, in the evenings, we tied the boat to a bank near a village and had a pub supper. Some mornings we bought fresh baked goods from the village. At the beginning of the trip, we tossed for sleeping quarters, and Dan and I won the double-bed, which was put together at bedtime by combining the benches and the table in the front of the boat. We all had to agree on bedtime before disassembling the dining area and retiring to our separate quarters.

One day I jumped off the boat onto the tow path and landed wrong on my left leg, crashing to the ground. The pain in my knee was instant and I wondered how I would get back on the boat, which was just five feet away. John backed up the boat and Dan and he got me back onboard. When we got to the first large turning basin, a taxi was hired to take me to the Wrexham Hospital. Jean went along with us and John stayed to man the boat. My leg was examined and I had an x-ray taken that showed no break, just a sprain. An Ace-bandage was applied. All this service was under the National Health Service, so it cost us nothing. That seemed incredible to us that foreign tourists were not charged. Dan made a donation. A lot of pain followed and sleeping in the bunk during the day was a help. My lower leg felt disconnected. It seemed as though I was dragging a heavy log. From that time on, I stayed on the boat. At some point, we found a handmade hawthorn cane which Dan purchased for me, and that was a tremendous help.

We hated to end our journey. John and Jean took us to their home in Dollar in Clackmannanshire, the seat of the Campbells. Dan and I had rail passes, which enabled us to continue to the top of England at John O' Groats. From there we took a ferry to the Orkneys, stayed in a comfortable hotel and took several day trips to explore the islands. We could not walk to get close to the famous standing stones there. Returning by ferry, we rented a car and drove as far as Dundee and took the train back to London.

The outstanding part of this trip to Great Britain was the canal boat adventure.

"Seven" Avenue Road

Avenue Road is a short tree-lined street in the Isleworth district of London (There are thirty Avenue Roads in the London directory). This one runs off London Road just a block from the Isleworth train station, providing good access to the city by way of Waterloo Station. Jack and Kay Cutting had a bed and breakfast at their home at 7 Avenue Road.

Their red brick semi-detached house had a number '7' set in the stained-glass transom over the heavy front door. A low iron fence surrounded the tiny front garden and an iron gate opened to the tiled walkway. Flowering plants filled the garden, leaving just enough space for the stepping stones that led around the side of the solid brick dwelling. Triple windows on both floors were to the left of the front entrance with its gleaming brass kick plate, heavy knocker and brightly polished door hardware. There was nothing to mark this as a bed and breakfast, nor could one guess at the gracious hospitality and the treasures that were inside.

We made our first reservations there on the advice of a young Minnesota woman at Northwest Airlines. We were asking about an inexpensive small London hotel. She asked if we had ever used bed and breakfasts. I said, "Of course, in English villages, but never in London." She gave us the details of this small B&B with such rave reviews that we never expected anything could live up to her description. We sent off a letter and deposit, received a brief confirmation and arrived at 7 Avenue Road for the first time.

The host, Jack, opened the door into a long hall, tiled in traditional black and white checked squares. An antique half-table with a fresh flower arrangement was immediately to the right. He took our bags and led us up the carpeted stairs past a group of handsomely framed colorful prints of regimental soldiers, which marched up the stair wall. Our bedroom overlooked the rear garden. He showed us the nicely carpeted room and carpeted bath next door. Matching bedroom furniture was traditional modern, with a double bed, two nightstands, an armoire and a mirrored vanity. Two windows had sheer curtains with heavy green velvet pull drapes.

We were invited to come downstairs when we were ready for a welcoming cup of tea – a pattern that was followed on all our repeat visits over the years. Here we met his wife, Kay, a friendly outgoing brunette. The Cuttings had met and married while they were both serving in the British Army. After WWII, they had stayed in the service and had been posted in many places, including Egypt and the Orient. Some of their exotic furnishings reflected this. During those years, they'd raised two sons and seen a lot of the world.

After retiring from the Army, they went into business and bought a rundown country pub. By working together energetically, they managed to make the pub into a popular and successful enterprise. It was located near an American airbase, which provided many of their patrons. Some years later, the airbase was moved to another location. Their loyal customers persuaded the Cuttings to sell up and move with them. They were able to sell the pub at a profit and then repeated their success in a new location.

In time, they ventured further into the hospitality business by purchasing a small country hotel. This involved staffing and they were hard put to find dependable employees who would be up to their own high standards. The hotel was sold and they moved to London, buying a house that had belonged to Jack's grandfather. He'd bought the house from a cousin who had inherited it. They restored the house and garden and started a "word of mouth" bed and breakfast with just two bedrooms. There was a small room on the second floor that was always locked that could have been used for storage.

There was a kitchen wing on the first floor and, apparently, their private quarters were downstairs. As friendly as the Cuttings were with us, we never saw the kitchen part of this "upstairs-downstairs" world. The lounge, where we were welcomed to tea, was carpeted and centered by an old-fashioned fireplace with an imposing array of shining brass fire tools, a gleaming fender and intricate brass fan. On one side was a handsome sideboard with Capodimonte porcelain candelabra and several antique clocks. A sizeable collection of Royal Doulton figures was discreetly displayed in both a corner cupboard and an antique hanging cupboard. Unobtrusively placed downstairs were a number of antique clocks, including several old water clocks that still worked, as our host demonstrated for us. It was only later that we learned that the television was concealed in a carved chest high cabinet.

Kay was a fan of Prime Minister Margaret "Maggie" Thatcher and they shared with us their expansive views on English politics, elections, taxes, etc. While they were now limiting their activities and travel, they continued their interest in world affairs. They had sold their Rolls Royce because they didn't want to give up any garden space to build a garage. We were given a heavy brass key to the front door and trusted to come and go at our leisure.

Breakfast was served at the time of our choice, before nine o'clock. We would come downstairs and go into the dining room where a single oblong table covered in a heavy white damask tablecloth had large, crisp napkins at our places. A striking arrangement of white tulips in a handsome glass compote centered the table. A slender parfait glass of orange juice was at each place, together with cornflakes in double-handled rosebud-patterned china bowls. Bread and butter plates and saucers were exactly in place. Matching jam jars held three kinds of preserves or marmalade and there was a bowl with artistic curls of butter. Trying to make these later at home, I bought the special tool needed to create the elegant curls, but never quite succeeded.

The dining room held more antiques and handsome figurines in addition to the substantial furniture. A double French door at the end of the room led to a glassed conservatory and then into the back garden. This was kept closed and didn't contain plants. They had collected impressive articles on their travels and then had added to their things by going to antique dealers and estate sales. There was even a history to the needlepoint fire screen against the dining room fireplace.

Jack seated us for breakfast and was always dressed in a coat and tie. After the cereal, he brought in heated cups, a teapot and the filled toast rack. We started on the tea and toast and then he served heated plates of fried egg, English bacon (actually, it was Danish), a grilled tomato, mushroom and a sliver of fried bread. The menu and service never varied. With that wonderful breakfast, we were set for our day's exploration of London.

After our first stay at 7 Avenue Road, under the expert attention of the Cuttings, we never considered staying anywhere else whenever we visited London. The price was right and it became a wonderful haven.

We learned the best way to get from Gatwick Airport by train to the station at the foot of the

Dan and I sitting outside at the National Theater in London before a show in 1983

road. We bought day tickets and had a choice of train, bus or underground each day. It was better to go see West End matinee shows, as transportation later at night was less readily available. There were several restaurants in walking distance and a number of shops. London became the starting point and return stop for many overseas trips and the Cuttings willingly stored suitcases for us. That was a great help. We would repack our bags to take only warm weather clothes for our trips to Italy, Egypt and Greece. On return trips, we could squeeze in short sightseeing excursions around London or spend time reconnecting with British friends.

Each year the most handsome Christmas greeting card we received was from the Cuttings. They were collector's items we enjoyed for many hours. Regretfully, one year Jack became ill and was in hospital. We had made our reservations months in advance and Kay didn't want to disappoint us, so she took us in, although they had closed their small business for guests. We ended up being the last guests that enjoyed their wonderful bed and breakfast. London was never quite the same without the Cuttings and 7 Avenue Road.

The Eton of Africa
Zimbabwe and Malawi – 1983

Our first big trip following retirement was to Malawi in East Africa at the invitation of our friends Jean and John Chaplin. John was the first headmaster of a new coeducational boarding school, Kamuzu Academy in Malawi, sponsored by the first president of the country, Dr. Hastings Kamuzu Banda. The teaching staff had been imported from the UK and housed in attractive brick ranch-style houses. The school was often called the "Eton of Africa." Aside from their son and daughter, no other family or friends had been able to visit the Chaplins since their move from Scotland to Malawi.

John suggested the best way to fly from London and the best time of year to visit was during the school's spring holidays. They met us in Harare, Zimbabwe and together we toured Zimbabwe visiting Lake Kariba, Victoria Falls and the Livingston tree, and Hwange Game Park for a wildlife safari.

They had arranged that we would all stay with their friends, the Wilsons, in their walled and gated modern house in Harare. He was the Scottish architect who had designed the recently completed Kamuzu Academy. His wife was a travel agent who had set up all of our tours for the trip. The Chaplins were coming to the end of their time in Africa and wanted see more of it with us as traveling companions.

Our first stop was at Lake Kariba, a man-made lake filling hundreds of acres behind a giant Italian-built dam on the Zambezi River. It had the capacity to provide hydro-electric power to one-third of Africa. We had an afternoon boat ride on the lake among a large group of hippos. I didn't realize at the time they were considered very dangerous. They would surface briefly and then disappear under water, only to resurface in a completely different spot. It was impossible get a picture of them without a telephoto lens.

We stayed at a pleasant inn overlooking the lake and the trees just outside were filled with nests of weaver birds. After a five-course dinner, there was a bright moon and John and I took a stroll on the surfaced road that led from the inn. Then we realized that this was not the well-known roads of our homelands. In Africa, we could not be sure of what wildlife might be out there in the dark, so, we turned back at a brisk pace.

We then flew into Hwange Game Park to spend two nights. This was not a safari camp but a luxurious hotel. The deluxe bedrooms all opened onto patios. There was a large open lobby and an elegant dining room with a sophisticated menu. An elevated wooden structure at the edge of the grounds had a bar called the "Water Hole." We didn't find it in service, but it was an ideal place to sit and watch the wildlife at night as they came to a lighted water hole in the ravine below. A deep moat separated that area from the hotel grounds. We were awakened early for a drive through the park, where we saw a rhino as well as many giraffes and zebras. Then, it was back to the hotel for breakfast. In the late afternoon, there was another drive with fewer sightings, though we never did see any lions.

The next flight was to Victoria Falls, which we could see long before we landed from the large cloud of spray in the air. We stayed outside the village in a hotel that claimed to have the largest thatched roof in Africa. It was on the banks of the Zambezi River where there were many monkeys playing in the trees and sometimes venturing as far as the swimming pool. In the afternoon, there was a sundowner boat ride on the river with many crocodiles lounging on the bank. That night, coming back from a performance at the back of Victoria Falls Hotel, our van driver stopped abruptly. The headlights showed wild buffalo crossing the road on their way to the river to drink. The driver kept his distance and we sat quietly until they were all past. The wild buffalo is a beast that can and does kill lions. Before we left Harare, we were driven to a bird sanctuary with many large, exotic species. We spent another night with the Wilsons who took us to the airport for the return to Blantyre, Malawi.

Upon arriving in Blantyre, we were escorted to the VIP lounge while our luggage was taken care of through customs and delivered to John's car, which was waiting at the airport for us. The first night, we stayed in the guest house of the Vice Chancellor of the University of Malawi, David Kimble. He and his wife entertained us with drinks as they were going out to dinner.

The next day we went for a recommended hike up Mount Sochi and a tour of the tea plantation at its base, and then to dinner at a place with a view that was non-existent when a heavy rain fell. The second night we stayed at the residence of the Resident British Consul, who was absent with his family in England. The servants had been instructed to receive us. From there we slowly progressed the 275 miles to Kasungu, sightseeing and shopping along the way for food and other things not available at the Academy, where John would return to his duties as headmaster. With luggage for four and the supplies for the Academy, the car was completely packed.

Kamuzu Academy was truly amazing. Impressive gates and smooth pavement greeted us, which was a welcome relief after the twenty-five miles of bumpy, dusty road from Kasungu. It is located in a rural area and the setting is touted as an excellent way to keep students focused on their studies. The rose-pink buildings were made of brick produced on-site and the extensive campus was coherent in style, unlike most U.S. schools and colleges, which tend to grow topsy-turvy over many years in many styles.

Kamuzu teachers were most hospitable and we met them at the Faculty Club, where there was a lovely swimming pool and social events. Invitations came for tea and dinner parties. There was a separate guest wing where they often housed visiting local educators or British consul, so that was where we stayed.

Miss Cecilia Kadzamira being escorted by Jean Chaplin through Kamuzu Academy

During our visit, Miss Cecilia Kadzamira, the president's official hostess, arrived for a visit and tour of the Academy. Dr. Banda was unmarried, and Miss Kadzamira, who was first a nurse in his medical practice and later his private secretary, had been granted the duties of the first lady. She was the president's confidante and her nickname among the Malawian people was Mama Kadzamira. Her appearance at Kamuzu Academy with the cabinet ministers' wives, which included Mrs. Ruth Tembo, her aunt, was a cause for a flurry of activity. There were drumming and dancing in costumes by the women workers. I was invited to dine with our exalted guests at a formal luncheon held for them after they inspected the school. Later, tea and coffee were served out on the patio for us by staff in white jackets.

The daughter of the assistant headmaster was visiting her parents from England while we were there. It was arranged one day for us to join her and her mother on a day-long trip to visit a game park in Malawi to search for elephants. The school driver and Land Rover were put at our disposal and we were off.

It seemed that we would never spot any elephants among the six-foot tall grass. The park was virtually deserted. We saw only two other cars and felt sorry for them. The Land Rover was high and gave us a view over the grasses. For an ordinary car, it must have seemed like driving through a tunnel. It was our driver who spotted the elephants first. We were even close to one on the road. We stopped at a safe distance and waited. Finally, they appeared in the distance. They were wild and free, nothing like trained elephants in the West.

The Art of Golfing

The British, and particularly the Scots, are passionate about golf. It is no surprise that there are golf courses everywhere in the world where the British have been. I've seen many of them in my travels. The highest golf course in the world is Gulmarg near Kashmir, India. You have to have excellent lungs to play there. You are aware of the altitude just from climbing the steps to the restaurant. The famous St. Andrew's Golf Club in Scotland would not win any prizes for its beauty. The same would be true of most courses in the United Kingdom, especially when compared to the lush green, manicured courses in the United States or even Japan where golf is highly regarded. The British rely on hazards such as patches of gorse. Once a ball goes into those thickets, it can never be recovered. Mullion Golf Club in Cornwall is along the sea buffeted by winds and bare of trees and bushes due to the wind. The fairways are minimal and situated between gullies of sand.

One afternoon during our visit to Malawi, my husband Dan and I went with our host John Chaplin to the Farmers Golf Club, where he was to meet a friend for their regular weekly golf outing. His wife, Jean, packed equipment for tea before we all set off. The club house was a low white building with minimal furnishings inside. The interior was dusty. The deep windows were largely open. One room was a library with shelves of tattered paperback books.

John and his friend each had two Malawians as caddies, for a total of four men assisting them, one caddie each to carry their golf bags and one caddie each to stand out in the field to spot where their balls landed. The fairways were dry, ten-inch-high stubble and it was not possible for the golfer to see where the ball was. The "greens" surrounding the holes were large circles of sand. There was a crude rake made of a flat piece of wood with a long handle to smooth the sand and make a path to the hole. The caddies went barefoot and had their shoes tied around their necks. Shoes were expensive and precious, to be worn as little as possible.

Jean and I visited in the shade of the thatched shelter while the game was played and laid out the tea equipment for the return of the golfers. It just proves that there is golf almost everywhere.

A Tunnel Cloud

We were on the deck of the MV *Ilalla* gazing toward the shores of Mozambique on a five-day trip on Lake Malawi. Growing up in Zelienople, I have an affinity for the letter Z. It seems to pop out on any printed page. Being able to travel from my youth in Western Pennsylvania to this place in Africa seemed a marvelous feat.

Preparing for the trip, we tried to read as much as possible about Malawi. One book described the best way to see the country was by traveling on the MV *Ilalla*, a motorized ship that still plies the waters of the lake today. The long lake was nearly half the size of the country and was the principal way of transport, since roads deteriorated the farther north they ran. It was only possible to purchase tickets locally. This was our one request to John, and not an easy one to fulfill.

The cabins on the first-class upper deck of the boat were booked up quickly by travel agencies in South Africa, since Malawi was a popular destination. White South Africans were not greeted warmly in most other African countries because of their support for apartheid. However, Malawi was a poor country and welcomed tourist dollars no matter where they came from. Several teachers at Kamuzu said they had enjoyed the lake trip.

John asked his secretary if she would call the steamboat company for reservations. The reply was that all cabins were booked, but something could be arranged for several weeks later. When she explained that these were guests from the United States who would be leaving soon, she was asked to call back later. A day later, she was told that his guests could have the forward cabin usually reserved for company directors. It had a simple private bath and two windows and was a duplicate of the captain's cabin on the other side of the deck.

One of the school's two Land Rovers and a uniformed driver were put at our disposal to take us the considerable distance to the dock. Enroute we had a luncheon appointment in Lilongwe, the new capital, with friends of our foreign service friend who were stationed at the United States Embassy there. Other than the resorts, President Banda enforced a strict dress code everywhere in the country. Thus, Dan wore a summer suit, white shirt and tie and I had a navy suit and hat when we lunched at the hotel. After lunch, there was a long drive to Salinas to board the boat. There was a wide concrete dock and so we were taken right to the gangplank, where we must have made a grand entrance in both attire and mode of arrival. When we were escorted to the director's cabin, the white South African passengers looked at us askance.

The boat usually stopped at night for unloading and loading, which was often noisy. Villagers came aboard during the evening stops and came to the upper deck bar for MGTs. These mild drinks were Malawi gin and tonics. The visiting locals were always quiet and well-mannered, as this was a special occasion for them. Dan was self-conscious about being a tourist and asked me to keep our camera in my purse so we would not be conspicuous. But a six-foot, 200-pound white man in a predominately black country could not avoid being noticed, even more than we were observing everyone else. People were friendly and delighted to have their pictures taken, even rushing over to get into a shot.

One magical night, we were awakened and looked out to see many lights reflected on the still water. Later. we learned that it was fishermen in small boats with flaming torches. We paid for our meals separately and sometimes skipped the four-course dinners served at lunchtime. There was always a delicious fish course, fresh from the lake. The boat made its way every week along the lake, carrying local passengers and produce and animals on the lower deck. It stopped at small villages without docks where the life boats served as lighters. We didn't always go ashore, but there was a stop at an island where there was a huge Anglican cathedral to see. Only a small chapel portion of it was being used. Livingstonia, the Presbyterian mission that Dr. David Livingston founded, could be seen from a distance on top of a hill. It was interesting to visit with our fellow passengers, with the exception of the South African group, who pointedly would not mingle with any black people.

Short rains and amazing rainbows appeared frequently. One afternoon on deck, there was what appeared to be a funnel cloud in the distance, although it was a bright day. It was the shape of a tornado and somewhat alarming. We were told that it was a swarm of insects above the lake. They did not bite but had been known to smother fishermen who were caught in a swarm. We hurried to close the cabin windows. The cloud did not come closer and dispersed as we moved on.

We had an unusual financial arrangement with John. He paid all our expenses and kept an accounting, and, on the final night, Dan was able to give him a check, which he could deposit in his American bank account. Malawi currency had no value outside the country. John was limited as to how much of his annual salary could be taken out of Malawi, as well. This meant that spending Malawi "kwacha" and paying him in dollars was a help to him. No currency conversion was needed on our part. Dollars could never repay the wonderful experiences in Malawi.

Elephants and Mahouts
India and Nepal – April 1985

Phyllis was a slim, light-haired English woman in her late forties. She was an experienced tour guide working for SAGA. This was a well-known travel agency that originated in Britain, first with day tours for seniors and then longer holidays and finally branching out to the United States. Their itineraries were longer and the stays were a minimum of two nights and sometimes a week in places that were ideal for retired travelers. Our tour was a month-long holiday flying to Delhi, India from London's Heathrow Airport. The flight took eleven hours, including a refueling stop at Dubai, where we did not deplane. The superb service of Japan Airlines took away any pain.

Our guide had taken groups to India before and really knew the ropes. She was most aggressive in protecting our health. We had cholera and typhoid shots in advance. We were told to drink only bottled water, not to eat any peeled fruit, nor eat any outside food until the third day when she would plan the menu for a special Indian dinner. A previous group had all suffered stomach problems. Nothing could be worse than being ill away from home and committed to a schedule of travel.

At each hotel, she checked out the swimming pool and no one was to use a pool until she had inspected and approved it. As our tour progressed, the weather became increasingly hotter as the season of the monsoon rains approached. In Agra, our day tours were very early in the day, then we had a siesta after lunch and no one was to use the pool until after four o'clock in the afternoon.

Most of the hotels had buffets with a European side and an Indian side. We sometimes went to the Indian side for rice. Just once, I ventured a small taste of something else on the Indian side to the burning regret of my throat. The cure for stomach problems was plain white rice and lots of tea.

Days four through six took us from Delhi to Jaipur, the Rose City, where many of the buildings are of a rosy stone. In addition to our day tours, this was where we met Dr. P.J. Sharma, a teacher at the University of Jaipur. He had studied in the U.S. under the sponsorship of a Duluth philanthropist who had put us in contact with him. He took us to a new Hindu temple and drove us around the university in his car that had a lace curtain in the rear window. Then we went to his home for tea with his wife and two daughters. During his study in North Carolina, his family had been with him for part of the time. They were most hospitable and proud of their modern kitchen, and also of the towels and sheets from the U.S. Touring their home, we went to the flat rooftop, which was where they slept in the hot weather.

Not far outside Jaipur was the Amber Fort, a combined castle and battlements on a high ridge. There was a cobblestone road winding up the hill to the fort. This was a chance to make a grand entrance under the extra tall gate by riding an elephant. There were steps up to a wooden platform from which we could mount a platform on the elephant's back, equipped with two forward-facing seats just behind the mahout, seated on the elephant's neck. Shortly after we started, Dan dropped his camera. It was not expensive but we were sorry to lose the pictures that were already taken in it. We looked down at the lost camera some nine feet below us. To our amazement, the mahout had the elephant back up and pick up the camera with his trunk, handing it back to the mahout who wiped it off and passed it back to Dan.

Over a week later, our tour took us to Katmandu, Nepal where there was another opportunity to ride elephants in a much different setting of the semi-tropical forest of the Royal Nepal Game Park. There were twelve of us on this outing and we were somewhat late in getting underway. We arrived at the park to find that the mahouts were bathing their decorated elephants, expecting to call it a day. I don't think they were too pleased to go back to work.

The three elephants were forty years old, fifty years old, and a youngster of just twelve years. These elephants were saddled with a railed platform and the passengers each sat at a corner with their legs straddling a post. This was a fairly long ride through a forest that had monkeys and exotic birds. The path was narrow and well-worn and the elephants were very surefooted. At one point we stopped, overlooking a deep ravine, so that someone on the leading elephant could take a picture. I was on an outside leg looking down at the drop below and wondering if the American Express insurance would cover an elephant crash in a Nepalese ravine.

The third young elephant seemed far behind us. When we got back to the end of our circuitous ride, we found the missing elephant and its riders waiting there. At some point the "youngster" had staged a revolt and, in spite of the mahout's best efforts, had turned back to the start of the trail. It was a clue to the elephant's personality.

From Nepal we flew back to Delhi for one night at the same hotel, the Maurya Palace Sheraton, where we had a peek at an elaborate Indian wedding. The groom arrived on a handsome white horse and there were torch-bearing attendants. Inside we could see the bride dressed in red and seated in a small room with many women.

During our weeklong stay on Lake Dal, we took a day trip to Gulmarg. which is known as the highest golf course in the world. In the winter, it is a ski resort and then a golf resort in summer. Since we were between seasons, there was simply a restaurant from which to enjoy the views. It would have been fun to have hit a few balls off the range.

The taxis that took us on our day tours were comfortable. We shared the same cab and driver for several days with our friends and relaxed as he negotiated the winding roads with none of the guard rails or warning signs that we are accustomed to. On a third trip, we looked for "our driver" only to be told that he was absent since he had smoked too much ganja and was unable to drive.

Night in Nepal

The highway from Katmandu, Nepal to Pokhara was actually a two-lane road of tightly packed gravel. It went up and down along ridges following the contour of the land without any need for landfill or bridges. There were no guard rails. The road was built by the Chinese, whose workers must have felt at home in familiar surroundings. Chinese landscape art had always seemed artificial and stylized to me until seeing this terrain with its terraced hills, rice paddies and mountains. Now I was seeing the real thing.

The hillside terraces ranged from two to six feet wide and were planted in barley and wheat. The level spaces were held in place by low stone walls built up over centuries of backbreaking labor. Everything had to be done by hand, from seeding to weeding to harvesting. Kansas wheat farmers would be appalled at such a challenge and United States farm aid in the form of tractors would be entirely useless here. There was a system of irrigation which was a mystery to me.

Our destination was Fishtail Lodge on an island lake in Pokhara. The lodge was reached by a short hand-operated ferry, which consisted of the raft on which we stood pulled along a steel cable. Helped off by the ferry man, he pointed to my husband Dan's size thirteen shoe and laughingly said, "Yeti!"

The name of the lodge was not related to the lake, but named for the famous mountain peak of the Annapurna Range that resembled a fishtail in its curve. There were small houses scattered lower on the mountainside among green fields. The point of the trip was to view the rising sun light up the opposite peaks and particularly Fish Tail. We were only there for one sunrise and would not be awakened if the morning was not clear. The lodge consisted of three low, round buildings, two of which held rooms and the third housed the kitchen and dining room. We dined on a simple stew and were served a wedge of what appeared to be pie. It had such a strange taste that everyone pushed away after one bite. The night was clear and about 2 a.m. we put on robes and had a private view of the moonlight on the glistening white mountain tops.

Pokhara is the center of the area where Britain has long recruited their famous mercenary troops, known as the Gurkhas. After foreign service, these veterans, returning to the local economy, were financially set for life. The town is the take-off point for mountain trekkers. A small shack bore a bookstore sign. It was crowded with used paperback books in many languages. Returning hikers would dispose of books and their climbing equipment here. There were traders in the shade of some large trees with their goods spread out on blankets.

We were nearing the end of our trip and this was an opportunity for me to do some bargaining. We always traveled with comfortable old clothing and then lightened our load on the homeward journey by disposing of some of it. The souvenir vendors presented a chance to try out my skills. I took over a small carry-on filled with shirts, a purse and a dress. The dress was a Diane Furstenberg cotton knit that had been purchased at St. Paul's church rummage sale in Duluth, Minn. especially for the trip. It was lightweight, non-crushable with long sleeves appropriate for temple visits. As I had checked out and paid for my $1 dress, I was told it had been donated by one of my friends.

It is amazing how a few words and sign language can accomplish trading. There were offers and counter offers. I was offered some of their items for my clothing and some cash. I counter-offered just the clothing, no cash. At the end I had a handful of small trinkets, a bracelet and some carvings

We left Pokhara by plane in the afternoon and were soon back at the comfortable Everest Sheraton. Katmandu has a sizeable Tibetan community. We visited a large stupa where we encountered young monks in their saffron-colored robes, a temple and a primitive rug weaving shop. The headquarters of the exiled Dali Lama were pointed out on the hillside. This was as close to the Tibet of my bedtime readings as I would ever get. Somehow there were no regrets at missing altitude sickness and yak butter tea.

Once back at home, I presented a simple carving of a snow leopard to the original owner of the dress with a card saying, "bread cast upon the waters will return unto you."

A Puzzle from Kashmir

The April week we spent in Kashmir living on a luxurious houseboat on Lake Dal was the highlight of our month-long trip to India and Nepal. Our thirty-day SAGA tour was split between two weeks in India, a week in Nepal and then back to New Delhi and on to Srinagar. Fruit trees were blossoming and the fields were a spring green in Kashmir. The air was fresh and cool, a delightful change from Benares. There, the heat of the day meant that any trips away from the air-conditioned hotel had to be made early in the morning. People were longing for the monsoon season to bring some relief from the heat.

Our houseboat, the Meena Bazaar, had carved paneling, Oriental carpeting, crystal side lights, a salon, dining room and four bedrooms, each with a private bath. The largest bathroom at the rear even boasted a bidet. Furnishings were ornate and bedspreads and draperies were made of a crewel fabric. The boat was anchored offshore to a small island where the cook shed was located. Only the movement of the crystal chandelier and side lights indicated that we were not on solid land.

Our travel companions were our good friends, my college roommate, Jean Rothermel, a librarian and her husband, Dan, a school principal. Early on, two knowledgeable English gentlewomen on the tour asked if they could join us on the houseboat, which was most agreeable. That left room for two more and so Jean invited a charming Englishman and his wife to fill the space. David was an architect and an artist and had been in charge of the conservation of the Mary Rose, the 15th-century warship of King Henry VIII's that had been recently raised and restored. His wife, Mary, had been a government clerical worker and was definitely not his equal. She found much to complain about, including the weather and the help. Her husband did not contradict her in public, but the couple in the next stateroom heard him rebuking her in private. We later discovered that she was a second wife. She was the only sour note in our congenial group. We often took turns at the bridge table in the salon in the evening. The two English ladies were expert bridge players.

Day tours were arranged by taxi cab as there were no buses in the region. When we returned from drives, tea was served on the front veranda with freshly baked sweet biscuits. Service was superb in every way. Each boat had a covered shikara, or water taxi, to ferry us around. Because the weather was cool, the boats had lap robes and hot water bottles for our comfort. It had soft cushions and was propelled by a man sculling it from the back.

The head servant was the khitmutgar who had two assistants. He consulted us as to our preferred menu choices, arranged the flowers, and laid out the table settings with a large repertoire of napkin folds; hardly what one would expect. All meals were served on the boat except for days when a picnic lunch was provided or we lunched at a nearby restaurant.

The khitmutgar took Dan aside after a few days and had several long conversations with him. He was a Muslim in what was a Hindu country. Even then there was unrest in the area. He wanted to know how he could get to the United States and better himself. Dan had no easy answer and said that, with his skills, he might find employment with Arabs of the same religion. His reply was that the Arabs were a cruel people, even though they were Muslim.

The servants were thrilled with pictures of themselves that we took with a Kodak instant camera, similar to a Polaroid. I found the camera heavy and awkward, so we did a trade of the camera and all the film I had left for a shawl and a skirt. Other shopping purchases were a pair of small Tibetan rugs in Nepal and an Oriental rug in Kashmir.

Many shikara boats were filled with merchandise and we bought leather gloves lined with rabbit fur during an exchange on the lake. Merchants besieged visitors and only a few sellers were invited aboard. One was a tailor/dressmaker and another man had papier-mâché objects. A shikara filled with flowers was beautiful, but we had no need to purchase since flowers were already provided on our houseboat.

One misty morning, we had a private tour of the maze of island waterways. It was amazing to see a scantily clad six-year-old boy singlehandedly and skillfully managing a type of canoe. We stopped at a woodcarver's shikara and bought a number of items as gifts since they could be sent home for us. To be certain that the same items that had been selected were delivered, we were told to sign the bottoms. It was some months later before they arrived in Duluth and since they were wooden, they had traveled safely.

A simple jewelry box was my choice because I admired the grain of the wood. It was a puzzle box and a section in the middle of the front had to slide to the right in order to open it. A puzzle from Kashmir returned with us to remind me of that magical time on Lake Dal.

Dinner at Rules

Rules is the oldest restaurant in London. Hosting a dinner there is not easy, since it is very small and reservations are hard to come by. Before leaving for a thirty-day tour of India and Nepal, we made reservations there for the night of our return. We wanted our travel companions, Jean and Dan Rothermel, who lived on the East Coast, to experience this unusual place. In addition, we wanted them to meet our London friends, Liz and Derek Parrish. Our homeward departures were set for a day later.

The tiny Fielding Hotel, where we were staying, sits on Broad Court in the heart of the theatre district, just in back of the Bow Street Magistrates Court. It was both convenient and quiet for there was no street traffic on the wide courtyard that extends between two streets. The front desk was minimal, as was the lounge. Breakfast was available in the basement for an additional charge. The accommodations were less expensive than large London hotels and it was close to the Royal Opera House. I had recommended it to our Duluth neighbors, who were planning a trip to England.

Imagine our surprise the afternoon we returned to London to find those Duluth friends, Biz and George Spencer, were already at the Fielding and waiting to see us. They were returning early from travelling around the UK. This was at George's insistence and Biz was miffed. I never heard what had gone wrong that made him so dispirited. But they were expecting us to act as guides in London, even though we only planned on being in the city for twenty-four hours.

It was impossible to include them in our dinner plans because the restaurant was so crowded. The building is timbered outside and beams crisscross the interior. Uneven plastered walls and battered furnishings make one aware of its age. Our party of six was wedged into a small nook on the second floor. Two others could not have been added at the last moment. Furthermore, this would not have been a congenial group of guests since George was extremely deaf and the Duluth couple had nothing in common with our other friends. It was an embarrassing situation. The best that I could do was to offer to take Biz to breakfast the next morning and guide her around as much of the immediate area as possible, spending time in Covent Garden and adjacent tented booths. George wanted to get home as soon as possible and was not interested in anything in London, so he did not join us.

Biz and I had breakfast at an interesting small spot, saw the Royal Opera House, the actors church and yard and did some shopping in the open-air market. At her urging, I bought a navy-blue wool cashmere blend coat, which I wore for years. She was satisfied that she had seen a significant section of London.

Dan and I had dinner at *Rules* on an earlier trip to London, but our dinner with our good friends was the most memorable.

A Bumpy Trip on the Silk Road
The Soviet Union – 1988

Samarkand, Tashkent, and Bukhara – the exotic and fabled cities of the ancient Silk Road lured us from Minnesota to the faraway places of Central Asia in the latter days of the USSR. Our tour group assembled in London and flew the Russian airline Aeroflot to Moscow in 1988. It qualifies as the worst airline we were ever on and we wondered why we couldn't just have been on British Air, which also served Moscow at the time.

The hostess gave the usual speech about the use of the safety vests provided for water rescue and said the vests were stored under the seat. When passengers felt under the seat, no one could detect a vest. The same instructions were given on the return flight and this time the hostess said the vests were in a bin by the cockpit. This was equally incredible.

Friends who had been to the USSR warned us about the food and so we took as many snacks as possible, most of which were used up quickly in the early days of the three-week trip, except for the jars of jam and peanut butter. These same people instructed us to be careful what we said in our room and said that if we needed something, we could "talk to the ceiling."

From Moscow we took a train to Leningrad. The scenery showed many white birch trees and evergreens similar to Minnesota. There were open fields and small villages with low, shabby-looking one-story fenced homes. We met our overall tour guide. She was an attractive young woman who spoke excellent English. Her job was to translate for us, to arrange for the hotel accommodations and meals. Later, it became apparent that she was not there to satisfy the tour members, but to make a profit for the government. Local guides would join the group at the different cities. The streets of Leningrad were strangely empty on what was a warm spring Saturday evening. Our first meal in the hotel was on a balcony in a smoke-filled night club atmosphere overlooking some entertainment. Just one night was spent in that hotel and then we flew back to Moscow.

At the end of the tour, we would spend four days in Leningrad at another hotel. We had a Sunday on our own and time to explore the neighborhood of the tourist hotel on the outskirts of Moscow. There was an attractive old church nearby, boarded up. We wandered into a grocery store, if it could be called that, since there was so little available – some dried-up carrots, a few potatoes and turnips, nothing fresh looking. The canned goods were in glass jars, not cans and were distinctly unappetizing looking. Some even showed mold. There was more business outside where some people were lined up bearing a variety of containers to purchase kvass from a truck. That is a mildly alcoholic drink made from rye bread, we learned. There were long gray apartment buildings in the area. The small bits of ground in front of the apartments were weedy and bare of grass. Perhaps that was also an indication of the upkeep of the interiors.

The tourist hotel was impressive in its lobby, which was designed by Swedish architects. There was a grand staircase leading to the second-floor dining room. Above those floors were the hotel rooms with uncarpeted corridors and bare walls. The bathroom had a stained sink, rusty pipes and thin cotton towels. The bedroom itself was like a cheap dormitory room with limp drapes, thin spreads, flat pillows and bare floors.

There was a visit to Red Square and the honor of joining the line to pass by and see the waxen-looking Lenin in his tomb. The colorful domes and turrets of the old church seen in Russian posters was the most impressive feature of the Square. Near the church were public water fountains with a single metal communal cup. A quick visit to several subways was really impressive with beautiful artwork and chandeliers and here there was cleanliness. Most of a day was spent at the Park of Science and Industry where the rocket Sputnik was a major display, so small and much simpler than I had imagined. Each part of the USSR had its own building and exhibits and the best lunch was at a hotel near the entrance. One evening was a folk dancing show at the beautiful Tchaikovsky Theatre. There was no problem finding the rest rooms…the smell told.

From everything read and seen about the food situation, we felt fortunate to have ample servings throughout the tour. But the food was simply terrible, with so many ways to make potatoes interesting that never happened. Potatoes were for making vodka, probably. We asked the waiter for only one plate to share, but that would have been deviating from practice and never happened. We were served chicken just once, and it was a challenging experience, for the chicken was not disjointed, but rather sliced across the whole body so that you couldn't tell just what part you were eating or where the bones were.

Opened bottles of warm, sweet Pepsi-Cola, warm, weak beer and warm mineral water were grouped together on the tables. We bought bottled water and were careful not to drink from the taps. At night, there was a big metal samovar near the elevator and we would fill glasses of boiled water and use that to brush our teeth at night and in the morning. There was a matron on each floor who looked you over and sometimes controlled the room keys. After this trip, Dan could never stand the taste of Pepsi again.

When at the airport to go to Tashkent, tourists were taken to a separate waiting room apart from the main terminal. There were no boarding passes or seat assignments. We were taken as a group and put on the plane ahead of other passengers standing by and seated in a block.

Tashkent, now part of Uzbekistan, was a huge industrial city and quite a surprise. The reason was that, during World War II, the munitions factories and the employees had been moved from the more vulnerable locations by the border of the Soviet Union to this distant central location. Here, the guide indicated a certain air of independence and freedom from the oppressive government of Moscow. Where the crossroads of the ancient trade routes met was now just a wide, open intersection. Streetcars ran outside the hotel. One evening, we witnessed an accident involving two streetcars and wondered how such a situation would be resolved. There was a visit to an ancient cemetery and a caravanserai.

In the ancient city of Samarkand, we were housed in a small hotel opposite the university. The hotel had a refrigerator opposite the elevator on our floor, to our short-lived delight. Alas, it was only window dressing for it was not connected!

We strolled there on limited grounds between low buildings and also made our way down a side street to find for ourselves the tomb of Tamerlane, a 13th century mausoleum known for its ornate architecture and azure-colored dome.

A daytime bus trip took us through rocky grassy country to an inn near the border of Afghanistan. That was as far as it was safe to go. The special treat there was a tiny glass of a strong plum wine that made one gasp. Some shepherds nearby were roasting meat over an open fire. It smelled wonderful and I was offered a piece which was tasty but mostly gristle. With a woman there, I did a trade of a pink necklace for something I offered from home. At a bustling marketplace there were piles of spices that were difficult to identify until the merchant showed me a book and pointed out the Latin name. He gave me several samples in a twist of newspaper. The most impressive building was a large madrassa, a combination of an Islamic school and mosque.

A greater sense of freedom prevailed in Central Asia for the guide here virtually ignored the group. She never ate with us and probably was enjoying better food than we were. One man in the group had special food needs and got little help from her with his problems. We realized that for her, too, the main responsibility was to ensure that the trip was profitable.

The overnight train ride that took us from Samarkand to Bukhara was all too short. There was hot tea served in glasses in decorative metal holders at our berths which seemed a special treat and Dan persuaded the porter to sell us one of them. We had to get up early and leave the comfortable train. There were camels in Bukhara and a whiff of the past of the transport of the historic Silk Road.

Our final Central Asia stay was in Alma-Ata, just 200 miles from the border with China and now called Almaty. It was an attractive city surrounded by beautiful mountains. The hotel had helpful signs in English and was the most comfortable. It had been readied for the World Speed Skating Cup and many of the Soviet Union's Olympians trained there. An optional tour was a trip to the site and luncheon in a yurt. By this time, most of the group were travel-weary and glad to be in a warm hotel. No one was interested in this outing. For the first time, our guide seemed aware of our feelings and practically begged people to sign up. We didn't!

Our peanut butter had held up well over the ensuing weeks, so we brought it to breakfast and shared it. Bread was the best food in the USSR and we were very popular that morning. I did get to go to a market one day alone with the guide. She was doing personal shopping for herself and friends in Leningrad since dried fruits and grains were cheaper and more readily available in Central Asia. She was buying in bulk quantities as I watched. A large shed housed the market and abundant produce was heaped on wooden tables. This was a far cry from what we had seen in that Moscow store.

The final days were in Leningrad and, since this was the guide's home city, we were in her hands. Special Russian food requests had been put off by her saying that the best food would be in Leningrad. That didn't happen. She was our guide at the famed Hermitage Museum and I wondered if she really knew much about it, since we were virtually on our own. The opulent settings, marble pillars, and marquetery floors detracted from the wonderful collection of impressionist painting there, as did the inadequate lighting. At a place where one could have spent days, we had only three hours.

Russian circuses are famous and none was scheduled. The group became vocal in asking for tickets for the circus. Our guide would make no promises and it was only at the last minute that we found out that we could attend. The place was packed and some of us were seated on the balcony steps, which would never have been allowed in the U.S. It was well-worth seeing and a satisfying evening to end what had been an unsatisfying trip.

Egyptian Brass

Most tourists see Cairo, the Pyramids and the Sphinx and then go to the Upper Nile, which is actually south from Cairo when you look at a map of Africa. The attractions there are Luxor, the Valley of the Kings, Aswan, Abu Simbel and Phyla Island. We were on a Thomas Cook Sun tour out of London to Cairo for two days and then out of Cairo by train instead of the slower but more luxurious riverboats on the Nile.

Our friend, Gladys Cooper, a personnel officer at the U.S. Embassy, joined us for dinner at our hotel. We made plans to meet at Aswan and then to stay with her following our tour, thereby extending our one-week trip to two additional weeks as her guests. Knowing Gladys' interest in music (she had a fine singing voice and we had been in the music department at Chatham together), I suggested the possibility of going to a Cairo Symphony Orchestra concert, which I had read about in an English language magazine on the plane. She laughed and said that she wouldn't recommend that based on her previous experience. The music was mediocre at best, and at intermission, the cats, which roamed the concert hall, would go on stage and sit in the musicians' chairs.

The most dangerous part of the trip was at the start when we joined our guide and had scarcely seen his face before he led our group swiftly through a sea of humanity at the Cairo train station to our car. If we had lost sight of him or the group that we didn't recognize, we would have indeed been marooned.

Our destination was Luxor to visit the Temples of Karnack, Luxor, the Valley of the Kings, the Theban necropolis and the ancient mosque. We were in an Oberoi Hotel and found that it was true what they said about the desert temperatures at night. The days were hot and, when you went to cool off in the hotel pool, it turned out to be extremely cold since the water had not recovered from the nighttime chill. The climate was

Posing with a replica sphinx at the Waterloo Bridge before flying off to Egypt to see the real one in person

so dry that a towel was not needed. The air dried your body quickly. That was a great help in taking care of the laundry that we tried to do along the way. We were putting some clothing out on our balcony and found a couple waving at us. It wasn't just a friendly greeting. They had stepped out on their balcony and the door had closed behind them. They were imprisoned there until help could come from the front desk. We bought and carried bottled water with us and it was refreshing even though it was not cold.

From Luxor, we traveled by air-conditioned bus, stopping at Esna, Edfu, and Kom Umbu. This was a chance to see the sometimes sandy, sometimes rocky country along the way. The Egyptian sky is golden haze from the dust that is always in the air. David Roberts has captured this in his paintings of Cairo. The dust is constantly on the move.

At Aswan, we stayed on Elephant Island and were joined by Gladys and her coworker, Mary Ann, a nurse from the U.S. Embassy. Together we had a delightful weekend with a sail on a farouche to Kitchener Island, where there was a botanic garden, and to the opposite shore, where there was a view of one of Aga Khans homes atop a sandy rise. We could have hired donkeys to ride there but declined. Gladys and Mary Ann opted for an afternoon tour to Philae while we stayed with the group who went to see the Aswan Dam. That was a big mistake, for a dam looks the same almost anywhere. It has had a tremendous impact on all the land. It provides electricity for most of the country and TV aerials are seen sprouting from the roof of mud huts. There is dim lighting in all the smallest villages. It has also changed the water table and endangered ancient sites. The effect of the Nile River itself is dramatic, as it is bordered on both sides by bright green and then, as if a ruler had been drawn, the sand appears. There is no gradual change.

We all returned to Cairo by sleeper train in spacious cars built by the Germans. The tour group returned to London, but we stayed on for an additional two weeks with Gladys in her spacious fourth floor apartment with a glassed-in sunroom overlooking the Nile, in a building beside the former Presidential residence. We had experiences above and beyond the Cook's tour from the week before.

Gladys had always sought out and enjoyed Middle East postings as part of the Foreign Service, and said she didn't mind the dust and heat "as long as the British had come first and trained the servants." In Cairo, her houseman was a six-foot-tall man of Nubian descent named Hassan. He wore a white djabella and fez and did everything from the cooking, cleaning, marketing and buying and arranging fresh flowers with ease. Gladys had a machine washer and dryer and preferred to do the laundry rather than risk the machines to the help. In addition to the sun porch, there was a reception room, a living room, dining room, galley-type kitchen, laundry, two bedrooms and two baths. An open rear balcony was used for storage, as most residents did so, that many expensive apartments had a derelict appearance from the street. Her place was beautifully furnished with items from the Embassy furniture storeroom. The Foreign Service provided this for its employees so that it only had to pay the moving cost for a few personal effects when people were transferred every two or three years.

Gladys' place was a block away from a botanic garden and close to the University of Cairo. It was across the Nile from the heart of the city and the river was quite broad here. While she went back to work, we were free to explore Cairo on our own and often crossed the Nile by the University Stop ferry. We walked three blocks along the river to the University ferry station where we could cross the river. The ferry fare was only about five cents. The boat went downstream at an angle taking passengers to the heart of Cairo and the main square where the Cairo Hilton and the Egyptian Museum face each other over an intersection so crowded that an elevated cross walk is needed for pedestrians.

During our stay with Gladys, we were included in two Embassy organized tours: one to the Souk and ancient Cairo houses and another to visit old mosques and churches. The Al-Azhar mosque is at the entrance to the Souk. Climbing to the roof of a mosque by way of a rickety staircase and looking out over the old city's rooftops, it seemed so derelict that it might have been in a war recently. Gladys took us to the Khan el-Khalili, the historical market in the middle of Islamic Cairo; so crowded and dark that it was intimidating. In the bazaar, we found prints on papyrus for a fraction of the cost the same prints were sold for in the giftshop on the tourist-oriented Nile houseboat. Bargaining was supposed to be the way to go but even for me, a seasoned haggler, that was more intimidating than the strange surroundings.

On a second visit to the market with Gladys and her friend Mary Ann, it all seemed less frantic and the booths that were selling brass gleamed like something out of Aladdin's Cave. Gladys had arranged to change dollars at a better-than-tourist rate, so it was possible to buy two heavy 13-inch candlesticks, two 10-inch candlesticks, a brass tray and some brass mugs. There was no fine Egyptian cotton to be seen, but I did buy a two-meter length of heavy cotton with a narrow satin strip of pale green for a possible evening skirt. Instead, it served as a table cover and was the altar cloth for my daughter Amy Jane's outdoor wedding many years later in Florida.

All of this would have been too heavy to carry home with us, but Gladys arranged for the courtesy of the Embassy mail pouch. It was free to send our purchases back to Duluth. When I polish the Egyptian brass candlesticks, the vivid market scenes come back to me.

One Sunday, we attended a farewell party for some Embassy staff. There was to be a convoy of cars going to a resort on the Suez Canal. Along the way, there was a chance to see how fertile the country could be with the use of irrigation machines. Gladys had hired a driver. The convoy seemed to become confused and split up along the way. Our group arrived at a resort and parked only to find it was the wrong place, so we piled back into our cars and then found the other group. It was a reminder of past Sunday School picnics.

There was an ample al fresco meal during which we watched boat convoys sailing past on the canal. Then we boarded a boat and had a short trip on the Suez, passing by the site of the six-day war with Israel, which was pointed out to us. It seemed incredible that blood could be spilled and fought over such arid desert land.

With Gladys' help, we hired a car and English-speaking driver for a day trip to Alexandria. The scenery along the way of the donkeys and farm workers in long garb were right out of Biblical illustrations. The streets of Alexandria were narrow and the three-story buildings seemed tattered. We stopped for coffee midway and also at the consulate to make a delivery there. The historic sites were impressive and most interesting was the drive along the corniche and a swing through the grounds of the former royal palace on the waterfront. We had a late lunch or early dinner at a restaurant on the water and were back at the apartment just after dark

Gladys and Mary Ann took me to their favorite beauty shop where I had my first pedicure. In a dusty country where sandals are worn, a pedicure takes precedence over manicures. When we entered the shop, we had to wait while the attendant completed her prayers in a back room. At the end of our visit, our tour allowed for another hotel night, which we enjoyed at a palatial spot near the airport. The gardens were beautifully lit at night and, for entertainment, we had a chance to see an Egyptian wedding. The bride and groom came slowly down a long curving stairway and scattered coins to their guests, followed by their wedding attendants.

Then it was back to London and an April house party in Stanton in the Cotswolds just three miles from Broadway. We had two weeks over the Easter holiday and sensational sunny weather at the cottage we had rented to gather and entertain our British friends. They were all former Nassau residents so they were a most congenial group.

St. Johns Cottages
Sandwich, Kent, England – 1997

The advertisement in the back of *In Britain* magazine was intriguing, as it promised a converted almshouse cottage in a garden. A three-week holiday in the UK was planned for May with some time in London, a week on the Isle of Wight, a visit to Bridge of Allan, in Scotland and a week in the countryside, then back to London for the famous Chelsea Garden Show. I phoned and made our reservations, the quickest way of getting information as to deposit, method of payment, location of cottage, etc. We were committed to the unknown!

We had a frightening adventure on the train ride from London. The train was nearly empty and we had ample room to put our bags beside us and in the next open compartment. Dan took a stroll through some of the other train cars. When he returned to our compartment, he noticed that his luggage was missing. We were horrified to think it had been stolen. This was at the very beginning of our holiday. Dan would be hard put to replace his missing clothes for he was tall, broad and much above the average size for English men's clothing stocks.

He hurried back to the baggage car where he found the train conductor to report the problem. It seemed that the conductor had thought it was unattended, dangerous baggage and had put it off the train at the last brief stop. He apologized and called that station to arrange to have it sent to Sandwich on the next train. Therefore, Dan had to wait at the station for his luggage to arrive. Pulling my bag by myself, I found the cottage easily, received the key and unpacked. I was alarmed when a couple of hours went by and Dan had not arrived. Had something happened to him? Those were anxious minutes before Dan appeared after a long, tiresome two-hour wait for his bag.

Our destination was St. Johns Cottages in Sandwich, Kent. The town was one of the Cinque Ports that were fortified to protect England from the French, centuries ago. It had been so long ago that the ports were no longer on the sea but were now inland, approached by stream from the ocean. The cottage was indeed in a garden that extended to the residence of the owners. It was also within sight of the old city hall and within yards of a fish and chip shop, as well as a bus stop and all the village stores. It was one of six small connected cottages that had been rescued from demolition by the adjacent owners, who promoted their preservation.

The entry door opened into a small sitting room that had a coal-burning fireplace. A loveseat, an antique gate leg table with ladderback chairs and a small chair furnished the room along with antique prints on the walls. A door to the rear of the room went to the tiny kitchen and through to a small walled courtyard. There was a compact "loo" at the foot of a steep curving stairway leading to the bedroom upstairs. The staircase was tiny and had a rope banister that was a help in navigating the steps. It was a cozy fit for two.

This was the ideal village to explore on foot. We went to the stream just outside a remaining ancient gatehouse where there was a marina. There were antique shops and, in one of them, I sold a sterling compact from the early 1900s. At an art show, I purchased drawing paper and mats and resisted anything else. By bus, we could visit nearby villages. Our bachelor headmaster friend, Malcolm Lawson, came one evening for supper with us and then another day took us on a day-long drive of the area, including a tour of Walmer Castle, which was a property of the Queen Mother Elizabeth.

The Chelsea Flower Show is a world-famous event for gardeners held in London annually. The May event is held on the grounds of the Chelsea Hospital, a war pensioners home. It is a five-day event with the first day's admission reserved for the Queen and other VIPs. The second and third days are open only to members of the Royal Horticultural Society, and Thursday and Friday are public days. At the end of the day on Friday, at the close of the show, there is a terrific stampede as the exhibits are dismantled and for sale.

My visit to see the Chelsea Flower Show was truly a long, difficult journey. I knew someone who was a member of the Royal Horticultural Society and had her secure a member's ticket for me by writing months ahead and sending a money order in Pounds Sterling currency to England. That meant that I actually attended under her name, but I could get in on the first members' day when the exhibits would be at their peak. Dan and I made special arrangements to extend our airline tickets for this date. Then, on the day of the show, the traffic was such that there were special show buses going from Victoria Station to the show grounds. There the queue for these buses was over a block long with a dedicated waiting time. I suggested to a couple in the line that we share a taxi and they agreed. No one questioned my identity as I presented my half-day ticket at the gate.

It was a huge crowd and seemed as though everyone in England was a member of the Royal Horticultural Society and was there that day. My thought of touring the exhibits and having a sit-down luncheon were soon dashed. The refreshment tents were filled to overflowing with not a vacant place to sit. There was a huge block-long tent of plants and floral displays and then acres of individual theme gardens to see. My head could not absorb it all and my feet could not stand it all. It was completely exhausting and I was glad that I had only invested in a half-day ticket.

Our landlady was a keen gardener who attended the Chelsea Garden show as a member of the Royal Horticultural Society regularly. One morning I was amazed to find her seated in a full tweed suit on a stool weeding. Along with her well-worn suit, she was wearing a hat and garden gloves – no pants or jeans for her.

She explained that she was beyond the age of jeans. I was too embarrassed to admit that, for my gardening, the sturdiest pants or jeans were my choice.

The grand furnishings of the cottage could be explained by the fact that she was a co-owner of an antique shop in a nearby village. She graciously invited me to tour their personal gardens and I was invited into their home for a brief visit. One long wall of the house's lounge was packed with bookshelves. Several round tables were filled with silver-framed photographs and a collection of antique silver. There must have been hired help to dust all this silver and polish the copper I saw as I passed through the kitchen and out into the back garden.

Outside, there was a koi pond and a round brick garden house just big enough for a desk and chair for reading and writing. The home reminded me of English garden designer and aristocrat Vita Sackville-West's retreat at Sissinghurst Castle, where she wrote about gardens, among other things. The May weather was with us. Time went all too quickly.

Back in Duluth, musing on our wonderful experience, I wrote a letter to the editor of *In Britain* for the monthly column recounting travel experiences in Great Britain. There was a book awarded for the best letter of the month. My letter about our week in Sandwich at St. John's Cottages was printed and given the monthly prize. At Christmastime, I sent a copy of the article to our hosts and received in return a thank you note. Also included was a copy of a stylized painting done by their son-in-law that showed the cottages, the gardens, the rear of their home and an inserted frontal view, as well as pictures of their family. It is a lovely souvenir of a special experience.

Twelve
Return to Zelie

Hankey Court

With retirement, there were no more company transfers. The final move we made was to the Passavant Retirement Community in Zelienople, where I had been born and had family roots. Unlike many isolated retirement places, the community is right in the center of a friendly, small town, convenient to banks, stores and eateries. In 1996, we traveled to Pittsburgh to see our family and stopped to see Dan's college friends, who were living at Passavant at the time. Following the visit, we put our names on a waiting list for a cottage for independent living. Our grown children and grandchildren lived in the Pittsburgh area, as well as my sister and some of her family, so, it made sense to move closer to them.

My sister, Ceil, who lived nearby, toured some cottages for us as they became available and offered pictures and suggestions while we were on the waiting list for two years. Meanwhile, we started to downsize, after twenty-five years living in our split-entry four-bedroom, three bath home with a two-car garage, two decks and family room overlooking the lake.

Dan and I settled in Hankey Court, a cluster of nine cottages for independent living on the upper edge of the retirement community campus in 1998. One side backed against a hill at the end of the property with a large field stretching out behind us. All but one of the cottages were two-bedroom homes. The other cottages were originally occupied by couples. It was a congenial but not too close group.

When someone on the Court had a birthday to celebrate, the Hankey-Panky Chorus met at their front doorstep with the unrehearsed, only number in their repertoire and sang Happy Birthday to the accompaniment of my small accordion. Some people would bring cards but we only lingered briefly at the door, as our duties were as carolers. Several years ago, we had a surprise birthday dessert party for one resident who had a day after Christmas birthday and never was serenaded. We often shared rides together for the monthly wine and cheese gatherings and other events at the Main Building.

Standing outside my cottage door in Zelienople

Our retirement community brought new opportunities to volunteer at the Zelienople Historical Society in town and on the campus. It was a chance to learn more of the local history and my own family's personal history, leading tours at the Passavant and Buhl houses maintained by the Society, and getting to portray my ancestress Fredericka Dorothea Goehring Buhl and town namesake Zelie Passavant in my own homemade 19th century costumes. On the campus, there was regular duty Thursday mornings in the library, various committees, computer, writing, and art classes (with a short painting career and art exhibit as "Grandma Warhola") and being an Ambassador to new residents.

I have lived long enough to see Zelienople celebrate its 175th anniversary, and once again, was given a special place of honor in the parade down Main Street – not as Miss Zelienople on a float this time – but instead as the Grand Marshal in a fancy horse-pulled white carriage!

My sister, Ceil, joined us here at Passavant to become my neighbor, a joyful, short-lived time that ended far too soon when she left me in November 2004. Her children, grandchildren and now great-grandchildren make the trek from all over the country to visit me still.

Dan was with me here for six years before spending the last three months in the campus nursing facilities when his prostate cancer returned. I was grateful I could be with him daily to the end.

Pilgrimages

There have been many pilgrimages in my travels. Some of them were planned and deliberate trips to places of personal interest. Many religious shrines were inadvertent visits – simply part of a tour in a foreign land. I didn't realize that the birthplace of Buddha was just outside Agra, India until we had arrived there.

We were in India and a highlight of that month-long trip was a visit to the Taj Mahal. Actually, there were two visits, one in order to appreciate it in the morning, and another to see it at sunset. In spite of all the photographs seen over the years of this incredible architectural shrine and in spite of crowds and vendors outside the gates, it does not disappoint. My husband was not a dedicated photographer but he was proud of his picture of the Taj Mahal.

Not many people realize that this beautiful tomb and mosque, erected over the course of sixteen years by a Persian emperor, was a tribute to a long romance with his wife, the woman who had borne him many children before dying in childbirth. When one of those children deposed him, he was imprisoned further along the river. From there he could gaze out and see his shrine to her every day.

London is full of historical and literary shrines. Everyone goes to see the Tower of London, Buckingham Palace, Covent Garden, Trafalgar Square, Westminster Abbey and the Houses of Parliament. Visits must be made to the Tate Gallery, the National Gallery, the National Portrait Gallery, which is as much history as art and, of course, the famous British Museum. If the light is on in the tower above Parliament, it indicates that it is in session and it is usually possible to get a seat in the visitor's gallery. I learned that each seat is equipped with a loudspeaker at the rear, so you shouldn't lean forward to try and follow the speeches, but lean back toward the speaker instead.

Personal interests led me to visit the Chelsea Physic Garden. It was not open to the public at that time, but I used my affiliation with the Herb Society of America to gain admission. That meant that the garden was almost empty except for a few gardeners and some artists doing botanical sketches. It was a special place I felt privileged to be able to stroll through on that fair English day.

There was an important garden show in Philadelphia that I had heard about for years and finally was able to attend after we moved back to Zelienople. The bus trip was organized by Pittsburgh's Phipps Conservatory and it seemed even more challenging than the renowned Chelsea Garden show, which had many outdoor gardens. The Philadelphia Flower Show was held in early March with everything indoors and all the flowers, shrubs and trees would be forced into leaf and bloom by the staff. The trip was well-planned with bag lunches provided for us and no time wasted for meal stops. Our bags were dropped at the hotel and the bus took us on to the show in the evening and back again the next morning.

The dooryard gardens were appealing, but many of the larger garden exhibits that advertised the skills of professional landscapers were much too exotic to be practical. They were in competition for the most original ideas. The main feature of the show, entitled Mother Earth, was so huge that you walked by it scarcely aware of the height. Lighting was a factor in creating the wondrous exhibit, and my digital camera was incapable of capturing it adequately.

The return trip took us to the Winterthur estate for lunch and a tour of the mansion and gardens. The mansion was the childhood home of horticulturist Henry du Pont, and he turned his collection of Americana and naturalist gardens into an extensive museum. Afterwards, we had a lovely drive through beautiful rural Eastern Pennsylvania before rejoining the turnpike to arrive in Pittsburgh at 10 p.m. It was enjoyable, but that is a pilgrimage that can be crossed off the list.

The last pilgrimage was a return to Nassau in 2007 with my family to scatter Dan's ashes off Rose Island, as he had requested. It was good to be together as a family, but not the happiest holiday, as we were mourning the recent loss of my younger granddaughter, Rachel, as well as Dan. There are many wonderful memories there but few friends are left. We were fortunate to have lived there in a simpler time.

Celebrating our 50th wedding anniversary with our family in Pittsburgh in 1994

Tree Watching

After fifty-four years, I am back in Zelienople, and, like Rip van Winkle falling asleep under the branches of a tree for decades, the houses are mostly the same, but the occupants have changed. It is comforting to drive around and recall the friends and relatives who lived there before.

The days when I marked the growth of our children with height marks on various kitchen doorways is long past. Now I am watching the growth of the trees around my retirement cottage. The spindly flowering crab apple sapling in front is a sad reminder of the beautiful pink blossoms on the old tree that blew over

340

during a windstorm. Photographs will record it now. A Cleveland pear tree beside the driveway flowers briefly in white, while growing tall and straight, impervious to the wind.

A volunteer crab apple tree at the base of the hill has benefited from pruning and puts out a show of pink on alternate years. Beside this is a corkscrew willow tree, grown from a rooted cutting and just eleven years old. Not only are all the branches twisted into interesting shapes, but the leaves are twisted as well. It is now twenty-five feet tall and has provided cuttings for other friends. I watch the progress of these trees with a bit of pride. Another variety of the corkscrew willow is the golden bark corkscrew. The difference in the bark is only obvious in winter when its leaves have been shed. It was purchased in a small pot and survived replanting when the plants were healed in pending construction. The golden bark is smaller but broad and is a good screen in back of the garden bench.

The small oak tree has also survived several moves and is now reaching ten feet. The leaves turned a deep red-brown and faded. The oak adds interest to the garden all winter, since it holds the leaves until March. Nearby is a river birch which has now grown to fifteen-feet tall. The sweeping branches are graceful in summer and in the winter the white mottled bark stands out.

Outside the bedroom window in back of the cottage is the maple tree, which is my great joy. Underneath, there is summer shade for a small flagstone platform with a glass-topped table and two chairs. It is an excellent spot for al fresco lunches and afternoon tea. Our family celebrated one of Dan's last birthdays there on a perfect June day, reciting poetry to the poet.

I like do some work in the herb garden, then sit under the maple tree, relax and ponder what needs to be done next. Some of the branches are low, but I keep them for the shade and privacy. In the spring, it is thrilling to see the buds swell, become dangles and finally swell into open leaves. Come fall the tree is in its full glory, with flaming orange-red leaves. Then, the ground is carpeted in orange leaves, soon to turn yellow and brown. A strong wind completely removes the remaining leaves in winter. On moonlit nights, its bare branches cast shadows on the snow and the sun can shine in on me by day.

Tree watching is not the same as the progression of flowers in the garden. The perennials appear like seasoned actors and take their place in order of bloom without prompting. The changes in the leaves are more subtle. When the flowers are gone, the shapes of the trees and their bark give the landscape life all year long.

Life has come full circle since leaving Zelienople over fifty years ago. It is good to be home.

www.ingramcontent.com/pod-product-compliance
Lightning Source LLC
Chambersburg PA
CBHW080042280326
41935CB00014B/1763